Family Life Education With Diverse Populations

Family Life Education With Diverse Populations

Editors
Sharon M. Ballard
Alan C. Taylor

East Carolina University

Los Angeles | London | New Delhi
Singapore | Washington DC

Los Angeles | London | New Delhi
Singapore | Washington DC

FOR INFORMATION

SAGE Publications, Inc.
2455 Teller Road
Thousand Oaks, California 91320
E-mail: order@sagepub.com

SAGE Publications Ltd.
1 Oliver's Yard
55 City Road
London, EC1Y 1SP
United Kingdom

SAGE Publications India Pvt. Ltd.
B 1/I 1 Mohan Cooperative Industrial Area
Mathura Road, New Delhi 110 044
India

SAGE Publications Asia-Pacific Pte. Ltd.
33 Pekin Street #02-01
Far East Square
Singapore 048763

Acquisitions Editor: Kassie Graves
Editorial Assistant: Courtney Munz
Production Editor: Brittany Bauhaus
Copy Editor: Megan Markanich
Typesetter: Hurix Systems Pvt. Ltd.
Proofreader: Lawrence Baker
Indexer: Scott Smiley
Cover Designer: Anupama Krishnan
Marketing Manager: Katie Winter
Permissions Editor: Adele Hutchinson

Printed in the United States of America

Library of Congress Cataloging-in-Publication Data

Family life education with diverse populations / [edited by] Sharon M. Ballard, Alan C. Taylor.

p. cm.
Includes bibliographical references and index.

ISBN 978-1-4129-9178-0 (pbk.)

1. Family life education. 2. Families. I. Ballard, Sharon M. II. Taylor, Alan C.

HQ10.F3418 2012

306.8507–dc23

2011033908

This book is printed on acid-free paper.

11 12 13 14 15 10 9 8 7 6 5 4 3 2 1

Contents

Preface

There is a constant need for more information and resources specific to the field of family life education. In this time of "evidence-based," "best practices," "outcomes," etc., it is apparent that there is a particular need for a resource that helps family life educators identify best practices within family life education. One of the cornerstones of family life education is the importance of meeting the needs of the target audience. The challenge is to understand and then to meet the unique needs of so many diverse audiences. Thus, the idea of a book that pulled together best practices in family life education specific to various populations was born. We decided to test the idea in a symposium at the annual conference of the National Council on Family Relations (NCFR). We had a successful symposium at the conference in 2009 and had much positive feedback. We immediately began soliciting chapter authors who would be able to provide valuable insights and contributions to a book on family life education with diverse populations. The result is a book that captures the essence of 11 different populations and provides practical information vital to anyone who works with families.

There are many potential audiences for this book. First, it can be used as a textbook for courses in family life education, family diversity, human services, and community practice. The book can be used in professional development or training activities with practicing family professionals. Finally, practicing family professionals within community agencies; cooperative extension services; or other local, state, or national organizations that work with diverse populations will find this book to be a valuable resource.

Judith Myers-Walls (2000) has suggested that family life education is faced with questions of family diversity from three perspectives: (1) What will an educator teach? (2) Whom will an educator teach? (3) How will an educator teach? (p. 359; please see the References in Chapter 1 for the full reference).

Our book, *Family Life Education With Diverse Populations*, addresses all three of these questions posed by Myers-Walls.

This book includes chapters on the following populations: rural families; prison inmates and their families; court-mandated parents and families; military families;

grandfamilies: grandparents raising grandchildren; American Indian families; Latino immigrant families; Asian immigrant families; Arab immigrant families; black families; and lesbian, gay, bisexual, and transgender (LGBT) families. We recognize that there are many populations omitted from this volume. However, great care was taken in selecting these 11 groups. First, we chose populations with clear parameters that might have unique needs. For example, immigrant family groups are included because of the specific issues related to language and cultural adaptation. Similarly, American Indian families are included because of the unique parameters of working on a reservation with Native families. We also make a conscious attempt to fill the gap in the literature. There are some populations for which there are more materials available or whose needs might not demand unique content or methods.

This book pulls together the best of what is known about working with these 11 populations in an effort to provide a foundation and a starting place for family life educators. The goal of this book is to provide clear information on what research has shown to work (best practices) when designing and implementing family life education programming with various populations. Each chapter is written by an author(s) who has some sort of experience with the respective population and describes this experience at the beginning of the chapter. Each chapter, other than the introductory (Chapter 1) and concluding chapters (Chapter 13), has a consistent format. Using the questions posed by Myers-Walls (2000) in thinking about serving diverse audiences, the first three sections of the chapter answer the question of "Whom will the educator teach?": (1) defining the population, (2) unique aspects of the population, and (3) strengths and assets of the population. This section lays the foundation for work with this population. There are many in-depth resources available that cover many of these populations. Consequently, the goal was not to duplicate them but to provide an overview of unique aspects of the population that might provide a foundation for programming as well as strengths of the population on which family life educators can build.

The next sections answer the questions "What will the educator teach?" and "How will the educator teach?" and includes the following specific headings: (1) Current State of Family Life Education With This Population, (2) General Needs of This Population and Rationale for Family Life Education, (3) Marketing/Recruitment, (4) Barriers to Participation, (5) Environmental Considerations, (6) Modes of Learning, (7) Educator Characteristics, (8) Ethical Considerations, and (9) Best Practices in Family Life Education Programming. The chapter concludes with Future Directions. Throughout these sections, authors were asked to glean best practices from the literature and to present a sample of successful or promising programs. We also asked authors to use examples from their own work to illustrate these best practices.

Chapter 1 further explores issues related to evidence-based practices (EBPs) and programs and the difficulties with which family life educators are faced in negotiating the need for an evidence-base in their work. A *Framework for Best Practices in Family Life Education* is introduced in an effort to clarify which components of family life education are truly essential for best practice consideration. Chapter 13 concludes the book with a discussion of important components of an effective family life educator and how we can move the profession of family life education forward.

HOW TO USE THIS BOOK

Information in this book can be used to do the following:

- Improve an existing program to better reflect the needs of a specific population
- Adapt a universal program to fit a specific population
- Develop a new program for a particular population
- Assess current programming efforts to see if it is adequate for the target audience
- Increase understanding of various populations, the importance of knowing your audience, and knowing which questions to ask and what program components should be considered when thinking of cultural relevance
- Increase capacity to adequately meet needs of particular participants within a mixed population (e.g., a parent education class with gay/lesbian parents, Latino immigrant parents, and grandparents raising grandchildren in the audience)
- Identify evidence-based programs that are available for a given population

Readers will benefit from the experienced eye of the authors as they present a balance of information and pull it together in a way that has, to date, not been done before. This volume is one that all family life educators will want on their shelf and that they will refer to often. It is our hope that this volume will assist family life educators to better meet the needs of diverse families, thereby strengthening and enriching families.

ACKNOWLEDGMENTS

As we finished this book, we recognized that we had been involved in this project for nearly 3 years. It was an e-mail exchange on September 19, 2008, from Sharon to Alan with an idea for a book that would fill a needed gap in the field of family life education. We look back at this journey as one in which we've each grown significantly in our personal and professional lives as family life educators and have a stronger understanding of family life education work with diverse populations than ever before. We've come to recognize that we now have more sympathy and compassion for anyone who has taken or will take on the task of editing scholarly books! With that said, we've been fortunate to work closely with some of the brightest and most experienced family life educators. They have written such thought-provoking and interesting chapters for this book. We thank them for their great contributions.

Along with the chapter authors, there are many other people we would like to thank who have helped to make this book a reality. First, we would like to thank Kassie Graves at Sage and her production team for their assistance, support, and guidance. We would like to thank the reviewers of the initial book proposal for their insightful feedback that immediately began to shape the book into its final product. We would like to thank Sarah Miller for her attention to detail and editorial assistance. Lorraine Blackman was an early contributor on the chapter addressing family life education with black families, and we thank her for her efforts.

Finally, we would like to thank our families. Sharon would like to thank her husband, Kevin Gross, and her son, Jamie Gross, for their love and continued patience and support during this project. Alan would like to thank his wife, Kelly, for being a wonderful partner and sounding board for his thoughts and ideas associated with this book. She was helpful in her critical review and feedback during the writing and editing process. Alan would also like to thank Kelly and his five children (Bronson, Holden, Camryn, Ethan, and Lauryn) for their constant love and support, particularly associated with this book project.

About the Editors

Sharon M. Ballard, PhD, CFLE, CFCS, is an associate professor in the Department of Child Development and Family Relations at East Carolina University. She has been a certified family life educator (CFLE) since 1998 and is serving her seventh year on the CFLE advisory board with the National Council on Family Relations (NCFR). After teaching Family and Consumer Sciences for 6 years at the high school level, Sharon completed her graduate work in Child and Family Studies at The University of Tennessee, Knoxville and started teaching at the university level. She has taught both undergraduate and graduate courses in family life education and family studies, and has conducted a variety of family life education programs in community settings. She has also authored or coauthored numerous journal articles, many of which are about family life education.

Alan C. Taylor, PhD, CFLE, is an assistant professor in the Department of Child Development and Family Relations at East Carolina University. Alan has taught family life education and family relationship curriculum at the university level for the past 14 years. He has worked within the community as a family life educator in a state prison setting and also as a court-mandated parenting instructor. Alan received his master's degree in family life education from Brigham Young University, his PhD in Family and Child Development from Virginia Polytechnic Institute and State University and has held the credential of CFLE since 1998. He has authored or coauthored numerous journal articles and book chapters within edited books.

About the Contributing Authors

Menatalla M. Ads, BA, is currently a clinical psychology PhD student at the University of Detroit Mercy. Her BA in general psychology and English language and literature was received from the University of Michigan–Ann Arbor. Her experience with ethnic populations includes community development projects in Cairo, Egypt, and Detroit, Michigan, and lived experience within multicultural communities. She is presently the teacher assistant of Dr. Libby Balter Blume, PhD, CFLE. Menatalla is contributing to Dr. Blume's current research with Arab American mothers and their daughters, which investigates family-level constructions of nationality, religion, and culture.

Kristy L. Archuleta, PhD, LMFT, is an assistant professor in the School of Family Studies and Human Services at Kansas State University. She has served as director and codirector of Women Managing the Farm since 2005 and is currently the director of the Institute of Personal Financial Planning Clinic. Kristy has authored several publications and presented workshops on the topics of money and relationships and rural populations and currently serves as coeditor of the *Journal of Financial Therapy*. One of Kristy's therapy specializations is working with rural families.

Eboni J. Baugh, PhD, CFLE, is an assistant professor in the Department of Child Development and Family Relations at East Carolina University. Eboni has taught undergraduate and graduate courses in family studies for 11 years and has 5 years' experience as a family and consumer sciences specialist within cooperative extension. She has authored, coauthored, and reviewed journal articles and extension curricula, in addition to training community volunteers and county extension faculty in many areas of family life education.

Andrew O. Behnke, PhD, CFLE, is an assistant professor and human development extension specialist in the Department of 4-H Youth Development and Family and Consumer Sciences at North Carolina State University. Andrew partners, designs, implements, and evaluates various family life education programs that foster healthy children, families, and communities. He conducts outreach efforts and publishes applied research in the areas of stress and resilience, teen issues, academic achievement among youth, parent involvement in academics, stress and parenting, and fatherhood. He is recognized in the field for his efforts to serve military families and Latino immigrant families via programs such as the Juntos program, the Illuminando program, and Essential Life Skills for Military Families.

Libby Balter Blume, PhD, CFLE, is a professor in the Department of Psychology at the University of Detroit Mercy where she directs the programs in CFLE, developmental psychology, and community development. She has been a member of the NCFR for 20 years and a CFLE since 1999. Libby teaches undergraduate and graduate courses in human development, family relations, environmental psychology, and women's and gender studies. She has edited family studies journals, coauthored two textbooks on middle childhood and adolescence, and has published book chapters on transnational families, multicultural and critical race feminisms, and the social construction of ethnic identities. Her current research with Arab American immigrant mothers and their teenage daughters explores family-level constructions of nationality, religion, and culture.

Elizabeth (Bettie Ann) B. Carroll, JD, CFLE, is an associate professor in the Department of Child Development and Family Relations at East Carolina University, Greenville, North Carolina. She earned her undergraduate degree at the University of Mississippi, master's degree in marriage and family therapy from East Carolina University, and doctor of jurisprudence from Mississippi College School of Law. She primarily teaches classes in family life education and family law and public policy. She is the principal investigator of the Healthy Marriage Life Skills: A Family Readiness Program, funded by HHS-ACF Healthy Marriage Initiative, which targets Reserve Component and National Guard service members and their families. She coauthored the *Essential Life Skills for Military Families* curriculum and research interests include family life education for military families, financial literacy, and family history. Before her academic career, she was bond director for the Mississippi Treasury Department and an attorney in the Mississippi Secretary of State's office.

DeAnna R. Coughlin, BS, is a graduate student in the Department of Child Development and Family Relations at East Carolina University. She is currently pursuing her master's degree with a specialization in sexuality studies. DeAnna received her bachelor's of science degree from Kansas State University in family studies and human services with a minor in women's studies. DeAnna plans on pursuing a career working with families with a focus on sexuality.

Saul Feinman, PhD, is professor emeritus of child & family studies (Department of Family & Consumer Sciences) and of sociology at the University of Wyoming and still teaches a variety of sociology courses in the summer session. He has taught at Dine College (formally Navajo Community College), which is the tribal college of the Navajo Nation, and at the San Juan Campus of the College of Eastern Utah (part of Utah State University), where around half of the students are Navajo or Ute. He has also worked as a consultant on issues of cultural diversity, primarily with a focus upon health care and higher education.

Shann Hwa (Abraham) Hwang, PhD, CFLE, is an associate professor in the Department of Family Sciences at Texas Woman's University. He has been a CFLE since 2000 and is serving his first year on the CFLE advisory board with the NCFR. Abraham has taught family life education and family studies courses at the university level (both undergraduate and graduate) for 10 years. He has also conducted a variety of family life education programs in community settings, particularly with the Asian population. He has authored journal articles, many of which are about family life education.

Lis Maurer, MS CFLE, is director of the Center for Lesbian, Gay, Bisexual & Transgender Education, Outreach, and Services at Ithaca College. Lis has provided family life education in diverse community settings: for students and teachers in the United States, peer educators in Namibia, Girl Scout troops, religious education classes, correctional facilities, day care providers, and communities of elders. The American Association of Sex Educators, Counselors and Therapists has designated Lis a certified sexuality educator and counselor. Maurer is Senior Advisory Editorial Board member of the *American Journal of Sexuality Education* and serves on the editorial board of *The Prevention Researcher.* Coeditor of *Doing Gender Diversity: Readings in Theory and Real-World Experience,* published by Westview Press, Maurer also teaches at the graduate and undergraduate levels.

Maureen T. Mulroy, PhD, is an associate professor emerita from the University of Connecticut. Cofounder of the Connecticut Parenting Education Network, she was instrumental in the development of the state's parenting educator credential. Currently residing in Tennessee, Maureen continues her work with and for families via pro bono private practice; board membership for children, families, and the community service agencies; and serving as the state representative to the American Psychological Association's (APA) ACT Against Violence initiative.

Judith A. Myers-Walls, PhD, CFLE, is a professor emerita in the Department of Human Development and Family Studies at Purdue University. She has been a CFLE since 1991 and was an extension specialist and university professor for more than 30 years. During that time period, she presented approximately 25 community or regional family life education programs each year; created curricula and developed programs for parents, families, and human service professionals; and taught family life education in the college classroom for 7 years. She helped to coauthor models such as the National Extension Parent Education Model and the National Extension Parenting Educators Framework and most recently cocreated the Domains of Family Practice model.

Charlotte Shoup Olsen, PhD, CFLE, is a professor and extension specialist in the School of Family Studies and Human Services at Kansas State University. She has authored or coauthored numerous publications and resources for the cooperative extension service that have been used nationwide in family life education settings. She also has conducted a variety of trainings for extension and community-based professionals on the process of planning, delivering, and evaluating family life education programming. In addition, Charlotte is a frequent workshop presenter for delivering family life education to audiences from diverse backgrounds. She has been a CFLE with the NCFR since 1994.

Dianne Duncan Perrote, MS, CFLE, works for Lux Consulting Group, Inc. in Silver Springs, Maryland. She has been a CFLE for 13 years. Dianne has over 19 years' experience in early childhood education including more than 18 years working with Native American communities. She has demonstrated skills of identifying and developing culturally enhanced methods and strategies based on research and applies them to work in parent involvement, curriculum, and program development. Throughout her career, Dianne has focused on strengthening communities by building collaborations and providing research-based information in order to strengthen capacity.

Annita A. Sani, PhD, is a clinical psychologist. She has lived and worked in Dubai, located in the United Arab Emirates (UAE), since 2001. Currently, she is an educational consultant in the Department of Special Education for the UAE Ministry of Education and develops policies, procedures, and professional development training programs for determining K through 12 students' eligibility for special education programs and services. Annita was an assistant professor at Zayed University in Dubai from 2001 until 2009 and taught undergraduate courses in psychology, individual and family assessment, and intervention to female Arab students. Prior to moving to the UAE, Annita lived and worked in Michigan and was adjunct professor at the University of Detroit Mercy where she taught undergraduate courses in developmental psychology and was a certified school psychologist. She has experience providing family life education and counseling services to Arab children and their families in Michigan and the UAE.

Paul L. Schvaneveldt, PhD, CFLE, is an associate professor in the Department of Child and Family Studies at Weber State University. He has taught in family science for 17 years and is a CFLE. Paul directs a family literacy program and a federally funded marriage education program serving primarily Latino populations. He was a Fulbright Scholar through the U.S. Department of State and taught, developed programs, and conducted research at universities in Ecuador. Paul served as the chair of the International Section of the NCFR and president of the Family Science Association. He has authored numerous journal articles and book chapters on Latino family dynamics.

Catherine Clark Morgan Smith, RN, MS, NFA, CFLE, CDON-LTC, with the Essential Life Skills for Military Families project at East Carolina University, is the first North Carolina state employee hired solely as a family life educator. She has presented nationally at numerous professional and military conferences on military family needs and resilience, taught at several community colleges, and was a hospital community education coordinator. Overseas she served as a U.S. Department of Defense school nurse and as the information and referral/site manager for a military family service center. Her association with the U.S. Navy, U.S. Air Force, and U.S. Marine Corps spans 30 years. Her areas of research include military family resiliency and aging within family systems. She has authored or coauthored journal articles, community health columns, health care organization policy and procedural manuals, and research-based curricula.

Chapter 1

Best Practices in Family Life Education

SHARON M. BALLARD, CFLE, AND ALAN C. TAYLOR, CFLE

According to *Standards & Criteria: Certified Family Life Educator (CFLE) Designation* (National Council on Family Relations [NCFR], 2011b), "Family life education is the educational effort to strengthen family life through a family perspective. The objective of family life education is to enrich and improve the quality of individual and family life" (p. 3). Family life education is relevant across the life span, is inclusive of all types of families, and is designed to meet the true needs of the target audience (Arcus, Schvaneveldt, & Moss, 1993). However, given the diversity of families, it is often difficult to determine the true needs of an audience, and many audiences may be hard to reach. According to Wiley and Ebata (2004), family life educators cannot effectively teach audiences of which they are unfamiliar or unaware. Beyond just knowing about diversity among individuals and families, family life educators also must be cognizant of the unique challenges and opportunities that arise from developing and implementing programs specifically for diverse populations.

This book examines 11 diverse populations and identifies the best practices for meeting the unique family life education needs of each of them. In this chapter, we begin by discussing diversity and diverse families. We then define best practices and distinguish best practices from other related terms. Specifically, we set the stage for the book by discussing three components of family life education practices: (1) *program content*, (2) *program design*, and (3) *the family life educator*. When set in the context of culture, strengths, and needs of the population, these three components comprise the *Framework for Best Practices in Family Life Education*.

WHO ARE DIVERSE FAMILIES?

Duncan and Goddard (2011) identified "reaching the neediest audience" as one of five issues within family life education that need attention along with "professionalism, program rigor, program effectiveness, [and] marketing" (p. 366). In order to increase professionalism and visibility within the field of family life education, family life educators must conduct programs that are rigorous and effective. As professionals, family life educators also have an ethical obligation to be sure that they are targeting and reaching audiences that have a demonstrated need for the programming (Wiley & Ebata, 2004). Similarly, Small, Cooney, and O'Connor, (2009) identified "socioculturally relevant" as a guiding principle of effective family life education programming and stated that programs must reflect the language, content, and culture as well as participants' experiences, developmental, and life stages. These are all aspects of diversity within families.

Family diversity can be defined according to family structure characteristics (e.g., grandparent-headed households), race/ethnicity (e.g., American Indian), or gender and sexual orientation (gay/lesbian families) and by family process characteristics (parent–child relationships, intergenerational relationship) (Wiley & Ebata, 2004). In addition to family structure characteristics, we take the contextual approach suggested by Myers-Walls (2000) and include societal contexts (e.g., military and prison), geographical locations (e.g., rural families), and societal constraints (e.g., court-mandated). We use these dimensions (i.e., structural characteristics, societal context) to identify populations included in this book. However, we are not advocating for a particular family form, making judgments about any of the populations included in this book, or attempting to provide an in-depth analysis of the various populations. There are many other good sources that provide in-depth coverage of particular populations, and many are referenced within these chapters. Our intent is to facilitate and improve family life education efforts with these populations with the ultimate goal of strengthening and improving family life. Although the chapters provide a foundation for understanding each of the 11 populations, reading these chapters does not take the place of conducting a needs assessment. It is vital for a family life educator to know his or her audience and often talking with actual participants (or potential participants) is the best way to achieve this understanding.

Within each chapter of this book, the authors focus on one main aspect that defines a particular group (e.g., military). However, Myers-Walls (2000) cautioned family life educators to recognize that there are "multiple and intersecting dimensions of diversity" (p. 364). Consequently, it is important to remember that most families fit into multiple categories. For example, a military family may be Latino and while the parents are deployed also may be a grandfamily. While we recognize that dimensions of diversity are not mutually exclusive, for the purposes of this book we are focusing on one prominent dimension of diversity for each chapter (e.g., rural). Yet we can't ignore the fact that many family life education programs will have a heterogeneous audience that represents many diverse families. Therefore, we do briefly address programming for mixed populations in Chapter 13, the concluding chapter of the book.

An ongoing issue in any discussion of diversity is whether to focus on differences or similarities and how to strike a balance between the two (Allen, Fine, & Demo, 2000). Each chapter in this book may touch on both similarities and differences as the authors establish the rationale for family life education with their respective population. Although all families share similarities, there are unique needs of particular families and unique aspects that influence programming efforts. As Demo, Allen, and Fine (2000) strived for in their *Handbook of Family Diversity,* we, too, have tried to achieve a "dynamic balance" between differences and similarities within families (p. 2). Yet the thrust of this book is to describe the unique aspects of various populations (i.e., differences) so that family life educators will be able to better meet their needs. However, it is important to avoid overgeneralization as there is much diversity within these groups. For example, there are tremendous differences among Chinese immigrant families and Japanese immigrant families; however, Hwang addresses best practices with all Asian immigrant families in Chapter 9.

EVIDENCE-DRIVEN CULTURE

Currently, there is a trend in both prevention and intervention programming to prove what works. This need to prove what works has resulted in many terms such as evidence-based programs, evidence-informed practices, Outcome-based, best practices, and more. Family life educators are inundated with messages regarding the need for their programs to be evidence-based. However, family life educators are not always sure how to decipher all of the terms or what the terms actually mean in regard to their work with families. It is clear that we live in an evidence-driven culture, and it is essential for family life educators to situate themselves within this culture.

Within this culture, there is a spectrum of family life education programming. On one end of the spectrum, some family life educators may advocate for the use of evidence-based programs, which can be defined as "well-defined programs that have demonstrated their efficacy through rigorous, peer-reviewed evaluation and have been endorsed by government agencies and well-respected research organizations" (Small et al., 2009, p.1). Although there are many advantages to evidence-based programs, they do not take the place of a needs assessment, nor do they take the place of a skilled family life educator. Family life educators often feel pressure to use an evidence-based program, but the available programs may not meet the needs of the target audience, or be a good fit for the educator. Often there is the perception that as long as you have an evidence-based program, anyone can be trained to teach it and it will be effective. This idea is not necessarily true and negates the importance of a trained family life educator.

On the other end of the spectrum, family life educators are conducting programs and using techniques for which there is little, if any, empirical support. Many of these programs may be based largely on the educator's own experiences, perceptions of a particular group (Kumpfer, Alvarado, Smith, & Bellamy, 2002), or are a "hodgepodge" consisting of a variety of things pulled together (Small et al., 2009) rather than implementing programs that are based on research and theory. Although the experience of the educator cannot be discounted, it is not enough. Family life education programming must be based on research and theory.

Finally, in the middle of the spectrum, family life educators may strive for a balance and use a variety of "evidence-based approaches" in their programs, practices, and principles (Oregon State University Family Policy Program, 2003)."Evidence-based programs, practices and principles are processes or procedures that are shown to reliably produce measurable and sustainable improvements in productivity, efficiency, or effectiveness" (Oregon State University Family Policy Program, 2003, p. 193). Evidence-informed is yet another term and refers to the idea of using practices informed by provider experience, theory, or research (Moore, 2009, p. 2). These practices can be implemented into existing programs rather than replacing existing programs with evidence-based ones (Small et al., 2009).

It is this last approach to programming that might be the optimal and most practical option for the field of family life education and it is this approach that is the focus of this book. Throughout the book, we use the term "best practices" to refer to those family life education methods that have evidence of effectiveness. Best practices moves beyond a focus on content and methods to include program format and features. Educators must be able to gain the trust of their target audiences and effectively recruit enough participants to attend program sessions in order for the program content to have the most impact. Best practices also can incorporate what we know about a particular population and what we know works in terms of methods and content for that population. Each chapter in this book includes a section on best practices in family life education. In this section, chapter authors present a combination of evidence-based programs, promising programs, programs that exhibit best practices, as well as best practices gleaned from the literature and their own practice with a particular population. Readers can incorporate some of these best practices into their own programming or identify a program that fits the unique needs of their audience.

Therefore, good family life programs based on best practices may be a combination of empirically supported content and program design along with experiences and skills of the family life educator. The key to meeting the needs of a diverse audience is to pay attention to all of these components and to recognize that these components are interrelated and interdependent in high-quality family life education programs. It is a skilled family life educator who can coordinate these pieces to provide family life education programming that meets diverse audience needs. Therefore, these three components (program content, program design, and the family life educator) set in the context of culture and needs and strengths of the population provide our *Framework for Best Practices in Family Life Education* (see Figure 1.1).

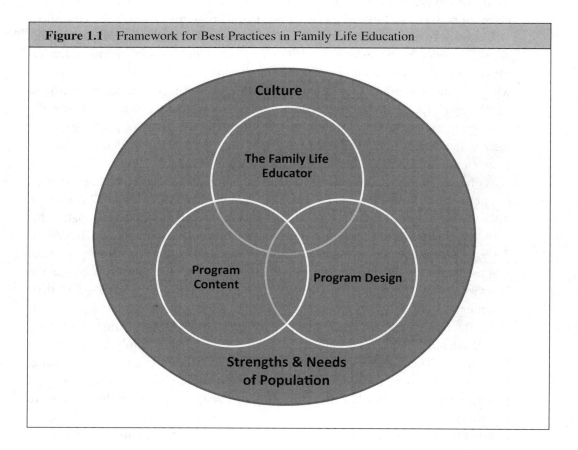

Figure 1.1   Framework for Best Practices in Family Life Education

We will discuss each of these three components (i.e. program content, program design, and the family life educator) in more depth and explore how they contribute to best practices.

Program Content

One of the principles of strong sustainable family life education programs identified by Duncan and Goddard (2005) is that "successful community programs are developmentally appropriate and based on current research" (p. 58). Duncan and Goddard elaborated on this by suggesting that this research foundation includes both empirical literature and needs assessments of the target audience. Small, Cooney, Eastman, and O'Connor (2007) distinguished between a research-based program and an evidence-based program in this way: "a research-based program has been developed based on research about the outcomes or processes it addresses. However, it has probably not been subjected to the rigorous evaluations and real-world testing that are needed to designate a program as evidence-based" (p. 4). We posit that there is a place for both research-based and evidence-based programs in family life education.

In regard to diverse audiences, program content also must be culturally appropriate in order to be effective (Wiley & Ebata, 2004). Specific to diversity, Myers-Walls (2000) recommended that family life educators look for two things when examining program content: "breadth-inclusiveness and applicability to participants" (p. 375). In other words, family life educators must determine the appropriate scope of their program and establish the relevance, or applicability, to their audience. One tool available to assist family life educators with this task is the *Framework for Life Span Family Life Education* (Bredehoft, 2009).

As family life education has progressed as a profession, one of the cornerstones has been the 10 content areas. First defined in 1987 and revised in 1997 and 2010, the *Framework for Life Span Family Life Education* has provided a foundation for both the preparation of family life educators and program development (Bredehoft, 2009). Currently there are over 120 universities and colleges in North America that use these nine content areas (plus family life education methodology) as the knowledge base for preparing students to work as family life educators in their communities (NCFR, 2011a). Through its initial development and subsequent revisions, the framework and content areas have been reviewed and critiqued by many (see Bredehoft, 2009, for complete history of the life span family life education framework). The recent practice analysis survey of family life educators (Darling, Fleming, & Cassidy, 2009) further validated these content areas as a basis for best practices within family life education. Although chapter authors in this book were not asked to specifically discuss these content areas in relation to their respective populations, these content areas were evident both explicitly and implicitly throughout the chapters. In this section, we briefly define each of these content areas and provide examples from the chapters of how this content relates to working with diverse populations.

Families and Individuals in Societal Contexts

Families and individuals in societal contexts can be defined as an understanding of families and their relationship to other institutions, such as the educational, governmental, religious, and occupational institutions in society (NCFR, 2010b). This knowledge includes having an understanding of how family structure has changed over time, the demands placed on society and the family, the shift in population sizes, dating courtship and mate selection decisions, the impact of societal trends on gender roles, and cultural variations within families. Allen and Blaisure (2009) discussed the importance of thinking contextually and globally when working with families. In order to better meet the needs of families, family life educators must be aware of current and future demographic trends as well as contextual influences on families in our society.

Consequently, each chapter in this book that addresses a specific population (Chapters 2–12) begins with sections that define the population and describe unique aspects, strengths and assets of the population, and general needs. This information provides an important foundation upon which family life educators can design and implement educational programs. For example, information regarding the historical forces that shaped black families today is shared in Chapter 11 by Baugh and Coughlin. Similarly, processes such as immigration patterns are significant to understanding Asian immigrant families and are discussed by Hwang in Chapter 9.

Internal Dynamics of Families

Internal dynamics of family is the understanding of family strengths and weaknesses and how family members relate to each other (NCFR, 2010b) on a micro level. It has also been referred to as the conceptual lenses through which family life education should view the individual within the family (e.g., family systems theory, human ecology theory, and life span development theory) (Walcheski & Bredehoft, 2009). This content area addresses family patterns and processes, family forms, and their own unique strengths and challenges. It also addresses the awareness and sensitivity to new family forms or relationships and the stress that might be felt among family members. Being able to see families through a theoretical lens and examine unique processes, strengths, and challenges helps family life educators avoid applying a "one-size-fits-all" model to their programming. Effectively using a theoretical lens is essential for family life educators to understand why families do what they do and how to develop and present an educational program to address the needs of the families involved.

A cornerstone of family life education is using a strengths-based approach to working with families. Helping people recognize their strengths and the opportunities they possess can generate a sense of empowerment and fortitude. In regard to family life education programming, certain family dynamics may be emphasized as familial strengths and may provide important clues to successful programming. Schvaneveldt and Behnke, in Chapter 8, discuss *familismo,* which refers to the strong connection among family members that is present among Latino immigrant families. *Familismo* can be considered a strength that can guide effective family life education practices. For example, designing parent education programming that involves the whole family rather than just the parents may be more effective when working with Latino families.

Conversely, internal dynamics of families also relates to family stress, which can point to the need for particular types of programming. In Chapter 7, Perrote and Feinman discuss the prevalence of domestic violence among American Indian families and the importance of addressing this issue in a culturally appropriate manner.

Human Growth and Development

Human growth and development is the understanding of the developmental changes (both typical and atypical) of individuals in families across the life span. This understanding is based on knowledge of physical, emotional, cognitive, social, moral, and personality aspects of an individual's development (NCFR, 2010b). Also included in this content area is the understanding of the various theories of development (e.g., Freud, Erikson, and Piaget) and how they relate to development of the individual over the life span.

Developmental transitions can be a key time for family life education. The manner in which one negotiates developmental stages intersects with his or her membership in a particular population. Maurer, in Chapter 12, takes a life span approach to understanding the needs of lesbian, gay, bisexual, and transgender (LGBT) individuals and families. She states that particular adolescent needs, such as information about pregnancy prevention, may be ignored among LGBT youth and that pregnancy prevention efforts with this population should not be overlooked but may need to be approached in unique ways.

Human Sexuality

Human sexuality encompasses an understanding of the physiological, psychological, and social aspects of sexual development across the life span, so as to achieve healthy sexual adjustment (NCFR, 2010b). In addition, sexuality education is a lifelong process of acquiring information and forming attitudes, beliefs, and values about identity, relationships, and intimacy. Sexuality education entails more than teaching young people about anatomy and the physiology of reproduction. It encompasses sexual development, reproductive health, interpersonal relationships, affection, intimacy, body image, and gender roles. There are many factors that play into an individual's understanding and belief about sexuality, including parents, peers, schools, religion, the media, friends, and partners (National Coalition to Support Sexuality Education, n.d.). An important aspect of human sexuality, of which family life educators should be aware, is both the emotional and psychological features of sexual involvement, sexual values and decision making, and the influence of sexual involvement on interpersonal relationships. In addition, it is essential for family life educators to be able to address these needs using a life span approach, as sexual issues impact children, adolescents, emerging adults, adults, and older adults.

When working closely with a diverse population, family life educators should respect the diversity of values and beliefs about sexuality that exists in each culture. In Chapter 10 on Arab American families, Blume, Sani, and Ads point out that topics such as sexuality often are considered inappropriate, particularly among Muslims. However, some Arab immigrant families may be accepting if the sexuality education is conducted in single-sex classrooms and the family life educator is the same sex as the students.

Interpersonal Relationships

Interpersonal relationships can be defined as the understanding of the development and maintenance of personal relationships (NCFR, 2010b). A relationship is normally viewed as a connection between two individuals, such as a parent–child relationship, or a romantic relationship. Individuals can also have relationships with groups of people, such as the relationship between a man and his church congregation, an aunt and her extended family, or an employee and her coworkers. Much of the interpersonal relationship programming focuses on romantic partners in pairs or dyads. These intimate relationships are, however, only a small subset of interpersonal relationships. A family life educator needs to have a comprehensive understanding of the development and maintenance of interpersonal relationships.

In regards to working with diverse populations, understanding interpersonal relationships is essential for family life educators in order to build relationships of trust with those they serve. More importantly, understanding interpersonal relationships allows family life educators to ascertain and meet participant needs through family life education programming. When providing education to a population that employs interpersonal communication skills differently than the larger population, programming activities would likely need to be adapted to meet the needs of the intended audience. Adaptations may include how participants listen to each other, provide self-disclosure, or even how conflicts are resolved. In Chapter 7, Perrote and Feinman discuss the importance of respect and of being trustworthy when working with American Indian populations. In Chapter 5, Carroll, Smith, and Behnke discuss some of the unique aspects of interpersonal communication within a military setting. For example, service members are introduced by their rank or title. Finally, Schvaneveldt and Behnke, in Chapter 8, point out the importance of *simpatia* among Latino immigrant families. *Simpatia* refers to politeness in social interactions and the avoidance of direct conflict or disagreement (Falicov, 2007). Having an understanding of unique cultural differences in regards to interpersonal communication can bring the family life education content closer to the participants' understanding.

Family Resource Management

Family resource management regards the decisions individuals and families make when it comes to developing and allocating resources, including time, money, material assets, energy, friends, neighbors, and space to meet their goals (NCFR, 2010b). It also entails knowing the basic skills needed to manage money and other family resources, developing financial literacy and making the types of financial decisions families are faced with on a daily basis, such as housing, transportation, food, clothing, and retirement. When working with diverse populations around resource management issues, family life educators may need to examine the values placed on certain resources. What might be considered an important resource to the educator might not be highly valued by the diverse participants or vice versa. An understanding of the decision-making structure (e.g., Does the husband make all resource decisions?) may also be an important aspect to understand.

Some of the needs of rural families identified by Olsen and Archuleta in Chapter 2 are financial concerns, availability of and /or access to community resources, lack of health insurance, and issues related to employment. These concerns relate directly to family resource management, and although these may not be unique to rural families, the rural context provides particular challenges for rural families that other families may not face. These concerns and challenges contribute to unique stressors among rural families and indicate the importance of acknowledging the role family resource management plays in the health of rural families.

Parenting Education and Guidance

Parenting education and guidance is the understanding of how parents teach, guide, and influence children and adolescents as well as the changing nature, dynamics, and needs of the parent–child relationship across the life span (NCFR, 2010b). This content area includes parenting changes over the course of time and the impact outside influences (media, peers, extended family members, work, religion, etc.) have on parenting decisions. There are many factors that influence how individuals view and practice parenting relative to diverse families. Acknowledging that parenting styles and behaviors vary greatly among various cultures and societies is important when developing and organizing educational programming. What may be considered harsh or inappropriate treatment by one group may be the norm for another. Baugh and Coughlin thoughtfully explore the role of spanking among black families in Chapter 11 and the importance of family life educators understanding the historical and cultural contexts for parenting practices among black families. Another example of the intersection of diversity and parenting practices is the unique parent education needs of incarcerated parents. Mulroy, in Chapter 3, explores parenting education efforts among prison inmates and their families.

Family Law and Public Policy

Family law and public policy is the understanding of legal issues, policies, and laws influencing the well being of families (NCFR, 2010b); encompassing issues relating to family formation, family dissolution, custody, and individual and family rights. Family life educators must understand how family policies and laws influence the structure of families (formation and dissolution) and influence family functioning (child rearing, family caregiving, and economic support) (Bogenschneider, 2006). With a solid base in this content area, family life educators possess the knowledge and skills to build more supportive policy environments for family members and can help families understand the formal support that is available to them. Many populations have unique legal issues such as those that grandfamilies face (Chapter 6) or the impact of laws such as the Defense of Marriage Act on LGBT families (Chapter 12). Laws and policies also may affect the availability and delivery of family life education as in court-mandated family life education described by Myers-Walls in Chapter 4.

Professional Ethics and Practice

Ethics refers to an understanding of the character and quality of human social conduct and the ability to critically examine moral questions and issues as they relate to professional practice (NCFR, 2010b). Ethics is concerned with human conduct and character, addressing the kind of people we are and how we relate to others (Arcus, 1999). Just like any helping professional, family life educators must be concerned with ethical conduct; signing a code of ethics specific to family life education is required for all CFLEs (NCFR, 2010a). In addition to the more general ethical standards relevant regardless of population, there are particular ethical considerations that may be unique to various populations. Each chapter includes a section on ethical consideration in which the chapter authors articulate particular ethical issues of which family life educators must be aware when working with that population. For example, family life educators must recognize the potential of dual relationships in rural communities (Chapter 2). Similarly, those working with military families (Chapter 5) should not let political affiliations and ideologies interfere with their work with service members and their families who are performing their duties within what is sometimes a controversial military environment.

Program Design

Content often is the primary emphasis within a program, yet participant needs extend beyond content to program design. Program design includes program format and features as well as methods. Family life education methodology is the understanding of the general philosophy and broad principles of family life education in conjunction with the ability to plan, implement, and evaluate such educational programs (NCFR, 2011b). Family life education methodology, along with the nine content areas covered in the previous section, is an area in which individuals must demonstrate competency in order to become a CFLE. Methods are the tools needed by family life educators to deliver the educational programming necessary for their intended audiences and these methods may differ based on the audience. The ability to adapt methods for diverse audiences is an important component of cultural competence (Allen & Blaisure, 2009; Wiley & Ebata, 2004).

Each of the population chapters in this book includes sections on modes of learning, recruitment and marketing, barriers to participation, and environmental considerations—all crucial components of program design. In these sections, chapter authors describe best practices drawing on the literature as well as their own practice. The consistent headings allow for structure throughout the book; however, they illustrate the differences among the various populations and the importance of embedding best practices within a cultural context and with an eye toward the strengths and needs of the population. For example, modes of learning may include the relevance of storytelling when working with American Indian populations (Chapter 7), the role that structure and hierarchical relationships play in the learning styles of military families (Chapter 5), or the use of small discussion groups rather than speaking in front of the whole class with Asian immigrant families (Chapter 9). In relation to environmental considerations, Myers-Walls points out that family life educators should be cognizant of the distribution of power between themselves and participants within court-mandated family life education (Chapter 4) and the importance of creating a safe and comfortable learning environment.

In addition to the sections on modes of learning, recruitment and marketing, barriers to participation, and environmental considerations, there are sections in each of the population chapters on the current state of family life education and best practices in family life education programming that include examples of promising and successful programs. Programs may vary in terms of program extensiveness. Dumka, Roosa, Michaels, and Suh (1995) emphasized the importance of program extensiveness in program planning and identified three aspects: (1) universal, (2) selective, and (3) indicated. Universal programs are designed for everyone in a particular population (e.g., a parenting education program that is designed for all parents). Selective programs are designed for a particular subgroup such as grandparents who are raising their grandchildren, or a subgroup who might be at risk (incarcerated parents). Indicated programs are intended for particular subgroups that are showing negative outcomes (e.g., court-mandated parent education). Dumka et al. (1995) cautioned that selective and indicated programs require an accurate method of identifying the target audience and that there is a risk of stigmatizing the participants by specifically targeting them. However, universal programs are often developed with the white, middle-class audience in mind and fail to meet the needs of families who don't fit this limited view. This book is focused primarily on selective programs or those programs that are designed for a particular audience. However, many of the best practices described in the chapters can be used to adapt existing universal programs.

This discussion of different program types leads to the issue of program fidelity (i.e., implementing a curriculum as it was developed), which is a central component of evidence-based programming. Many evidence-based programs have core components that are thought to be integral to the effectiveness of the program and cannot be altered. O'Connor, Small, and Cooney (2007) provided some guidelines on program adaptation while maintaining program fidelity. Generally, adaptations at the surface level, such as language, relevant scenarios or examples, or replacing images to reflect the target audience, are acceptable revisions and do not threaten program fidelity. However, "deep level" changes such as changing the dosage (i.e., length of the program), removing content, or changing implementation strategies such as number of facilitators are more likely to compromise program fidelity and should be done in conjunction with the program developers. This focus on fidelity often overlooks the importance of needs assessment.

Family life educators are trained to assess the needs of their target audience and adapt content and methods to meet varying audiences. However, a program designed for a specific cultural subgroup might still miss the mark because of the great heterogeneity among specific subgroups; family life educators must still rely on their training and expertise to design and adapt programs that truly meet audience needs.

Although many standards of efficacy (e.g., Flay et al., 2005) have been established, many of the family life education programs described in the best practices sections of the chapters in this book may not meet these standards of efficacy but may still be effective. Flay et al. identified a difference between efficacy and effectiveness: "Efficacy refers to the beneficial effects of a program or policy under optimal conditions of delivery, whereas effectiveness refers to effects of a program or policy under more real-world conditions" (p. 153). Similarly, Small et al. (2007) cautioned that because an evidence-based program has been tested under particular circumstances, it is important to implement the program under similar circumstances. Effectiveness may be more relevant than efficacy to many family life education efforts. The reality is that many family life educators may not have the luxury of providing family life education programming within the strict conditions outlined by curriculum developers. When dealing with real people, it is difficult to have consistent standards or to deliver programming in prescribed ways. Family life educators are trained to meet the needs of the target audience. The target audience often does not know that they are supposed to behave in a certain way to meet certain conditions! Family life educators also may have resource constraints that may prohibit their ability to implement a program with fidelity. For example, inadequate funding might lead to a 12-week program being offered for 8 weeks or only using one facilitator instead of two. Kumpfer et al. (2002) reviewed the limited research on culturally adapted programs as compared to culturally specific programs and found that there is some empirical support for the effectiveness of culturally adapted prevention programs, particularly in regard to engagement within the program and recruitment and retention of ethnic families. Therefore, although evidence-based programs may be considered the ideal, it may be most appropriate and practical to focus on the use of best practices and culturally adapting programs to correspond with the real-world conditions that are common within most family life education practices.

The Family Life Educator

Family life education has always been challenged by the fact that everyone has a family and therefore may think that they are experts. Armchair philosophy abounds, and it often seems that everyone has advice to share. Think of a couple transitioning to parenthood and the plethora of advice they may hear—very little of which may have a research base. But there may be a place for personal experience and advice within a family life education program. Support and sharing of experiences and feelings among participants can be an important aspect of many family life education programs. Additionally, although no family life education program should be based solely on experiences, we contend that we don't want to ignore the experience of the family life educator both in terms of content and in practice.

Throughout this book, authors lend their expertise in working with a particular population and blend their personal experience with what evidence supports in programming with this population. This experience in combination with evidence-based approaches is vital in helping family life educators more effectively reach and serve diverse families.

Research is obviously important, and providing research-based information is one of the primary things that make family life educators different than Grandma giving advice. Yet is research-based information enough? A family life educator may have research-based content, but it may not represent the information needed by the target audience at that time or be presented in a way that makes sense to the participants. If all parents could read the latest research articles and apply the information to their own parenting situations, there would be little need for parent education. Family life educators must pull the "teachable ideas" out of the latest research and present it in a way that is relevant and appropriate for the parents in your audience (Duncan & Goddard, 2011, pp. 33–34). This idea again reinforces the crucial role of the family life educator. The family life educator must not only identify relevant and "teachable" material that is empirically based but also must be able to then deliver this information in an effective manner.

Others have advocated for qualified educators within family life education (Arcus et al., 1993; Small et al., 2009). Yet, too often, family life educators are trained to work with white, middle-class families and then have trouble when they are faced with families that don't fit this mold. There is growing agreement that family professionals need more skills training and more training in working with diverse families along with building knowledge in the various family life education content areas (e.g., Smart, Keim, Pritchard, & Herron-Miller, 1995; Wiley & Ebata, 2004). This training should also encompass cultural competence.

Allen and Blaisure (2009) defined cultural competence as "practices that reflect an understanding and appreciation of diverse ethnocultural contexts, and the value such diversity brings to our lives and work" (p. 211). Allen and Blaisure also identified three assumptions regarding cultural competence and family life educators:

> (a) Given the increasing complexity of family life, [family life educators] FLEs have a critical role to play in promoting family well being in the 21st century; (b) As society's families become increasingly more diverse, FLEs must acquire skills and knowledge that allow them to work effectively and ethically; (c) Cultural competence is an essential component of professional FLE competence. FLEs must be able to function effectively and ethically in increasingly diverse settings. (pp. 209–210)

This book provides support in realizing these assumptions and can help family life educators to increase their cultural competence. The importance of the educator is recognized within each chapter in a section called "Educator Characteristics" in which characteristics specific to working with that target population are discussed. For example, in Chapter 5 on military families, Carroll, Smith, and Behnke explain that the military prefers a family life educator who has some type of military experience. Mulroy, in Chapter 3, cautions that not all family life educators are cut out for work in a prison setting. Educators must be "strong, determined, and confident individuals." In order to better elaborate on the characteristics needed by family life educators, each chapter is written by an author or authors who have experience with the respective population and describe this experience at the beginning of the chapter.

The importance of the family life educator in the success of programming is often overlooked. Yet we contend that the family life educator is a crucial piece in what constitutes best practices and is a piece that is missing from much of the discourse. A skilled family life educator effectively uses best practices in program content, program design, and program implementation.

SUMMARY

In this chapter, we have presented the *Framework for Best Practices in Family Life Education* (see Figure 1.1), which emphasizes the intersection of program content and program design with the family life educator. This framework provides a guide for the upcoming chapters and is designed to help you understand, interpret, and apply the information with each of these 11 chapters. The framework is revisited in Chapter 13 where we focus on the family life educator component and discuss strategies for strengthening family life educators through skills, knowledge, and experience.

Family life educators who are designing programs for diverse groups must create materials and use approaches that are inclusive for heterogeneous audiences (Myers-Walls, 2000). In addition, educators must also be on target with materials developed and adopted for homogenous groups. It is only through an awareness of and an appreciation for the diversity of cultures and populations that family life educators will achieve the goal of helping families live life to its fullest potential within the context of their particular circumstances, as well as within the umbrella culture of society at large (Forehand & Kotchick, 1996).

REFERENCES

Allen, K. R., Fine, M. A., & Demo, D. H. (2000). An overview of family diversity: Controversies, questions, and values. In D. H. Demo, K. R. Allen, & M. A. Fine (Eds.), *Handbook of family diversity* (pp. 1–14). New York: Oxford University Press.

Allen, W. D., & Blaisure, K. R. (2009). Family life educators and the development of cultural competency. In D. J. Bredehoft & M. J. Walcheski (Eds.), *Family life education: Integrating theory and practice* (pp. 209–220). Minneapolis, MN: National Council on Family Relations.

Arcus, M. (1999). Ethics education in family science: Strengthening programs in higher education. *Family Science Review, 12*(1), 49–64.

Arcus, M. E., Schvaneveldt, J. D., & Moss, J. J. (1993). The nature of family life education. In M. E. Arcus, J. D. Schvaneveldt, & J. J. Moss (Eds.), *Handbook of family life education: Foundations of family life education* (pp. 1–25). Newbury Park, CA: Sage.

Bogenschneider, K. (2006). Teaching family policy in undergraduate and graduate classrooms: Why it's important and how to do it better. *Family Relations, 55*(1), 16–28.

Bredehoft, D. J. (2009). The framework for life span family life education revisited and revised. In D. J. Bredehoft & M. J. Walcheski (Eds.), *Family life education: Integrating theory and practice* (pp. 3–10). Minneapolis, MN: National Council on Family Relations.

Darling, C., Fleming, M., & Cassidy, D. (2009). Professionalization of family life education: Defining the field. *Family Relations, 58*, 330–345.

Demo, D. H., Allen, K. R., & Fine, M. A. (Eds.). (2000). *Handbook of family diversity*. New York: Oxford University Press.

Dumka, L. E., Roosa, M. W., Michaels, M. L., & Suh, K. W. (1995). Using research and theory to develop prevention programs for high risk families. *Family Relations, 44*, 78–86.

Duncan, S. F., & Goddard, H. W. (2005). *Family life education: Principles and practices for effective outreach.* Thousand Oaks, CA: Sage.

Duncan, S. F., & Goddard, H. W. (2011). *Family life education: Principles and practices for effective outreach* (2nd ed.). Thousand Oaks, CA: Sage.

Falicov, C. (2007). Working with transnational immigrants: Expanding meanings of family, community, and culture. *Family Process, 46*(2), 157–171.

Flay, B. R., Biglan, A., Boruch, R. F., Castro, F. G., Gottfredson, D., Kellam, S., et al. (2005). Standards of evidence: Criteria for efficacy, effectiveness, and dissemination. *Prevention Science, 6*(3), 151–175.

Forehand, R., & Kotchick, B. A. (1996). Cultural diversity: A wake-up call for parent training. *Behavior Therapy, 27*, 187–206.

Kumpfer, K. L., Alvarado, R., Smith, P., & Bellamy, N. (2002). Cultural sensitivity and adaptation in family-based prevention interventions. *Prevention Science, 3*(3), 241–246.

Moore, K. A. (2009). Programs for children and youth in a community context. *Child Trends research-to-results*, Publication #2009-35. Retrieved from http://www.childtrends.org/Files/Child_Trends-2009_07_16_PI_ProgramsContext.pdf

Myers-Walls, J. A. (2000). Family diversity and family life education. In D. H. Demo, K. R. Allen, & M. A. Fine (Eds.), *Handbook of family diversity* (pp. 359–379). New York: Oxford University Press.

National Coalition to Support Sexuality Education. (n.d.). *Sexuality education resources.* Retrieved from http://ncsse.com/index.cfm?pageId=941

National Council on Family Relations. (2010a). *Family life educators code of ethics.* Retrieved from http://www.ncfr.org/sites/default/files/downloads/news/CFLE_CODE_OF_ETHICS_2010_0.pdf

National Council on Family Relations. (2010b). *Family life education content areas: Content and practice guidelines.* Retrieved from http://www.ncfr.org/sites/default/files/downloads/news/CFLE_Content_and_Practice_Guidelines_2010_0.pdf

National Council on Family Relations. (2011a). *Academic program approval*. Retrieved from http://www.ncfr.org/cfle-certification/academic-program-approval

National Council on Family Relations. (2011b). *Standards & criteria: Certified family life educator (CFLE) designation*. Retrieved from http://www.ncfr.org/sites/default/files/downloads/news/Standards_2011.pdf

O'Connor, C., Small, S. A., & Cooney, S. M. (2007). Program fidelity and adaptation: Meeting local needs without compromising program effectiveness. *What works, Wisconsin-Research to practice series*, Issue #4. Retrieved from http://whatworks.uwex.edu/attachment/whatworks_04.pdf

Oregon State University Family Policy Program. (2003). *Evidence based programs, practices and principles support children, youth, and families*. Retrieved from http://www.oregon.gov/OCCF/Documents/HealthyStart/MeetingNotes/Community_Mobilization/Appendix2.pdf?ga=t

Small, S. A., Cooney, S. M., Eastman, G., & O'Connor, C. (2007). Guidelines for selecting an evidence-based program: Balancing community needs, program quality, and organizational resources. *What works, Wisconsin-Research to practice series*, Issue #3. Retrieved from: http://whatworks.uwex.edu/attachment/whatworks_03.pdf

Small, S. A., Cooney, S. M., & O'Connor, C. (2009). Evidence-informed program improvement: Using principles of effectiveness to enhance the quality and impact of family-based prevention programs. *Family Relations, 58*, 1–13.

Smart, L. S., Keim, R. E., Pritchard, M. E., & Herron-Miller, A. C. (1995). Professional development during college: A comparison of out-of-class experiences in two majors. *Family Science Review, 8*, 129–141.

Walcheski, M. J., & Bredehoft, D. J. (2009). Internal dynamics of families. In D. J. Bredehoft & M. J. Walcheski (Eds.), *Family life education: Integrating theory and practice* (pp. 123–130). Minneapolis, MN: National Council on Family Relations.

Wiley, A. R., & Ebata, A. (2004). Reading American families: Making diversity real in family life education. *Family Relations, 53*(3), 273–281.

Chapter 2

Family Life Education With Rural Families

CHARLOTTE SHOUP OLSEN, CFLE, AND KRISTY L. ARCHULETA

If you have ever listened to the lyrics of the song "Down Home," recorded by country music sensation Alabama in 1991, you have heard the ideals and values placed on the simple life of living in rural America. However, if you are not from a rural community or familiar with rural life, you may not be able to fully appreciate the sentiments that the lyrics provoke. Rural families are often portrayed as independent, hardworking, and honest. With these positive attributes, rural people sometimes gain a negative reputation and are viewed as narrow-minded, uneducated, and stressed for various reasons. Rural families may or may not possess some or all of these characteristics, but one thing is for certain ... rural families face unique challenges and share opportunities that may be difficult for nonrural family life educators and other helping professionals to understand.

As chapter authors, we wish to acknowledge our appreciation for being born into rural, farm, and ranch families. Both of us were born in the Plains states to parents who were totally immersed in small agricultural communities. We learned how to drive tractors, large trucks, and combines at an early age to help with the farming operations of our families. During adulthood, we each have continued to be involved with farming and ranching enterprises with our husbands and/or families of origin. As personal and professional lives often intersect, we have found as faculty members that our outreach and research interests include targeted efforts to address the contemporary needs of rural families. Our initial work together was establishing an annual conference for Kansas and Oklahoma women, Women Managing the Farm, that continues to thrive today. Out of these types of outreach efforts have come quantitative and qualitative data that help us more clearly understand the varied situations of agricultural families as well as rural families not directly tied to agricultural operations. We have great hope for rural America and what the environment can provide for increasingly diverse families and the rural communities that support them.

DEFINING THE POPULATION

To begin to understand rural families, it's helpful to first understand the definition of *rural*. Most people envision "rural" as farms, ranches, open spaces, and small towns (Cromartie & Bucholtz, 2008). However, defining the term *rural* is a difficult task. Depending on the definition used, the U.S. rural population ranges from 17% to 49% (Cromartie & Bucholtz, 2008). Official government offices have given multiple definitions of rural populations, making it a difficult task to distinguish rural from urban among researchers and policy makers. According to Cromartie and Bucholtz (2008), there are three major ways to determine urban versus rural boundaries: (1) administrative, (2) land-use patterns, or (3) economics. The term *administrative* is used by "many USDA [U.S. Department of Agriculture] rural development programs [and] defines urban along municipal or other jurisdictional boundaries" (Cromartie & Bucholtz, 2008). The term *land-use* identifies urban areas based on density or how densely settled the area is. This definition is used by the U.S. Census Bureau. The "economic" concept is the most widely used definition in rural research projects and recognizes the influences of cities on labor, trade, and media markets that extend well beyond densely settled cores to include broader "commuting areas." The economic concept is used by the U.S. Office of Management and Budget (OMB).

In the definition given in the 2002 Farm Bill, rural populations are generally characterized by any area other than (1) cities or towns made up of 50,000 or more people and (2) the urbanized areas contiguous and adjacent to such a city or town (Womach, 2005). The U.S. Census Bureau defines rural areas as open country and settlements with fewer than 2,500 residents; areas designated as rural can have population densities as high as 999 per square mile or as low as 1 person per square mile (Womach, 2005). The OMB describes nonmetro counties outside of the boundaries of metro areas and further subdivides them into micropolitan statistical areas centered on urban clusters of 10,000 to 50,000 residents and all remaining noncore counties (Womach, 2005). The Economic Research Service (ERS) allows researchers to break out the standard metropolitan and nonmetropolitan areas into smaller residential groups (Womach, 2005).

Rural and frontier communities comprise nearly 90% of the land in the United States (Howarth, 1996). Interestingly, nearly 75% of the U.S. population resides in 2% of the land mass. Howarth stated that 90% of America's population now earns salaried incomes, primarily in urban settings. The remaining 10%, who still produce resources, generate 20% of the world's coal, copper, and oil; 10% of its wheat; 20% of its meat; and 50% of its corn. These percentages reflect the movement toward commercialized farming rather than single-farm families.

Rural American communities are diverse racially, ethnically, religiously, socially, economically, educationally, and politically, as well as in language (Townsend, 2010). This chapter addresses the diverse families living in rural areas, family life education practices, and exemplar programs that deal with the unique challenges of rural families and embrace and strengthen the ideals and values of rural life.

Unique Aspects of Rural Families

Rural communities are comprised of both farming and nonfarming families and are increasingly aging as the younger population leaves rural areas (Townsend, 2010). Sawyer, Gale, and Lambert (2006) described rural areas as being characterized by low population, limited economic base, cultural diversity, high rates of poverty, limited access to cities, and residents who can have serious mental and behavioral health problems such as depression, suicide, and alcohol and substance abuse. Furthermore, American Community Survey reports that there is a consistent national pattern of higher divorce rates in rural populated states than in highly populated states. However, the report indicates that this finding cannot be taken at face value as a higher rate of common-law marriages and cohabiting couples in urban areas may be a confounding variable (National Center for Family and Marriage Research, 2009).

Townsend (2010) and Conger (1997) reported that rural communities are diverse across the United States. Conger noted that rural communities are as diverse as more urban areas, from the Native Americans who live in rural areas across the country, the Hmong tribes people from Southeast Asia residing in rural Iowa, to African Americans who live in the southeast corner of the United States. Townsend noted that people of color comprise between 15% to 17% of the rural population. Approximately 23% of the total white population lives in rural areas, too. More specifically, the 2002 U.S. Census Bureau reported African Americans comprising 12.5% of the entire population, which was an increase from the 2000 U.S. Census. African Americans are more likely to reside in southeastern states (e.g., Georgia, Alabama, South Carolina, Louisiana, and Mississippi). In 2000, Hispanic Americans comprised 5% of the total rural population, and this appears to be increasing rapidly, showing a growth rate of 71% since the 1990 U.S. Census. In mostly southern or midwestern states, the rate of growth among the Hispanic rural population has nearly doubled. Almost 70% of the Hispanic population lives in Texas, New Mexico, California, Arizona, Colorado, Washington, Florida, and Kansas. Native American and Alaska natives comprise about 1.5% of the population. Native Americans are more likely to live in rural areas than other racial/ethnic groups. In fact, nearly 42% of all Native Americans live in rural areas with the majority living in Oklahoma, Arizona, New Mexico, Alaska, North Carolina, South Dakota, and Montana. Asian Americans make up about 1% of the rural population. Over 50% of Asian/Pacific Island Americans are concentrated in rural Hawaiian counties. Approximately 80% of white Americans comprise the rural population. A large number of white Americans live in Southern Highlands and the Appalachian region of the United States.

Strengths and Assets of Rural Families

In an area where "everybody knows your name," rural Americans face many stressors and challenges, but they also encounter many opportunities that are unique. Most of the literature addresses stressors or problems from living in rural America. In fact, very few research studies note the positive aspects of living in a rural community. In a study about attitudes of psychology doctoral students' attitudes of working in a rural area, Jameson, Blank, and Chambless (2009) found that doctoral students had more of a positive attitude towards working in a rural area than the researchers originally expected. Most notably, these doctoral students who mostly grew up in nonrural communities and went to school in nonrural areas believed that rural areas offered a safe place for family and a pace of life that was less stressful. Danbom (1996) stated that rural America is America's "field of dreams," a place where "people live genuine lives, where both individualism and community thrive and where physical and mental health are restored. It's the heartland of American values of liberty and equality" (p. 17). Rural America has also been seen as the identity and strength of the republic and place where people escape the values of urban culture.

Townsend (2010) noted that rural high school graduation levels match or exceed urban levels. This might be explained by the higher teacher–student ratio. Typically, rural schools have more teachers per student, which allows additional one-on-one tutoring and assistance with special needs. Unfortunately, because fewer students attend rural schools, rural schools are being affected by major budget reductions.

Because there is a sense of a "Mayberry Syndrome" i.e., everyone knows everyone else's business in small towns, there is an impeccable challenge of learning to get along with others. In rural communities, children learn to navigate the social culture and get along with peers at a very early age. If ties are severed with one peer group, there are no or few alternative peer groups to join. Creighton (2010) stated that urban people are able to self-select their peers and avoid people they don't like. If you have options of where to shop and go to school and a choice of children's activities, you can do something different if you don't like it. However, rural adults do not have the same luxury. In a small town, "the same people are part of every group. Anonymity or starting fresh is not an option" (Creighton, 2010, para. 7). Civic virtue is learned when you are forced to work with others, especially those who you may not like. Creighton (2010) suggested that this may be the "essence of community [because] community comes before friendship. Getting things done together comes before getting along. The good news is that getting things done often leads to getting along" (para. 10). As Townsend (2010) said, "They care for their own (in rural communities); have strong community supports and relationships, even while holding onto personal privacy" (p. 31).

FAMILY LIFE EDUCATION PRACTICES

Current State of Family Life Education

The Cooperative Extension Service has been a leader over time in delivering family life education to rural families in the United States, mainly in the agricultural sector. This entity dates back to 1914 when federal legislation, the Smith–Lever Act, created the Cooperative Extension Service as an outreach arm of each state's land grant university. The Cooperative Extension Service was designed to receive local, state, and federal financial and organizational support to deliver informal community education based on university research findings. Its purpose was to disseminate practical and useful information to persons throughout the United States on content relating to agriculture and family and consumer sciences (formerly known as home economics) and to encourage the adoption of recommended practices (McDowell, 2001). Youth development and 4-H programming also reside within the extension system. In more recent times, extension offices in each county within the United States are not always the norm as Cooperative Extension Services and its local, state, and federal partners adjust to changing economic conditions and increasingly diverse needs of rural populations. However, Rogers (2003) called the extension model, using local change agents called extension agents or educators, one of the oldest and definitely one of the most successful diffusion systems for delivering educational innovations in the United States.

Extension agents/educators in the family life area as well as their 4-H/youth development extension counterparts are collaborating with other community family professionals to more effectively reach and meet the multiple needs of rural audiences living both in small towns and on farms and ranches (Rodman, Sheppard, & Black, 2008). These community workers are not working in isolation from each other. Local health departments, rural mental health centers, public and private school systems, community development organizations, private- and publicly funded social service agencies at the county and state levels, religious organizations and coalitions, after school and child care services, private foundations, homeless and domestic violence shelters, the extension service, and other entities created to address the needs of rural individuals and families are increasingly working in community collaborations.

Family life programming in rural areas covers the life span—early and middle childhood, adolescent youth, young and middle adulthood, and aging. The programs are as diverse as the communities in which programs are delivered. Initiatives on caregiving are more prevalent in areas where the majority of the population is older adults (Bailey & Paul, 2008) as compared to rural areas where immigrant populations are moving into communities that have employment opportunities (i.e., meatpacking industry). In the latter communities, family life educators are recognizing the need to design and implement culturally specific programs to meet family needs (Skogrand, Barrios-Bell, & Higginbotham, 2009).

Increasingly, programming can reflect national initiatives that provide competitive grant dollars to tackle local community needs. Operation: Military Kids is a national initiative funded by the U.S. Army to address the needs of National Guard and Army Reserve rural youth and children impacted by deployment, living away from the support systems offered at military installations. As part of a 4-H/Army Youth Development Project, rural community partners connect military children and youth with local resources in order to achieve a sense of community support and to enhance their well-being (Operation: Military Kids, 2009).

The Healthy Marriage Initiative funneled millions of dollars into rural communities in the past decade "to help couples, who have chosen marriage for themselves, gain greater access to marriage education services, on a voluntary basis, where they can acquire the skills and knowledge necessary to form and sustain a healthy marriage" (Administration for Children and Families [ACF], n.d.). The initiative was specifically targeting low-income, unmarried parents.

Rural family life educators, just as their urban and suburban counterparts, are being trained to understand how nonprogrammatic research and theory are essential for program development and refinement, implementation, and program research to inform subsequent and successful educational initiatives (Higginbotham, Henderson, & Adler-Baeder, 2007). A comprehensive training model that had federal funding support through the extension system was hosted by the Ohio State University Extension in 2006 for relationship and marriage enrichment educators, predominately from rural areas. This effort evolved into a national effort in creating a guide for community programming. It has relevance not only for relationship education but for parenting education and other family life content areas. The guide emphasizes the importance of the following:

- Understanding the content area to more readily ensure that the family life educator will do no harm to the audience when implementing a program
- Using nonprogrammatic research and theory to inform practical and ethical programmatic decisions as well as to explain the programming results
- Working with community collaborations to make good use of available resources, understand the community, ensure adequate needs assessment, and increase likelihood of positive program impact and sustainability
- Understanding the target audience (diverse family structures, low-resource and culturally diverse, youth, adults, etc.) to more effectively meet the targeted population's family needs and how they are most likely to be recruited, to be cognizant of their learning styles, and to be aware and respectful of cultural values that impact their receptivity to family life programming
- Understanding other related topics for successful community initiatives such as clearly defining program leadership with an appropriate communication mechanism, having shared and clear mission and goals, creating a viable implementation plan with shared responsibilities, and evaluating and documenting impact (Futris, 2007; Higginbotham et al., 2007; Olsen & Shirer, 2007; Skogrand & Shirer, 2007).

General Needs of This Population and Rationale for Family Life Education

Lovelace (1995) described nine major stressors for rural families: (1) financial situation, (2) personal illness, (3) inadequate social institutions (e.g. schools, hospitals, and recreation areas), (4) generational/family pressure (e.g. pressure to return home and maintain a family farm or business or pressure to excel or become more educated), (5) occupational unpredictability (both economic and natural), (6) Mayberry Syndrome, (7) lack of health insurance, (8) lack of access to medical/social support systems, and (9) occupational hazards. These stressors are listed in order from most to least stressful. More recently, Waldman (2008) found six very similar stressors in her study of associations between stressor events and depressive symptoms among rural, low-income single mothers, including (1) parenting hardships/worries; (2) financial concerns; (3) availability of and/or access to community resources; (4) health; (5) interactions with family, friends, and others; and (6) employment. This finding suggests that over the course of 12 years, very little has changed in terms of types of stressors that rural families experience.

Johnson and Booth (1990) found that when farm couples face economic hardship, thoughts of divorce increase, which was largely mediated by depressive symptoms. In other words when financial issues rise, farm husbands are likely to experience depressive symptoms and begin thinking about divorce. Johnson and Booth suggested that the close relationship between the economic unit of the farm and the family unit serve as a barrier to marital dissolution. Therefore, when the economic unit of the farm is threatened, a potential barrier to marital breakup is weakened.

In 2004, Evans reported that rural women often have higher rates of depression than the general population. These women are often characterized by low educational levels and poverty. More specifically, research conducted by the Rural Families Speak project found that low-income rural women reported having fewer opportunities for employment, and less access to child care, transportation, and health and mental health resources (Bauer & Katras, 2007). Lack of access to these resources in return impacts women's ability to obtain and maintain employment.

Kosberg and Sun (2010) reported that rural men face many similar problems as urban men and rural women, such as marriage, divorce or separation, family losses, unemployment, illness and aging, and caregiving responsibilities. Rural men are more likely to encounter specific social, economic, and mental and physical health problems resulting from the dependency on their work, such as farming, fishing, and herding. These occupations are prone to stressors beyond one's control, such as weather, economic, and political climates (Garkovich, Bokemeier, & Foote, 1995). In addition, farming has been named in the top three most dangerous occupations with the highest fatality rate (U.S. Department of Labor, 2004).

Courtenay (2006) suggested that "rural male culture" portrayed in the media as rugged, strong, and tough influences rural men on how they should act and behave. Rural men often engage in unhealthy activities such as smoking, drinking, and eating poorly and are likely not to seek help when physical or mental symptoms arise (Kosberg, 2005). Rural men experience a great sense of independence and pride and view seeking help as making one appear too weak to handle their own problems (Courtenay, 2006). Instead, they are likely to engage in destructive coping mechanisms (Kosberg, 2005). Like rural women, rural men are prone to depressive symptoms but at higher rates. In fact, national suicide rates are three to five times higher for rural men than national averages (Courtenay, 2006). In a place where "everybody knows your name," everybody also knows your business—or at least thinks that they do—which can impede on the functioning of the community, leadership, social support, and help-seeking.

A prevalent problem in rural America is substance abuse. Conger (1997) suggested that urban substance abuse lends itself to rural substance abuse both for illicit and licit drugs. Urban drug dealers have found new markets in rural areas, and drug manufacturers can move to rural areas to develop their practice in a more isolated area; rural drug manufacturers can then find new outlets in urban areas to sell their drugs.

Rural areas have faced many years of economic decline, which appears to have contributed to the rising rates of alcohol and drug abuse and depleting available resources to treat, prevent, and educate in the area of substance abuse (Conger, 1997; Sloboda, Rosenquist, & Howard, 1997). Substance abuse is not only a concern for adults but also for youth (Conger, 1997; Cutrona, Halvorson, & Russell, 1996; Sloboda et al. 1997). According to Cutrona, Halvorson, and Russell (1996), alcohol consumption tends to be higher among rural youth than urban youth. Conger (1997) reported that the smaller the rural community and the higher the involvement and supervision of parents or adults with children lead to decreased substance use. However, he noted that rural youth are three times more likely to use alcohol and drugs than metropolitan youth. Substance abuse is not the only risky behavior that the literature points out. Rural youth also have higher rates of risky sexual behavior (Yawn & Yawn, 1993). Townsend (2010) indicated that 20% of teen pregnancies occur in rural areas, and suicide rates among rural youth ages 10 through 24 are consistently higher than the national average.

Poverty is an important concern among those studying and educating rural families. Many rural families travel 50 miles to work off-farm. Townsend (2010) reported that less than 10% of rural Americans live on farms, and nonfarm employment accounts for nearly 80% of rural jobs. Rural working families are likely to be poorer than urban working families with a major contributing factor being that rural employment income is less than in urban areas (Townsend, 2010). Townsend reported that 23% of rural counties are classified as persistent poverty counties by the U.S. government, and she noted that recent economic downturns have worsened behavioral health issues, particularly in communities affected by factory and plant closings.

Another major challenge that often arises for rural families is caregiving for both children and older adults (Bauer & Katras, 2007; Kosberg & Sun, 2010). For example, at the time of this writing, a small town in rural south central Kansas called a special town meeting in order to discuss a major problem: no child care facilities. The last child care provider quit in order to pursue other opportunities, and now the working families in the area with young children were left facing a major crisis. Women were shown to have high commitment to both work and childcare and were willing to find strategies with their limited resources that reduced the conflict of maintaining employment and obtaining child care. The lack of or access to child care facilities is just one of the unique stressors that rural Americans face that nonrural families may have difficulty understanding. Another challenge is the caregiving of parents or adult relatives with special needs. The burden of caregiving can seem overwhelming.

Yee and Schulz (2000) found that male caregivers may experience similar levels of burden and depression as found for caregiving females. As gender role norms relax in rural areas, it's likely that more men will take on the responsibility of care-giving (Kosberg, 2005). Rural families may feel isolated; lacking social support and access to health and resources is difficult. Those in the "sandwich" generation may find it difficult to balance employment if there is a lack of child care facilities and at the same time tending to the needs of older adult relatives.

Serving rural families requires an understanding of the local demographics, economic base, and group dynamics of the specific community in which a family life educator is working. The needs can be varied, but family life educators have the background and capacity to have a working knowledge of a rural commu-nity's human, cultural, and social dynamics and, therefore, can be an invaluable resource in bringing content areas such as parenting, caregiving, family financial management, family stress, youth development, and family communication and dynamics to the table to address documented rural family and community issues as mentioned previously. In fact, community survival factors were found to be more concentrated in these types of issues than with infrastructure challenges such as housing, transportation, utilities, water, etc. (Fritz, Boren, Trudeau, & Wheeler, 2007). Rural family life educators understand developmental needs across the life span within the context of rural culture. They understand how to build upon fam-ily strengths in helping rural families facing formidable challenges (e.g. living in poverty, abusing substances, caregiving, having family intergenerational pressures, and having gender role conflicts). Furthermore, family life educators are well grounded in building community collaborations to bring a diverse array of people together to work on issues of concern. For instance, Fetsch (2006) suggested the partnering of extension agents and mental health practitioners when working with farm and ranch families to reduce their depression and stress levels and enhance their "native self-sufficiency."

Marketing/Recruitment

Connecting with other community professionals who have trusted relation-ships with rural families is advantageous in marketing a program (Bailey & Paul, 2008). Partnerships with schools, religious institutions, and rural businesses are important factors in reaching rural families, especially from diverse cultural groups (Viramontez Anguiano & Kawamoto, 2003). Having multiple organizational part-ners working together on an educational endeavor for rural families brings together a vast array of skills and cross-disciplinary knowledge for designing a project that is relevant to the audience. Collaboration enhances the potential for under-standing the audience's needs as well as marketing and recruiting of participants. Furthermore, such collaborations build professional connections for networking on other projects (Jones & Field, 2005; Olsen, Jones, Jost, & Griffin, 2009). One key to this successful partnership is having a designated leader who is responsive to the needs of each partnering group, is highly organized, and has effective group processing skills that are imperative for productive planning meetings (Archuleta & Olsen, 2008). To quote Letiecq and Bailey (2003), "If project staff do not collaborate with these local professionals (from other agencies, etc.), the result can be interagency conflicts, political reprisal, and professional isolation" (p. 3).

Rogers (2003) also found that the most successful diffusion projects use change agents who have similarities with the target audience. He labeled this similarity "homophily." This allows the change agent to personally reach out to potential clients to market and recruit and also opens the door to working with "opinion leaders" or respected community leaders within the target population.

Jones and Field (2005) found that marketing a program for caregivers of agricultural workers with disabilities was one of the most challenging aspects of their family life education efforts. Their success in getting participants to show up was working with local community members to make personal contacts with individuals and with the local news media.

PSAs of testimonies by persons well known to the target population such as politicians, athletes, and tribal and community leaders has been suggested for reaching rural men in need of services (Kosberg & Sun, 2010).

Family life education focus group participants have shared their recruitment preferences for personal approaches—first choice was word of mouth or invitations and second was through the media (posters, newspapers, radio, etc.). Participants also wanted to meet where they were, such as at home or in the workplace, with low or no-cost participant registration (Duncan & Marotz-Baden, 1999). If using focus groups to ascertain audience needs and effective marketing approaches, it is of utmost importance that persons are trained in focus group data collection methods. Furthermore, using appropriate listening and probing techniques allows professional service providers to more fully understand the context of a community and services needed to make a difference in the lives of rural families (Boleman & Cummings, 2005; Bowling & Brahm, 2002).

Barriers to Participation

For rural families involved in the agricultural sector, barriers to participation could be inconvenient timing because of specific farming/ranching/hunting/fishing operations (e.g. calving or harvest season), inclement weather conditions, travel requirements, separation from family, and personal financial situations. Technological discomfort and lack of Internet availability are barriers for online distance education participation (Archuleta & Olsen, 2008). Trust issues within the target population, particularly as it relates to rural families from multiple cultural and ethnic backgrounds, prohibit persons from participating in or voluntarily sharing information in family life education programs (Skogrand, Hatch, & Singh, 2009; Viramontez

Anguiano & Kawamoto, 2003). Closely connected community members may not want to share intimate details or personal challenges in front of each other. Furthermore, potential participants may consider the family life educator an outsider to their community who has no business in requesting personal family information, regardless of the program's goal of providing information to help families in their decision making. Immigration issues also can profoundly affect trust issues among some families within a community.

Letiecq and Bailey (2003) found that "dangerous driving conditions" (snowfall) and long distances requiring overnight stays can make it tough not only for the audience but for family life educators to deliver and evaluate a program. Furthermore, populations can be "leery of the university, our motives, and what the outcomes will mean to their communities and programs" (p. 3).

Lack of available child care and transportation options have frequently been cited as barriers to participation, especially among limited resource audiences (Olsen & Shirer, 2007; Richardson, Williams & Mustian, 2003). In general, rural areas do not have mass transportation systems for traveling from town to town. In counties with small populations, a family life education event held in the county seat is likely not to attract residents from the farthest reaches of the county. In rural America, there are many remote locations that require the family life educator to travel to the family.

Providing child care for limited resource audiences makes the event financially feasible for the parents to attend. From a cultural perspective, Olsen and Skogrand (2009) reported that Latino families are not likely to attend an educational event unless the whole family can attend. Furthermore, if the parents and children are separated throughout part of the event, the parents do not want to physically be far removed from their children.

Cultural minority groups may be biased from utilizing available resources because of differing values and history of the sponsoring agencies. There may be a history of conflict with governmental agencies or of being treated unfairly for African Americans, Native Americans, Hispanics, and others (Kosberg & Sun, 2010). A historical distrust does not easily dissolve despite the efforts of family life educators to make their programs accessible and available. Furthermore, language barriers and cultural conflict between long-term residents and new immigrants of the same ethnicity create additional layers of distrust within rural communities. More information and details on culturally-diverse families can be found in other chapters within this book.

Environmental Considerations

Viramontez Anguiano and Kawamoto (2003) called for a "rural paradigm shift" when serving rural Asian American and Latino families. The key lessons they learned in being culturally sensitive within rural communities are as follows:

1. learn the rural geographic region and its historical influence on the target groups;

2. understand cultural resources and characteristics that have evolved for these groups;

3. understand their relationship with local, state, and federal government; and

4. understand the importance of the concept of time in these rural communities. (p. 2)

These approaches are intuitively understood for rural audiences who have traditionally lived in the community but take a dedicated effort by a family life educator when serving families new to rural areas, especially if new groups encounter a discriminatory community climate.

"Tumultuous environmental disruptions" such as droughts, earthquakes, floods, fires, tornados, or hurricanes can affect the livelihood of farmers, ranchers, fishermen, and herders for brief or extended periods of time (Kosberg & Sun, 2010). Small-town businesses also suffer in the wake of a disaster, creating stress among families and their communities. Likewise, global and national economic indicators hit rural towns, too. When the rural population experiences an economic downturn, small factories and plants that manufacture many things such as livestock trailers and other agricultural equipment may be forced to downsize, lay off workers, or even shut their doors when the customers are not coming through the doors. Rural community employment trends affected by factory or plant and livestock feedlot closings cannot be ignored by family life educators. It can present opportunities for analyzing the shifting community needs and the types of educational interventions that would be timely and well received (e.g. stress management, managing on a limited budget, and family dynamics in hard times).

Anonymity is a big issue in small towns (Gorman et al., 2007). The community will see marketing flyers about town, read the upcoming events in the weekly town or county newspaper, or hear about a family life education program on area radio/ TV stations or through the Internet. People know each other's vehicles. Thus, families can be labeled as having a problem if their vehicle is parked where it is known that an educational event is being held.

However, people will more likely come to a place they trust, such as a church building. Fetsch (2006) also reminded extension agents who collaborate with mental health practitioners who are addressing messy intergenerational farm family issues to meet in a setting that is considered neutral by all family members.

Modes of Learning

The modes for learning related to rural families are diverse. A conference setting with keynote speakers, small concurrent sessions, networking time based on similar farming roles, and exhibit booths for commercial and professional resources has proven to be successful in addressing multiple learning styles for women in agriculture (Archuleta & Olsen, 2008). Rural women involved in agricultural operations were surveyed for the types of learning formats that they preferred (Barbercheck et al., 2009). The respondents indicated that not only did they want to learn more about farm topics but they wanted parenting and family communication information, too. Their preferred learning formats were seminar/workshop (85%), on-farm demonstration at local farm (80%), at home (74%), written materials (51%), online courses (48%), electronic materials (47%), and presentations during regular community meetings (45%). Duncan and Marotz-Baden (1999) also found that rural respondents wanted a learning mode that did not take much time from the family, whether it be mini-classes and workshops offered during children's school hours or at the workplace, short reading materials, or using the local media.

In Montana, an Alzheimer's caregiving educational intervention has been more successful in moving from a one-time event to a series of seminars but within short travel distances (Bailey & Paul, 2008). Among the Latino population, Skogrand, Barrios-Bell, et al. (2009) reported that personal relationships are important in how persons learn and that plenty of time should be allowed for talking and discussion in small group settings. Again, family life educators in rural settings are reminded to understand "cultural syndromes and expressions outside of Western norms" (Townsend, 2010, p. 32). Rogers (2003), in studying the most successful ways to educate rural audiences in general, emphasized that the change agent or educator needs to be person-centered with a strong orientation toward the client's needs rather than to assume the agency's orientation.

Educator Characteristics

A family life educator who truly embraces being a rural community change agent must work to understand the context of the families that are being served, especially when having a different cultural and socioeconomic background. Rogers (2003) has found that change agents have more success when they do as follows:

- Align with the audience's needs rather than focus solely on needs of their employer.
- Make repeated direct contacts with the target audience over time.
- Offer programming that is compatible with the audience's needs.
- Show empathy toward the audience.
- Have credibility in the eyes of the audience.
- Have homophily (similarities) with the audience—if not, using paraprofessionals from the target audience can bridge the gap.
- Work effectively with leaders within the target community.
- Use the target audience to evaluate programming effectiveness.

Ethical Considerations

"Maintaining participant privacy is very difficult in small towns and on reservations where most activities are visible to extended family members and community members. Unfortunately, few recommendations regarding confidentiality in rural communities have been identified in the literature" (Letiecq & Bailey, 2003, p. 3). For instance, if a family life educator would casually mention participants' comments to a community friend or family member without thinking, confidential information could spread throughout the community. Thompson (2003) shared an example where a community professional might be a natural confidant for a one-on-one family life consultation; however, the professional's spouse is known to talk a lot. Thus, confidentiality has to be guarded whether a family life educator is in a formal or informal setting.

In addition to issues of confidentiality, rural communities also may be prone to problems of dual relationships. The nature of small communities might lead the family life educator to play multiple roles, and it might not be possible to avoid these dual relationships. However, the family life educator must be aware of the potential impact of intersecting boundaries. The following quote illustrates how rural providers may have to manage personal and professional boundaries in "unique ways as compared to urban providers":

> We do a lot of things that you just would not do in the lower forty eight or anywhere else. We have to watch what we say, of course, due to confidentiality issues. As far as the ethical part, there is a large spectrum and what may be inappropriate in an urban area is not in a rural area. We have whole families in therapy for one thing or another, and then we are invited to their kids' birthday. What do you do? It would be insulting if we did not go. We do keep those mental boundaries and try to respect them. To some extent, I think the system underestimates client awareness of these situations. It is all about legalities and due to liability. It depends on the culture, and it changes from culture to culture depending on where you go. It is important to be aware of that. (Gifford, Koverola, & Rivkin, 2010, p. 17)

Best Practices in Family Life Education Programming

The Strengthening Families Program: For Parents and Youth 10 to 14 is a youth, parent, and family skills-building curriculum originally designed for rural families to "prevent teen substance abuse and other behavior problems, strengthen parenting skills, and build family strengths." This rigorously studied program has proven effective in the following:

- Delaying the onset of adolescent substance use
- Lowering levels of aggression

- Increasing the resistance to peer pressure in youth
- Increasing the ability of parents/caregivers to set appropriate limits and show affection to and support of their children (Iowa State University Extension, 2009)

The program has been scientifically evaluated in a randomized, controlled test through the Institute for Social and Behavioral Research at Iowa State University using multi-method and multi-informant measurement procedures. Data were collected at pretest, posttest, and multiple follow-ups after the pretest. This program received extensive external funding and has been nationally recognized for its positive impact on families.

Few family life education programs for rural families, if any, have been tested for their effectiveness as extensively as the Strengthening Families Program. What can be learned from this evidence-based program that could be applied to numerous educational initiatives addressing the needs of families in rural communities?

- There is a "fidelity of implementation," meaning that the program is delivered to the group for whom it was intended. For this program, it is families with youth ages 10 to 14.
- The program activities are based on nonprogrammatic research and theory related to individual, family, peer, school, and community risk and protective factors.
- Facilitators are rigorously trained, and they must have strong facilitation and presentation skills and prior experience working with youth or parents. They learn about the goals and background of the program as well as tips on recruiting and working with difficult situations during program sessions. (*Note: This program requires facilitator certification to insure program fidelity.*)
- The activities are delivered in the same matter as proven effective through the longitudinal research.
- The sessions are highly interactive, using role-plays, video vignettes with realistic parent and youth scenarios, learning games, discussions, and parent–youth family projects.
- The intervention is delivered in seven weekly 2-hour sessions with parents and youth meeting separately during the first hour and meeting together with parent–youth activities during the second hour.
- The program is delivered in the evenings at a community setting that is familiar to the audience.
- It requires at least 2 months of program planning with community collaborators prior to the first session.
- About 8 to 13 families are optimum for program delivery.

- It also has proven effective with ethnically diverse families although consideration needs to be given to video scenarios that represent the ethnicity and cultural background of the participants.
- Recruitment procedures have included identifying a target group such as a school class, religious group, or families receiving services from an agency, inviting four to six parents from the target group to a short informational meeting, showing a promotional video and having a sample activity, asking parents to be "program shepherds" by inviting one to two families to the program, and/or getting referrals from a family-serving organization or agency.
- Incentives such as providing the evening meal, child care, transportation if needed, store coupons, etc., can help promote attendance if grant money is available. If not, volunteers can also be helpful in providing these incentives.
- Simple pretest and posttest evaluations are appropriate for this program since it has proven its effectiveness through more rigorous testing.

Four booster sessions are available between 3 to 12 months after the 7-week sessions if families feel a need for additional intervention (Bode, Hanlon, & Santiago, 2008; Iowa State University Extension, 2009).

FUTURE DIRECTIONS

Family life educators who work with rural families will continue to be pulled in multiple directions by the diverse populations and their multiple needs as previously noted. Family caregiving will be an increasingly difficult issue. Adult children or grandchildren may not be living within easy driving distance to look after the day-to-day needs for their aging relatives in rural communities. Aging friends and siblings within the same community may not be an option for the elderly population as these natural caregivers could be having their own caregiving challenges. Family life educators who understand the multiple issues of caregiving, including long-distance caregiving, can be a valuable asset to rural communities with aging populations.

Rural communities may need to position themselves for traumatic brain injury education for both survivors and caregivers not only for the elderly population with their frequent falls and subsequent head injuries but also for veterans returning to their rural home communities, especially National Guard and Army Reserve personnel who may not live near a military installation. Traumatic brain injury is the "signature injury" for soldiers who have been deployed in Operation Iraqi Freedom and Operation Enduring Freedom (de Riesthal, 2009). Educational programs need to include knowledge about the physical, behavioral, emotional, and cognitive changes of traumatic brain injuries; effects upon the persons themselves as well as family and community; and helpful resources, services, and linkages to others with similar situations (Sellers & Garcia, 2010).

Rural communities that offer employment opportunities in the agricultural and construction sectors have traditionally attracted immigrants from diverse cultures. These populations, often more vulnerable than those families established in a rural community, will continue to receive family life education opportunities that inform them when they need family-related services, what options are available, and how to access and pay for them (Townsend, 2010). These audiences, coming from numerous ethnicities, racial groups, educational levels, religions, languages, and political beliefs, will require a family life educator to be increasingly culturally competent to understand how to deliver culturally relevant and appropriate educational services. This is especially poignant for families where the youth are socially living in two cultures simultaneously and serving as the English interpreter for adult family members.

Since family life educators understand a rural community's intangible capitals, such as human and social behaviors, they have the skill set to be integrated into diverse collaborations for many rural audiences. For instance, intergenerational farm transfer is an overwhelming issue that has traditionally been addressed by agricultural economists, lawyers, bankers, and accountants. Family life educators have a niche in partnering with these types of professionals for helping families understand communication dynamics in difficult situations (Olsen et al., 2009). Another example is youth development educators being tapped by school districts and community leaders for help in building upon the strengths of their youth in avoiding risky behaviors (gang activity, substance abuse, etc.).

Long-distance technology will be included in most service delivery plans of the future, not only for marketing but for the content delivery, too. Face-to-face programming will never totally dissolve, but Internet-based delivery systems will increasingly be used as wireless Internet access reaches remote rural areas. Woolverton (2003) was using videoconferencing several years ago to connect specialists hundreds of miles away with families who had children with special needs. Ever since that time, there are countless examples of more advanced technologically driven service delivery modalities.

Philanthropic-research practitioners' partnerships have "great promise" in creating models of "effective service delivery to underserved populations," such as those previously named (Kohler, Tarr, Nix, & Greenberg, 2003). The authors provided a model that has been used to improve health and well-being of rural low-income children. These types of partnerships will enhance the interrelatedness of research and programming for documenting impact based upon sound research questions.

Professional development training will become more sophisticated in helping family life educators understand help-seeking behaviors of rural audiences based on updated evidence-informed programs and practice experiences (Kosberg & Sun, 2010). Such training will include professionals becoming more aware of how their own personal issues can reverberate and negatively impact providing ethical services.

In conclusion, providing family life education to rural audiences will never be static. Similar to urban environments, individual and family issues and challenges change within the context of their rural community as well as the bigger society. The rural family life educator can never be complacent to think that rural audiences are all the same and are prone to stay the same. Change is inevitable even among rural populations.

REFERENCES

Administration for Children and Families. (n.d.). *The healthy marriage initiative.* Retrieved from http://www.acf.hhs.gov/healthymarriage/about/mission.html#ms

Archuleta, K., & Olsen, C. (2008, April). *Support systems for women in agriculture.* Paper presented at the meeting of the National Women in Agriculture Educators Conference, Oklahoma City, OK.

Bailey, S., & Paul, L. (2008). Meeting the needs of rural caregivers: The development and evaluation of an Alzheimer's caregiving series. *Journal of Extension, 46*(1). Retrieved from http://www.joe.org/joe/2008february/a1.shtml

Barbercheck, M., Brasier, K. J., Kierman, M. E., Sachs, C., Trauger, A., & Findeis, J. (2009). Meeting the Extension needs of women farmers: A perspective from Pennsylvania. *Journal of Extension, 47*(3). Retrieved from http://www.joe.org/joe/2009June/a8.php

Bauer, J. W., & Katras, M. J. (2007). *Rural prosperity: A longitudinal study of rural communities and rural low-income families.* Retrieved from http://www.cehd.umn.edu/fsos/assets/pdf/RuralFamSpeak/NRICGPFinalReport.pdf

Bode, M., Hanlon, E., & Santiago, A. (2008, May). *Addressing risk and protective factors in the strengthening families program for parents and youth ages 10–14.* Paper presented at the CYFAR Conference, San Antonio, TX.

Boleman, C. T., & Cummings, S. R. (2005). Listening to the people—A strategic planning model for Cooperative Extension. *Journal of Extension, 43*(3). Retrieved from http://www.joe.org/joe/2005june/tt3.php

Bowling, C., & Brahm (2002). Shaping communities through Extension programs. *Journal of Extension, 40*(3). Retrieved from http://www.joe.org/joe/2002june/a2.php

Conger, R. D. (1997). The social context of substance abuse: A development perspective [NIDA Monograph, 168]. In E. B. Robertson, Z. Sloboda, G. M. Boyd, & L. Beatty (Eds.), *Rural substance abuse: State of knowledge and issues* (pp. 6–36). Rockville, MD: National Institute on Drug Abuse. Retrieved from http://archives.drugabuse.gov/pdf/monographs/Monograph168/Monograph168.pdf

Courtenay, W. H. (2006). Rural men's health: Situating men's risk in the negotiation of masculinity. In H. Campbell, M. Mayerfeld-Bell, & M. Finney (Eds.), *Country boys: Masculinity and rural life* (pp. 139–158). University Park: Pennsylvania State University Press.

Creighton, J. (2010, May 3). Required civic virtue. *Washington Times.* Retrieved from http://communities.washingtontimes.com/neighborhood/dispatches-heartland/2010/may/3/required-civic-virtue/

Cromartie, J., & Bucholtz, S. (2008). *Defining the "rural" in rural America.* Retrieved from http://www.ers.usda.gov/AmberWaves/June08/PDF/RuralAmerica.pdf

Cutrona, C. E., Halvorson, M. B. J., & Russell, D. W. (1996). Mental health services for rural children, youth, and their families. In C. E. Heflinger & C. Nixon (Eds.), *Families and the mental health system for children and adolescents: Policy, services and research* (pp. 217–237). Thousand Oaks, CA: Sage.

Danbom, D. B. (1996). Why Americans value rural life. *Rural Development Perspectives, 12*(1), 15–18.

de Riesthal, M. (2009). Treatment of cognitive-communicative disorders following blast injury. *Perspectives in Neurophysiology & Neurogenic Speech & Language Disorders, 19*(2), 58–64.

Duncan, S., & Marotz-Baden, R. (1999). Using focus groups to identify rural participant needs in balancing work and family education. *Journal of Extension, 37*(1). Retrieved from http://www.joe.org/joe/1999february/rb1.html

Evans, G. D. (2004). Improving behavioral health services in rural America. *Rural Mental Health, 29*(1), 13–16.

Fetsch, R. (2006). Practical strategies for extension agents to partner with mental health professionals in providing family consultation for farm/ranch families. *Journal of Extension, 44*(5). Retrieved from http://www.joe.org/joe/2006october/iw3p.shtml

Fritz, S., Boren, A., Trudeau, D., & Wheeler, D. (2007). Low resources in a high stakes game: Identifying viable rural community partners. *Journal of Extension, 45*(4). Retrieved from http://www.joe.org/joe/2007august/rb2.shtml

Futris, T. (2007). Building community collaborations to support healthy and stable marriages. In T. Futris (Ed.), *Cultivating healthy couple & marital relationships: A guide to effective programming* (pp. 65–74). Washington, DC: USDA Cooperative State Research, Education and Extension Service.

Garkovich L., Bokemeier, J., & Foote, B. (1995). *Harvest of hope.* Lexington: University Press of Kentucky.

Gifford, V., Koverola, C., & Rivkin, I. (2010). Factors contributing to the long-term retention of behavioral health providers in rural Alaska. *NARMH Rural Mental Health, 34*(1), 12–22.

Gorman, D., Bulkstra, E., Hegney, D., Pearce, S., Rogers-Clark, C., Weir, J., et al. (2007). Rural men and mental health: Their experiences and how they managed. *International Journal of Mental Health Nursing, 16,* 298–306.

Higginbotham, B., Henderson, K., & Adler-Baeder, F. (2007). Using research in marriage and relationship education programming. In T. Futris (Ed.), *Cultivating healthy couple & marital relationships: A guide to effective programming* (pp. 19–26). Washington, DC: USDA Cooperative State Research, Education and Extension Service.

Howarth, W. (1996). The value of rural life in American culture. *Rural Development Perspectives, 12*(1), 5–10.

Iowa State University Extension. (2009). *Strengthening families program: For parents and youth 10–14.* Retrieved from http://www.extension.iastate.edu/sfp/index.php

Jameson, J. P., Blank, M. B., & Chambless, D. L. (2009). If we build it, they might come: An empirical investigation of supply and demand in the recruitment of rural psychologists. *Journal of Clinical Psychology, 65*(7), 723–735.

Johnson, D. R., & Booth, A. (1990). Rural economic decline and marital quality: A panel study of farm marriages. *Family Relations, 39,* 159–165.

Jones, P., & Field, W. (2005). Caregiving in the heartland: Outreach through adaptation and collaboration. *Journal of Extension, 43*(3). Retrieved from http://www.joe.org/joe/2005june/iw4.php

Kohler, J. K., Tarr, J. E., Nix, R., & Greenberg, M. T. (2003). Improving the health and development of rural low-income children: A philanthropic-research-practitioner partnership in Centre County, Pennsylvania. *National Council on Family Relations Family Focus on Rural Life, FF17.*

Kosberg, J. I. (2005). Meeting the needs of older men: Challenges for those in helping professions. *Journal of Sociology and Social Welfare, 32,* 9–31.

Kosberg, J. I., & Sun, F. (2010). Meeting the mental health needs of rural men. *Rural Mental Health, 34*(1), 5–11.

Letiecq, B. L., & Bailey, S. J. (2003). Weaving a feminist approach into program planning and evaluation in rural communities. *National Council on Family Relations Family Focus on Rural Life, Issue FF17.*

Lovelace, D. (1995). Stress in rural America. *Journal of Agromedicine, 2,* 71–78.

McDowell, G. R. (2001). *Land-grant universities and Extension into the 21st century: Renegotiating or abandoning a social contract.* Ames: Iowa State University Press.

National Center for Family and Marriage Research. (2009). *Divorce rate in the U.S., 2008* (FP-09-02). Bowling Green, OH: Author. Retrieved from http://ncfmr.bgsu.edu/family_%20 marriage_lit/Family%20Profiles/Divorce%20in%20US_2008.pdf

Olsen, C. S., Jones, R., Jost, J., & Griffin, C. (2009). Integrating economics, management, and human relationship issues into training for successful farm family businesses. *Journal of Extension, 47*(5). Retrieved from http://www.joe.org/joe/2009october/iw6.php

Olsen, C. S., & Shirer, K. (2007). Offering relationship and marriage education in your community. In T. Futris (Ed.), *Cultivating healthy couple & marital relationships: A guide to effective programming* (pp. 27–36). Washington, DC: USDA Cooperative State Research, Education and Extension Service.

Olsen, C. S., & Skogrand, L. (2009). Cultural implications and guidelines for extension and family life programming with Latino/Hispanic audiences. *The Forum for Family and Consumer Issues, 14*(1). Retrieved from http://www.ncsu.edu/ffci/publications/2009/v14-n1-2009-spring/ olsen-skogrand.php

Operation: Military Kids. (2009). *Creating community connections and touching lives...Before, during and after deployment.* Retrieved from http://www.operationmilitarykids.org/public/ home.aspx

Richardson, J. G., Williams, J. Y., & Mustian, R. D. (2003). Barriers to participation in extension expanded foods and nutrition programs. *Journal of Extension, 41*(4). Retrieved from http:// www.joe.org/joe/2003august/a6.php

Rodman, J., Sheppard, C., & Black, J. (2008). Family and consumer sciences—A valuable resource to public schools in parent and community engagement. *Journal of Extension, 46*(5). Retrieved from http://www.joe.org/joe/2008october/iw2.php

Rogers, E. M. (2003). *Diffusion of innovations* (5th ed.). New York: Free Press.

Sawyer, D., Gale, J., & Lambert, D. (2006). *Rural and frontier mental and behavioral health care: Barriers, effective policy strategies, best practices.* National Association for Rural Mental Health. Retrieved from http://www.contracosta.networkofcare.org/library/Rural%20and%20 Frontier%20Mental%20Health_Barriers_2006.pdf

Sellers, D., & Garcia, J. M. (2010). *Traumatic brain injury (TBI): Promoting public knowledge.* Unpublished USDA-NIFA grant application. Manhattan: Kansas State University.

Skogrand, L., Barrios-Bell, A., & Higginbotham, B. (2009). Stepfamily education for Latino couples and families: Implications for practice. *Journal of Couple and Relationship Therapy, 8*(2), 113–128.

Skogrand, L., Hatch, D., & Singh, A. (2009). Strong marriages in Latino culture. In D. Abbott, J. Johnson, R. Dalla, & J. DeFrain (Eds.), *Strengths and challenges of new immigrant families: Implications for research, policy, education, and service* (pp. 117–134). Lexington, MA: Lexington Press.

Skogrand, L., & Shirer, K. (2007). Working with low-resource and culturally diverse audiences. In T. Futris (Ed.), *Cultivating healthy couple & marital relationships: A guide to effective programming* (pp. 57–64). Washington, DC: USDA Cooperative State Research, Education and Extension Service.

Sloboda, Z., Rosenquist, E., & Howard, J. (1997). Introduction: Drug and alcohol abuse in rural America [NIDA Research Monograph, 168]. In E. B. Robertson, Z. Sloboda, G. M. Boyd, & L. Beatty (Eds.), *Rural substance abuse: State of knowledge and issues* (pp. 1–5). Rockville, MD: National Institute on Drug Abuse. Retrieved from http://archives.drugabuse.gov/pdf/monographs/Monograph168/Monograph168.pdf

Thompson, T. (2003). Improving health and human services in rural America. *National Council on Family Relations Family Focus on Rural Life, FF17.*

Townsend, W. (2010). Recovery services in rural settings: Strengths and challenges influencing behavioral healthcare service delivery. *Rural Mental Health, 34*(1), 23–32.

U.S. Department of Labor, Bureau of Labor Statistics. (2004, September 22). *National census of fatal occupational injuries in 2003*. Retrieved from http://www.bls.gov/news.release/archives/cfoi_09222004.pdf

Viramontez Anguiano, R., & Kawamoto, W. (2003). Serving rural Asian American and Latino families and their communities: A call for a rural paradigm shift. *Journal of Extension, 41*(1). Retrieved from http://www.joe.org/joe/2003february/iw1.shtml

Waldman, J. B. (2008). *Stressor events, resources, and depressive symptoms in rural, low income mothers*. Unpublished master's thesis, University of Maryland, College Park, MD.

Womach, J. (2005). *Agriculture: A glossary of terms, programs, and laws,* 2005 edition. CRS Report for Congress. Retrieved from http://ncseonline.org/nle/crsreports/05jun/97-905.pdf

Woolverton, M. (2003). One rural family's experience with telehealth. *National Council on Family Relations Family Focus on Rural Life, FF17.*

Yawn, B. P, & Yawn, R. A. (1993). Adolescent pregnancies in rural America: A review of the literature and strategies for primary prevention. *Family & Community Health, 6*, 36–45.

Yee, J. L., & Schulz, R. (2000). Gender differences in psychiatry morbidity among family caregivers: A review and analysis. *The Gerontologist, 40*(2), 147–164.

Chapter 3

Family Life Education With Prison Inmates and Their Families

MAUREEN T. MULROY

Although the decades-long growth of the U.S. prison population continues to profit from much public and political support, the negative economic consequences are causing many to question the efficacy of the system. This chapter summarizes the far-reaching but largely hidden impact of incarceration on the children and extended families of inmates, as well as on the prisoners themselves.

Based upon personal and professional experiences with incarcerated parents and their families, I propose that family life educators are professionally prepared to analyze and negotiate this country's fragmented judicial and penal systems. Family life educators are in a prime position to advocate for and to develop the type of multifaceted, family-nuanced programs that are needed to alleviate some of the damage and suffering currently visited upon those who are innocent and those who may be guilty.

DEFINING THE POPULATION

With 1 in 100 adult citizens currently behind bars, the U.S. rate of incarceration is the highest in the world (Pew Center on the States, 2008). In fact, it is almost four times the world average (Hartney, 2006)! These figures have powerful implications for American children and families because 60% of these 2+ million imprisoned men and women are parents of minor-age children (Harrison, 2003; Mumola, 2000). Because many inmates have multiple minor-age children, it is estimated that over 1.7 million, or 2%, of U.S. children have at least one parent in prison (Glaze & Maruschak, 2008). This figure is twice the percentage of similarly affected children in other Western industrialized nations such as Great Britain (Murray, 2007) and Australia (Quilty, Butler, & Levy, 2005).

Experts agree that the growth in the U.S. prison population began in the mid-1980s and continues to rise. For example, numerous reports indicate that the number of men and women in prisons and jails doubled between 1987 and 1998 (Garfinkel, McLanahan, Meyer, & Seltzer, 1998; West & Sobol, 2008). This dramatic increase in conviction and imprisonment rates coincided, not surprisingly, with a nationwide outcry for law enforcement to "get tough on crime" and for legislators to enact habitual offender laws (i.e., "three strikes, you're out") that used incarceration as the primary means of punishment (Hallinan, 2001; King & Mauer, 2002; Scalia, 2001). Indeed, many criminologists point to the increased power prosecutors were given during this period, in terms of plea bargaining and the use of fixed mandatory minimum sentencing guidelines, to explain the upward spiral of U.S. conviction and imprisonment rates (Arditti & McClintock, 2001; Austin & Irwin, 2001; Beck & Harrison, 2001; Scalia, 2001).

In recent years, the wisdom, expense, and efficacy of the "three strikes" laws and "mandatory minimums" have been called into question. The fiscal and psychological costs associated with the incarceration of the over 1 million criminals affected by these mandates have been staggering (Arditti & McClintock, 2001; Austin & Irwin, 2001; Irwin, Schiraldi, & Ziedenberg, 1999; King & Mauer, 2002; Travis, McBride & Solomon, 2005). Prisons and jails needed to be expanded or constructed; corrections personnel had to be recruited, hired, and trained; families disrupted by the incarceration of a spouse or parent required public assistance; and some children of inmates needed to be placed into state care (Hairston, 2003). In some states, the costs related to incarceration rivaled the costs of public education (Greenwood, Modell, Rydell, & Chiesa, 1996)!

Because legislatively mandated minimum guidelines often resulted in lengthy sentences, financial and emotional hardships related to imprisonment were not short-term in nature. A large percentage of inmates, convicted during this period, received sentences of 10 to 12 years in federal and state prisons and local jails for offenses that involved neither harm nor threat of harm to a victim (Austin & Irwin, 2001; Bales & Dees, 1992; Beck & Harrison, 2001; Irwin et al., 1999; King & Mauer, 2002; Lynch & Sabol, 2000; Tonry & Hatlestad, 1997).

By early 2000, researchers, policy makers, police officials, and social justice and family advocates began to argue the judiciousness of using harsh criminal sanctions for nonviolent offenders. Reports by a variety of state and federal agencies contributed to this discourse by noting the unprecedented increases in the number of women inmates, the disproportionate numbers of imprisoned African American males, the high recidivism rates, and the challenges communities faced as hundreds of thousands of prisoners were removed from or reunited with families annually (Davies, Brazzell, LaVigne, & Shollenberger, 2008; Haj 2003; LaLiberte & Snyder, 2008; Mumola, 2000; Scalia, 2001).

Unique Aspects of Prison Inmates and Families

The U.S. Department of Justice (2004) report *Survey of Inmates in State and Federal Correctional Facilities* provides invaluable statistical insight into the lives of prison inmates and their families:

- While 48% of state and 38% of federal prisoners reported never being married, 55% of the state and 63% of the federal inmates did report having children under 18 years of age. Eighty-six percent of the prisoners' minor age children were under 10 years old, and 22% were under the age of 5.
- Sixty-four percent of the mothers in state facilities and 84% of mothers in federal facilities reported living with at least one of their minor age children prior to incarceration. Approximately 33% of these women lived alone as a single parent with their children, and 16% reported living with their children and a spouse or partner prior to being jailed.
- Forty-four percent of state-imprisoned fathers and 55% of the federally imprisoned fathers reported residing with a child prior to their admission. Of these fathers, 25% reported living with their children and a spouse or partner prior to incarceration, and only 4% reported living as a single parent.
- Over 90% of imprisoned fathers reported that their children were currently living with their children's mother(s). Other reported child-living arrangements were grandparents (11.6%), other relatives (5%), friends (5%), and foster care (1.5%).
- Incarcerated mothers reported their children as currently living with fathers (29.5%), grandparents (49%), other relatives (30%), and friends (29.5%), and in foster care (6.5%).

Other reports indicate that parent inmates are typically young (57% under the age of 35), educationally limited (75.7% have a high school diploma or less), have few or inadequate employment skills, and are disproportionately poor and minorities (Chesney-Lind, 1997; Pollock, 2002; U.S. Department of Justice, 2002, 2003, 2004).

Strengths and Assets of Prison Inmates and Their Families

Despite these life challenges, prison inmates are not without familial and personal assets. Most parents in both state (80%) and federal (93%) prison reported having had some form of contact with their children since their admission either via telephone (71%), mail (76.5%), or personal visit (49.6%) (Mumola, 2000).

Because of the expense involved in these forms of contact, the communication between inmate parents and their children had to be supported by adults with an expressed interest in helping either the child or the parent, for example, nonincarcerated spouses, parent partners, grandparents, relatives, and friends (Hairston, Rollins, & Jo, 2004; Pollock, 2002). It appears that if some degree of positive alliance existed between the inmate and his or her children, spouses, partners, or kin relatives prior to incarceration then continued contact and support during the period of incarceration is quite likely (Loper, Carlson, Levitt, & Scheffel, 2009).

Depending upon the inmate and the penal facility to which he or she is admitted, the experience of being imprisoned can become the foundation upon which important life skills are developed and the cycle of recidivism broken. Over 90% of state prisons, all federal prisons, 90% of private prisons, and 60% of local jails provide educational programs in secondary and basic adult education and vocational training and well over 50% of state and federal inmates participate in them (Harlow, 2003). In some facilities, inmates may also receive substance abuse treatment and choose to participate in recovery education, literacy, and anger management classes and volunteer to engage in family reunification and community reentry preparation programs. Many inmates participate in these types of programs because they see them as avenues for improving their ability to find employment as well as mending their relationships with families and friends after being released (Vacca, 2004).

FAMILY LIFE EDUCATION PRACTICES

To understand the current state of family life education programming for incarcerated parents and their families, readers must first realize that the term *family life* has rarely been applied to the programs, projects, and initiatives that have been designed to improve the life trajectories of inmates and their families. Then readers must acknowledge the very real impediments associated with the replication of prison- and community-based education and intervention programs, such as the varying and restrictive prison policies, challenging profiles of inmate and family risk, and the psychological and logistical difficulties surrounding family visitation and reengagement. Finally, readers will need to look beyond the flawed evaluation methods common to many of the cited studies (e.g., failure to use pre- and post-assessments, validated tests and measures, or "wait-listed" comparison groups). Upon accepting these limitations, astute readers will be free to discover a wealth of research informed findings, recommendations, and suggestions that can be utilized to construct model programs and to establish best practices for incarcerated parents and families. They will also uncover a field of study ready for the focused attention and sustained engagement of family life education researchers and practitioners.

Current State of Family Life Education

Although there may be other types of family life education programs offered in prison settings, such as those related to personal well-being (e.g., life skills, and anger management), this chapter will focus specifically on parent education programs. Programs specifically designed for incarcerated parents and their families fall into four main categories: (1) parenting classes for incarcerated parents, (2) parent–child visitation programs, (3) mentoring for children of incarcerated parents, and (4) school and community-based counseling and support groups for the children of incarcerated parents.

Parenting Classes for Incarcerated Parents

These classes primarily focus on the needs of men and women parenting from a distance rather than on preparation for family reunification. They are typically designed to teach principles of child development and/or the development of effective parenting skills, such as positive communication and guidance and discipline techniques, in anticipation of release and reunification. A few have additional foci such as understanding children's responses to parental incarceration and the challenges and restrictions of parenting from prison. Courses for fathers may also present information on child support payments and may cover anger management and domestic violence (DV) issues. The overall goal of these courses is to help participants become better parents and to improve outcomes for their children (Bushfield, 2004; Frye & Dawe, 2008; Hairston, 2007).

Parent–Child Visitation Programs

Visitation programs allow incarcerated parents—usually mothers—to spend extended time with one or more of their children within the prison environment. This type of program uses a variety of strategies to strengthen the parent–child relationship, such as the provision of structured and enriched environments in which parents and children can meet and interact (Block & Potthast, 1998; Weilerstein, 1995), opportunities for children to participate in "sleepovers" and extended visits (Block & Potthast, 1998; Luke, 2002; Snyder, Carlo, & Coats Mullins, 2001), and in-prison nurseries for women and their infants (Carlson, 1998, 2001). Visitation programs have been found to result in a higher frequency of parent–child contact, reports of greater closeness in the relationship, higher levels of parental satisfaction and esteem, and in the case of the nursery programs, higher levels of custodial contact after release (Carlson, 2001; Moore & Clement, 1998; Showers, 1993; Snyder-Joy & Carlo, 1998).

Mentoring for the Children of Incarcerated Parents

The primary aim of this type of mentoring program is to break the cycle of intergenerational incarceration. Although specific goals vary between programs, most mentoring programs for children of inmates focus on reducing antisocial behaviors, improving school outcomes, and creating positive relationships with an unrelated adult volunteer. Typically children are matched with a mentor who commits to spending at least 1 hour per week for at least 1 year. Mentoring for children of prisoners has been promoted by the federal government as an effective, low-cost approach to helping children and as a means of involving faith-based and other community organizations in preventing crime (Boudin, 2003; Hairston, 2007; Shlafer, Poehlmann, Coffino, & Hanneman, 2009).

School and Community-Based Counseling and Support Groups for the Children of Incarcerated Parents

These programs, typically moderated by a trained adult, are designed to give children an opportunity to meet with peers in their community who have a parent in prison, to speak openly about their feelings and experiences, and sometimes to provide them with social and recreational activities. These programs face significant challenges in terms of referral, recruitment, and retention of participants, and the program facilitators have to work hard to gain the trust of caregivers and children alike (Weissman & LaRue, 1998).

It should be noted that most of these program types are organized to coincide with the period of parental imprisonment. Although inmates and family members report high levels of confusion, stress, and emotional upheaval during the arrest and adjudication process and at the time of subsequent release, community reentry, and family reunification, few programs have been developed to help either the incarcerated parent or his or her family during these equally critical phases (Davies & Cooke, 1999; Frye & Dawe, 2008; Travis & Waul, 2003).

General Needs of This Population and the Rationale for Family Life Education

Parental incarceration is associated with a complex array of legal, financial, social, emotional, relational and educational issues, as well as consequences for the parent, parenting partner(s), children, family members, and other caregivers. The crime committed by the parent, the length of the sentence, the number and types of existing family configurations, the quality of the pre-arrest family relation-ships, the phase of parental incarceration (i.e., pre-arrest criminal phase, arrest and adjudication phase, prison admission and incarceration phase, the pre-release or community transition phase, and the community reentry and family reunification phase) as well as the gender of the parent and his or her children are some of the factors that influence the type of needs that can be addressed by family life educa-tion professionals (Hairston, 2003; Nesbith & Ruhland, 2008).

The experience of imprisonment requires a dynamic family life approach to help meet the myriad needs of the incarcerated parents and their family members:

- Parents in prison need instruction on how to maintain, reestablish, or forge healthy bonds with their families; communicate in honest, supportive, and developmentally appropriate ways; and to appreciate and collaborate with their children's caretakers. Their spouses, partners, children, and other sup-porting family members, on the other hand, need help processing the legacy of harm resulting from the criminals' activities and behaviors. They also need support and guidance in evaluating the consequences of reestablishing communication with the prisoner (Cecil, McHale, Strozier, & Pietsch, 2008; Eddy et al., 2008; Greenberg, 2006).

- Parenting from prison is very different from parenting on the outside. Therefore, efforts must be made to ensure that the parenting education offered to inmates and their families reflect prison-specific realities. Each audience needs to learn how to make the best of the "allowable" forms of contact (Greenberg, 2006).

- Inmate parents and their family members need to be provided with a forum to process their intense feelings of guilt, sadness, anger, and shame in a safe and constructive manner. They can also benefit from peer support and sup-port from institutional and community agents (Cecil et al., 2008; Eddy et al., 2008; Greenberg, 2006).

- Parenting programs, in and out of prison, need to help participants develop realistic goals and expectations about the type of parenting and family sup-port that can be provided by the inmate parent and his or her caregiving part-ners (Cecil et al., 2008; Eddy et al., 2008; Hairston et al., 2004). Both groups must learn to be flexible and creative in their plans for parenting. Problems such as a prison "lockdown," a child's illness, or a car that breaks down are unavoidable and must be handled without animosity and recrimination.

- A generic "one size fits all" approach to parenting education will not meet the needs of incarcerated mothers and fathers. There is ample evidence suggest-ing that men and women require different parenting solutions and practical training techniques because of the differing levels of connection with their children and children's caretakers. Unlike women, men frequently reported ιaving no legal or biological relationship to children yet still felt a connection ecause of their relationship with the children's mothers (Bushfield, 2004; ¹agaletta & Herbst, 2001; Tripp, 2001).

As Klein, Bartholomew, and Bahr (1999) noted, implementing educational programs to help inmates strengthen family ties before, during, and after incarceration is an important goal for several reasons. First, inmates who learn how to repair and maintain their family relationships have reduced disciplinary problems within the prison system and are less likely to accept the norms and behavior patterns of hardened criminals. Secondly, maintenance of family and community ties during imprisonment is positively related to post-release success. Finally, the period of incarceration may be a time when inmates and their families are motivated to improve their lives and take steps to rehabilitate, preserve, and/or strengthen their marital and family relationships.

Marketing/Recruitment

Any family life education corrections-based program designed for incarcerated parents and their families will have to be vetted by the state or federal prison where it will be used. The receptivity to family life education programs will vary from prison to prison. Institutional barriers in the guise of policies and regulations should be expected and will most likely hamper program development, marketing, and recruitment efforts (Arditti, 2008). Similarly, interest in and receptivity to participation in a family life education program will vary from one child and family to the next. For the children and families of incarcerated parents, the "Five S's"—stigma, shame, separation, secrecy, and silence—play a significant role in marketing programs and recruiting participants (Greenberg, 2006). Family life educators need to understand that for many families the imprisonment of a loved one results in a profound sense of personal and familial shame that is often accompanied by real or imagined stigmatization and separation from friends, neighbors, or society in general. To cope with these harsh realities, many children and families of inmates resort to a code of silence and secrecy and attempt to distance themselves from any connection with the prison inmate and the prison system (Greenberg, 2006; Hairston, 2002).

Prison inmates themselves must also be recruited to participate in family life education activities and programs. Although educators may view these individuals as a willing, "captive audience," the majority will not be mandated to attend any relationship or parenting programming. It will likely be their choice to attend and participate. While there might be some inmates truly wanting to learn about the principles and concepts that a family life education program might provide in regards to relationships and parenting, there are some who also might decide to participate for the sole purpose of having the program activity look positive at their next parole meeting. A certificate of completion given to persons completing a required number of classes and fulfilling the assigned activities might be a good method for family life educators to utilize for recruiting and retaining participants over time. A certificate incentive may also motivate them to fully participate and engage throughout the education sessions.

Barriers to Participation

Barriers to designing, implementing, and evaluating family life education programs for incarcerated parents include the incarcerated parent's refusal of contact with family members (Hairston, 1991; Tripp, 2001); irreparable preprison damage to relationships with spouses, partners, children, and other family members (Bloom & Steinhart, 1993; Hairston & Oliver, 2007); or because family members, particularly children, are kept ignorant of the incarceration and are therefore unavailable for participation (Hairston, 2007). Many families also indicate that the distance from the prison, lack of affordable and reliable transportation, and the costs attending visitation preclude frequent visitations and direct involvement with the incarcerated parent (Simmons, 2000). Prison policies and conditions such as restraints on the number, type, and duration of "allowable" telephone calls, visits, and visitors; the experience of visitor "pat downs" and "put downs"; and the lighting and cleanliness of the waiting and meeting areas have all been reported as barriers to participation (Arditti, 2008; Hairston, 1991).

Environmental Considerations

Many incarcerated parents present challenging participant profiles—low literacy and educational achievement, lack of viable economic skills, long histories of substance abuse and mental illness, familial histories of intergenerational family dysfunction including incarceration, as well as children living in a variety of relative, nonrelative, and state care (Mumola, 2000). However, family life educators need to understand that distinct demographic differences exist between and among parents housed in federal and state prisons and jails. They need to be prepared to respond in accordance with these differences.

In addition, family life educators should comprehend and adjust accordingly to the established structures of each federal and state correctional facility with which they work. They can expect different sets of visitation policies, regulations, and environments; different and nonvarying established schedules of inmate routines; and different degrees and types of institutional resources (e.g., counselors, educators, library, AV equipment, and computer access). Working within a correctional facility also means that the content and process of parent education may be altered by the frequent intrusion of loudspeaker announcements, delays in program start times due to unscheduled/unannounced prisoner "head counts," poor understanding of the value and processes of parenting programs by some institutional staff manifesting in their refusal to provide access to AV equipment or allow the dimming of room lights to aid in the viewing of a training slide, as well as restrictions on the types of materials inmates are allowed to use, read, or keep. Understandably, these factors, which vary from prison to prison, will influence the type of programs and services that can be designed and offered to inmates and their families (Hairston, 2007; Schram & Morash, 2002). Prison programs also may differ in their level of financial and institutional support, and the prison's security level may limit the range of training and inmate contact opportunities, with fewer options available at high-security institutions (Loper & Turek, 2006).

Family life educators interested in establishing an "in-house" program must gain approval from the appropriate authorities that in some settings may take as long as a year to obtain. If child or family visitation is an approved part of a parenting or family life education program, family life educators will most likely encounter barriers and obstacles that have the potential for undermining the value of the experience for the participants. Common problems include the following:

- Lack of or unreliable means of transportation—particularly problematic when an inmate is housed far from home
- Cost—the expenses surrounding getting to the prison (e.g., gas, air, and public transportation fares), attending to basic needs during the visit (e.g., purchasing meals, snacks, and beverages from visiting room vending machines), or keeping in contact between visits (e.g., telephone and postal charges)
- Parenting stress—resulting from nonsupportive interactions with prison staff and fellow inmates or institutional restrictions on the amount and type of allowable physical contact with visitors (e.g., glass-partitioned visits only, across a table visit with/without hand-holding, side-by-side bench sitting but no children on laps)
- Child and family distress—resulting from conditions that are intimidating (e.g., package and purse searches and physical "pat downs"), uncomfortable (e.g., long waits before a visit in dark, dirty, and overcrowded rooms) and humiliating (e.g., visitation rooms that are crowded, noisy, and dirty and often unfriendly and restrictive to children and family members (Arditti, 2008; LaVigne, Davies, & Brazzell, 2008).

Modes of Learning

Although no research has been conducted on the preferred teaching and learning experiences of inmates and their families, there is growing evidence that family life education programs that combine classroom lessons with visitation-facilitated skill-building exercises and experiences tend to have positive outcomes

(Block & Potthast, 1998; Sandifer, 2008). A family life educator will have to conduct a variety of institutionally approved environmental and participant assessments to determine the types of programs that can and need to be offered; the modes of learning that are preferred, practical, and permissible; and the means for maintaining consistent, satisfying, and economical family communications.

It should be noted that many programs for incarcerated parents and their children have not acknowledged or included the nonincarcerated parent or caregiver, so little is known about their level of interest in participating in a family life education program. There is evidence many spouses, former partners, and relatives feel a great deal of anger and resentment toward the inmate and are reluctant to maintain contact for fear of recrimination and further deterioration in their relationship with the imprisoned. Just like the data pertaining to children, these caregivers are concerned by the stigma surrounding incarceration as well as the problematic consequences of continuing their association with the inmate (Hairston, 2002, 2007). While there are growing numbers of community-based mentoring, counseling, and support and advocacy programs that have been established to help the families of prisoners, especially children, their effects are often short-lived, narrow in focus and address, and have not been critically scrutinized (Boudin, 2003; Hairston, 2007).

Educator Characteristics

There is surprisingly little information about the men and women who are hired, assigned, or volunteer to serve as educators or facilitators within the prison setting. The available information comes from the few published research studies that note the qualifications, affiliations, and/or professional orientation of the class facilitators, such as experienced therapists, a consumer and family life skills educator, graduate students in social work, volunteers from community or faith-based organizations, correctional educators, and mental health staff (Frye & Dawe, 2008; Loper & Turek, 2006; Sandifer, 2008).

Evidence indicates the need for intensive and specialized training for whoever assumes the responsibility of instructor and trainer for incarcerated parents and their families. Besides having knowledge of normal and atypical child development and family systems, these instructors should also be familiar with issues pertaining to substance abuse and recovery, post-traumatic stress disorder (PTSD), and inmate "survival" skills such as the "Don't Talk," "Don't Trust," and "Don't Feel" credos that can provide an inmate with an initial sense of security. These instructors should also receive direction on locating and utilizing the resources provided by many local and national volunteer organizations dedicated to helping inmates and their families (Frye & Dawe, 2008; Greenberg, 2006; Magaletta & Herbst, 2001).

Given their educational background, professional training experiences and researcher and practitioner skill sets, family life educators are one of a few professional groups uniquely qualified to design, implement, and evaluate the types of dynamic, family-contextualized, prison, and community-situated programs needed to assist families involved with and affected by this country's criminal justice system. However, it is imperative that family life educators who choose to work in prison settings be strong, determined, and confident individuals. Those who are weak or timid will be zeroed in on as victims by certain inmates who know how to take advantage of and/or manipulate people. Working in this type of setting is not for all family life educators.

Ethical Considerations

The numbers of families impacted by incarceration, the well-documented adverse consequences of incarceration and recidivism, evidence of overt racism and sexism imbued in the criminal justice system, and a prevailing public sentiment that "forfeiture of family" is a legitimate punishment and natural consequence of criminal activity (Clement, 1993) point to several ethical considerations. Clearly, family life educators and researchers have a professional obligation to plainly articulate and represent the realities and needs of these "invisible" American families.

Family life education researchers and practitioners can provide evidence-based recommendations for and direction to sentencing reform, alternatives to incarceration, children's advocacy, parenting classes, contact visitation programs and policies, as well as the need for transitional training to aid prisoners and their families after the inmates' release from prison (Bloom, 1995; Smith, 1995). Family life educators can also help define parenting situations and circumstances that require a "do no harm" policy. Although the explicit goal of many parent education programs is to enhance the connection between an incarcerated parent and his or her child, there are contexts (e.g., parental history of physical and sexual abuse, DV, and child and family abandonment) in which parents, children, and families may be better served if the relationship were not encouraged (LaVigne, Davies, & Brazzell, 2008; Loper & Turek, 2006; Zierbert, 2006).

Best Practices in Family Life Education Programming

Research on incarcerated parents and their families has not been extensive. The methodological flaws in many studies prevent a clear articulation of best practices. However, a consistency of findings can inform the efforts of family life educators as they develop efficacious family life programs, namely the following:

- Inmates need strategies and skills that support the financial, social, and emotional well-being of all family members during the period surrounding their arrest, incarceration, parole, community reentry, probation, and family reunification (Hairston, 2007; Snyder et al., 2001).

- In-prison programs need to teach effective skills for parenting and coparenting from a distance and for reassuming (for some inmates assuming for the first time) parental and family roles upon release.

- In-prison programs that allow parents and their children to spend extended time together doing parent–child or family type activities appear to have the most beneficial effects for both the parent and the child (Block & Potthast, 1998).

- Challenges identified for working with inmates and their families alike include recruiting and retaining participants, managing the stigma and risks associated with participation in a prison-based program, gaining trust and cooperation, handling logistical problems related to transportation of family participants to the training site, and managing the need for different types of programming depending upon the ages of the children and the points of parental involvement with the corrections systems (Robertson, 2007; Weissman & LaRue, 1998).

- Imprisoned fathers and nonincarcerated, single-parent, male head of household families are rarely recognized as requiring or benefiting from in-prison or out-of-prison family life education programs (Rosenberg, 2009), so little is known about their particular wants or needs. Needs assessments developed for fathers and nuanced for fathering and male heads of household families need to be designed and used.

- "Being a parent" is a social and central identity adopted by many incarcerated parents. It is also one of the few prisoner "recognized and approved" reasons for participating in a prison-sponsored program. As such, parenting programs can help inmates address serious emotional and mental health issues (e.g., depression, stress, guilt, and low self-esteem) that are often linked to family relationships (Sandifer, 2008).

As these findings indicate, the issues facing incarcerated parents and their families are multifaceted and complex, involving psychological, developmental, educational, and environmental factors. Because of this, successful family life education interventions will need to focus on and teach strategies that (1) replace profiles of risk with profiles of resiliency; (2) process painful and harmful experiences through lenses of personal insight, moral reasoning, and cognitive and emotional understanding; (3) forge, maintain, or renew family connections and support for those living within and outside the shadows of prison; and (4) help construct multiple levels and systems of support for all those affected by imprisonment (Klein et al., 1999).

Family life educators interested in working with or designing programs for incarcerated parents and their families are referred to the following research and web-based resources:

- *Purposeful Parenting: A Manual for Extension Educators Working with Incarcerated Parents* (DeBord et al., 2008) is a manual designed to prepare educators to work with prisoners and within prison settings. It provides an educational framework, a starter kit of activities, and tips for conducting an effective program.
- The CCIP Clearinghouse is a collection of over 3,500 documentary and audiovisual items relating to families in the criminal justice system, including the Prison Parents' Education Project (PPEP) core curriculum with particularizations for use with parolees and offenders in residential programs (Center for Children of Incarcerated Parents, n.d.).
- Parenting Inside Out (PIO) is an evidence-based parenting skills training program for parents involved with the criminal justice system. The prison version is appropriate for both incarcerated mothers and incarcerated fathers who are parenting from prison. The community version is appropriate for parents on parole or probation (Parenting Inside Out [PIO], n.d.).
- *Faith Community and Criminal Justice Collaboration: A Collection of Effective Programs* is a report that describes over 30 field-tested programs that were designed for use across the entire criminal justice system. Each program outlines an approach that has proven effective in reconciling, nurturing, and restoring offending individuals back into their families and communities (National Crime Prevention Council, 2005).

FUTURE DIRECTIONS

The aforementioned published reports and studies attest to the fact that many people, agencies, and organizations recognize and are responding to the singular needs of incarcerated parents and their families. Unfortunately, few of these efforts are organized within the theoretical or empirical framework of family life education. Thus, there are numerous opportunities for professional engagement and contribution by an experienced family life educator. Table 3.1 outlines the various ways in which family life educators can engage in and contribute to this important and underserved population.

Interested family life educators can, for example, contribute to public discourse and criminal justice and legislative decision making by disseminating unbiased, fact-based reports that focus attention on the family impact costs and

Table 3.1   Incarcerated Parents and Their Families: Areas for Professional Contribution and Engagement by Family Life Educators

Areas for Professional Contribution	*Areas for Professional Engagement*
Theory	• Sharing theoretical lenses and models such as: 　○ Family Systems Theory 　○ Ecological Model 　○ National Extension Parenting Education Framework
Research	• Designing, implementing, and evaluating evidence-based intervention studies that are: 　○ Developmentally appropriate for the targeted groups 　○ Educationally and methodologically sound 　○ Gender and culturally sensitive and respectful
Policies	• Conducting educational forums for correctional and legislative policy makers, highlighting the costs and benefits of instituting policies and procedures that address family needs at the local, state, and national level
Curriculum development	• Developing educational modules and materials that address the specific needs of the following: 　○ Incarcerated parents 　○ Children of prison inmates 　○ Family members and other caretakers
Training methods	• Aiding correctional staff and volunteer teachers in conducting training programs that are: 　○ Educational and not therapeutic in nature 　○ Grounded in adult learning theory and methods 　○ Inmate and family supportive
Partnerships	• Collaborating with professionals in associated, relevant disciplines for the purpose of designing and testing multidisciplinary approaches and interventions that address the needs of incarcerated parents and their families
Advocacy	• Sponsoring professional development opportunities that help raise awareness about our country's most "invisible" citizens (i.e., prison inmates and their families) • Designing public awareness campaigns that promote a range of options that support and strengthen family bonds throughout the criminal justice system

benefits of policies related to the sentencing, incarceration, and community reentry of parent offenders. Likewise, by sharing the results of studies designed to assess the efficacy of and conditions surrounding the use of family life education programs, curricula, and resources inside and outside of prison settings, family life educators can provide valuable, research-informed guidelines and recommendations to local, state, and national organizations established for and dedicated to addressing the needs of imprisoned parents, their parenting partners, and children.

Finally, because of their "family lens" orientation, family life educators are uniquely qualified to offer classes, workshops, and in-service training attuned to the nuanced and differential impact of an offender's age and stage of development, his or her sentence length, or phase of incarceration. In addition, because of their skills as experienced trainers, family life educators can expect to offer these programs of education to audiences comprised of correctional staff, inmates, volunteers, and community-based prisoner and family visitors interested in broadening the focus, effectiveness, and strength of their educational and outreach efforts.

REFERENCES

Arditti, J. (2008). Parental imprisonment and family visitation: A brief overview and recommendations for family friendly practice. In T. LaLiberte & E. Snyder (Eds.), *CW360: A comprehensive look at a prevalent child welfare issue: Children of incarcerated parents*. St. Paul: University of Minnesota.

Arditti, J., & McClintock, C. (2001). Casualties of the war: Drug policy and families. *Marriage and Family Review, 32,* 11–32.

Austin, J., & Irwin, J. (2001). *It's about time: America's imprisonment binge*. Belmont, CA: Wadsworth.

Bales, W., & Dees, L. (1992). Mandatory minimum sentencing in Florida: Past trends and future implications. *Crime & Delinquency, 38,* 309–329.

Beck, A., & Harrison, P. (2001). Prisoners in 2000. *Bureau of Justice Bulletin* (NCJ 188207). Washington, DC: U.S. Department of Justice, Office of Justice Programs.

Block, K., & Potthast, M. (1998). Girl Scouts beyond bars: Facilitation parent-child contact in correctional settings. *Child Welfare, 77,* 561–579.

Bloom, B. (1995). Imprisoned mothers. In K. Gabel and D. Johnston (Eds.), *Children of incarcerated parents*. New York: Lexington Books.

Bloom, B., & Steinhart, D. (1993). *Why punish the children? A reappraisal of the children of incarcerated mothers in America*. San Francisco: National Council on Crime and Delinquency.

Boudin, K. (2003). Children left behind. *Nation, 277*(9), 5–7.

Bushfield, S. (2004). Fathers in prison: Impact of parenting education. *Journal of Correctional Education, 55*(2), 104–116.

Carlson, J. (1998). Evaluating the effectiveness of a live-in nursery within a women's prison. *Journal of Offender Rehabilitation, 27,* 73–85.

Carlson, J. (2001). Prison Nursery 2000: A five-year review of a prison nursery at the Nebraska Correctional Center for Women. *Journal of Offender Rehabilitation, 33*(3), 75–97.

Cecil, D., McHale, J., Strozier, A., & Pietsch, J. (2008). Female inmates, family caregivers, and young children's adjustment: A research agenda and implications for corrections programming. *Journal of Criminal Justice, 36,* 513–521.

Center for Children of Incarcerated Parents. (n.d.). *Center Educational Projects*. Retrieved from http://e-ccip.org/services.html

Chesney-Lind, M. (1997). *The female offender*. Thousand Oaks, CA: Sage.

Clement, M. (1993). Parenting in prison: A national survey of programs for incarcerated women. *Journal of Offender Rehabilitation, 19*(1–2), 89–100.

Davies, E., Brazzell, D., LaVigne, N., & Shollenberger, T. (2008). *Understanding the needs and experiences of children of incarcerated parents.* Retrieved from http://www.urban.org/url .cfm?ID=411615

Davies, E., & Cooke, S. (1999). Neglect or punishment? Failing to meet the needs of women post-release. In S. Cook & S. Davies (Eds.), *Harsh punishment: International experiences of women's imprisonment.* Boston: Northeastern University Press.

DeBord, K., Head, S., Behnke, A., Wicher, K., Kernadle, P., & Jones, S. (2008). *Purposeful parenting: A manual for extension educators working with incarcerated parents.* Retrieved from http:// www.ces.ncsu.edu/depts/fcs/pdfs/incarguide.pdf

Eddy, M. J., Martinez, C. R., Schiffman, T., Newton, R., Olin, L., Leve, L., et al. (2008). Development of a multisystemic parent management training intervention for incarcerated parents, their children and families. *Clinical Psychologist, 12,* 86–98.

Frye, S., & Dawe, S. (2008). Interventions for women prisoners and their children post-release. *Clinical Psychologist, 12*(3), 99–108.

Garfinkel, I., McLanahan, S., Meyer, D., & Seltzer, D. (1998). *Fathers under fire: The revolution of child support enforcement.* Thousand Oaks, CA: Sage.

Glaze, L., & Maruschak, L. (2008). Parents in prison and their minor children. *Bureau of Justice Statistics Special Report (NCJ 222984).* Washington, DC: U.S. Department of Justice, Office of Justice Programs.

Greenberg, R. (2006). Children and families: Mothers who are incarcerated. *Women & Therapy, 29*(3–4), 165–179.

Greenwood, P., Modell, K., Rydell, C., & Chiesa, J. (1996). *Diverting children from a life of crime: Measuring costs and benefits.* Santa Monica, CA: Rand.

Hairston, J. (1991). Family ties during imprisonment: Important to whom and for what? *Journal of Sociology and Social Welfare, 18*(1), 87–104.

Hairston, J. (2002, January). *Prisoners and families: Parenting issues during incarceration.* Paper prepared at the "From Prison to Home" conference.

Hairston, J. (2003). Prisoners and their families: Parenting issues during incarceration. In J. Travis & M. Waul (Eds.). *Prisoners once removed: The impact of incarceration and reentry on children, families, and communities* (pp. 259–282). Washington, DC: Urban Institute Press.

Hairston, J. (2007). *Focus on children with incarcerated parents: An overview of the research literature.* Baltimore MD: Annie E. Casey Foundation.

Hairston, J., & Oliver, W. (2007). *Domestic violence and prisoner reentry: Experiences of African American men and women.* New York: Vera Institute of Justice.

Hairston, J., Rollins, J., & Jo, H. (2004). Family connections during imprisonment and prisoners' community reentry. In *Children, families, and the criminal justice system.* Chicago: University of Illinois at Chicago.

Hallinan, J. (2001). *Going up the river: Travels in a prison nation.* New York: Random House.

Harlow, C. (2003). Education & correctional populations. *Bureau of Justice Statistics Special Report* (NCJ 195670). Washington, DC: U.S. Department of Justice, Office of Justice Programs.

Harrison, P. (2003). Prison and jail inmates at midyear, 2002. *Bureau of Justice Statistics Special Report* (NCJ 198877). Washington, DC: U.S. Department of Justice, Office of Justice Programs.

Hartney, C. (2006). U.S. rates of incarceration: A global perspective. *Fact sheet: Research from the National Council on Crime and Delinquency.* Retrieved from http://www.nccd-crc.org/nccd/ pubs/2006nov_factsheet_incarceration.pdf

Irwin, J., Schiraldi, V., & Ziedenberg, J. (1999, March). *America's one million nonviolent prisoners.* Washington, DC: Center on Juvenile and Criminal Justice.

King, R., & Mauer, M. (2002, September). *Distorted priorities: Drug offenders in state prisons.* Washington, DC: Sentencing Project.

Klein, S., Bartholomew, G., & Bahr, S. (1999). Family education for adults in correctional settings: A conceptual framework. *International Journal of Offender Therapy and Comparative Criminology, 43*(3), 291–307.

LaLiberte, T., & Snyder, E. (Eds.) (2008). *CW 360: A comprehensive look at a prevalent child welfare issue: Children of incarcerated parent.* St. Paul: University of Minnesota.

LaVigne, N., Davies, E., & Brazzell, D. (2008, February). Broken Bonds: Understanding and addressing the needs of children with incarcerated parents. Urban Institute, Justice Policy Center. Retrieved from http://www.urban.org/UploadedPDF/411616_incarcerated_parents.pdf

Loper, A., Carlson, W., Levitt, L., & Scheffel, K. (2009). Parenting stress, alliance, child contact and adjustment of imprisoned mothers and fathers. *Journal of Offender Rehabilitation, 48,* 483–503.

Loper, A., & Turek, E. (2006). Parenting programs for incarcerated parents. Current research and future directions. *Criminal Justice Policy Review, 17*(4), 407–427.

Luke, K. (2002). Mitigating the ill effects of maternal incarceration on women in prison and their children. *Child Welfare, 81,* 929–948.

Lynch, J., & Sabol, W. (2000). Prison use and social control. *Policies, Processes, and Decisions of the Criminal Justice System, 3,* 7–44.

Magaletta, P., & Herbst, D. (2001). Fathering from prison: Common struggles and successful solutions. *Psychotherapy, 38*(1), 88–96.

Moore, A., & Clement, M. (1998). Effects of parent training for incarcerated mothers. *Journal of Offender Rehabilitation, 27,* 57–72.

Mumola, C. (2000). Incarcerated parents and their children. *Bureau of Justice Statistics Special Report.* Retrieved from http://bjs.ojp.usdoj.gov/content/pub/pdf/iptc.pdf

Murray, J. (2007). The cycle of punishment: Social exclusion of prisoners and their children. *Criminology and Criminal Justice, 7,* 55–81.

National Crime Prevention Council. (2005). *Faith community and criminal justice collaboration: A collection of effective programs.* Retrieved from http://www.ncpc.org/resources/files/pdf/volunteering/faith%20community_complete.pdf

Nesbith, A., & Ruhland, E. (2008). Children of incarcerated parents: Challenges and resiliency, in their own words. *Children and Youth Services Review, 30,* 1119–1130.

Parenting Inside Out. (n.d.) Retrieved from http://www.parentinginsideout.org

Pew Center on the States. (2008). *One in 100: Behind bars in America 2008.* Retrieved from http://www.pewcenteronthestates.org

Pollock, J. (2002). Parenting programs in women's prisons. *Women & Criminal Justice, 14*(1), 131–152.

Quilty, S., Butler, T., & Levy, M. (2005). The magnitude of experience of parental incarceration in Australia. *Psychiatry, Psychology and Law, 12,* 256–257.

Robertson, O. (2007). *The impact of parental imprisonment on children.* Retrieved from http://www.quno.org/geneva/pdf/humanrights/women-in-prison/ImpactParentalImprisonment-200704-English.pdf

Rosenberg, J. (2009, July). Children need dads too: Children with fathers in prison. *Human Rights & Refugees Publications.* Retrieved from http://www.quno.org/geneva/pdf/humanrights/women-in-prison/CNDT%20internet-1.pdf

Sandifer, J. (2008). Evaluating the efficacy of a parenting program for incarcerated mothers. *Prison Journal, 88*(3), 423–445.

Scalia, J. (2001, August). Federal drug offenders, 1999 with trends 1984–99. *Bureau of Justice Statistics Special Report* (NCJ 187285). Washington, DC: U.S. Department of Justice, Office of Justice Programs.

Schram, P., & Morash, M. (2002). Evaluation of a Life Skills Program for women inmates in Michigan. *Journal of Offender Rehabilitation, 34*(4), 47–70.

Shlafer, R., Poehlmann, J., Coffino, B., & Hanneman, A. (2009). Mentoring children with incarcerated parents: Implications for research, practice, and policy. *Family Relations, 58,* 507–519.

Showers, J. (1993). Assessing and remedying parenting knowledge among women inmates. *Journal of Offender Rehabilitation, 20,* 35–46.

Simmons, C. (2000). *Children of incarcerated parents.* Sacramento: California Research Bureau, California State Library.

Smith, G. (1995). Practical considerations regarding termination of incarcerated parents' rights. In K. Gabel & D. Johnston (Eds.), *Children of incarcerated parents.* New York: Lexington Books.

Snyder, Z., Carlo, T., & Coats Mullins, M. (2001). Parenting from prison: An examination of a children's visitation program at a women's correctional facility. *Marriage & Family Review, 32*(3–4), 33–61.

Snyder-Joy, Z., & Carlo, T. (1998). Parenting through prison walls: Incarcerated mothers and children's visitation programs. In S. L. Miller (Ed.), *Crime control and women: Feminist implications of criminal justice policy.* Thousand Oaks, CA: Sage.

Tonry, M., & Hatlestad, K. (1997). Race and sentencing. In M. Tonry & K. Hatlestad (Eds.), *Sentencing reform in overcrowded times: A comparative perspective* (pp. 217–218). New York: Oxford University Press.

Travis, J., McBride, E., & Solomon, A. (2005). *Families left behind: The hidden costs of incarceration and reentry.* Washington, DC: Urban Institute Justice Policy Center.

Travis, J., & Waul, M. (2003). Prisoners once removed: The children and families of prisoners. In J. Travis & M. Waul (Eds.), *Prisoners once removed.* Washington, DC: Urban Institute Press.

Tripp, B. (2001). Incarcerated African American fathers: Exploring changes in family relationships and the father identity. *Journal of African American Men, 6*(1), 13–18.

U.S. Department of Justice, Bureau of Justice Statistics. (2002). *Profile of nonviolent offenders exiting state prisons.* (NCJ 207081). Washington, DC: Author.

U.S. Department of Justice, Bureau of Justice Statistics. (2003). *Education and correctional populations.* (NCJ 195670). Washington, DC: Author.

U.S. Department of Justice, Bureau of Justice Statistics. (2004). *Survey of inmates in state and federal correctional facilities, 2004.* ICPSR04572-v1. Ann Arbor, MI: Inter-university Consortium for Political and Social Research, 2007-02-28.

Vacca, J. (2004). Educated prisoners are less likely to return to prison. *Journal of Correctional Education, 55,* 297–305.

Weilerstein, R. (1995). The prison MATCH program. In K. Gabel, & D. Johnston (Eds.), *Children of incarcerated parents.* New York: Lexington Books.

Weissman, M., & LaRue, C. (1998). Earning trust from youths with none to spare. *Child Welfare, 77*(5), 579–594.

West, H., & Sobol, W. (2008). Prisoners in 2007. *Bureau of Justice Statistics Bulletin*, (NCJ 224280). Retrieved from http://bjs.ojp.usdoj.gov/content/pub/pdf/p07.pdf

Zierbert, R. (2006). *No easy answers: The effects of parental incarceration on children.* Milwaukee, WI: Alliance for Children and Families.

Chapter 4

Family Life Education With Court-Mandated Parents and Families

JUDITH A. MYERS-WALLS, CFLE

Most family life education efforts are aimed at adults and use adult education principles. These principles were dubbed "andragogy" by Malcolm Knowles (1984) and include several assumptions: (1) adult learners are self-directed, so they need to know why the topics in educational settings are important; (2) they need to learn experientially; (3) they enter learning with specific problems they want to solve; and (4) they want to be able to apply the learning to their lives immediately (Kearsley, 2010). Those assumptions are challenged in some family life education situations, however. Sometimes family life education participants do not direct their own learning or are not allowed to focus on their self-perceived needs. They may not participate voluntarily but rather are coerced or mandated in some way to participate. In spite of violations of some of the key adult education principles, the other principles are still important guides for educating these adults. This chapter will focus on nonvoluntary participation in family life education.

My experience with mandated family life education programming began when I served as a state specialist for the Cooperative Extension Service. County staff members were asked by local judges to provide leadership for abusive and neglectful parents and other families in high-risk situations. I collaborated with them to design programming that would address the unique situations and needs of nonvoluntary audiences and in evaluating, adjusting, and improving the programs to maximize the success levels for the participants and the educators by using basic family life education principles and guidelines. Some of those collaborative efforts led to the development of new curricula (see Myers-Walls, Newcom, & Berkope, 2009).

There are many terms that have been used for requiring parents or families to participate in programming related to family life education, including coerced, court-referred, or legally referred (Polcin, 2001); required (Chamberlain, Price, Reid, & Landsverk, 2008); mandated (Brandon, 2006); court-mandated (Arbuthnot & Gordon, 1996); court-ordered (Schaffner, 1997); and court-connected (Cambron, Yankeelov, & Brown, 2000). Each term has a different legal connotation, but participants are often unaware of those differences (Polcin, 2001), and the educational environment may not differ much across the various situations.

The bottom line for the parents or family members is that someone is forcing them to participate. They are informed that they must attend an educational program in order to achieve or retain a parenting or family role or in order to avoid a fine or some other negative consequence. Because the focus of this volume is family life education, the chapter will not address mandated treatment programs (e.g., mandated drug or mental health treatment or anger management training), although some of the literature in those areas provides important insights for the issue of mandated education. In addition, it will not address family life education for parents and families in incarcerated settings; those participants are mandated to be in the setting but usually not mandated to participate in family life education. (Note that family life education for incarcerated audiences is addressed in Chapter 3.) The chapter will also not address mandates for agencies, systems, or organizations to offer certain education programming to families, and it will not address mandated reporting of abuse and neglect or other dangerous behaviors. The focus is specifically on mandated participation in family life education-related programming.

DEFINING THE POPULATION

The situations that may lead to parents and families being mandated to participate in family life education fall into three categories: (1) parents or families choose to take on a role or set of responsibilities and are required to complete training in order to continue with the legal or regulatory aspects of the new role; (2) parents or families are in a situation that has been judged as putting children or families at risk for negative outcomes, so they are required to participate in educational programming before they can progress legally; or (3) parents or families have been identified as performing inadequately in their family roles and are required to participate in family life education to be allowed to continue in their family roles or possibly to avoid other penalties. The kinds of parents and families who find themselves in each of those categories are likely to be quite different from each other. Thus, the content and delivery of each type of family life education should also be quite different, so populations representing each category will be defined separately.

- *Mandatory education for a voluntary role.* One situation included in this category is the training of foster and adoptive parents. Individuals who express an interest in adopting or fostering children are required to attend training in order to gain legal caregiver status. In some kinship adoption or foster care processes, the situation may be less voluntary than in other situations, but the individuals in these educational programs are usually self-selected. Although not involved with the courts, other groups may have similarities with this category. For example, families preparing to accept a foreign exchange student or couples in premarital education workshops may share many of the characteristics of this population: They are required by an agency or institution to attend a training session or series because of a new role they will be assuming. Because the programming mandated for these populations could be considered a type of job training, participants are likely to be generally accepting of and open to the programming.

- *Education for risky family situations.* A common example of this type of training is mandated education for divorcing couples. Some jurisdictions have blanket mandates: All couples with children in a particular municipality, county, or state who are filing for a divorce must participate in a program. Other mandates are issued only to divorcing couples with contested custody or visitation cases. In other situations, judges may issue individual mandates to couples who are judged to be at risk for family conflict or repeated court involvement (Pollet & Lombreglia, 2008). (It may be argued that those with individual mandates would more appropriately fall into the next category.) In most cases, couples need to show proof of attendance in order for the legal procedures to move forward. Another example of training in this category is for families preparing to take a child home after a medical procedure; training is not court-mandated, but a hospital may require family members to participate in specific training before returning the child to the family's care.

- *Mandated education for parents or families judged as inadequate.* Probation departments or judges may require parents who have been found to be abusive and/ or neglectful to participate in parenting education programs. Other families in this category are parents who have been involved in domestic violence cases or parents of children in the juvenile justice system. In these cases, parents and families are identified individually as needing targeted education and training. Parents may need to complete the educational program in order to maintain or regain custody of their child(ren) or sometimes the education is an alternative to a fine or incarceration.

Unique Aspects of Court-Mandated Parents and Families

This section outlines some key characteristics indicative of each category of mandated parents and families. The scope of this chapter does not allow for an exhaustive description of any of the populations. In addition, these descriptions are illustrative only; other groups could fall into these categories as the practice of courts and other authorities choosing to require family life education becomes more common.

Mandatory Education for a Voluntary Role

In 2008, there were 463,000 children in foster care in the United States, and 123,000 children were adopted (U.S. Department of Health and Human Services [DHHS], 2009). In 2003, there were 155,355 nonrelative foster homes licensed to care for those children (Van Camp, 2004), but there is a chronic shortage of placements available for children who need such care. Although extensive statistics are available on the *children* in foster care, it is difficult to find information about the foster care *providers*. Some minimal information may be assumed because, although regulations differ by state, it is common for states to require that foster parents be at least 21 years of age. In addition, foster parents must pass criminal and Child Protective Services (CPS) background checks, and they must have a regular source of income (Bigner, 2010). In all but two states, they also must participate in foster parent workshops and basic first aid and CPR training (Chamberlain et al., 2008).

There are three types of foster care, although the distinction is not always identified. "Traditional/regular foster care" is the provision of basic care and support for children on their way to permanent placements, while "treatment foster care" is designed for the needs of behaviorally disturbed children and youth and includes additional training and financial support for the foster parents (Dorsey et al., 2008). Foster parents involved in this type of care are seen as "frontline therapeutic agents" (Dorsey et al., 2008, p. 1404). Although foster care often leads to adoption by the foster parents in other situations, such an outcome is not nearly as likely in treatment foster care. The third category of care is "kinship foster care" and entails family members serving as foster parents. Some of these parents receive no training, while others are treated as fitting into one of the other foster care categories.

Some published evaluations of adoptive parent and foster care trainings may provide hints about some characteristics of this population, but it is not possible to determine how representative the samples are. Puddy and Jackson (2003) reported that the mean age of their group of 62 foster and adoptive parents was 34.7, 63% were female, 83% were married, 77% had less than a college education, and almost one third had no parenting experience. Chamberlain and colleagues (2008) enrolled 700 foster caregivers (34% kin and 66% nonrelative) in a training program. The participants' mean age at baseline was 48.6 years with a range from 19 to 81. In their sample, 93% were female, 55% were currently employed, 38% had a high school education or less, 49% had some college education, and they had an average of 3.5 other children in the home, with other foster children accounting for the largest part of that number.

Regarding the children in these situations, American Foster Care Resources (Henry, Cossett, Auletta, & Egan, 1991, as cited by Puddy & Jackson, 2003) have estimated that 70% of children in foster care placements have suffered physical abuse and neglect in the past, while about half have been sexually abused. This leads to significant challenges for foster care parents who need to help the children deal with the ramifications of earlier trauma, feelings of rejection and loss, and a sense of personal failure (Puddy & Jackson, 2003). Previous abuse can potentially lead to both internalizing and externalizing behaviors that demand the foster parents use specialized child behavior management techniques (Chamberlain et al., 2008; Van Camp, 2004), whether the setting is considered "regular" or treatment foster care.

What these numbers tell us more than anything is that foster care parents and their situations are diverse. It can be assumed that foster parents are relatively stable—if not, they would not be allowed to participate in the foster care system. As is true in much of the programming related to parenthood, most participants in trainings are likely to be female. However, it is also likely that male caregivers are involved as well in caring for foster children and could be included in training with creative recruitment and programming methods. What we do know about foster care providers is that they have taken extra steps to care for children for whom they were not legally responsible before they entered the system. They could be either valiant heroes who care for children who need help or reluctant kin who agree to step in when a relative did not or could not, but in short, they all have agreed to care for children who have been in difficult situations.

More extensive information is available on adoptive parents than foster parents. According to Jones (2008), between 1973 and 2002 the percentage of all U.S. women who had adopted a child ranged from only 1.3% to 2.2%. Men in 2002 were more than 2.5 times as likely to have adopted a child (3.8%). More than one quarter of women who had not delivered a child and had pursued fertility treatments had adopted a child. Never-married women were less likely to have adopted than married women, but still, 100,000 single women in the United States did adopt in 2002. Adoption is more frequent in families with higher incomes, but a significant number of families under 150% of the poverty level also adopt children. In 1992, it was estimated that 42% of adoptions were by stepparents or other relatives (Kreider, 2003). Some parents move from fostering children to adopting them; among children adopted out of foster care, 54% are adopted by the former foster parents (U.S. DHHS, 2009).

It can be expected in groups of adoptive parents that many of them have worked long and hard to become parents, many of them have mourned or are mourning their inability to bear children, and some of them have spent significant amounts of money on adoption. Others have both biological and adopted children, and some have accepted responsibility for older children with special needs or a history of maltreatment or neglect, sometimes after serving as foster parents.

Education for Parents and Families in Risky Situations

This category—particularly when it represents programs for divorcing parents—comprises the largest percentage of mandated family life education programming currently. In 2009 an estimated 1,100,401 children under 18 in the U.S. lived with parents who became divorced that year (U.S. Census Bureau, 2011). The largest percentage of those parents (29% of men and 30% of women) were between the ages of 35 and 44, and 64% were classified as White, non-Hispanic. Many of the parents who divorced that year—especially the women—lived under the poverty level: 11% of men and 22% of women.

Many negative outcomes have been identified for children who experience the divorce of their parents (Amato, 2000; Wallerstein, 1991). A factor that seems to be especially important in children's adjustment is their exposure to interparental conflict and aggression (Amato, 1993). While a minority of divorces include high levels of conflict and aggression, it is this aspect of divorce that has been the primary concern of many courts and community agencies, which has led to the rapid growth of mandated family life education for divorcing parents (Pollet & Lombreglia, 2008). Virtually all divorcing couples do deal with financial strain; the relocation of at least one family member; anger; and perceptions by others and themselves of failure, loss, and defeat. Children can feel caught in the middle of parents who are struggling with those challenges and blaming each other for the problems.

As mentioned before, mandates for these parents to attend educational programs vary across states and municipalities. The approaches that are taken for referring parents to programs will result in very different group compositions. If all divorcing parents are required to attend the programs, there will be a wide range of participants, some of whom are adjusting well and others who are struggling. It is logical to assume that parents who are part of a blanket mandate are not likely to feel singled out, but they still may resent the requirement to attend classes if the divorce is smooth and the relationship between the parents is congenial. In situations where only parents with contested custody or visitation cases are required to attend or when judges refer only the couples who have a history of conflict and aggression, the resentment may be higher because the parents may rightly take the mandate personally. However, a plus is that participants in this scenario may be more likely to recognize their need for assistance and guidance—at least eventually.

Mandated Education for Parents and Families Judged as Inadequate

Mandates that are applied at this level are individual and based on reports or assessments that indicate that the parents or other family members are performing their role in ways that put the children at risk for negative developmental outcomes. Reports from the National Child Abuse and Neglect Data System (U.S. DHHS, 2010) stated that, in 2008, 2 million reports of child abuse and neglect involving 3.7 million children were investigated by CPS workers across the United States. Almost one quarter (23.7%) of the reports resulted in a finding that at least one child was abused or neglected. An estimated 1,740 children died that year as a result of maltreatment. Children under 1 year of age were the most common victims. In 60% of the cases, the finding was one of neglect. Approximately 80% of the perpetrators were found to be the child's parents and of those, 90% were the biological parents, and slightly more than 75% were under age 40. More than 20% of the children were placed in foster care as a result of the investigation. Reflecting a more preventive approach (albeit tertiary prevention), it has been reported that at least 400,000 parents in the child welfare services system participate in voluntary or mandated parent training each year (U.S. DHHS data cited by Barth et al., 2005).

A number of characteristics have been identified as common among the population of abusive and neglectful parents. Many are overreactive to children's misbehavior, have unrealistic developmental expectations of their children, are socially isolated, have high stress levels, have an external locus of control, (meaning that they feel other people or fate control their behaviors and outcomes) and are likely to depend on physical punishment as a primary method of childrearing (Barton, Baglio, & Braverman, 1994; Bradley & Peters, 1991; Janko, 1994; Shannon, n.d.). Neglectful parents are also likely to experience low levels of self-esteem. Women who have been involved in domestic violence hold many of these same characteristics, and they are very likely to report having been abused themselves as children (Seamans, Rubin, & Stabb, 2007). Parents who sexually abuse children tend to possess different characteristics, but those parents are not likely to be mandated into parenting programs, as their needs are not likely to be met with educational interventions.

When abusive and neglectful parents are required to attend parenting programs, it is logical to expect them to be defensive and angry. Because many abusive parents do not understand the causality of children's behaviors, they may believe that they simply got a "bad child," so they will not grasp the purpose of education. Defensiveness also comes from the fact that they were individually targeted as needing to be "fixed."

Across all three categories of mandated parents and families, some participants may see the requirement to receive family life education as a welcome opportunity to gain answers to difficult family situations. Others may see the requirement as an undeserved intrusion that robs them of basic rights and independence. Yet others may view the training as preparation for a new and demanding role they have chosen, while others may look forward to getting through this necessary hurdle so that they can continue on with the next step, whether that is adopting a child or finalizing a divorce. It is critical for programmers to assess the participants' characteristics and attitudes carefully in order to provide effective programming.

Strengths and Assets of Court-Mandated Parents and Families

It can be challenging to identify the strengths and assets of parents and families who are mandated to participate in family life education; in many cases, families are required to attend the programs based on either identified or likely weaknesses or vulnerabilities, not strengths. A strengths-based approach may be critical in order for the educational intervention to be successful, however (Bundy-Fazioli, Briar-Lawson, & Hardiman, 2008). In spite of the inherent deficit model, there are some strengths that may be population-wide and predictable. For example, foster and adoptive parents experience screening and need to meet basic criteria, so educators can expect a minimal level of functioning across the population. Many foster and adoptive parents offer to care for children with special needs, difficult histories, and behavior problems, so those participants are likely to reflect high levels of self-efficacy, commitment, and optimism. Strengths in the other groups and in some foster and adoptive parents may be more idiosyncratic, and it may be necessary to become acquainted with individual families to uncover those assets; there is extreme diversity among the groups that are mandated to attend family life education. Making the effort to uncover individual strengths in each participant may take time but will enhance the positive outcomes of the programming.

Common assets identifiable across mandated audiences can provide a springboard for building strengths-based programming. First, all of the groups previously described may be at a turning point in their family lives. They may be taking on responsibility for a new child, losing custody of a child, building a new life after divorce, or experiencing the shock of having been declared abusive or neglectful. These major events or crises disrupt the status quo and may make the individuals stressed, angry, and/or upset, but these pivotal events also may leave them open to education and information, at least after any resentment and anger have dissipated. Expanding on the Brazelton concept of "touchpoints" (see http://www.touchpoints .org/approach.html), families periodically encounter developmental or imposed changes that will not allow interaction patterns to proceed as before. Those families need to develop a new normal, and those situations can be fertile ground for educational interventions.

Another asset of these populations comes from the mandates themselves. If parents and families respond to the mandates by actually enrolling in the course, walking in the agency door, or opening their own door to an educator, there are possibilities. There is no hope of making a difference if there is no contact. Court orders, requirements, or mandates can provide a kick in the pants or a shove down the road. Participants may enter programs angry and resentful, but they move beyond that point quickly when the program proves to be useful, and many then report that it was beneficial that they were required to attend (Pollet & Lombreglia, 2008; Van Camp, 2004). Many participants feel positive about the programming once it is underway or complete. Another asset in many mandated programs is that, in order for the program to operate, community linkages among courts, agencies, and educators need to be established. Those networks can lead to strong outcomes for families in need (Shannon, n.d.).

FAMILY LIFE EDUCATION PRACTICES

Current State of Family Life Education

The practice of requiring parents and families to participate in family life education programs rarely appeared in literature until the 1980s and 1990s. In recent years, many areas of mandated programming have developed as courts and probation departments attempt to increase the effectiveness and accountability of their programming related to vulnerable children and families. It is interesting to note that the emphasis in most of these mandated programs is the well-being of children. Some of the programs mention family functioning or parent interests, but most of those concerns return to the matter of children being given a safe and nurturing environment. It seems that children's vulnerability is a critical factor that has allowed governmental and social agencies to justify choosing to mandate family life education.

It should also be noted that most of the programs do not use the term *family life education* and are rooted in a variety of disciplines, such as social work or corrections and are not directly connected to the field of family life education. Many are conducted by court personnel, some by social workers, and some by probation officials. It is possible to also find programs run by university personnel, medical professionals, and Cooperative Extension staff. Each category of mandated programming has a unique developmental track, so the status of each will be described separately.

Adoption and Foster Care Training

Federal guidelines require foster parents to participate in training programs as part of the licensing process, and that requirement is supported by legislation in all but two states (Chamberlain et al., 2008; Dorsey et al., 2008). Federal guidelines stipulate that foster parents must receive appropriate preparation before beginning their role and then must participate in continuing education each year, although the amount, content, and organization of both the pre-service and in-service training are flexible; there is more focus in the guidelines and legislative directives regarding hours and frequency of training than on its content (Dorsey et al., 2008). Adoptive parents are often included in these trainings, but that is most likely to occur when parents are adopting children who have been in foster care or have been removed from the homes of other caregivers. Reviews have indicated that there is very little consistency in adoptive and foster care parenting programming, and outcome studies have provided weak and inconsistent evidence of the effectiveness of the existing programs (Chamberlain et al., 2008; Dorsey et al., 2008; Puddy & Jackson, 2003).

Two programs are mentioned most often in the literature and are considered the "gold standards" for the field (Dorsey et al., 2008): Model Approach to Partnerships in Parenting/Group Selection and Participation of Foster and/or Adoptive Families® (MAPP/GPS) and Foster Parent Resources for Information, Development, and Education® (PRIDE). Approximately half of the states require that one or the other of those programs be offered. MAPP/GPS was developed in the mid-1980s and was revised in the early 1990s by the Child Welfare Institute. PRIDE was developed with the idea of filling in the gaps left by MAPP in 1993 and was revised 10 years later by the Child Welfare League of America (Dorsey et al., 2008). In spite of their widespread use, there is very weak evidence available to demonstrate their impact. For the preparation of parents providing treatment foster care, Multidimensional Treatment Foster Care (MTFC) was created by Chamberlain and colleagues in the mid- to late 1990s (see Chamberlain, 1998; Chamberlain & Mihalic, 1998) and seems to be the only training program for this population. Its use appears to be increasing.

The content of all three curricula includes dealing with new and unexpected changes, managing children's challenging behaviors, and dealing with the child-serving system (Dorsey et al., 2008). Beyond that basic core, MAPP focuses on the impact of foster care on foster parents and families, while PRIDE concentrates more on the importance of meeting the needs of children. MTFC, on the other hand, focuses more on teaching the specific techniques and approaches of treatment foster care. The relative lack of training for dealing with difficult child behaviors is consistent with some of the concerns expressed by other authors who have voiced a need for training that provides skills-based education for dealing with behaviorally challenging children (Chamberlain et al., 2008; Van Camp, 2004).

Participants in training sessions for adoptive and foster parents generally report feeling positive about the training, suggesting that there is little or none of the anger and resentment that has been attributed to participants in other mandated trainings. In spite of their positive feelings, however, there is limited evidence that the trainings have built requisite skills and knowledge. Puddy and Jackson (2003) concluded that MAPP serves as a better preservice tool to help families decide whether to enter the foster care role than as a tool that teaches the skills necessary to the role. Overall, it appears that mandating training for foster and adoptive parents is a successful strategy for helping participants to make decisions about beginning the role, but more guidance and care is needed in determining the content and focus of the training, especially in preparing foster parents for dealing with children who bring significant challenges to the relationship.

Education for Divorcing Parents

One of the first mandatory divorce education programs in the United States was offered in Kansas in 1976 (Pollet & Lombreglia, 2008). Almost 20 years later, a 1994 survey of over 3,000 counties in the United States found that almost one quarter of the responding counties offered court-connected group parenting education programs with a primarily educational purpose (Blaisure & Geasler, 1996). Just 4 years later, the percentage had increased to 48%—a 180% increase (Geasler & Blaisure, 1999). In 2008, Pollet and Lombreglia reported that mandated programs were in operation in 46 states. Some authors have referred to this growth as "the latest trend for family courts" (Salem, Schepard, & Schlissel, 1996, p. 9). One survey found that 65% of divorcing parent programs are comprised of mandated attendees (Cambron et al., 2000). In most cases, mandated parents need to complete the class before a divorce hearing will be scheduled or a final decree issued.

In the early 1990s, an attempt was made to distribute books on parenting after divorce to parents and measure the impact (Ogles, Lambert, & Craig, 1991). The results showed that the use of any of the books was associated with improved emotional outcomes for the parents, but no parenting skill measures were used. Formal divorce education programs began after that time. Programs vary from single, 2-hour sessions to a series lasting for 15 sessions, with most consisting of either

2 or 4 hours (Pollet & Lombreglia, 2008). Geasler and Blaisure (1999) reported that programs in the late 1990s concentrated on reducing children's exposure to interparental conflict (64%), improving parenting skills (55%), and decreasing the number of legal complaints (32%). There are several face-to-face curricula that have been discussed in the literature. Children in the Middle is a video-based program created in the early 1990s; it is billed as a coparenting program focused on raising children in two homes (Craig, 1998). Twelve years after the classes began, an online version of Children in the Middle was offered. Helping Children Succeed after Divorce: A Court-Mandated Program for Divorcing Parents (Petersen & Steinman, 1994) began in the mid-1990s and focuses on providing parents with specific, concrete actions to reduce conflict and support children's positive development. Parenting Apart: Strategies for Effective Co-Parenting (Mulroy, Sabatelli, Malley, & Waldron, 1995) is a 6-hour program created by Cooperative Extension professionals and other faculty at the University of Connecticut and is aimed at helping parents negotiate the changes of divorce. The Cooperative Parenting and Divorce program (Boyan & Termini, 1999; Cooperative Parenting Institute, 2009) is an 8-session, 16- to 20-hour program with video/DVD and leaders guide and bills itself as the "first and only comprehensive parenting coordination training program" (Cooperative Parenting Institute, 2009). It offers training programs, leader preparation, and written materials. All of the programs that were previously described focus on lowering parental conflict and improving child outcomes. The programs vary in length, the amount of focus on knowledge transmission versus skill-building, and the specific programming materials and components.

The majority of the divorce education programs conducting any sort of evaluation have relied heavily on customer satisfaction surveys. In those surveys, parents indicated that they learned something new and that they appreciated the program (Arbuthnot & Gordon, 1996; Brandon, 2006; Whitehurst, O'Keefe, & Wilson, 2008). Those studies have found that parents say the program is helpful and that they would recommend it to others. When programmers measure outcome data, those data are often also based on self-report. Some examples of how parents say they have changed their behavior include not sending messages to the other parent through the children and not fighting or arguing in front of the children (Brandon, 2006), saying they have a more positive relationship with the other parent (Whitehurst et al., 2008), or adjusting to the divorce better after the program (Pollet & Lombreglia, 2008).

A few programs have used experimental designs with comparison groups. For example, Whitehurst and colleagues (2008) found that parents who participated in Cooperative Parenting and Divorce rated their relationships more positively, improved their coparenting abilities more, and more successfully lowered their maladaptive behaviors compared to a delayed-treatment group. Pollet and

Lombreglia (2008) have called for more research to begin to assess the impact of the programs in light of the timing of the program, the content and teaching strategies used, the amount of conflict found in the couple, and the length of program.

Mandated Training for Abusive/Neglectful Parents

According to the U.S. Department of Health and Human Services (DHHS) (2010), over 3 million children received "preventive services" in 2008. These are "services … provided to parents whose children are at-risk of abuse or neglect" (p. 77). The services usually focus on teaching developmental stages and improving childrearing competencies. According to one review, at least 400,000 parents each year participate in either voluntary or mandatory educational parenting programs, and placing parents in such classes is reported to be the primary approach used by Child Welfare Services (Barth et al., 2005). There are many parenting education programs offered across the country; Carter and Kahn (1996) estimated several years ago that there were then over 50,000 programs reaching millions of parents and caregivers every day. Some of these programs are associated with child welfare programs and others are not, but many of the programs aim to prevent or reduce child maltreatment. There is very little information about the number of programs that include mandatory participation, however. When mandated parents are integrated into mainstream parenting programs, it is very difficult if not impossible to describe the mandated programming in any distinct way. It is known, however, that parent training is a common aspect of court orders involving parents. It is often required that parents complete the training in order for the case to be dismissed (Barth et al., 2005).

The ultimate objective of parent training programs run by child welfare agencies is to preserve or reunite families (Barth et al., 2005). In some cases, the approach of the programs used with mandated parent audiences is to teach the parents techniques for managing or altering children's inappropriate behavior and thereby attempting to reduce the likelihood that the child will experience more negative outcomes (Incredible Years, 2009; McMahon, 2006). Other programs assist parents in understanding and negotiating with the child welfare system (Barth et al., 2005). Many other programs used with mandated parents are aimed at general improvement of parenting skills, such as providing real limits in a fun way (Love and Logic Institute, 2011); preventing and treating child abuse and neglect (Nurturing Parenting [Family Development Resources, 2007]); using effective communication techniques, encouragement, and natural and logical consequences (STEP Publishers, n.d.); reducing or eliminating instances of child maltreatment by increasing positive parenting practices (Myers-Walls et al., 2009); reducing problem behaviors and increasing communication and family unity

(Parenting Wisely [Family Works, 2003]); or teaching children and their parents the skills necessary to get along without abuse and neglect (Project 12-Ways [Southern Illinois University Carbondale, 2003]). In a number of situations, parenting programs may include both mandated and nonmandated parents, even though some authors have argued that such integration is likely to compromise the effectiveness of the programs (Barth et al., 2005; Myers-Walls et al., 2009).

Barth and colleagues (2005) have outlined four primary components of programs for parents in the child welfare system: (1) assessing parent problems, (2) teaching parenting skills, (3) parents applying the skills to their children, and (4) parents receiving feedback about how the new skills are working. These components reflect the child welfare roots of much of the programming with high-risk parents; in contrast, individual assessment and monitoring are not normally part of the family life education process. In their description of "The Universe of Parenting Education: A Typology," Carter and Kahn (1996) included a category called "multiple and complex needs" (p. 12). In that category are topics such as abuse/neglect, antiviolence, and CPS. (Note that divorce and separation, foster care, and adoption—the other target topics covered in this chapter—are also included in this category.) Carter and Kahn stated that programming in this category will involve intensive levels of service, specialized training, higher levels of supervision, and collaboration with agencies and services. This is in contrast to another of the Carter and Kahn categories—normative parenting education programs, which are primarily promotional in design, lowest in intensity, and most prevalent among middle-class communities. It is important for each program leader to consider his or her role and clarify when it moves from normative parenting education to more intense involvement and when it is family life education versus case management (Myers-Walls, Ballard, Darling, & Myers-Bowman, 2011).

Very few programs have been designed specifically for abusive and neglectful parents. For example, many mandated parents participate in Parenting with Love and Logic (Love and Logic Institute, 2011), Systematic Training for Effective Parenting (STEP Publishers, n.d.), or Parenting Wisely (Family Works, 2003)—programs that were either developed for "normative parenting" or are used for both mandated and voluntary participants. One set of programs that have attempted to meet the unique needs of abusive/neglectful parents is the Nurturing Parenting Programs (Family Development Resources, 2007). In these programs, Steven Bavolek has maintained a specific goal of preventing or reducing child abuse. Reports indicate that these programs have been used with a wide variety of parents, including mandated audiences, although none of the programs is advertised as being designed specifically for that group, and no evaluations of the Nurturing Parenting Programs when used with mandated audiences could be found. Parenting

12-Ways (Southern Illinois University Carbondale, 2003) is marketed as a parenting and therapy program, and The Incredible Years was designed for parents with children with serious behavior problems, although it is unclear whether those programs have addressed the issue of mandated audiences (Incredible Years, 2009).

In the late 1990s, I encountered difficulties in finding appropriate programs when working with a county extension educator who had been asked by the courts to provide mandated programming for abusive/neglectful parents. After much frustration, the creation of the program Parenting Piece by Piece, now in its 4th edition, resulted (Myers-Walls et al., 2009). An evaluation of Parenting Piece by Piece, when used with mandated audiences, found several changes from pre- to post-assessment. After the program, participants reported they were more confident as parents, used more positive parenting techniques, spanked their children less, and were more likely to take care of their own needs (Myers-Walls et al., 2009). This evaluation was based on self-report, albeit using a comparison of reports of actual behavior frequency in the recent past at the beginning and end of the program.

Other programs are much less structured and may not use identifiable curricula. Schaffner (1997) reported on a mandated program for parents with teens in the juvenile justice system. The program was offered in a local county probation department by a probation officer using guest speakers and videos. Informal, ad hoc programs like this may be quite common, but it is difficult to estimate how common in the absence of nationwide data. What is clear is that there are very few programs designed specifically for this audience.

A related set of parenting education programs is mandated for parents who have been involved in domestic violence. One such program is Men Engaged in Nurturing Strategies (MENS) out of SAFEchild (United Way of the Greater Triangle, n.d.) in North Carolina. Another is the Family Violence Accountability Program (Insight Counseling, n.d.) in Michigan. Parenting education is mandated for those parents based on research that identifies the children in those families as being at risk for violence and maltreatment. No outcome evaluation reports could be found from these programs.

General Needs of This Population and Rationale for Family Life Education

As mandated audiences, all participants must first come to terms with the fact that they are required to participate. The reaction to the mandate could range from gratitude and relief to resignation, anger, and hostility. The participants most likely to react with anger and hostility may be those who have been judged as being inadequate and who have lost rights and privileges until they have met the expectations of the authorities. However, the interpretation of the mandates may be very individual. All of the populations that have been mandated to attend parent and family life education programs have been judged to have a lack of information and skills related to parenting and family relationships, so education is determined to be something they need. Unfortunately, few needs assessments have informed these judgments.

Programs for adoptive and foster parents define the needs of the audience in part by the legislation that governs the foster care and adoption systems. Foster parents need to know the regulations and expectations that they will face. Some authors have also pointed out that this population needs additional assistance with responses and techniques for dealing with difficult child behaviors, because 70% of children in foster care are estimated to have those characteristics (Van Camp, 2004). These parents are also likely to deal with the legal system related to the various complications that led the child to be placed in their care. Evaluations of foster care training programs show that the issue of child behavior management is the area in which foster parents feel least well prepared (Puddy & Jackson, 2003; Van Camp, 2004).

Divorcing parents are in need of understanding the impact of divorce on children, strategies to avoid putting their children in the middle of parental conflicts, and methods for establishing appropriate communication strategies and reducing hostility with the child's other parent (Brandon, 2006; Pollet & Lombreglia, 2008). These parents also may need information about the legal system and how they will be interacting with it, although that aspect of programming has not been shown to be the most impactful. It is important to keep in mind that many of the parents in these programs are likely to be dealing with significant life changes that could contribute to high stress levels, so it may be important to build stress-reduction techniques into the program.

For parents mandated to attend parenting programs due to abuse and neglect, it is important to remember that needs will vary by the type of abuse and neglect, the numbers and ages of children, whether the child has been removed from the home or not, and the unique characteristics of the individual parents (Barth et al., 2005). Leaders should investigate whether the participants are literate or not, whether they will need child care during the program, and whether they have previously participated in parenting programs. In a paper on the National Parenting Education Network website that reviews best practices for programs aimed at preventing child abuse, Shannon (n.d.) has stated that these parents need increased knowledge about children and parenting, a chance to practice using the information and skills they have learned, techniques for managing their children without abusing them, stress management strategies, and suggestions on improving their relationships with others so they can reduce their isolation.

Marketing/Recruitment

When participants are mandated to attend programs, recruitment and marketing take a very different turn than when programs are trying to attract participants. Although not all mandated individuals will participate, mandating people to attend is one of the most effective means for getting them through the door. The real marketing task may be in establishing support and cooperation from the agency or jurisdiction that will issue the mandates, orders, or referrals.

Cookston, Sandler, Braver, and Genalo (2007) looked at the readiness of court systems to adopt evidence-based programming. They looked specifically at family courts establishing mandated divorce education, believing that the courts were an especially appropriate home for the educational programs. They based their argument on the facts that the mandates would be issued by judges, and the courts have shown an increasing interest. After surveying 128 courts, they discovered that the most important factors indicating readiness to adopt evidence-based programs were (1) the presence of champions advocating for the programs (and the absence of opponents), (2) community attitudes that were supportive of expanding the court's programming, and (3) being in a smaller county. The authors speculated that one of the reasons for greater support coming from smaller counties was the fact that larger counties may have had the resources to create their own programming and therefore were less likely to seek evidence-based programs from other sources. The authors also cited previous work that showed that judges and advocacy groups would supply very strong support for effective parenting programs and very few would oppose them, while almost one quarter of state legislators might oppose such programs.

Cambron and colleagues (2000) suggested a list of questions to answer when considering the possibility of establishing a court-connected divorce education program. The list should be viewed with caution, because the basis of the items is unclear, but the questions could provide a starting point and an organizing structure when combined with other literature. The questions are paraphrased here:

1. What are the goals of the program?

2. What are the needs of the target population?

3. What components should be part of the program? Does a curriculum exist or need to be created? How much does it cost?

4. What support is available for the program from judges, community leaders, the clerk's office, and agencies?

5. Who will manage the program and serve as facilitators?

6. What funds are available? Will there be fees for participants? If so, what will happen if fees are not paid?

7. What will qualify people to be mandated? What will they be told? When could they be exempted? How will attendance be documented? What happens to dropouts?

8. How will the program handle participants with special needs and language differences? Will security personnel be necessary?

9. How will the program be evaluated and for whom? What kinds of outcomes will be measured? Who will conduct the evaluation? How will evaluation costs be covered?

Although the Cookston and colleagues study (2007) and the list of questions from Cambron and her collaborators (2000) looked only at divorcing parent education, the results are likely to have implications for all mandated family life education. It appears to be critical to identify champions and build coalitions of supporters—both at the local level and with legislators. Mandated programming is multifaceted and requires attention to the contributions and roles of families, mandating officials, service providers, legislators, and funding sources. It also is necessary to identify effective programs, which means conducting more and stronger evaluation studies that look not only at "customer satisfaction" and self-report reactions but that also assess behavior change and the impact of the programming on families and communities. It also may be helpful to educate policy makers and program leaders to recognize quality programs and materials, possibly using a tool like the Family Life Education Materials Quality Assessment Tool (Myers-Walls, 2010).

Barriers to Participation

In spite of being mandated, not all participants attend programs, participate in activities, or continue attending after they start. Leaders' responses to attendance behaviors vary. In some foster parent programs, staff will follow up with absent participants and compensate for missed sessions in another visit (Chamberlain et al., 2008). This may reflect the power balance in foster parent training. Because the foster care system needs more willing parents, staff often experience negative consequences if participants do not complete the program, so they take extra steps to help participants complete the training. In less accommodating settings, researchers have found that parents who did not comply with mandated parenting programming had lower incomes, were single or separated, were more likely to have an aggressive male in the household and a transient lifestyle, and they had higher drug and alcohol use levels, more partner violence, and a higher incidence of criminal behavior (Butler, Radia, & Magnatta, 1994). This suggests that leaders need to be sensitive to those participants facing significant life obstacles and try to lower those obstacles in order to encourage better attendance.

When officials require attendance at these programs, they are assuming that it will be helpful for individuals to attend. To explore whether attendance influences program outcomes, Nix, Bierman, and McMahon (2009) collected data on participants in a Parent Management Training program called Fast Track (not mandatory). They measured attendance and quality of participation in two different components of the program as well as completion of take-home activities. They discovered that *quality* of participation was more powerful than the frequency of attendance in predicting successful program outcomes. In the end, however, demographic characteristics, severity of children's problems, and stressful family situations predicted success better than attendance and participation in the Fast Track program. The Fast Track program instituted several conditions to encourage and support attendance, however. Applying this research to mandated audiences suggests that it is not enough to just get the participants to show up, but that engaging them actively in the educational environment is critical.

Van Camp (2004) explored attendance issues with a sample of participants in the MAPP program for biological, adoptive, and foster parents. She noted that 36% of participants dropped out of the program before the end. About one half of the foster parents, just under half of the biological parents, and a few of the adoptive parents were mandated or received incentives (babysitting reimbursement or $45 payment) for attending the sessions. The adoptive parents had the highest rates of attendance, while the biological parents attended least often. Mandating participation clearly increased attendance; combining the mandate with reimbursement for babysitting costs was most effective with encouraging and maintaining attendance. It is interesting that paying participants to attend (without other incentives) was only moderately effective.

Research with a related population offers insights into the impact of mandating attendance. Polcin (2001) looked at the impact of coercing people abusing drugs into drug treatment versus allowing them to enter voluntarily. Most studies have found that positive outcomes were not increased or decreased based on whether participation was mandated; apparently, being mandated to attend drug treatment does not either cancel out or guarantee results. The authors concluded that coercion is a continuous and not a dichotomous variable. Many participants in drug treatment receive pressure from family, friends, self, and professionals to enter treatment, so coercion can come from many sources, and users may not perceive coercion when others feel it is present. The author cited a study that found that 35% of mandated drug treatment participants reported that they did not feel coerced. This suggests that the perceptions of the parents and families in court-mandated family life education are at least as important as objective measures of mandates or requirements. The more a facilitator can help a participant see attendance as his or her idea, the greater the commitment and the lower the resistance.

This background suggests that mandating attendance in family life education programs is likely to increase attendance but that attendance alone will not guarantee active participation or positive impact of programs. Some participants want to passively "do their time" and move on. Schaffner (1997) talked about parents who "entered the court-ordered classes obviously very angry and sat defiantly silent with their arms across their chests" (p. 328). Yet several studies found that participants may enter a program angry and resentful after being required to attend but later support the mandate and say they wish it had started earlier or lasted longer (Brandon, 2006; Pollet & Lombreglia, 2008). So mandates seem to increase attendance, but it is up to the atmosphere of the group to encourage participation and true engagement in the educational environment.

Environmental Considerations

Cookston and colleagues (2007) pointed out that divorce education programs could be offered in schools, universities, community service agencies, and family courts. Salem and colleagues (1996) stated that leaders of those programs could be "judges, lawyers, college professors, community volunteers, researchers, mental health professionals, graduate students, family court mediators, and parents" (p. 16). Some argue that the court setting is really the best setting (Cookston et al., 2007), but others make different arguments. Myers-Walls and colleagues (2009) and Salem and colleagues (1996) suggested that it is important for program leaders to separate themselves from the mandating bodies and officials. If parents and families are angry and resentful, it could be helpful for the program to be in a different setting besides the mandating organization so that participants can resolve those negative feelings more quickly. Such a setting can help participants engage more honestly and openly in discussions and activities, facilitating the effectiveness of the program. On the other hand, holding programs in the official agency setting can enable the mandating authorities to monitor attendance, and participants may take the mandate more seriously. They could be more motivated to demonstrate improvement to those who have determined that they need to attend programming.

A very important environmental consideration is the distribution of power in the program leader–participant relationship. Mandated participants begin the relationship several steps down. Some authors have noted that there are often large numbers of minorities in participant populations while the majority of program leaders are white and middle-class (Schaffner, 1997; Van Camp, 2004). If leaders are also presented as experts with all the answers, it is not surprising that participants feel resentful and angry. Using good family life education programming principles, leaders should create environments that are comfortable, safe, and free of unnecessary distractions. Setting up an environment of punishment will not facilitate learning and success in program outcomes.

Another environmental consideration is the makeup on the target audience for the programs. There is controversy regarding whether groups should consist of only mandated participants or a mixture of mandated and voluntary. Barth and his coauthors (2005) commented on one type of group heterogeneity when they stated that "combining open and closed in-home cases in parenting groups generates substantial heterogeneity with regard to motivation and issues of expectations" (p. 358). Parenting Piece by Piece (Myers-Walls et al., 2009) has taken the position that mandated parenting programs should be made up of only mandated parents, perhaps supplemented with some additional high-risk referrals. This recommendation is based on several issues. First, it is important for programs to address the anger and resentment related to the mandate, and it would be difficult to do so if the group were mixed. Second, the educational needs of high-risk and low-risk groups are quite different, and it is difficult to meet both sets of needs simultaneously. A third issue is the stigma that may accompany mandates. If only some of the participants are mandated to attend, they may feel nervous and self-conscious about being discovered and may resist participation. If the entire group is mandated, this fear does not arise. Experience indicates that mixed groups may also have negative outcomes related to who constitutes the larger part of the group. If most of the group is not mandated and a few are, it is likely that the mandated parents will feel intimidated by the other parents and will sit back and participate only enough to get credit for attending. Because they are only passive participants, program topics and solutions are not likely to meet their needs. If the mandated parents form the majority of the group, the voluntary participants may wonder what kind of group they have found themselves in and quickly drop out, or they may take on a quasi-leader position and try to "save" the high-risk parents.

Others have taken a different approach to this issue and advocated for mainstreaming at-risk parents and families with other groups. They believe that this mixture provides good role models for the struggling parents and helps them transition into other community programming. The underlying belief is that both groups can be served with programming that falls under the Carter and Kahn (1996) category of normative parenting and that parenting and family needs are standard and predictable. This means that basic curricula will meet the needs of all parents and families. With these arguments in mind, group leaders should consider whether to restrict membership to either mandated or nonmandated or mix the two. Whatever a program leader decides, the fact remains that it is critical for any leader to become familiar with the audience and tailor programs to their needs.

Modes of Learning

Because of the issues of control in mandated programming, it could be easy for a leader to slip into a mode of didactic learning with specific content and inflexible curriculum outlines. This is especially true if particular curricula are required as the only acceptable guides. Top-down programming can also result if there is no established curriculum and the leaders conduct sessions on an ad hoc basis. But several authors have noted the importance of including active learning approaches and collaborative agendas (Pollet & Lombreglia, 2008; Puddy & Jackson, 2003). Those authors and Shannon (n.d.) also have used evaluation results to determine that more active learning styles that address and provide opportunities to practice specific skills are likely to be most effective.

As with any family life education programming, it is critical to know the audience and how they learn. Some programs have used booklets and other written materials as the primary educational strategies and have found them to be effective in divorce education (e.g., Ogles et al., 1991). Some participants in high-risk situations may be functionally illiterate, however, making the use of written materials ineffective. Other approaches have been the use of electronic media and web-based materials (Cooperative Parenting Institute, 2009; Craig, 1998; Pacifici, Delaney, White, Nelson, & Cummings, 2006). The advantages of these varied delivery methods are their flexibility regarding timing and location. Flexibility can be especially important to some families who are anxious to have children returned to the home, to get on with the divorce proceedings, or complete the adoption process. The disadvantage of distance-learning options is the reduced opportunity to discuss issues with others and normalize reactions and behaviors as well as the possible lack of a viable computer among participants. There are also possibilities in group programs to set up supportive networks, and participants can model the behaviors of others who have successfully dealt with the resentment of being required to attend (Polcin, 2001) or who have found useful approaches for dealing with family challenges. The distance-learning setting also makes it much more difficult to monitor the needs, understanding, and participation of parents and families.

Educator Characteristics

As stated earlier, many different types of professionals have been involved in leading mandated family life education programs for parents and families (Cookston et al., 2007; Salem et al., 1996). Myers-Walls and her coauthors (2009) recommended that leaders of Parenting Piece by Piece have experience with parenting education and/or experience with working with mandated audiences. In addition, they state that ideally leaders will have "a degree and work experience in child development, family studies, family life education, social work, counseling, or a related field" (p. 2) but that a degree is not necessary. Salem and his colleagues (1996) noted some authors have said that a mental health background is most important for divorce education leaders, and some programs require at least a master's degree in a mental health field. What Salem and his coauthors emphasized, however, is having skills in group work. They express concern about putting too much emphasis on academic background. As they stated, "In addition to a substantive knowledge base, programs selecting presenters should strongly consider background in adult education theory, group facilitation skills, and public speaking" (1996, p. 16). Bundy-Fazioli and colleagues (2008) conducted a qualitative study with child welfare workers and mandated parents and found three key worker characteristics that were valued by the parents: (1) a positive disposition, (2) compassion, and (3) authenticity.

Carter and Kahn (1996) stated in their analysis of parenting education that "to those individuals considered national leaders, parenting educators . . . are considered to be inadequately prepared for the responsibility they carry" (p. 45). Since that time, the requisite skills for parenting education programming in general have been captured by the National Extension Parenting Educators Framework (NEPEF) (DeBord et al., 2002). In this model, professionals are expected to *GROW* in the field by participating in professional development and socialization; *FRAME* the content by learning to understand and apply the primary theoretical frameworks and philosophies of parenting education; *DEVELOP* programs using needs assessments, behavioral objectives, creative activities and program components, and appropriate evaluation plans; learn how to deliver the program effectively and *EDUCATE* parents and families using proven teaching and learning strategies; *EMBRACE* a variety of parent and family backgrounds, forms, and cultures; and *BUILD* the field of parenting education by advocating for the needs of parents and families at community, regional, national, and international levels. These skills were identified for parenting educators in a variety of settings, and they define abilities that are critical for leaders of mandated programs as well.

As previously stated, mandated parent and family programs have spanned a number of professional settings and disciplines. The professionals from these settings have very different areas of expertise. The danger in multidisciplinary situations is that one discipline may not recognize, understand, or take advantage of the expertise of another. For example, Salem and colleagues (1996) wrote an article titled "Parent Education as a Distinct Field of Practice." The authors seemed to be totally unaware of the fact that parenting education has a long history and well-established theoretical, research, and practice base separate from the court-connected context of the article. Further, the authors considered only divorce education programs in the manuscript, ignoring other emphases in parenting education programs both inside and outside of the court context. As Carter and Kahn (1996) put it, "Parenting education is a cross-disciplinary exercise that still needs to establish a common language and conceptual framework that can be embraced by each of those disciplines" (p. 100).

As previously mentioned, the professional skills outlined in NEPEF could apply to all of the mandated programming that involves parents. However, it may be important to embellish the NEPEF skills when used in mandated settings. For example, perhaps the GROW component needs to be expanded to include training in the legal system. The ideal situation in this multidisciplinary setting would be for the various professionals involved in these programs to work closely together, recognizing and honoring the unique expertise held by each discipline. Child development and parenting experts should provide background in children's developmental needs and parent–child relationships, while lawyers and court officials should provide their insights into legal precedent and reasonable use of power. When collaborating, professionals need to know and claim what they know and also know what they don't know. The complex situations of children and families at risk are much better faced by a united, multidisciplinary force than by isolated groups of practitioners, researchers, or advocates.

Ethical Considerations

The ethical considerations associated with programming for mandated audiences are closely entwined with appropriate use of power. The fact that someone can make someone else do something means that there is an unequal power distribution. Program leaders in this situation may be tempted to focus on the negative assessments of the participants and pronounce judgments, telling participants what to do rather than working together to build skills and find solutions. As Schaffner (1997) reported, she observed leaders saying things such as the following:

> You have got to get control of your kid!... Discipline is important—or you are going to have a child runnin' the streets! and *Kids do not survive divorces!* Divorces are not "okay"! When a father leaves a family, a *kid* feels abandoned, too. (pp. 422–423)

While statements like these could be shared among peers in informal conversations, their negative and defeatist tone can have unintended consequences when expressed by program leaders.

It is critical for program leaders to examine their own attitudes and opinions when delivering these programs. Knowing themselves and their biases will help the leaders to avoid allowing those attitudes to impinge inappropriately on participants. Schaffner (1997) identified three perspectives in her unstructured observations of a probation-operated parenting series for parents with children in the juvenile justice, divorce court, or CPS systems. The first perspective, held by most of the probation department representatives, was that the probation department could "parent" better than the biological parents who were deviant or delinquent. The second perspective was a defensive reaction to the first: Although the parents recognized they didn't have the answers to their problems, they did not feel they were getting answers from the probation department either. The third perspective was sometimes held by both parents and probation personnel. This perspective was a kind of demonization of the children (primarily older children), blaming the children for being bad or uncooperative. None of these perspectives is helpful and can be considered unethical if held by professionals. Professionals who are respectful of and collaborative with the participants are more likely to achieve positive outcomes.

Another ethical pitfall to avoid is conflict of interest. This can occur if professionals hold more than one position in relation to the families in the programs. Schaffner (1997) found that probation officers would recommend that parents testify against their children in court proceedings—an approach that is helpful from the perspective of probation department goals but not from parenting education perspectives. Salem and colleagues (1996) warned about the dangers of leading programs that include parents who have or could be clients in the law practice responsible for the program. This concern also argues against having staff from the probation, court, or CPS system lead educational programs.

In looking closely at power relationships between parents and child welfare workers, Bundy-Fazioli and her colleagues (2008) found that "how workers and parents choose to interact may influence service outcomes" (p. 2). They say that workers rarely receive training or assistance to learn how to balance power with clientele and avoid a hierarchal approach in spite of the fact that equitable relationships are encouraged. One finding of the study was that both parents and workers felt powerless. The parents felt controlled and judged by the courts and CPS, and the workers wanted to see their programs as voluntary, but in actuality they needed to admit that the parents had been mandated to attend. In fact, the workers were told that they were to be the "eyes and ears" of the court. They were to monitor the participants' activities and let the court know how the families were doing. This situation created the conflict of interest previously mentioned as the leaders tried to reconcile those two very different functions.

So a unique ethical challenge of leading mandated programs is to try to maintain a strengths-based, empowerment approach in a system of court-based power, mandates, and judgments. Educators receive the advantages of programming to a mandated audience, freeing them from recruitment tasks, but they need to avoid letting that freedom allow them to ignore the process of making programs inviting, collaborative, and effective. They also need to try to separate the roles of educator, monitor, and adjudicator as much as possible.

Best Practices in Family Life Education Programming

None of the domains of programming discussed in this chapter is fully developed and well established regarding best practices. Addressing mandated programs for abuse/neglect, Barth and colleagues (2005) reviewed parent training and support efforts using the standards of evidence as set by the American Psychological Association (APA) and found that "there is not a single intervention that has generated a published peer-review article based on a study in which they accepted referrals from a child welfare agency, randomly assigned them to a treatment condition, and evaluated the outcome" (p. 359). At the same time, these authors reported that a number of the programs listed in this chapter met somewhat less stringent requirements. In lieu of meeting APA evidence-based expectations, they suggested criteria such as accessibility of manuals, face validity of the content, good administrative support, successful on-the-ground experience, basic evaluation data, brevity, low cost per family, no requirement of advanced training for leaders, recognition that some parents will have their children at home and others will not, and concepts that are easy for participants to grasp.

Another similar but broader approach to determining the quality of curricula used for family life education in general is called the Family Life Education Materials Quality Assessment Tool (Myers-Walls, 2010). This tool could be applied to any materials to be used with mandated or nonmandated parents or families. The criteria considered important for curricula include author/creator qualifications, the inclusion of citations supporting the research base of the material and a clear connection between the research base and the program, a clear indication of the intended level of impact of the program, clear and measurable objectives, an explicit values orientation, inclusion of statements communicating the importance of the information for the program participants, appropriateness of activities and topics for the target audience, clear and easy-to-follow instructions for the leader, attractive and useful handouts, a variety of activities, suggestions of additional materials and resources for participants, labeling of statements as facts or theories or opinions, inclusion of results of previous evaluation studies, inclusion of strategies and forms to support the collection of evaluation data from participants, inclusion of all materials necessary for the program, and a recognition of the context of children and families that would impact the application of the program skills and recommendations. These criteria can guide both the assessment of materials and the creation of new curricula items.

More specific guidelines are available to advance the state of adoptive and foster care training—particularly regarding treatment foster care. The Foster Family-Based Treatment Association: Program Standards for Treatment Foster Care state the following criteria of excellence: "...a strengths-based approach, an affirmation of children's natural families and their needs for permanent homes, and of cultural diversity" (Dorsey et al., 2008, p. 1406). Those value-related principles along with the more general criteria previously listed provide a structure for beginning to evaluate programs and for developing new ones.

Best practices for programs targeting divorcing parents have been suggested by some authors, but the content of those recommendations varies by the perspective of the author. The same is true for programming aimed at abusive and neglectful parents and parents of children in the juvenile justice system. Shannon (n.d.) has listed several best practices for programs aimed at preventing child abuse:

- Target as many risk factors as possible.
- Try to impact knowledge, attitudes, skills, and aspirations of participants.
- Work with parents often and for an extended period of time.
- The quality of the leaders and parent educators is critical.
- Work with other agencies and organizations as appropriate.
- Tailor the services to meet the particular needs of individual participants as appropriate.
- Engage in careful and purposeful planning.

Carter and Kahn (1996) described parenting education, a term into which all three categories of mandated programming described here could fit, as an "emerging discipline" (p. v). Collaborative, research-based efforts can help the field and its demonstrated effectiveness to grow.

FUTURE DIRECTIONS

There are several controversies and questions that define the future directions for mandated programs for parents and families.

1. How can individuals be given choices and a sense of control when being mandated to attend family life education programs?

2. Should mandated and nonmandated program participants be combined in the same program groups?

3. Should both members of a divorcing couple be included in the same divorce education sessions together?

4. How can professionals from different disciplines work effectively together to serve the needs of parents and families?

REFERENCES

Amato, P. (1993). Children's adjustment to divorce: Theories, hypotheses, and empirical support. *Journal of Marriage and Family, 55*(1), 23–38.

Amato, P. R. (2000). The consequences of divorce for adults and children. *Journal of Marriage and Family, 62*(4), 1269–1287.

Arbuthnot, J., & Gordon, D. A. (1996). Does mandatory divorce education for parents work? A six-month outcome evaluation. *Family and Conciliation Courts Review, 34*(1), 60–81.

Barth, R. P., Landsverk, J., Chamberlain, P., Reid, J. B., Rolls, J. A., Hurlburt, M. S., et al. (2005). Parent-training programs in child welfare services: Planning for a more evidence-based approach to serving biological parents. *Research on Social Work Practice, 15*(5), 353–371.

Barton, K., Baglio, C. S., & Braverman, M. T. (1994). Stress reduction in child-abusing families: Global and specific measures. *Psychological Reports, 75,* 287–304.

Bigner, J. J. (2010). *Parent-child relations: An introduction to parenting.* Columbus, OH: Merrill.

Blaisure, D. R., & Geasler, M. J. (1996). Results of a survey of court-connected parent education programs in U. S. counties. *Family and Conciliation Courts Review, 34,* 23–40.

Boyan, S. B., & Termini, A. M. (1999). *Cooperative parenting and divorce: A leader's guide and parent guide to effective co-parenting.* Marietta, GA: Active Parenting.

Bradley, E. J., & Peters, R. D. (1991). Physically abusive and nonabusive mothers' perceptions of parenting and child behavior. *American Journal of Orthopsychiatry, 61*(3), 455–460.

Brandon, D. J. (2006). Can four hours make a difference? Evaluation of a parent education program for divorcing parents. *Journal of Divorce & Remarriage, 45*(1), 171–185.

Bundy-Fazioli, K., Briar-Lawson, K., & Hardiman, E. R. (2008). A qualitative examination of power between child welfare workers and parents. *British Journal of Social Work,* 1–18.

Butler, S. M., Radia, N., & Magnatta, M. (1994). Maternal compliance to court-ordered assessment in cases of child maltreatment. *Child Abuse & Neglect, 18*(2), 203–211.

Cambron, M. L., Yankeelov, P. A., & Brown, J. H. (2000, Fall). Developing court-connected parent divorce education programs: Guidelines for communities. *Juvenile and Family Court Journal,* 17–26.

Carter, N., & Kahn, L. (1996). *See how we grow: A report on the status of parenting education in the U.S.* Philadelphia: Pew Charitable Trusts.

Chamberlain, P. (1998, October). Treatment foster care. *OJJDP Juvenile Justice Bulletin,* 1–11.

Chamberlain, P., & Mihalic, S. F. (1998). *Blueprints for violence prevention, book eight: Multidimensional treatment foster care.* Boulder, CO: Department of Health and Human Services.

Chamberlain, P., Price, J., Reid, J., & Landsverk, J. (2008). Cascading implementation of a foster and kinship parent intervention. *Child Welfare, 87*(5), 27–48.

Cookston, J. T., Sandler, I. N., Braver, S. L., & Genalo, M. T. (2007). Predicting readiness to adopt evidence-based programs for divorcing families: Champions, attitudes, and access to funding. *American Journal of Orthopsychiatry, 77*(4), 573–581.

Cooperative Parenting Institute. (2009). *Cooperative parenting institute: Recognizing the unique needs of separating families.* Retrieved from http://www.cooperativeparenting.com/index.html

Craig, B. (1998). *Children in the middle.* Retrieved from http://www.childreninthemiddle.com/index.htm

DeBord, K., Bower, D., Goddard, H. W., Kirby, J., Kobbe, A. M., Myers-Walls, J. A., et al. (2002). *National extension parenting educators' framework.* Retrieved from http://www1.cyfernet.org/ncsu_fcs/NEPEF/index.htm

Dorsey, S., Farmer, E. M., Barth, R. P., Greene, K., M., Reid, J., & Landsverk, J. (2008). Current status and evidence base of training for foster and treatment foster parents. *Children and Youth Services Review, 30,* 1403–1416.

Family Development Resources. (2007). *Nurturing program.* Retrieved from http://www.nurturing-parenting.com/home.php

Family Works. (2003). *Parenting wisely.* Retrieved from http://www.familyworksinc.com/about/index.html

Geasler, M. J., & Blaisure, K. R. (1999). 1998 nationwide survey of court-connected divorce education programs. *Family and Conciliation Courts Review, 37,* 36–63.

Incredible Years. (2009). *The incredible years.* Retrieved from http://www.incredibleyears.com/

Insight Counseling. (n.d.). *Family violence accountability program.* Retrieved from http://www.insightcounselingoftecumseh.org/FamilyViolenceAccountabilityProgam.htm/

Janko, S. (1994). *Vulnerable children, vulnerable families.* New York: Teachers College Press.

Jones, J. (2008). *Adoption experiences of women and men and demand for children to adopt by women 18–44 years of age in the United States, 2002.* National Center for Health Statistics. *Vital and Health Statistics* 23(27). Retrieved from http://www.cdc.gov/nchs/data/series/sr_23/sr23_027.pdf

Kearsley, G. (2010). *The theory into practice database.* Retrieved from http://tip.psychology.org

Knowles, M. (1984). *The adult learner: A neglected species* (3rd ed.). Houston, TX: Gulf Publishing.

Kreider, R. (2003). *Adopted children and stepchildren: 2000: U.S. Census Bureau Special Reports.* Retrieved from http://www.census.gov/prod/2003pubs/censr-6.pdf

Love and Logic Institute. (2011). *Love and Logic.* Retrieved from http://www.loveandlogic.com/what-is-for-parents.html

McMahon, R. J. (2006). Parent training interventions for preschool-aged children. In R. E. Tremblay, R. G. Barr, & R. DeV. Peters (Eds.), *Encyclopedia on early childhood development* (pp. 1–9). Montreal, Quebec: Centre of Excellence for Early Childhood Development. Retrieved from http://www.enfant-encyclopedie.com/Pages/PDF/McMahonRJANGxp.pdf

Mulroy, M., Sabatelli, R., Malley, C., & Waldron, R. (1995). *Parenting apart: Strategies for effective co-parenting.* Storrs: University of Connecticut Cooperative Extension.

Myers-Walls, J. A. (2010). *Family life education materials quality assessment tool (FLEMat QAT).* West Lafayette, IN: Purdue University Extension. Retrieved from http://www.extension.purdue.edu/purplewagon/FLEMat-QAT/FLEMat-QAT.htm

Myers-Walls, J. A., Ballard, S. M., Darling, C. A., & Myers-Bowman, K.S. (2011). Reconceptualizing the domain and boundaries of family life education. *Family Relations (60),* 357–372.

Myers-Walls, J. A., Newcom, T., & Berkope, S. (2009). *Parenting piece by piece.* West Lafayette, IN: Purdue Cooperative Extension. Retrieved from http://www.cfs.purdue.edu/extension/children_families/parenting_piecebypiece.html

Nix, R. L., Bierman, K. L., & McMahon, R. J. (2009). How attendance and quality of participation affect treatment response to parent management training. *Journal of Consulting and Clinical Psychology, 77*(3), 429–438.

Ogles, B. M., Lambert, M. J., & Craig, D. E. (1991). A comparison of self-help books for coping with loss: Expectations and attributions. *Journal of Counseling Psychology, 38,* 387–393.

Pacifici, C., Delaney, R., White, L., Nelson, C., & Cummings, K. (2006). Web-based training for foster, adoptive, and kinship parents. *Children and Youth Services Review, 28,* 1329–1343.

Petersen, V., & Steinman, S. B. (1994). Helping children succeed after divorce: A court-mandated educational program for divorcing parents. *Family Court Review, 32*(1), 27–39.

Polcin, D. L. (2001). Drug and alcohol offenders coerced into treatment: A review of modalities and suggestions for research on social model programs. *Substance Use & Misuse, 36*(5), 589–608.

Pollet, S. L., & Lombreglia, M. (2008). A nationwide survey of mandatory parent education. *Family Court Review, 46*(2), 375–394.

Puddy, R. W., & Jackson, Y. (2003). The development of parenting skills in foster parent training. *Children and Youth Services Review, 25*(12), 987–1013.

Salem, P., Schepard, A., & Schlissel, S. W. (1996). Parent education as a distinct field of practice: The agenda for the future. *Family and Conciliation Courts Review, 34*(1), 9–22.

Schaffner, L. (1997). Families on probation: court-ordered parenting skills classes for parents of juvenile delinquents. *Crime & Delinquency, 43*(4), 412–437.

Seamans, C. L., Rubin, L. J., & Stabb, S. D. (2007). Women domestic violence offenders: Lessons of violence and survival. *Journal of Trauma & Dissociation, 8*(2), 47–68.

Shannon, L. C. (n.d.). *Best practices for parent education programs seeking to prevent child abuse.* Retrieved from http://www.npen.org/pdfs/BestPra.pdf

Southern Illinois University Carbondale. (2003). *Project 12-ways.* Retrieved from http://www .p12ways.siu.edu/

STEP Publishers. (n.d.). *The STEP program.* Retrieved from http://www.steppublishers.com/

United Way of the Greater Triangle. (n.d.). SAFEchild agency details. Retrieved from http://volunteer .truist.com/triangle/org/17135642.html

U.S. Census Bureau (2011). *Marital events of American: 2009: American community survey reports.* Retrieved from http://www.census.gov/prod/2011pubs/acs-13.pdf

U.S. Department of Health and Human Services. (2009). *Adoption and foster care analysis and reporting system (AFCARS) FY 2008 data (October 1, 2007 through September 30, 2008).* Retrieved from http://www.afterschool.ed.gov/programs/cb/stats_research/afcars/tar/ report16.htm

U.S. Department of Health and Human Services, Administration for Children and Families, Administration on Children, Youth and Families, Children's Bureau. (2010). *Child maltreatment 2008.* Retrieved from http://www.acf.hhs.gov/programs/cb/pubs/cm08/index.htm

Van Camp, C. M. (2004). *Behavior analysis in child welfare: A preliminary program evaluation.* Unpublished doctoral dissertation, Louisiana State University, Baton Rouge.

Wallerstein, J. (1991). The long-term effects of divorce on children. *Journal of the American Academy of Child Adolescent Psychiatry, 30*(3), 349–360.

Whitehurst, D. H., O'Keefe, S. L., & Wilson, R. A. (2008). Divorced and separated parents in conflict. *Journal of Divorce & Remarriage, 48*(3), 127–144.

Chapter 5

Family Life Education With Military Families

ELIZABETH B. CARROLL, CFLE, CATHERINE CLARK MORGAN SMITH, CFLE, AND ANDREW O. BEHNKE, CFLE

Family life education with military families offers unique settings and opportunities for innovative programming and projects. We are part of a collaborative project titled "Essential Life Skills for Military Families." Our perspective is informed by research, shaped by our personal experiences with the military, and humbled by their sacrifices. One of us, the daughter of a World War II veteran, has spent the past 7 years engaged in family life education with military families, first with the Citizen Soldier Support Project and later as director of the Essential Life Skills for Military Families project. Another, the wife of a navy chaplain, has 30 years associated with the military including experiences as the manager for a family support center, as a nurse, and as a family life educator. Yet another worked at Purdue's Military Family Research Institute where he helped research factors influencing the well-being of military families. All three of us are trainers for the Essential Life Skills for Military Families curriculum, collaborate in the implementation of training and workshops for reserve and National Guard families, and work daily to inspire community educators to support military families through education. As chapter authors, we honor those soldiers, sailors, marines, airmen, and their families who sacrifice personal and family time, energy, resources, and often their lives to keep us safe.

DEFINING THE POPULATION

The U.S. Department of Defense (DOD) is the United States' largest employer, with over 1.4 million active duty, 1.1 million National Guard and reserve component forces, and 718,000 civilian personnel (Military OneSource Center, 2009). The U.S. military consists of five active duty services and their respective guard and reserve units. Despite close ties and similarities, each service is uniquely different in regard to mission, customs, traditions, and uniforms. The largest service, the U.S. Army, is the primary land combat force. The U.S. Air Force defends in the air, while supporting sister services with air cover and transporting troops, weapons, and supplies. The U.S. Navy protects our interests on the water and supports land forces with weapons, supplies and personnel transport. The U.S. Marine Corps, part of the U.S. Navy, is primarily a highly skilled amphibious force. The U.S. Coast Guard provides maritime law enforcement, search and rescue, police operations, and inspections of cargo and ships.

The reserve component is composed of each state's National Guard and reserve forces from each service. Their lifestyles are mainly civilian. They serve part-time, drilling one weekend a month and 2 weeks per year. Historically, the National Guard and reserve forces have been less likely than their active duty counterparts to identify themselves as military families (U.S. Department of Defense [DOD], 2009). The National Guard has traditionally provided assistance within its own state; however, they may be mobilized to meet federal needs. During the past 10 to 15 years, the reserve component has shifted away from a part-time commitment to one in which service members may expect to deploy for 1 to 1.5 years approximately every 5 years (Griffith, 2009).

Each service has more enlisted personnel than officers. For example, approximately 10% of the Marine Corps serve as commissioned officers; 90% are enlisted. Commissioned officers are leaders, planners, and problem solvers who are responsible for the welfare, morale, and professional development of the enlisted troops in their command.

To function effectively, the U.S. military requires strict obedience to commanding officers, known as command and control. The hierarchy begins with the individual service member and continues upward through the ranks to the secretary of defense and the president of the United States as commander-in-chief. The DOD strives to instill in every person in uniform the core values of leadership, professionalism, and technical expertise. Nonconformity can result in disciplinary action. Commitment and a common value system permeate almost every aspect of a member's home and family life (Riccio, Sullivan, Klein, Salter, & Kinnison, 2004).

Demographics

As the armed forces' perspective on families changed over the past 50 years, the families themselves also changed. Today's active duty military is an all-volunteer force. It is better educated, more likely to be married, and has more female members and more minorities than the draft-era military. Overall, African Americans and whites who serve in the military are significantly more likely to marry than are their comparable civilian counterparts. Unlike the civilian community, there is little difference between blacks and whites in the likelihood of marriage (Lundquist, 2004). The number of dual service couples has grown, with 42% of the army's uniformed wives being married to servicemen (Shinseki, 2003). By the end of the 20th century, nearly half of the active duty forces were under age 26, over half were married, and 43% had children. By 2004, 60% had some sort of responsibility for children (Weinstock, 2010). As a group, they are predominately young and, if not married, many are in long-term relationships. Marriages frequently occur immediately before deployments. Sole parents with primary custody emerged as a discernible group (Shinseki, 2003), and female soldiers increased from 9% in 1982 to 15% by 2002 (Harris, Simutis, & Gantz, 2002). Most (95%) enlisted members had a high school diploma or had passed the General Educational Development (GED) high school equivalency test. More than half (69.4 %) of army spouses had some college, and almost 80% of the soldiers had completed some college by their second enlistment (Shinseki, 2003). Two thirds of active duty families live near but not on base (U.S. General Accounting Office, 1996), and 10% to 25% of military families relocated when the military spouse was deployed (Granovsky, 2002). At the opposite end of the spectrum are other active duty and reserve component families who live away from base. Their affiliation with the military is often not even known by neighbors or friends.

Based on current statistics, the military maintains a force that is somewhat representative of the ethnicity of the nation. By 2003, the active army reported its soldiers were 58.7% white, 25.1% African American, 9.5% Hispanic, and 6.7% other. This was comparable to the general 17- to 19-year-old civilian population of 66.7% white, 14.5% African American, 13.7% Hispanic, and 5.1% other. African American women were four times more likely to join the military service than were their white counterparts. In 2003, they represented almost 42% of the army's uniformed women (Shinseki, 2003.) The military appears closer to achieving their goal of equal representation than in times past (Armor, Gilroy, & Curtis, 2010). Compared to the civilian sector, the active duty military is composed of younger workers. For example, in 2005, 88% of new recruits were between 18 and 24 years old, compared to 37% of the general population in the same age range. On average, new recruits were about

20 years old (Lee & Mather, 2008). Among young enlistees, a family life educator might expect to see more minorities from single-parent families. Enlistment rates were highest among men from one-parent families (Bachman, Segal, Freedman-Doan, & O'Malley, 2000). These young troops often accept remarkable responsibilities requiring highly trained technical skills, personnel management, and leadership expertise not experienced by the civilian counterparts (Bowen & Martin, 2011).

Unique Aspects of Military Families

Although military families face a myriad of issues, several unique challenges are particularly noteworthy. Geographical isolation limits availability of services. With the unprecedented level of activation and deployment of reserve and guard members during recent operations, the delivery of quality support services for the "geographically dispersed" has proven difficult. Effective partnerships and systems must be developed with federal, national, state, local, and private agencies to encourage collaboration with support services near dispersed families.

Along with geographic isolation, separation is an intrinsic factor in military families. Changes in duty station, known as Permanent Change of Station (PCS), results in families that are twice as likely to move as nonmilitary families (Segal & Wechsler, 2004). Families may accompany their service member depending on the type of assignment. Periodic separations also occur for training or temporary duty assignments (TDYs). The family may reside stateside while their service member serves an overseas tour. The family may live far from base, and the service member becomes a geographical bachelor, joining the family only periodically. Families may live apart for years, waiting for children to graduate from high school or trying to sell a home they purchased. For the dual military couple, this is an important issue in respect to joint domicile assignments and family care planning if both uniformed parents deploy at the same time (Shinseki, 2003).

With every move or separation, parents experience challenges. Moving often requires securing new housing, placing belongings and vehicles in long-term storage, or shipping items overseas. Families frequently sell vehicles and relinquish pets. Weight limits may require eliminating household items. One military wife described how she limited the size of the items she owned to those that could fit in the largest shipping box. Each move causes a lengthy interruption, loss of job tenure, and often the need to meet location-specific licensing certification for working spouses. The moves mean the loss of established social support networks and the need to reestablish them in the new location. The frequent moves may also negatively affect the civilian spouse's career. Reserve component families are more likely to stay home while their service member is activated and have even fewer resources (Segal, 1986).

Relocation affects children in the areas of education and relationships. Just as their parents experience moves, military children experience frequent moves with the transient rate for Department of Defense Education Activity (DoDEA) schools at 35% (U.S. DOD, 2009). Military children from active-component families move on average 2.5 times more often than civilian children and may change schools nine times before graduating from high school. Constantly changing schools, curriculums, peer groups, and friends are the hallmarks of a military childhood (National Governors Association, 2008). DOD has emphasized increasing academic standards in DoDEA schools, involving parents in decision making and facilitating smooth transfers between DoDEA schools and local school districts (Department of Defense Education Activity [DoDEA], n.d.).

Deployment

Families experiencing their first deployment encounter additional stress. Those with more than three deployments are at higher risk for mental health problems and work-related problems than those on their first or second (Mental Health Advisory Team V, 2008). Back-to-back or poorly managed deployments are problematic for military families (Shinseki, 2003). Boundary ambiguity frequently exists during deployments (Boss & Greenberg, 1984). Families have difficulty perceiving who is in or out of the family and who is performing what roles and tasks within the family system. Often this boundary ambiguity was associated with concern over the member's safety and redistribution of roles and responsibilities. The extent to which families closed their boundaries varied in relation to the level of ambiguity the family was experiencing (Faber, Willerton, Clymer, MacDermid, & Weiss, 2008). Parental loneliness, depression, the ability of the nondeployed parent to cope, communication with the away parent, the age of the child, living arrangements, and other factors all contribute to the effects of deployment on children (U.S. DOD, 2009).

Most spouses of military personnel (85%) in a recent survey listed foreign deployments as the most stressful situation they had experienced in the past 5 years. Raising children in their husbands' absence was described often (Dimiceli, Steinhardt, & Smith, 2009). Research has shown that women whose husbands deployed for 1 to 11 months received more diagnoses of depressive disorders, sleep disorders, anxiety, acute stress reaction, and adjustment disorders. Among army wives, the prolonged deployment of spouses has been associated with increased mental health diagnoses (Mansfield et al., 2010).

Families often experience emotional and behavioral changes with the deployment of their service member. Known as the emotional cycle of deployment, some services describe five stages of the cycle; others describe seven stages

(Morse, 2006). As outlined in the seven-stage cycle: Stage 1 is the anticipation of departure. Stage 2 involves detachment and withdrawal. Stage 3 is emotional disorganization. Stage 4 consists of recovery and stabilization. Stage 5 is identified as the anticipation of return. Stage 6 moves into return adjustment and renegotiation. Stage 7 is reintegration and stabilization. Stabilization of the family takes time, sometimes 6 months or longer, which can be increasingly stressful with back-to-back deployments. Families may reenter Stage 1 before stabilizing from a prior deployment (Morse, 2006).

Stress and Mental Health Issues

Skills that keep warriors safe may be less constructive in the civilian world. Munroe (2005) identified specific battlefield skills that are necessary for warriors but frequently make life challenging when service members return home. Time in harm's way requires the service member to be constantly alert to danger. After returning home, the service member may experience safety, control, and hypervigilance issues that are confusing to family members.

In addition, returning from an environment where the service member is used to taking commands, service members may be hesitant to make decisions and have difficulty balancing priorities. Cooperative decision making and taking time to weigh the possibilities that are frequently the norm in a family may become a source of conflict.

Downrange service members must be able to react immediately to threats. They must have equipment clean, orderly, and readily available. Environments that are messy or disorganized may threaten the warrior sense of safety. Their response to the perceived threat may frighten or intimidate family or coworkers. At the same time, warriors have learned to vary their routines and schedules and have learned to withhold information. Employers, spouses, and children expect routines, schedules, and the sharing of information (Munroe, 2005). This dichotomy can be challenging for all involved. Service members may numb responses to combat as a survival mechanism, also affecting relationships on arrival home (La Bash, Vogt, King, & King, 2009).

While the risk of injury or death is the greatest during times of war, there is a potential for injury or death during training maneuvers as well. Over 75% of soldiers and marines who were surveyed reported being in nonwar situations where they could be killed or seriously injured; 62% to 66% knew someone who was seriously injured or killed. Over one third of those surveyed were able to describe an event, which caused them intense horror, fear, or helplessness (Mental Health Advisory Team IV, 2006). The good news is that a greater percentage of our wounded are surviving injuries than in previous wars, with 90% of wounded soldiers surviving their injuries. However, higher percentages are returning with traumatic brain injury (TBI) and severe post-traumatic stress disorder (PTSD) (Yaffe et al., 2010).

Strengths and Assets of Military Families

Military children and families are often stereotyped rather than being appreciated as the multifaceted and diverse populations that they are (Cozza, Chun, & Polo, 2005). Many times these assumptions are biased, rooted in a lack of understanding of the military community or preconceived ideas of the vulnerability of the population. In general, military families and children appear to be a strong and healthy group.

The lifestyle on base can be highly supportive and enjoyable. DOD installations have shops, gas stations, schools, child care, recreational facilities, and restaurants. Many military families live in base housing, shop at the facility's grocery store, attend school, take college courses, work, go bowling, attend church, and participate in Scouts entirely within the boundaries of a military base. For these active duty families, social events, television programming, and the newspaper may be military sponsored. Research on the psychological well-being of military spouses whose partners were absent due to work (Orthner & Rose, 2009) indicates that the informal support assets such as living in a close community and having close friends was associated positively with the spouse's psychological well-being.

Military families have the advantage of living within a system that values and supports them. As an employer, DOD strives to strengthen its families. Thus, despite high deployment rates, the quality of life for military families has been found to be high, and with it, retention and readiness rates remain high (Shinseki, 2003). Improved family policies and support has increased the level of commitment of both service members and their families to the military (U.S. DOD, 2009). The 2002 Social Compact is continually updated and revised to keep pace with the changing expectations of the military families.

Leadership and Unit Support

The military has found that caring leadership, values, camaraderie, traditions, sense of purpose, and a feeling of self-worth within members offset the rigors of military life (Bourg & Segal, 1999). Concerned leadership and sharing the common experiences of military life encourage bonding, and this bonding seems to moderate the stresses associated with military life (Martin & Orthner, 1989). Leaders are charged with being responsible for everything within their command, extending to the responsibility for the well-being of service members and their families. Their family issues become the commander's issues (Shinseki, 2003). The leader promotes informational support and assistance among unit members and their families, which in turn promotes and sustains their own well-being (Bowen, Mancini, Martin, Ware, & Nelson, 2003).

Child Care

Child care is a huge issue for this young, mostly married population who make up the average military family. Having reached a low point in 1983, evidence mounted that child care adversely affected recruitment, morale, and retention (Shinseki, 2003). DOD has worked diligently to improve this issue by aligning with national agencies to institute standards of care/education with child development centers (CDCs) and home child care providers. Because of these measures, the DOD child care system has improved its quality of care and high level of trained and educated care providers (Schwarz, MacDermid, Swan, Robbins, & Mather, 2003). Compared to only 8% of nonmilitary child care centers, 95% of the military child care centers meet the standards of the National Association for the Education of Young Children (NAEYC) (Campbell, Appelbaum, Martinson, & Martin, 2000). DOD serves the largest number of children on a daily basis than any other U.S. employer (DoDEA, n.d.). This excellent, subsidized child care often has waiting lists at nearly all DOD installations (Zellman, Gates, Moini, & Suttorp, 2009).

FAMILY LIFE EDUCATION PRACTICES

Current State of Family Life Education

The military tends to specify licensed mental health professionals and those with military family life experience when hiring individuals to provide family life education for its families. Most family life educators working with military populations are employed in one of five capacities: (1) Military Family Life Consultants (MFLC), (2) parent support specialists as part of New Parent Support Program (NPSP), (3) victim advocates with the Family Advocacy Program (FAP), (4) center staff with one of the military's CDCs, or (5) outside partner or contracted employee for a particular program or need.

Measures to improve readiness include identification of resiliency factors and subsequent family education (Weinstock, 2010). Family Readiness Groups (FRGs), Family Assistance Centers (FACs), predeployment resilience training, emphasis on the use of mental health resources, and the availability of chaplains and family life consultants are measures in place to help build resilience and coping skills. Each of the armed services has FRGs, which are often led by military spouses who volunteer to assist the unit. An FRG is a mechanism for creating a sense of community for the units' spouses and improved communication among geographically dispersed members and families (Granovsky, 2002). Family readiness groups may be known by different names depending on the branch of the military.

The MFLC program is charged with providing education. Established by the Office of the Secretary of Defense (OSD), the goal of the MFLC program is "to prevent family distress by providing education and information on family dynamics, parent education, available support services, and the effects of stress and positive coping mechanisms" (Baker, 2006, p. 1). The OSD recognized an emerging need to offer educational support to service members and their families as a means of supplementing existing counseling services at military facilities. MFLCs are "licensed clinicians with Masters Degrees and at least five years experience in Social Work, Counseling, or a related clinical discipline" (U.S. Army, n.d.). They are trained on military-specific topics such as military culture, the chain of command, and the deployment cycle. Active duty soldiers and mobilized army reserve and National Guard members and their families are allowed six prepaid, confidential face-to-face counseling sessions covering issues such as family, marriage, and relationship issues; stress; anxiety; depression; anger management; and parent–child communication.

Consistent with the view that those who understand the military should offer programming, unit chaplains offer marriage enrichment weekends through the Strong Bonds program (Stanley, Allen, Markman, Rhoades, & Prentice, 2010). Chaplains are service members who serve the faith-based needs of the unit. They have graduate degrees in theological or religious studies and must meet rigorous requirements before being accepted as a chaplain in one of the services.

General Needs of the Population and Rationale for Family Life Education

The relationship between the armed forces and the service member's family has fluctuated for more than two centuries. From 1990 to 1995, the army had downsized 750,000 service members to fewer than 500,000 personnel; consequently, family issues became increasingly important (National Center for Post-Traumatic Stress Disorder & Walter Reed Medical Center, 2004). Moving into the Afghanistan War, 2001, and Iraqi War, 2003, family services received increasingly greater resources, gained momentum and matured (Shinseki, 2003). According to General John A. Wickham, "The Army enlists Soldiers, but it re-enlists families. If you do not take care of the family, you're not going to encourage the Soldier to stay in…" (Collins, 2009, para. 9).

Research has consistently indicated that healthy families are the key to service members' performance on the battlefield and in meeting military objectives. The 1979 Families in Blue Study documented the link between family satisfaction and air force objectives (Tarpley, 2009). As early as 1973, research (Belenky, Sodetz, & Tyner, 1983) found that low morale and prior, or ongoing, civilian stress can predispose a soldier to battle shock, especially true if the stress was family turmoil. In the 1973 Arab Israeli War, prior ongoing stressors were found in 80% of battle shock cases. Those with cumulative stress were more vulnerable. Colonel Larry Ingraham, PhD, noted that families are important because healthy families keep service members alive. Soldiers who go into combat preoccupied with personal or family problems are at increased risk. "We have known for a long time that troubled families produce troubled soldiers who create troubles in their units" (Ingraham, 2002, p. 1). Despite valuing families, funding for family services must be weighed against other DOD financial commitments. Defense budget allocations must be balanced between family programming and ensuring service members receive the necessary equipment, training and support to complete their mission (Wickhman, 1983).

Readiness

Flexibility and preparedness is key in the military. Service members are expected to maintain a constant state of readiness, a condition of preparedness to meet the demands of the mission. The member, and by extension his or her family, must continually maintain numerous requirements to ensure readiness. Before deployment, additional tasks must be completed. Depending on the type, length, location, and the mission itself, preparation may include completing legal, parental, and financial tasks. Military parents, whether speaking of a single service member, dual military parents, or family situations in which one parent is a service member and the spouse is a civilian, must attend to guardianship, custody, and child care issues. Adequate preparation for deployment includes items such as education, realignment of tasks, attending unit functions, and developing appropriate support systems (Granovsky, 2002). Families must understand that family readiness directly affects survival in combat. Stress is cumulative, and the individual who is entering combat worried or preoccupied by thoughts and concerns about loved ones at home is at greater risk. It is critically important that military personnel feel confident about the health, security, and safety of their family members (Martin & Orthner, 1989).

Marriage Education

The military consumes a sizable share of the U.S. workforce, so it is a major setting for family life education. Marriage education in the military may be more advanced than employer-supported marriage education in the private workforce.

The justification for marriage education in the military is similar to reasons the corporate world would offer marriage education. Military service, especially deployment, places stresses on marriages and relationships, and marital problems affect mission readiness (Hawkins, Carroll, Doherty, & Willoughby, 2004).

Therefore, military couples are especially at risk for relationship problems and ultimately marital dissolution. In an analysis of veterans over the past century, Ruger, Wilson, and Waddoups (2002) found that combat has a significant influence on the length of a veteran's marriage. As a survival mechanism, troops may numb their responses to combat, which in turn affects their relationships upon returning home. These hard realities point to the need for effective marriage and relationship education. Marriage education over the past two decades has taken off in the various branches of the military (Hawkins et al., 2004).

Family Resource Management

The financial well-being of members of the U.S. Armed Forces is a significant readiness issue and offers opportunities for family life education. Traditionally, military families have survived on an income far below that of their civilian counterparts. In 1999, the unemployment rate among military spouses compared to an equivalent civilian population cohort was twice the national rate for men and three times the national rate for women. Surveys show that most enlisted families are dual income earners because they need the money for basic living expenses. Many (41%) employed military spouses reported that their pay represented a major contribution to their families' income. By 2004, 69% of active duty spouses worked, most of whom were working to meet basic expenses (U.S. DOD, 2004). Therefore, family resource management topics such as money management, budgeting, and consumer issues are important topics to consider for family life education programming with military populations.

Marketing/Recruitment

Morris, Cooper, and Gross (1999) asserted that family life educators should put more effort and resources into marketing their programs using the five Ps of the marketing mix: (1) price, (2) product, (3) place, (4) people, and (5) promotion. Because so many military family services are free as benefits of being in the military, family life educators in civilian agencies who want to charge for their services will have to find a way to be reimbursed through grants or by a benefactor or sponsoring organization that will underwrite the cost of classes.

The product, or program, has to be tailored to military families. There is a trend in DOD to make programming "purple," meaning it is joint, inclusive of all of the armed services. One sees more all-services terms like "warriors" and "service members" being used. Despite these efforts, the various branches of the armed forces like their individuality and thus programs focusing on one branch should be careful to understand and cater to the nuances of that branch. For example, marines prefer to be referred to as marines and the word airman is vital to someone who happens to be in the U.S. Air Force or U.S. Air National Guard.

In terms of the people aspect of marketing, having a key influential individual recommending the program may have the most impact on attendance. In the military, that key person will be either the unit commander or training sergeant. The selling point to the unit commander is that a service member who is preoccupied with family issues will not be focused on "the mission." Accomplishing the mission is every commander's primary objective.

Finally, promotional materials should be engaging and nongender-specific. One family life education program found that it was useful to have service-specific pictures with the same written information printed on rack cards.

Barriers to Participation

Military culture will strongly influence participation in family life education programming (Drummet, Coleman, & Cable, 2003). There are three primary barriers that might prevent service members and their families from taking advantage of educational opportunities. These include the lack of confidentiality (perceived or real), the fact that commanders may take an active role in "problem cases," and the fear that participating in services will negatively impact their military career (Vernez & Zellman, 1987).

Service members are concerned about how any mental health service, including family life education programming, will be perceived by both their peers and their superiors. They are afraid that seeking out such services will have a negative impact upon their careers. Negative stigma associated with seeking mental health services continues to be an issue, although less so than in the past. However, access to mental health services and especially access in the combat zone or by geographically dispersed service members on their return home are ongoing challenges (Mental Health Advisory Team V, 2008). Those meeting clinical benchmarks of needing help were twice as likely as those not needing mental health services to report a fear of being stigmatized by seeking mental health services (Hoge et al., 2004). Britt (2000) reported that over half the participants studied believed their military careers would be damaged if they reported mental health issues. Civilian services may be utilized because military families do not want the commander to learn of their problems (Vernez & Zellman, 1987). Assurances that instructors do not discuss classroom sharing should help to reduce fears. Additionally, to avoid stigma, family life educators should put the emphasis on the educational nature of programming without focusing on pathology (Drummet et al., 2003).

Environmental Considerations

One environmental consideration will simply be the service with which the family life educator is interacting. "The environmental stresses and demands for quality-of-life and support programs differ among the four armed services. What works in the Air Force, in other words, may not work in the Army" (Vernez & Zellman, 1987, p. vii). In addition to the approximately 450 active duty military institutions in the United States (National Park Service, n.d.), there are about 3,200 U.S. Army National Guard units located in 2,700 communities across the country. Likewise, some 1,700 U.S. Army Reserve units are situated around the United States (Wisher, Sabol, & Moses, 2002). These units train in armories or in reserve or readiness centers. Armories were originally built to provide local militia a place to train and store equipment. Readiness centers, as they may be called today, still perform the same functions, providing training space, room for administrative functions and storage of materials for the military units assigned to it. Some double as a community resource by providing space for public meetings or for educational programming. The space typically includes an administration area (offices, mail-room, and conference room), classroom area (tables and chairs, audiovisual equipment and blackboards), and assembly area (assembly hall and food preparation, serving and storage areas) (Hewitt, 2010).

When planning a program, family life educators should anticipate the military families' concept of safe and comfortable. They are used to drill halls or classrooms at military facilities, and they may enjoy more comfortable surroundings. For example, many couples enjoy the all-expenses-paid weekend retreats of the Strong Bond programs offered by the army at a nice resort.

Many military families live on and around bases and posts throughout the United States and the world. Some on-base facilities provide very comfortable accommodations; others are austere. In preparation for working on base or at a reserve center, family life educators should do their homework.

- Visit the site to look at the room; determine logistical support with the primary military contact and agree on classroom rules prior to a presentation. Although a site may have computers and projection equipment, they may be kept secure and prove unavailable for use. Usually civilian flash drives are not allowed in DOD computers.
- Air-conditioning may not be available. Large fans may be very noisy, and rooms may have windows but no blinds so videos cannot be seen easily.
- Projection screens, microphones, and podiums may not be available. Equipment may need to be carried up multiple flights of stairs.
- Weapons may be worn, and attendees may come to class in uniform.

- Participants may be removed during programs for mandatory physical training or roll calls, and instructors may be told programs must be halted so participants can leave and get chow (food).
- Educators must learn the requirements necessary to enter federal property and where to park vehicles.

In addition to understanding the issues of the educational environments at a military instillation, awareness of military customs will increase a civilian family life educator's comfort level. The military has a rich cultural history that includes traditions, language, dress, and etiquette. Prescribed codes of courtesy, precedent, and protocol govern military, ceremonial, and official functions (U.S. Department of the Army, 2001). Military rules of etiquette are important to learn and follow, but allowances are made for civilians. A few guidelines can reduce anxiety and promote mutual respect when collaborating with military representatives (Jones, 2009).

Each service, with colors and emblems displaying its history, is proud of its uniqueness, achievements, and accomplishments. A person addressing a marine as a soldier or vice versa will lose all credibility. As mentioned previously, addressing members of the armed services by their specific branch's names is a sign of respect, and slang terms (e.g., "grunt," "jarhead," or "squid") should be avoided. On military installations, "Saluting the Colors" refers to paying tribute to the U.S. flag. The flag is raised at 8:00 a.m. and lowered at sunset. The "National Anthem" is played during the morning ceremony, and at sunset, "Retreat" or the "National Anthem" is heard. If you are outside during "Colors" and able to view the flag or hear the anthem, stop what you are doing, face the flag or music, and stand until the music finishes playing and the colors pass. Civilians place their right hand over their heart; active duty and veterans salute. If a civilian is in a vehicle and the ceremony commences, he or she should stop the car, observe those in cars nearby, and follow their actions. Do not continue traveling until "Colors" has completed. Talking during "Colors" is considered disrespectful.

When entering some reserve centers or bases, documents may be required to prove your identity, as well as vehicle registration and insurance. A military sponsor may need to make arrangements with security before guests are allowed to enter a military installation or vessel. Punctuality is critical with military colleagues. A military colloquialism states, "If you arrive 15 minutes early you are already late." Cell phone interruptions are not acceptable.

Enlisted personnel's uniforms are indicated by chevrons, the upside down *V* shape emblem, and the curved shaped rockers on the sleeves (Institute of Heraldry, 2011). Officers wear bars, stars, oak leaves, or eagles, and striped bars denote warrant offices. Officers are addressed by their rank—for example, "General Smith," or as sir or ma'am—whereas enlisted personnel are addressed by their rate or rank or as "Mr." or "Ms." Introduce service members by their rank or title, especially when introducing an enlisted person to an officer. Professionally, officers and enlisted personnel do not address each other by first names. When meeting with military representatives, a protocol visit to a unit commanding officer is usually conducted first. After the initial visit, guests usually meet with similarly ranked personnel to conduct formal business. Thank-you notes are sent immediately after first meetings.

Modes of Learning

There is not a clear-cut style of learning that applies to all service members and their families. Just like the population as a whole, military personnel are varied in their preferences. Depending on their Military Occupational Specialty (MOS) rank, patterns emerge. The typical service member (Rife & Hansen, 1998) appreciates efficiency, achievement, and competence. He or she is conservative, professional, goal-and task-oriented, obsessed with details, and extremely time-conscious. Early to everything, service members believe in rehearsals. They are mission-focused, self-motivated, and independent. Generally they are not patient, intuitive, or empathetic listeners. Teamwork and uniformity are essential, and high professional and personal standards are demanded.

Considering the Carl Jung–based Myers-Briggs Type Indicator, among military officers the great majority (85%) prefer *thinking* to *feeling,* two thirds favor *sensing* to *intuition,* and fewer than one third (30%) are intuitive thinkers (Ehrman & Oxford, 1990). Similarly, in a study at the U.S. Air Force Academy, cadets were more often classified as sensing, thinking, judgment (STJ) on the Myers-Briggs Type Indicator, meaning the majority preferred thinking logically rather than being intuitive, and they wanted structure (Williams, 1999). Air Force officers are likely to be cognitively flexible, convergent thinkers, and field-independent. As such, they are pragmatic, logical, analytical, and individualistic; prefer solitary activities; and are unemotional, focused, and good at processing visual and spatial information (Whyte, Karolick, & Taylor, 1996). In contrast, maintenance troops who had recently finished basic training seem to prefer learning through kinesthetic methods (Jordan & Curtis, 2009).

The military is a hierarchical organization. Orders are given with the expectation that they will be obeyed. The great majority of families and service members in the military have no control over the choices made by those in command. Their job is to follow orders, and this idea may even trickle down to the learning environment. For example, one family life educator described how she had placed all the training materials at each participant's place. One document was the pretest that she wanted them to complete. The reserve unit with which she was working was composed of both officers and higher-ranking enlisted personnel. Not one of the participants sitting at the tables would pick up a pencil and begin the pretest until she instructed them to do so.

In contrast to participant behavior in a civilian environment, a practice that an educator might observe is a service member getting up and standing at the rear of the classroom. This is an acceptable practice in the military. Military instruction is often passive, lecture-based, and supported by visual slides. The practice of standing in the back allows service members to "stretch their legs," while remaining engaged in the learning session. This behavior is so ingrained as an acceptable practice to military personnel that one participant at a civilian conference reportedly stood quietly in the back of the room. The participant was a retired army officer.

Because most classroom-based military instruction is passive, service members and families often enjoy and appreciate a change of pace with an active learning approach. Providing opportunities for hands-on experiential learning activities to reinforce what is being taught received positive evaluations from military families. As such activities are developed, the educator should be responsive to both expressed as well as implied feedback. For example, when implementing the Essential Life Skills for Military Families program, we, the authors, used balloons in one activity to symbolize juggling one's expenses in meeting a budget. Instructors found that when the balloons popped in a drill hall, service members reacted like it was a gun being discharged. Developers opted to substitute beach balls for the balloons. Sensitivity to service members' unique needs is essential for successful programming.

The approach to family issues by the base and by the individual units will directly affect whether families are encouraged to or discouraged from taking advantage of available services (Vernez & Zellman, 1987). By army regulation, the unit commander is responsible for assuring that many aspects of family support are made available. Another challenge for the family life educator is that generic marriage education programs may not be applicable or relevant to the unique challenges military families face (Hawkins et al., 2004). While respecting appropriate copyright restrictions, family life educators should take the time necessary to adapt presentations to meet the specific needs and concerns of their audience. Remember one military family is not the same as the next, so adaptations may also be necessary depending on the context and unit being served.

Educator Characteristics

In addition to being well grounded in the substantive material and family life education methodology, there is a strong preference in the military for educators who have a background in military life. A personal history and experience with the military brings a perspective that is appreciated by many military families.

Selecting instructors that have served in the armed forces, been married to, or been the child of a service member gives a certain legitimacy to a family life education presentation. There is a sense that the instructor has experienced their lifestyle and understands the challenges of military life.

As a practical matter, there is an initial conversation that will occur at some point, as the instructor gets to know both the decision makers in a unit as well as the participants and as they develop trust in the instructor. Even if the educator has not been active in the military or reserve, knowing one's military pedigree, such as one's father's, brother's, sister's, or other relative's service in the armed forces, will greatly facilitate the instructor's ability to join with the participants.

Educators should be comfortable with service members and in military environments. They need a basic understand of both rank and protocol. Acronyms feature prominently in military conversation. The educator who takes time to learn the basic acronyms will often feel more comfortable with military families.

Ethical Considerations

Family life educators should remain politically neutral with regard to conflict or military actions. Service members and their families face enough challenges without the need to feel defensive regarding the professional obligations placed upon them by the government. The vast majority of service members and their families are proud of their service to this country and these families should be honored for their sacrifices.

Confidentiality is another important consideration when working with military families. Families may worry that the difficulties they experience or the life choices they make may influence their ability to be promoted, if they are shared with other military members. Mental health treatment, suicidal ideation, family violence, and substance abuse require educators to become aware of the policies and protocols associated with each issue. Assuring confidentiality, while following applicable state statutes and military requirements, is necessary. Military members are being encouraged to seek counseling and therapeutic support, and they have been assured that such assistance will not negatively impact advancement.

Best Practices in Family Life Education Programming

Markman et al. (2004) suggested that best practices in marriage education be incorporated into a more inclusive approach to providing services. One example is the Army Family Team Building (AFTB) program (U.S. Department of the Army, 2005). This is a worldwide educational program whose main objective is to enhance the general readiness of the army by educating soldiers and their family members to adapt to army life through a consistent, developmental, and sequential educational program. The mission of the AFTB program is to educate and empower service members and their families to develop skills that strengthen self-reliance, will enhance readiness, and promote retention. Of particular concern were the young and new-to-the-army spouses. The AFTB program has grown into the army's principal program to educate army family members and impart the skills and knowledge to increase family readiness (U.S. Department of the Army, 2005). It utilizes a train-the-trainer approach for instructors from within the military community being trained by Department of the Army–certified master trainers.

Marriage and Relationship Education

One of the most successful programs regarding marriage education in the military is the Strong and Ready Families Program/Strong Bonds Program. For married couples it uses an adaptation of *Prevent and Relationship Enhancement Program (PREP)* (Stanley et al., 2010) and is delivered by trained Army chaplains. It is a research-based approach to teaching premarital and married couples how to improve communication.

For single soldiers, the Strong Bonds Program utilizes the PICK a Partner program, also known as "How to Avoid Falling for a Jerk(ette)" which has received positive evaluations. PICK is an acronym for Premarital Interpersonal Choices & Knowledge. A relationship education program for singles, it was offered to single soldiers as a complement to existing well-being programs in the U.S. Army. Evaluation data indicated that educating single army soldiers on how to develop healthy, romantic relationships was advantageous to their dating and marital satisfaction and their satisfaction with military life in general. After finishing the PICK program, soldiers demonstrated an increased understanding of the important areas to discuss in a premarital, dating relationship (Van Epp, Futris, Van Epp, & Campbell, 2008).

Chaplains serving marines deliver the Prevention and Relationship Enhancement Program (PREP) and "How to Avoid Falling for a Jerk(ette)." In addition, chaplains offer the *Chaplain's Religious Enrichment Development Operations (CREDO)* to help marine families with spiritual growth work toward improved family functioning and group responsibility. Religious retreats enhance personal growth, marriage enrichment, and team building (Marine Corps Community Services, n.d.).

Another unique opportunity for family life educators is relationship education with reserve component families. Vogt, Samper, King, King, and Martin (2008) found that reserve component families are often less prepared to deal with the conflicts accompanying military service, family life, and civilian employment. Reserve component families often lack access to many of the services and programs that active duty military members and their families enjoy. The Essential Life Skills for Military Families (ELSMF) (Carroll, Robinson, Orthner, Matthews, & Rotabi,

2008) program is the first program in the nation designed specifically to meet the needs of reserve component families and individuals to help them improve couple relationships, financial preparedness, and legal well-being. This community-based program has been shown to contribute to positive intimate relationships among military service members (Carroll et al., 2008).

The program is fun and interactive and uses four 2-hour modules that promote practical steps to (1) increase positive communication, (2) encourage identification and use of community resources, (3) build family financial readiness, (4) improve understanding of legal protective measures, (5) deal more effectively with the emotional cycle of deployment, and (6) build healthier relationships. Interwoven throughout the program are opportunities for participants to practice new communication skills, to better understand stress management, and to learn coping skills. Participants actively engage in financial goal setting, role-play activities, and other hands-on exercises (Carroll et al., 2008).

In regard to parenting education, the voluntary NPSP was created to help families expecting a child or with a child under the age of 6. A team of nurses and social workers provides support through home visitation, support groups, and classes. Mom's Basic Training, Parenting Classes, and Daddy's Baby Boot Camp and Positive Parenting are some of the classes offered through this program (Military Home Front, n.d). Kelley, Schwerin, Farrar, and Lane (2006) evaluated the U.S. Navy's NPSP at 27 bases. Results from this evaluation indicated that the majority of participants in the study believed the NPSP enhanced parenting skills, reduced stress related to parenting, advanced their quality of life, and improved military readiness.

In addition to relationship education and parenting education, there has been family life education programming in the area of family resource management. For example, the Texas Cooperative Extension collaborates with Fort Bliss and Fort Hood where agents provide training to noncommissioned officers to teach fiscal responsibility to soldiers in their units. The basic financial education is part of an educational program to help new soldiers and families to be successful financially. Educational programming in budgeting, insurance, and protection against scams are other areas in which agents in Texas have provided programming (Texas AgriLife Extension Service, 2009).

FUTURE DIRECTIONS

In this final section, we offer some suggestions for future work with military families. Many opportunities lie in the support of reserve component families. Yellow Ribbon efforts emphasize the couple relationship following deployment. However, these efforts could be redoubled through coordinated and considerate efforts from community leaders and partners. Ruger et al. (2002) suggested that public officials need to have a better understanding of how military service impacts the troop's marital stability and consider greater efforts to support troop's reentry into society and their marriages following combat.

Marriages need support following a long separation like deployment, but additional supports for children, parents, and other loved ones also merit new and creative approaches. The DOD generally defines "military dependents" as the service member's spouse, children, and parent if the parent is dependent upon the service member for more than half of their support. However, military families also include service members' parents, siblings, other relatives, and partners (University of Minnesota, 2010). Consequently, there are opportunities to provide family life education to extended family members who generally cannot have access to base service. Most family members who have not been military have neither an understanding of the issues their service member relatives are facing, nor do they know how to provide adequate support to the spouse or child of a service member.

Family life educators may also find great opportunities working with Wounded Warriors and their families. We have mentioned that many more military members today return from tours of duty with injuries that change their ways of life. Whether an amputee or a serviceman struggling with PTSD, there are many opportunities to support these resilient individuals and their families. Few programs focus on helping the whole family, all of whom are affected by their loved one's battle wounds.

We suggest educators direct more efforts to serving the whole family. Younger children require assistance, and family life educators are ideally trained to assist parents in their efforts to support their children. Numerous programs exist within the military to support and educate military children from developmentally appropriate perspectives (e.g., military CDCs, Head Start programs, YMCAs, Boys & Girls Clubs of America [BGCA], and 4-H clubs). Programs for parents on coping skills, signs of mental health issues, and how to work with schools during a parent's deployment are worth considering. Joint programs for parents and children could be assisted to identify positive ways to cope with separation.

Adolescents' needs are different from the needs of younger children. Huebner and Mancini (2005) suggested that professionals develop materials to educate parents about discussing deployment and war information in a developmentally appropriate way with adolescents. Topics might include behavioral changes that might occur in adolescents; the importance of modeling stress reduction and self-care; the range of emotions an adolescent might experience; signs of mental health issues in adolescents; and the importance of consistent expectations about behavior and schoolwork, family rituals, continuing pleasurable family activities, and documenting those that were missed by the deployed family member. For adolescents themselves, Huebner and Mancini (2005) suggested providing skill-building classes such as cooking, babysitting, learning to do laundry, learning how to do yard work, or making repairs so that adolescents feel prepared for additional responsibilities. Education could include what to expect from the returning parent following the deployment. Reciprocal education could be provided to the deployed parent about what changes might have occurred in their son or daughter. It's not inconceivable that the parent will return to a son who is a foot taller than when he or she left and now needs to shave!

Another issue likely to take on increasing importance in the military is the need for policies about elder care. Although service members tend to be young, the longer that one stays in the military, the greater the likelihood the issue of taking care of their parents or grandparents will affect them. Senior military personnel will be the ones most likely to provide financial and custodial responsibility for aging parents (Segal & Harris, 1993).

In this chapter, we have identified key strategies and factors that may better help family life educators to understand and work effectively with military families. Though this chapter has only tapped the surface of what it means to be a military family and what these families are looking for in educators, the best way to gain a deeper understanding is through reaching out and serving these families. It's the highest of honors to serve those who serve us all so well.

REFERENCES

Armor, D. J., Gilroy, C. L., & Curtis, L. (2010). Changing minority representation in the U.S. military. *Armed Forces & Society, 36,* 223–246.

Bachman, J. G., Segal, D. R., Freedman-Doan, P., & O'Malley, P. M. (2000). Who chooses military service? Correlates of propensity and enlistment in the U.S. Armed Forces. *Military Psychology, 12*(1), 1–30.

Baker, A. E. (2006). *Standing operating procedures soldier family life consultants.* Retrieved from http://www.arfp.org/skins/ARFP/display.aspx?ModuleID=2a285ab0-5db1-4f36-9b91-f2263c973c32&Action=display_user_object&Mode=user&ObjectID=f53c45bd-b41d-486b-935d-d6215d9cb21b

Belenky, G. L., Sodetz, F. J., & Tyner, C. F. (1983). *Israeli battle shock casualties: 1973 and 1982* (Report WRAIR NP-83-4). Washington, DC: Walter Reed Army Institute of Research.

Boss, P., & Greenberg, J. (1984). Family boundary ambiguity: A new variable in family stress theory. *Family Process, 23,* 535–546.

Bourg, C. & Segal, M. W. (1999). The impact of family supportive policies and practices on organizational commitment to the army. *Armed Forces & Society, 25,* 633–652.

Bowen, G. L., Mancini, J. A., Martin, J. A., Ware, W. B., & Nelson, J. P. (2003). Promoting the adaptation of military families: An empirical test of a community practice model. *Family Relations, 52,* 33–44.

Bowen, G. L., & Martin, J. A. (2011). The resiliency model of role performance for service members, veterans and their families: A focus on social connections and individual assets. *Journal of Human Behavior in the Social Environment, 21,* 162–178.

Britt, T. W. (2000). The stigma of psychological problems in a work environment: Evidence from the screening of service members returning from Bosnia. *Journal of Applied Social Psychology, 30,* 1599–1618.

Campbell, N. D., Appelbaum, J. C., Martinson, K., & Martin, E. (2000). *Be all that we can be: Lessons from the military for improving our nation's child care system.* Washington, DC: Women's Law Center. Retrieved from http://eric.ed.gov/PDFS/ED441582.pdf

Carroll, E. B., Robinson, L. C., Orthner, D., Matthews, W., & Rotabi, K. S. (2008). Essential life skills for military families: Mobilizing the cooperative extension service in North Carolina. *Journal of Family and Consumer Sciences, 100*(1), 52–57.

Collins, E. M. (2009, June 26). Retired Gen. Wickham recalls army family action plan. *Army News Service.* Retrieved from http://www.army.mil/-news/2009/01/23/16043-retired-gen-wickham-recalls-army-family-action-plan/

Cozza, S. J., Chun, R. S., & Polo, J. A. (2005). Military families and children during Operation Iraqi Freedom. *Psychiatric Quarterly, 76*(4), 371–378.

Department of Defense Education Activity. (n.d.). *DoDEA schools span the globe.* Retrieved from http://www.DoDea.edu/back_to_school/2010_11.cfm?cId=Globe

Dimiceli, E. E., Steinhardt, M. A., & Smith, S. E. (2009). Stressful experiences, coping strategies, and predictors of health-related outcomes among wives of deployed military servicemen. *Armed Forces & Society, 36,* 351–373.

Drummet, A. R., Coleman, M., & Cable S. (2003). Military families under stress: Implication for family life education. *Family Relations, 52,* 279–287.

Ehrman, M., & Oxford, R. (1990). Adult language learning styles and strategies in an intensive training setting. *Modern Language Journal, 74,* 311–327.

Faber, A. J., Willerton, E., Clymer, S. R., MacDermid, S. M., & Weiss, H. M. (2008). Ambiguous absence, ambiguous presence: A qualitative study of military reserve families in wartime. *Journal of Family Psychology,* 222–230.

Granovsky, N. (2002). *The Army leader's desk reference for soldier/family readiness.* College Station: Texas Cooperative Extension. Retrieved from http://www.gordon.army.mil/acs/Deployment/Army_Leaders_Reference.pdf

Griffith, J. (2009). Being a reserve soldier: A matter of social identity. *Armed Forces & Society, 36,* 38–64.

Harris, B. C., Simutis, Z. M., & Gantz, M. M. (2002). *Women in the US Army: An annotated bibliography.* Alexandria, VA: US Army Research Institute for Behavioral and Social Science. Retrieved from http://www.hqda.army.mil/ari/pdf/WomenInTheArmy-DrHarris.pdf

Hawkins, A. J., Carroll, J. S., Doherty, W. J., & Willoughby, B. (2004). A comprehensive framework for marriage education. *Family Relations, 53,* 547–558.

Hewitt, O. L. (2010). *Armories.* Retrieved from http://www.wbdg.org/design/armories.php

Hoge, C. E., Castro, C. A., Messer, C., McGurk, D., Cotting, D. I., & Koffman, R. L. (2004). Combat duty in Iraq and Afghanistan, mental health problems and barriers to care. *New England Journal of Medicine, 351*(1), 13–22.

Huebner, A. J., & Mancini, J. A. (2005, June). *Adjustment among adolescents in military families when a parent is deployed: Final report submitted to the Military Family Research Institute and the Department of Defense Quality of Life Office.* Falls Church: Virginia Tech University.

Ingraham, L. H. (2002). Backgrounder: Caring is not enough. In N. Granovsky (Ed.), *The Army family readiness handbook—Revised.* College Station: Texas Cooperative Extension. Retrieved from http://riley.army.mil/documents/frg/Army_Family_Readiness_Handbook-OperationREADY.pdf

Institute of Heraldry. (2011). *U.S. Navy Awards Section.* Retrieved from http://www.tioh.hqda.pentagon.mil

Jones, L. C. (2009). *Protocol and etiquette corner.* Retrieved from http://dcp.psc.gov/ccbulletin/articles/Protocol_05_2009.aspx

Jordan, J. D., & Curtis, C. K. (2009). *Training maintenance troops: A study of factors affecting airman performance in a learning environment.* Wright-Patterson AFB, OH: Air Force Research Laboratory. Retrieved from http://handle.dtic.mil/100.2/ADA515366

Kelley, M. L., Schwerin, M. J., Farrar, K. L., & Lane, M. E. (2006). A participant evaluation of the U.S. Navy parent support program. *Journal of Family Violence, 21,* 301–310,

La Bash, H. A. J., Vogt, D. S., King, L. A., & King, D. W. (2009). Deployment stressors of the Iraq War: Insights from the mainstream media. *Journal of Interpersonal Violence, 24*(2), 231–258.

Lee, M. A., & Mather, M. (2008, June). U.S. labor force trends. *Population Bulletin, 63*(2). Retrieved from http://www.prb.org/pdf08/63.2uslabor.pdf

Lundquist, J. H. (2004). When race made no difference: Marriage and the military. *Social Forces, 83,* 731–757.

Mansfield, A. J., Kaufman, J. S., Marshall, S. W., Gaynes, B. N., Morrissey, J. P., & Engel, C. C. (2010). Deployment and the use of mental health services among U.S. Army wives. *New England Journal of Medicine, 382,* 101–109.

Marine Corps Community Services. (n.d.). *Marine Corps Community Services Leaders Guide.* Retrieved from http://www.usmc-mccs.org/aboutmccs/downloads/MCCS_Leader_Guide.pdf

Markman, H. J., Whitton, S. W., Kline, G. H., Stanley, S. M., Thompson, H., St. Peters, M., et al. (2004). Use of an empirically based marriage education program by religious organization: Results of a dissemination trial. *Family Relations, 53,* 504–512.

Martin, J. A., & Orthner, D. K. (1989). The "company town" in transition: Rebuilding military communities. In G. L. Bowen & D. K. Orthner (Eds.), *The organization family: Work and family linkages in the U. S. military* (pp. 163–177). New York: Praeger.

Mental Health Advisory Team IV. (2006, November). *Mental Health Advisory Team (MHAT) IV Report: Operation Iraqi Freedom 05-07.* Washington, DC: Office of the Surgeon, Multi-National Force-Iraq and Office of the Surgeon General, United States Army Medical Command. Retrieved from http://www.armymedicine.army.mil/reports/mhat/mhat_iv/MHAT_IV_Report_17NOV06.pdf

Mental Health Advisory Team V. (2008, February). *Mental Health Advisory Team (MHAT) V Report: Operation Iraqi Freedom 06-08: Iraq; Operation Enduring Freedom 8: Afghanistan.* Washington, DC: Office of the Surgeon Multi-National Force-Iraq and Office of the Command Surgeon and Office of the Surgeon General, United States Army Medical Command. Retrieved from http://www.armymedicine.army.mil/reports/mhat/mhat_v/Redacted1-MHATV-4-FEB-2008-Overview.pdf

Military Home Front. (n.d.) *New Parent Support Programs.* Retrieved from http://www.military-homefront.dod.mil/tf/newparentsupport

Military OneSource Center. (2009, January). *Report of the 2nd Quadrennial quality of life review.* Retrieved from http://cs.mhf.dod.mil/content/dav/mhf/QOL-Library/PDF/MHF/QOL%20Resources/Reports/Quadrennial%20Quality%20of%20Life%20Review%202009.pdf

Morris, M. L., Cooper, C., & Gross, K. H. (1999) Marketing factors influencing the overall satisfaction of marriage education participants. *Family Relations, 48,* 251–261.

Morse, J. (2006, July). *The new emotional cycles of deployment.* San Diego, CA: Deployment Health and Family Readiness Library. Retrieved from http://hooah4health.com/deployment/familymatters/Emotional_Cycle_Support.pdf

Munroe, J. (2005). *8 battlefield skills that make life in the civilian world challenging.* Retrieved from http://www.50thpsb.com/frg_reint_8%20Battlefield%20Skills%20that%20Make%20Life%20in%20the%20Civilian%20World%20Challenging.pdf

National Center for Post-Traumatic Stress Disorder & Walter Reed Medical Center. (2004). *Iraq War Clinician Guide* (2nd ed.). Retrieved from http://www.ptsd.va.gov/professional/manuals/manual-pdf/iwcg/iraq_clinician_guide_v2.pdf

National Governors Association. (2008). *HHS-10. Supporting military personnel and their families.* Retrieved from http://www.nga.org/portal/site/nga/menuitem.8358ec82f5b198d18a2781105010

10a0/?vgnextoid=287a9e2f1b091010VgnVCM1000001a01010aRCRD&vgnextchannel=4b18f
074f0d9ff00VgnVCM1000001a01010aRCRD

National Park Service. (n.d.). *Military bases in the continental United States MAP INDEX*. Retrieved from http://www.nps.gov/history/nagpra/DOCUMENTS/BasesMapIndex.htm

Orthner, D. K., & Rose, R. (2009). Work separation demands and spouse psychological well-being. *Family Relations, 58,* 392–403.

Riccio, G., Sullivan, R., Klein, G., Salter, M., & Kinnison, H. (2004). *Warrior ethos: Analysis of the concept and initial development of applications* (Report No. 1827). Vienna, VA: Wexford Group International, Inc.

Rife, R. L., & Hansen, R. (1998). *Defense is from Mars, State is from Venus: Improving communications and promoting national security* (Research Report No. ADA351032). Carlisle Barracks, PA: US Army War College. Retrieved from http://www.dtic.mil/cgi-bin/GetTRDoc?AD=ADA 351032&Location=U2&doc=GetTRDoc.pdf

Ruger, W., Wilson, S. E., & Waddoups, S. L. (2002). Warfare and welfare: Military service, combat and marital dissolution. *Armed Forces & Society, 29,* 85–107.

Schwarz, R. L., MacDermid, S. M., Swan, R., Robbins, N. M., & Mather, C. (2003). *Staffing your child care center: A theoretical and practical approach*. Retrieved from http:// www.mfri.purdue.edu/content/reports/Staffing%20Your%20Child%20Care.pdf

Segal, D. R., & Wechsler, M. (2004). America's military population. *Population Bulletin, 59*(4). Washington, DC: Population Reference Bureau. Retrieved from http://www.prb.org/ pdf04/59.4AmericanMilitary.pdf

Segal, M. W. (1986). The military and the family as greedy institutions. *Armed Forces & Society, 13*(1), 9–38.

Segal, M. W., & Harris, J. J. (1993, September). *What we know about army families* (Research Report No. ADA271989). Retrieved from http://handle.dtic.mil/100.2/ADA271989

Shinseki, E. K. (2003). *The Army family: A white paper*. Retrieved from http://www.whs.mil/library/ dig/ar-m620u_20080912.pdf

Stanley, S. M., Allen E. S., Markman, H. J., Rhoades, G. K., & Prentice, D. L. (2010). Decreasing divorce in army couples: Results from a randomized controlled trial using prep for strong bonds. *Journal of Couple Relationship Therapy, 9*(2), 149–160.

Tarpley, A. (2009). *Deployment and the military family*. Deployment Health Clinical Center: Reserve Component Resource Center. Retrieved from www.pdhealth.mil/reservist/downloads/ symp-at2.ppt

Texas AgriLife Extension Service. (2009). *Military program summary: Fort Bliss and Fort Hood*. Retrieved from http://fcs.tamu.edu/families/military_families/military_program_summary.htm

University of Minnesota. (2010). *Healthy generations: Health of military families*. Minneapolis, MN: Center for Leadership in Education in Maternal and Child Public Health. Retrieved from http:// www.epi.umn.edu/mch/assets/downloads/GH_Sum10_HiRES_final.pdf

U.S. Army. (n.d.) Basic pay: Active duty soldiers. Retrieved from http://www.goarmy.com/benefits/ money/basic-pay-active-duty-soldiers.html

U.S. Department of Defense. (2004, May). *Modernized social compact: Report of the First Quadrennial life review*. Retrieved from http://www.militaryhomefront.dod.mil/12038/MHF/ pdf/QQLR.pdf

U.S. Department of Defense. (2009). *Plans for the department of defense for the support of military family readiness*. Retrieved from http://cs.mhf.dod.mil/content/dav/mhf/QOL-Library/Project%20 Documents/MilitaryHOMEFRONT/Reports/2010%20Report%20to%20Congress%20 NDAA%20Sec%20581.pdf

U.S. Department of the Army. (2001). *A guide to protocol and etiquette for official entertainment*. Retrieved from http://www.ushistory.org/betsy/images/p600_60.pdf

U.S. Department of the Army. (2005). *Army Family Team Building (AFTB)*. Retrieved from http:// www.apd.army.mil/pdffiles/r608_48.pdf

U.S. General Accounting Office. (1996, September). *Military family housing: Opportunities exist to reduce costs and mitigate inequities.* Washington, DC: GAO. Retrieved from http://www.gao.gov/archive/1996/ns96203.pdf

Van Epp, M. C., Futris, T. G., Van Epp, J. C., & Campbell, K. (2008). The impact of the pick a partner relationship education program on single army soldiers. *Family and Consumer Sciences Research Journal, 36,* 328–349.

Vernez, G., & Zellman, G. L. (1987). *Families and mission: A review of the effects of family factors on Army attrition, retention and readiness.* Santa Monica, CA: Rand.

Vogt, D. S., Samper, R. E., King, D. W. King, L. A., & Martin, J. A. (2008). Deployment stressors and posttraumatic stress symptomatology: Comparing active duty and National Guard/Reserve personnel from Gulf War. *Journal of Traumatic Stress, 21,* 66–74.

Weinstock, M. (2010). *The deployment cycle and its impact on service members and their families.* Retrieved from http://www.deploymentpsych.org/training/training-catalog/the-deployment-cycle-and-its-impact-on-service-members-and-their-families-1

Whyte, M., Karolick, K., & Taylor, M. D. (1996). *Cognitive learning styles and their impact on curriculum development and instruction.* Paper presented at the 18th National Convention of the Association for Educational Communication and Technology, Indianapolis, IN. Retrieved from http://eric.ed.gov/PDFS/ED397846.pdf

Wickhman, J. A. (1983). *White paper 1983: The army family.* Retrieved from http://www.whs.mil/library/dig/ar-m620u_20080911.pdf

Williams, D. L. (1999). Frequencies of Myers-Briggs Type Indicator (MBTI) among military leaders. *Journal of Leadership & Organizational Studies, 5,* 50–56.

Wisher, R. A., Sabol, M. A., & Moses, F. L. (2002, May). *Distance learning: The soldier's perspective* (ARI Special Report 49). Alexandria, VA: U.S. Army Research Institute for the Behavioral and Social Sciences. Retrieved from http://www.ncohistory.com/files/NCOH00005.pdf

Yaffe, K., Vittinghoff, E., Lindquist, K., Barnes, D., Covinsky, K. E., Neylan, T., et al. (2010). Posttraumatic stress disorder and risk of dementia among U.S. Veterans. *Archives of General Psychiatry, 67,* 608–613.

Zellman, G. L., Gates, S. M., Moini, J. S., & Suttorp, M. (2009). Meeting family and military needs through military child care. *Armed Forces & Society, 35,* 437–459.

Chapter 6

Family Life Education With Grandfamilies

Grandparents Raising Grandchildren

EBONI J. BAUGH, CFLE, ALAN C. TAYLOR, CFLE, AND SHARON M. BALLARD, CFLE

As chapter authors, our understanding and knowledge of older adults, grandparents, and grandfamily relationships have come from many diverse experiences and situations. As coauthors, we bring together several academic, community, research, and work-related experiences that have enlightened us and opened our minds to the complexities, challenges, and joys that come with those associated with grandfamilies. With a background in marriage and family therapy and experience as a family life state extension specialist, Eboni has developed, implemented, and evaluated family life education programs for grandfamilies over the past several years. In addition to programming, Eboni has conducted research on grandfamily parenting, social support, and overall well-being. For a number of years now, Alan has conducted research on grandparenting issues and particularly grandfather involvement. In addition, he has taught multiple undergraduate and graduate gerontology classes during which grandfamilies were discussed in great detail. Finally, Alan has experience providing personal and group family life education for grandparents who were given custodial responsibilities of their grandchildren. Sharon's experience comes primarily from her research on family life education with midlife and older adults along with her teaching of gerontology classes. It is through a sharing and combining of these varied experiences that we discuss within this chapter family life education programming with grandfamilies.

DEFINING THE POPULATION

Within the literature, several names exist for households of grandparents caring for grandchildren: coresident grandparents and grandchildren (Hayslip & Kaminski, 2005; Simmons & Dye, 2003), grandparent caregivers (Grinstead, Leder, Jensen, & Bond, 2003; Kolomer, 2008), grandparents living with grandchildren (Simmons & Dye, 2003), custodial grandparents (Bachman & Chase-Lansdale, 2005; Hayslip & Goodman, 2007; Marx & Solomon, 2000), grandparents as parents (Stevenson, Henderson, & Baugh, 2007; Thomas, Sperry, & Yarbrough, 2000), and most commonly, grandparents raising grandchildren (Bunch, Eastman, & Moore, 2007; Dunne & Kettler, 2008; Hayslip & Goodman, 2007; Hayslip & Kaminski, 2005; Kropf & Kolomer, 2004; Minkler & Fuller-Thomson, 2005; Silverstein, 2007). This chapter will propose the use of *grandfamilies* (Generations United, 2010) as a systemic and comprehensive term appropriate for defining the approximately 2.5 million grandparents responsible for the care of one or more grandchildren under the age of 18 (U.S. Census Bureau, 2008). Although variations exist among grandfamilies, this chapter will focus on grandparents with formal and/or legal custody and responsibility for the primary care of their grandchildren.

Within grandfamilies, 38.5% have been primary households for grandchildren for 5 years or more (U.S. Census Bureau, 2008). Grandparents become primary caregivers due to parental incarceration, death (Marx & Solomon, 2000), substance abuse (Musil, Schrader, & Mutikani, 2000; Ross & Aday, 2006), mental illness (Jendrek, 1994), military deployment (Bunch et al., 2007), domestic violence, divorce, and other forms of parental absence (Generations United, 2007a; Henderson, 2004; McGowen, Ladd, & Strom, 2006; Mutchler, Baker, & Lee, 2007).

Both grandparents and grandchildren are at risk for economic hardships in grandparent-headed families. Children in grandfamilies, in comparison to children who do not live with grandparents, are twice as likely to live below poverty, three times as likely to receive public assistance, and are at greater risk for lacking adequate health care (Fields, 2003; Kreider, 2008). More children live in households headed by grandmothers (48%) than those in two-grandparent (47%) or grandfather-only (5%) households (U.S. Census Bureau, 2009). Dolbin-MacNab (2006) found that many custodial grandparents are raising their grandchildren without the support of a partner. Irrespective of marital status, grandmothers tend to provide the majority of care (U.S. Department of Health and Human Services [DHHS], 2007), thus increasing their economic burden. Single grandmothers fare worse economically as they have lower rates of education and employment (Mullen, 2000) and are more likely to be minority (Park, 2005).

Although similarities exist, grandfamilies are a very diverse population. The majority of caregiving grandparents are under age 65 (Gist & Hetzel, 2004) with

35% aged 50 to 59, 7% aged 30 to 39, and 1% over the age of 80 (Simmons & Dye, 2003). Grandparents aged 60 to 69 are most likely to care for grandchildren for 5+ years, the longest of any grandparent caregiver (Simmons & Dye, 2003). Caregiving grandparents are also mostly Caucasian (47%), African American (29%), or Hispanic (17%). Racial/ethnic groups less likely to parent grandchildren are Asians (3%), American Indian or Alaskan Natives (2%), and those identifying as some other race (2%) (American Association of Retired Persons [AARP], 2007; U.S. Census Bureau, 2000).

Despite greater numbers of Caucasian grandfamilies, a disproportionate number of African Americans and Hispanics are caring for their grandchildren (Fuller-Thomson & Minkler, 2000). Caregiving is a common occurrence in the African American community as 40% of grandparents live with two or more grandchildren (Mutchler, Lee, & Baker, 2003), and more than half of coresident grandparents are responsible for grandchild care (Simmons & Dye, 2003). In African American grandfamilies, grandmothers are more likely to be single, unemployed or low-income, and living below the poverty line (Minkler & Fuller-Thomson, 2005) in comparison to other African Americans. However, the importance of the role of caregiver within this community appears to reduce many negative effects of the aforementioned challenges (Pruchno & McKenney, 2002). Resiliency, cultural ideals, and informal resources (e.g., extended family, spirituality, and community) found in African American grandfamilies help to counteract the effects of poverty by supporting each family member's needs (Stevenson et al., 2007).

Within the Hispanic population, grandchild care is also quite common (Thomas et al., 2000). In comparison to African American grandfamilies, Hispanic grandparents are more likely to be married and coparent with their adult children, yet they still remain at an economic disadvantage (Goodman & Silverstein, 2002). More than 50% of Latino custodial grandparents are below 150% of the poverty threshold, more than 20% have physical limitations, and more than 65% are foreign-born (Mutchler et al., 2003). Culture, language barriers, and immigration status also impede access to and receipt of services for this group (Kropf & Kolomer, 2004).

Unique Aspects of Grandfamilies

As most aging adults are focusing on their life's contributions and preparing for retirement, grandfamilies are parenting for the second time. Reentry into parenthood often causes conflict with their position in the life cycle. Their "time disordered" (Seltzer, 1976, p. 111) roles, which includes out-of-sequence caregiving responsibilities, may contradict with the enjoyment of retirement, relationship reestablishment, and self-reflection (Walsh, 2005). Instead of occupying the traditional grandparenting roles of family historian, support provider, family nurturer, or social companion (Bigner, 2009), grandparents in grandfamilies experience ambiguity and conflict (Landry-Meyer & Newman, 2004) as they become full-time parents again.

This transition into the role of parent has positive and negative outcomes for grandparents. Grandchildren are a source of pleasure for grandparents as they provide companionship (Kropf & Burnette, 2003), opportunities for new activities, and a renewed focus on life (Waldrop & Weber, 2001). Dolbin-MacNab (2006) reported that the positive parenting experiences of grandmothers were due to increased wisdom, relaxation, and having extra time for grandchildren. As they are often the last option before foster care, grandparents value the opportunity to contribute to a child's development and keep their family together. Maintaining family stability and keeping children from exposure to foster homes enhances grandparent confidence and satisfaction (Dellman-Jenkins, Blankenmeyer, & Olesh, 2002). Children's success and positive behaviors as a direct result of being in a stable home environment (Dunne & Kettler, 2008) serve to offset many challenges associated with caregiving.

Conversely, challenges such as unstable family environments, increased stress, and health problems due to aging (Dolbin-MacNab, 2006; Giarrusso, Silverstein, & Feng, 2000) provide areas of concern for grandfamilies. The negative effects of parenting appear to be influenced by events that lead to the grandparent assuming primary care. Dealing with grief from the loss of a child, family conflict, and other crisis events (Goodman & Silverstein, 2006) impedes satisfaction for grandparents.

What appears influential to many aspects of grandparent life is the perception of their role as a parent. Research supports a relationship between well-being, specifically physical and mental health, and grandparent beliefs about parenting. Conway, Magai, Springer, and Jones (2008) found that optimism was a salient predictor of health for young and older grandparents who, as a result, had fewer reports of insomnia, hypertension, and depression. Other research reports that a history of healthy psychological functioning can reduce stress and facilitate favorable views of parenting (Giarrusso et al., 2000).

Additional predictors of well-being for grandparents are related to socioeconomic status, household composition, and health care. In 2007, adults ages 45 to 64 did not receive (8.3%) or received delayed (10.3%) medical care and/or did not get prescription drugs (9.1%) because they could not afford it. In addition, 5.8% of children under age 18 have no source of health care; the number increases (9.1%) for children living in poverty (U.S. DHHS, 2010).

Children in grandfamilies have unique characteristics separating them from children in other households. They are twice as likely to live in poverty, at the greatest risk for lack of health insurance, and more likely to receive public assistance due to their reliance on grandparents' limited income (Fields, 2003). Grandfamily children also struggle with physical and mental health issues, behavioral and academic problems, and negative emotions as a result of circumstances causing a need for grandparent care. Grandchildren report feelings of abandonment, isolation from peers, and negative relationships with their parents (Dolbin-MacNab, & Keiley, 2009; Messing, 2006). As a result of parental alcohol and drug abuse, grandchildren may experience disabilities, behavioral problems, anger toward parents, and feelings of guilt and shame (Kropf & Kolomer, 2004). Approximately 33% of children referred for behavioral issues reside in grandfamilies, and many meet diagnostic measures for ADHD, depression, and oppositional defiant disorder (Grant, 2000).

Strengths and Assets of Grandfamilies

Grandparent caregivers possess distinctive characteristics that separate them from their non-caregiving peers. With the needs of grandchildren as their main concern, grandparents disrupt their own lives to provide a secure environment during challenging family situations (Smith & Dannison, 2001). The dedication to keeping the family intact gives grandparents a sense of pride and accomplishment, both assets in their role as caregiver (Dellman-Jenkins et al., 2002).

Stevenson and colleagues (2007) described personal esteem as a strength for black grandmothers. Personal esteem has three core concepts: (1) *adaptive pride*, or self-respect, from the satisfaction gained in caring for grandchildren; (2) *self-reliance,* or autonomy, and strength in their ability to provide for grandchildren; and (3) *personal resources* such as spirituality, the ability to locate resources, and gratefulness. The gratification attained from giving care to a grandchild serves as a facilitator of resiliency and strength in the grandfamily (Stevenson et al., 2007). Black grandmothers also create new family identities through seven techniques: (1) communicating effectively, (2) stressing the role of education, (3) giving socio-emotional support, (4) involving the grandchild in the community, (5) being aware of grandchild fragility, (6) utilizing extended family, and (7) confronting parental absence (Gibson, 2005).

In addition to dedication to family, grandparent caregivers use varied methods of coping during times of stress and crisis. Spirituality (Smith-Ruiz, 2008), the perception of the caregiving role, and the amount of social support are assets that reduce stress and increase overall grandparent well-being (Sands, Goldberg-Glen, & Thornton, 2005). Ross and Aday (2006) reported that African American grandparents who focused on personal growth as coping mechanisms and those who sought social support from counselors and school programs had lower levels of stress. In addition, having a positive outlook (Moore & Miller, 2007), accomplishing goals, discussing feelings, working hard, focusing on grandchild needs, and volunteering help to alleviate stress (Waldrop & Weber, 2001).

Grandparents assuming the role of primary caregiver benefit society at large. Not only do grandparents contribute to the community by keeping children off the street but they decrease child welfare costs and save taxpayers billions (Silverstein, 2007). Contrary to common misconceptions of weakness and fragility, custodial grandparents are resilient, cultural heroes shielding grandchildren from the child welfare system (Kropf & Burnette, 2003).

Emotional bonding, wisdom, and previous parental experiences aid grandparents in their relationships with grandchildren. McGowen and colleagues (2006) studied grandmother well-being and found that 41% reported being more patient and relaxed as they were parenting for the second time. Prior parenting experience taught grandparents to focus on a grandchild's needs and spend more time enjoying activities.

The role of grandparent as primary caregiver can be rewarding and beneficial for grandparent caregivers. Grandparents report happiness and companionship, which brings meaning to their lives as they provide an important social and familial role when caring for grandchildren (Kropf & Burnette, 2003). Custodial grandfathers enjoy a sense of generativity gained from participation in grandchild activities and the passing on of family information and life lessons (Patrick & Tomczewski, 2007).

FAMILY LIFE EDUCATION PRACTICES

Current State of Family Life Education

As the numbers of grandfamilies increase, family life education programs are being tailored to the specific needs of this population. Programming in this area has historically focused on issues of aging (Brubaker & Roberto, 1993), nutrition (Sahyoun, 2002), and other health-related needs (Grinstead et al., 2003) of older adults, as information about parenting appears less prevalent. Cooperative Extension Services (Brubaker & Roberto, 1993) has been a leader in providing parent education programs for grandparents raising grandchildren (Kaplan et al., 2008) and is preferred and applicable to many diverse community audiences (Price & Brosi, 2006). Extension agents provide community programs that use theory- and evidence-based curricula, fact sheets, and web materials (Duncan & Goddard, 2005) to educate grandfamilies and provide resources regarding other community resources. A comprehensive report is provided by the Cooperative State Research, Education, and Extension Service (CSREES), which highlights national extension efforts to provide educational resources for grandfamilies (Cooperative State Research, Education, and Extension Service [CSREES], 2008).

Other family life education programs for grandfamilies are delivered through numerous organizations such as small business, health, educational, government or military, and faith-based institutions (Family Life Education Institute, n.d.) and by educators from varied backgrounds. To date, there has been no comprehensive evaluation of resources available to grandfamilies or an extensive examination as to program effectiveness. Despite this lack in the research, there has been progress in the implementation and delivery of grandfamily family life education programs. Historically, support groups have been a prevalent intervention method (Kolomer, McCallion, & Overendyer, 2003; Smith & Dannison, 2003; Strom & Strom, 2000). Current grandfamily programming appears to be more content-oriented, providing parent education using technology (Brintnall-Peterson, Poehlmann, Morgan, & Shlafer, 2009; Segrist, 2004) and information specific to grandfamily needs.

In spite of advances in family life education programming, grandparents consistently report a lack of available services or frustrations in dealing with service providers. There appears to be a disconnect between grandfamilies' knowledge of, access to, and interest in appropriate services. Many are unaware of available services or have limited access (Scarcella, Ehrle, & Geen, 2003) to those in their community. Of the grandfamilies who do receive services, many find them to be ineffective, uninteresting, or unable to meet specific needs (Duay & Bryan, 2008).

General Needs of Grandfamilies and Rationale for Family Life Education

It is vital to understand the various developmental, social, and environmental needs of middle-aged and older adults and incorporate these needs into custodial grandparent programs.

It is important to remember that there are no "typical" grandparents raising grandchildren today. Using an "all-encompassing" family life education program might not meet the individualized needs of these adults or address their challenges. However, there are some common challenges and needs that may help guide family life education programming with regard to this population.

Grandfamilies are at risk for challenges to their overall well-being, which may be determined by their level of need and the amount of legal issues they face (Butts, 2005).

Research suggests that grandfamily programs incorporate a variety of content areas, including those that participants find relevant and those that add new insight to previously known topics (Duay & Bryan, 2008; Hayslip & Kaminski, 2005; Strom, Carter & Schmidt, 2004). Kropf and Burnette (2003) suggested that the following areas enhance the content of grandfamily programs: (1) generational issues, such as role transition and confusion resulting from becoming parents again and how this transition affects the entire family, and (2) policy issues in relation to child welfare, health care, economics, and legal concerns, which may impact grandparents' decision making on behalf of their grandchild. In addition, Dolbin-MacNab (2006) suggested that programs focus on specific grandparental health needs, their changing family roles, and effective handling of societal influences on parenting.

Smith and Dannison (2001) examined the experiences of family life educators who reported the following areas of challenge expressed by participants within current grandfamily programming: (1) financial issues, (2) difficulty communicating with adult children and extended family, (3) feelings of social isolation, (4) health and employment concerns, and (5) successful negotiation of the school system and other support providers. Family life educators concluded that grandfamilies were in need of information on all of the previous topics in addition to receiving positive feedback from their group facilitators and referrals to social services (Smith & Dannison, 2001). Grandparents also reported difficulty talking with grandchildren about sensitive topics such as sexual activity, drug use, violence, and gang involvement. Providing information on sexuality, pregnancy, STDs, and contraceptives can increase opportunities for communication and problem-solving in grandfamilies (Cornelius, LeGrand, & Jemmott, 2009).

Additionally, we don't want to neglect the needs of the grandchildren. These needs may include early intervention, educational resources, support services, community involvement, disability assistance, mentoring, physical and mental health care, youth development programming, and quality child care (Butts, 2005; Generations United, 2010; Whitley & Kelley, 2007).

Marketing/Recruitment

As with any population, marketing family life education programs and recruiting participants are keys to success and there are strategies that have been found to be effective with this particular population. The National Council on Aging (2007) has suggested using incentives to encourage attendance and participation of older adults in community programs. Ballard and Morris (2005) found that a need for information, a desire for social connection, and an enjoyment for learning were the highest rated motivators to program attendance and might serve as effective marketing strategies. Ballard and Morris also found that those in the midlife (50–64) or young old (65–74) categories were more likely to attend a family life education program; therefore, marketing efforts targeted toward younger grandparents might be more successful than those targeting older grandparents.

Research with grandfamilies highlights common methods used for recruitment such as advertisements on websites; in newspapers, churches, schools, community agencies, senior centers, libraries, and health clinics; and by word of mouth (Duay & Bryan, 2008; Office of Services to the Aging, 2003; Strom et al., 2004; Waycie,

2006). Word of mouth appears to be most effective, as grandparents are often wary of other methods, fearing that services will be unavailable, being involved in too many other services, and the possibility of encountering the threat of removal of grandchild from home (McCallion, Janicki, Grant-Griffin, & Kolomer, 2000).

Watson (1997), in a study of African American grandparents that compared those grandparents who expressed interest in grandparent education and those who did not express interest, found that both grandmothers and grandfathers were interested in grandparent education. In particular, those who were younger, African American, had fewer economic resources, lived with their grandchildren, felt strongly about their role as a family teacher, and desired more information about their grandchildren were more interested in grandparent education. Watson encouraged the use of this information to tailor marketing strategies as well as for use in program development.

Barriers to Participation

In a study of barriers for midlife and older adults to participating in family life education programs, Ballard and Morris (2005) found that cost of the program and driving at night were the two biggest deterrents to program attendance. In this same study, personal barriers to participation such as poor health and not enough energy were more important stumbling blocks for older rather than younger age groups.

Gladstone, Brown, and Fitzgerald (2009) found the age and experience of the facilitator, level of trust, and organizational policies were additional barriers to a grandparent's utilization of child welfare services. A history of involvement in the social service system appears to significantly affect grandparent participation. Those who distrust the social system, feeling powerless and underrated, are less likely to seek or utilize resources (Gladstone et al., 2009). Furthermore, those grandparents who do utilize services often report receiving incorrect information and feeling that they are not recognized as authority figures capable of making decisions for grandchildren, despite being the children's legal guardians (Wallace, 2001).

Even taking into account such issues as health status, program location, time, cost, and age barring grandparent participation, the best predictors of involvement in an educational program are prior participation and educational level (Truluck & Courtenay, 1999). Grandparents are more likely to engage in activities with which they are familiar. As educational levels increase, so do interest and willingness on the part of grandparents to participate. Consequently, pairing family life education programs with more familiar activities (e.g., church or community events) might be an effective marketing strategy, particularly for those grandparents with lower educational levels who might not feel comfortable in traditional educational settings.

Additional barriers to participation include grandparent age-related health status, child care, transportation, time of the class, finances, and cultural issues. Older grandparents may encounter difficulty in access to services due to their location and/or level of accessibility. Younger grandparents, still in the workforce, may find meeting times inconvenient for their busy schedules. Service providers should make sure that buildings are accessible and assess older adults' physical situations before and after program delivery. Programs should also have flexible meeting times, including those when grandchildren are in school, and provide on-site child care for times when children are out of school (Kolomer, 2008).

Many grandfamilies do not have reliable or consistent transportation or cannot afford available transportation, which makes program participation impossible. A greater variety of transportation and parking options can increase attendance, especially if grandfamilies are reminded of them before each meeting (Kolomer et al., 2003). Participants should also receive vouchers, transfers, or other free or reduced transportation resources when available.

Culturally competent programs can reduce additional barriers to program participation. Due to increased representation of minorities within grandfamilies (Brubaker & Roberto, 1993) and underserved rural and foreign-born audiences, services should be tailored to the specific needs of each culture. Increasing access to existing programs, providing participants with culturally specific resources, and modifying services to fit each individual are strategies that may enhance the cultural quality and increase participation of minority audiences (Wiley & Ebata, 2004).

Environmental Considerations

Comfortable chairs, good lighting, a location with no stairs, and a low amount of background noise may be important factors to consider when choosing a program location (Morris & Ballard, 2003). Hearing loss is common in later life, and it is recommended to reduce background noise, as well as raise voice volume and lower the pitch of your voice in an effort to accommodate these changes in hearing. Time of day is an important consideration for midlife adults (Morris & Ballard, 2003) because of work and home responsibilities. In turn, time of day may be important to older age groups because going out in the evenings is not always desirable.

Setting is important, and many older adults like to attend a program in an environment that is familiar to them. Therefore, many family life education programs have been conducted at churches, synagogues, and senior centers. Also, as Watson (1997) pointed out, more and more grandparents are volunteering in their grandchildren's classroom; therefore, elementary schools have become an increasingly popular site for programming.

Modes of Learning

Participation in educational programs provides benefits for the entire grand-family. Continual learning for grandparents can delay the onset of Alzheimer's, increase physical and mental health outcomes, and reverse losses in intelligence (Strom, Strom, Fournet, & Strom, 1997). Grandchildren experience increases in social skills (Edwards & Daire, 2006), self-esteem, reading behaviors, and perceived relationships with grandparents (Smith & Dannison, 2003) following educational interventions.

The limited research conducted with midlife and older adults indicates that learning styles become less pronounced as we age and that there is more variation in preferred learning styles (Truluck & Courtenay, 1999). Truluck and Courtenay (1999) went on to suggest that older adults engage in more reflective learning. Therefore, it might be beneficial to incorporate a variety of learning activities and to include the opportunity for reflective learning.

Duay and Bryan (2008) examined perceptions of older adults with regard to learning. The number and types of activities, the personality of the instructor, and the topics covered were of concern to older adults. Programs with interactive activities, discussions, role-playing, crosswords, reading books, volunteering, and other exercises were preferred.

Midlife and older adults have expressed interest in family life education materials that they could utilize independently, such as newsletters or self-help books (Morris & Ballard, 2003). Consequently, older age groups may be an ideal audience for alternative delivery forms such as newsletters, videos, or home visits. More print materials relating to topics of interest for older age groups need to be developed and made easily available at places such as senior centers, retirement communities, doctors' offices, community centers, or area businesses.

Additionally, the use of technology is encouraged with aging populations. Using web-based fact sheets, grandparents reported increased knowledge and opportunities to give grandchildren a "better life" (Brintnall-Peterson et al., 2009, p. 5). The material gave support to isolated grandparents who felt alone. Grandparents also reflected on the value of web-based materials, as they are easy to duplicate and share with others. Among the participants, 46% planned to use the information with their families, and 37% were going to share it with support groups (Brintnall-Peterson et al., 2009).

Educator Characteristics

Older adults reported the most important factor in a program was the instructor. Classes with motivating, respectful, and open-minded instructors saw consistent and repeated participation from seniors (Duay & Bryan, 2008). Instructor characteristics such as knowledge, attitude, behavior, and authority can influence their effectiveness, likability, evaluation, and receptivity of students to learn (Chitranshi & Agarwal, 2010), With respect to comfort and attitude toward learning, educator characteristics are vital to older adult program participation and learning. Segrist (2004) found that educators using one-on-one, experiential teaching methods encouraged positive attitudinal changes toward learning in older adults learning new computer skills.

In a study of older adult learners, Duay and Bryan (2008) discovered educator characteristics preferred by this population. Educators should have the following characteristics:

- Enthusiasm—To keep audiences engaged, educators must be lively and enjoy teaching.
- Knowledge—Older adults want to learn new information and enhance what they already know; therefore, educators should be able to handle concerns and refer learners to sources of assistance.
- Clarity—Physical and cognitive changes of aging result in a need for clear and upbeat information using terminology sensitive to age and level of education.
- Respect—Older adults want their own life experiences included in the learning environment, and they prefer educators who value the expertise of participants and acknowledge their capacity to grasp new information.
- Flexibility—Educators should be open to change and allow for learning dependent on participant interest. Older adults report wanting relevant information with less focus on things that do not apply to their caregiving situation.

Ethical Considerations

Grandfamilies are a unique population in that they are comprised of older adults and children—both vulnerable groups. Additionally, most grandparents become primary caregivers as a result of family instability or crisis, thereby increasing the number of complex family issues participants face. Family life educators should be adept at dealing with a multitude of family and ethical concerns that may arise, such as confidentiality, dual relationships, respect, and legal issues.

Communication of sensitive information should be handled with respect and confidentiality. During support groups, participants may share stories of personal or grandchild sexuality, drug use, crime, or other illegal behaviors. Other situations occur in which participants may seek advice, and educators worry about crossing the line from teacher to counselor. While fostering an environment of respect and communication, educators must abide by ethical principles and protect themselves and their participants.

Custody, visitation, and other legal rights and responsibilities faced by this group are complex issues that could prove troublesome for those without a legal background. Despite having working knowledge of legal matters, educators should refrain from giving legal advice to grandfamilies. Legal experts (e.g., attorneys, child welfare workers, and child advocates) can be invited to provide information and answer grandparents' questions.

Dolbin-MacNab and Targ (2003) suggested that family life educators should be equipped to deal with a variety of issues, even those with which they have little to no previous training. As grandfamily advocates (Cox, 2007), family life educators should collaborate with others (Ballard & Morris, 2005) for help with topics outside their area of expertise. Providing appropriate referrals can help reduce harm (Edwards & Ray, 2010) and risk for unethical practices.

Given the high likelihood that there will be ethical issues when working with grandfamilies, it is imperative that educators create a safe environment based on trust and respect. In addition to educating and advocating, family life educators should (1) handle personal information with sensitivity, (2) seek help from other professionals when in doubt, (3) resist the temptation to form dual relationships, (4) make every effort to reduce harm, (5) respect grandfamily diversity in experience and family dynamics (Smith & Dannison, 2001), and (6) utilize a theoretical framework to guide ethical practice.

Best Practices in Family Life Education Programming

Dolbin-MacNab and Targ (2003) suggested that family life education programs with grandfamilies should (1) address multiple issues, (2) collaborate with other professionals, (3) remove barriers, (4) create environments of respect, (5) foster effective group interaction, (6) include extended family members, (7) attend to differences in culture, (8) ensure safety, and (9) support the parental role.

In keeping with the principles suggested by Dolbin-MacNab and Targ (2003), there are four programming components for grandfamilies that emerge from the literature as being effective: (1) support groups, (2) respite care, (3) parent education, and although outside the scope of family life education, (4) psychotherapy. Many programs incorporate these components in combination and in collaboration with other professionals. For example, parent education may take place within a support group format and respite care may be offered as one component of a more comprehensive program. We outline best practices with each of these programs in the following sections.

Support Groups

A large number of programs use support groups as educational and psychological resources for grandfamilies (Glass & Huneycutt, 2002; Hayslip & Kaminski, 2005). Whether peer-led or facilitated by a professional, support groups allow grandparents to combat feelings of isolation, share ways to reduce stress, and voice their frustrations (Dellman-Jenkins et al., 2002) in a comfortable environment among peers.

The reciprocal exchange of emotion and encouragement occurring in support groups improves the mental health status (Giarrusso et al., 2000; Hayslip & Kaminski, 2005) and caregiving capacity (Butts, 2005) of participating grandparents. These groups also provide formal support to encourage activity in the areas of policy and reform (Musil et al., 2000) and educate on navigating legal, educational, and health care systems on behalf of grandchildren (Kropf & Kolomer, 2004). Grandchildren also benefit from support groups as they can form relationships with peers from similar situations (Dellman-Jenkins et al., 2002).

To maximize the effectiveness of support groups, facilitators and grandfamilies should (1) encourage optimism and productivity, (2) define goals for all participants, (3) learn and use group process skills, and (4) make education a priority (Strom & Strom, 2000). Attendance and participation increase when groups support and connect with each grandparent, allow for participant input on topic areas, make regular visits to grandfamily homes, and provide incentives, refreshments, and child care (Waycie, 2006).

Despite the documented benefits of support groups, there is some discussion as to the effect of using the term *support group*. A review of kinship caregiver support groups suggested that using "get-together" (Casey Family Programs, 2007) instead of "support group" could increase group success and decrease the likelihood of participant discomfort.

Respite Care

Respite is a necessary component of successful grandfamily programming (Dolbin-McNab, 2006; Fuller-Thomson & Minkler, 2000) and is often provided within support groups or other family life education programs. The objectives are to decrease stress and delay or suspend the need for hospitalization of grandparent or removal of grandchild from the home (Generations United, 2007b). The primary benefit of respite care is the decrease of many negative aspects associated with caregiving (Bachman & Chase-Landsdale, 2005). Breaks from caregiving allow grandparents, especially those with health issues (Marx & Solomon, 2000), time to focus on their own health needs, opportunity to decrease stress levels (Grinstead et al., 2003), and methods of coping. There are many options for respite care: (1) frequent short breaks and occasional long breaks; (2) in-home providers; (3) summer, afternoon, and weekend programs for grandchildren; and (4) vouchers or referrals for paid services (Generations United, 2007b).

According to the Family Strengthening Policy Center (2007), optimal grandfamily respite services are those that are family-centered, strengths-based, and allow grandfamilies to (1) participate in planning and delivery of program, (2) assist in training of service providers, and (3) select services best for their needs. Additionally, facilitators should provide respite services that are (1) built on family strengths; (2) age-appropriate, educational, and fun; (3) focused on participant outcomes; and (4) community-based and sustainable.

Parent Education

Parent education or skills training is an integral part of most grandfamily family life education programs. Grandparents can receive information on child development (Britnall-Peterson et al., 2009), discipline (Dolbin-McNab, 2006; Kropf & Burnette, 2003), communication (Brintnall-Peterson et al., 2009; Cox, 2002; Strom & Strom, 2000), legal issues (Cox, 2002; Glass & Huneycutt, 2002), accessing resources (Cox, 2002; Smith & Dannison, 2001), and health care (Landry-Meyer, Gerard, & Guzell, 2005; Smith & Dannison, 2001) as fundamental areas of knowledge for grandfamily well-being.

Strom and Strom (1992), in some of their classic work on grandparenting education, identified five key features of their curriculum: (1) group discussion, (2) problem solving, (3) practical principles, (4) self-evaluation, and (5) intergenerational conversations. Overall, Strom, Beckert, and Strom (1996) identified the importance of grandparents having a clearly defined role. Depending on the circumstances that led the grandparents to become primary caregivers for their grandchildren, there may be ambiguity regarding their role. Helping grandparents to clarify the blurred lines between the grandparent role and the parent role is crucial for them to feel empowered to enact these roles successfully.

Psychotherapy

Although most family life education programs do not employ psychotherapy, research has consistently stressed the need to increase grandfamilies' access to psychotherapy services (Bachman & Chase-Lansdale, 2005; Giarrusso et al., 2000; Glass & Huneycutt, 2002; Leder, Grinstead, & Torres, 2007). When used in conjunction with family life education, psychotherapy can be an additional effective method to increase the mental and emotional well-being of grandparents and their grandchildren. Psychotherapy (interventions or referrals) can reduce stress for grandparent caregivers (Goodman & Silverstein, 2006) and can provide the opportunity to address specific areas of concern.

Individual, family, and group therapies help increase coping skills, reduce conflict, strengthen family relationships, and define role hierarchy (Roberto & Qualls, 2003). Increased accessibility to formal and informal support resources and reframing negative situations are psychotherapy outcomes that enhance grandparent health and well-being (Sands et al., 2005). With psychotherapy, grandchildren can rebuild trust and address negative emotions subsequent to the removal from parental care (Edwards & Ray, 2010).

Successful Programs

Over the past few years, several grandparenting curricula have been developed. Although evaluation data are limited, the following programs show promise in their effectiveness in working with grandparents.

Empowering Grandparents Raising Grandchildren (Cox, 2002; e.g., Bjelde, 2004)

This 14-session program includes topics such as building grandchild self-esteem; dealing with grief and loss; communication about drugs, sex, and HIV; behavior problems; and legal issues. Used by Cooperative Extension, and family life and parent educators, this curricula includes an evaluation of each session and the entire training. Grandparents reported learning a lot about parenting from this program, and many were inspired to become grandparent advocates, delivering program information throughout their communities.

A Tradition of Caring: Information, Resources, and Support for Kinship Families (Kinship PRIDE)—Child Welfare League of America (e.g., Child Welfare League of America, n.d.)

Delivered by family life and parent educators, this nine-session program addresses kinship issues, child development, resources, family dynamics, lifelong connections, and the child welfare system.

Grandparents Raising Grandchildren: Doubly Stressed, Triply Blessed—Penn State University (Kaplan, Hanhardt, & Crago, 2002; Penn State Cooperative Extension, 2011)

During four 3-hour sessions, this program addresses issues such as becoming a grandparent raising grandchildren, common issues faced by grandfamilies, resources, and community action. Used by Cooperative Extension agents, family life educators, and community facilitators, this multimedia program contains an evaluation of the entire training. This curriculum has recently been updated for online delivery in an effort to reach a larger audience.

Parenting a Second Time Around (PASTA)—Cornell University (Cornell University, 2006)

PASTA contains 2-hour workshops on child development, discipline, and guidance; self-care; how to rebuild the family; how to live with teenagers; legal issues; and advocacy for grandfamilies. This program has been used in 24 states by Cooperative Extension agents, social workers, and adult educators and has been well received by participants.

Second Time Around ... Grandparents Raising Grandchildren—Western Michigan University (Dannison & Nieuwenhuis, 1994)

Using an 8- or 16-session format, this program deals with becoming parents again, strengthening grandfamily well-being, using parenting skills, working with school and community, tackling finances, dealing with legal issues, and addressing how grandfamilies look to the future. Cooperative Extension agents and parent educators ask participants to complete weekly evaluation sheets and outcome logs. Group leaders and grandparents report that this curriculum contains information that helps in parenting grandchildren, and in some cases, grandparent groups continued to meet after the evaluation (Ness, Dannison, & Smith, 2000).

FUTURE DIRECTIONS

With regard to future directions for both programming and research, the following are seven key areas that should be addressed within family life education with grandfamilies:

1. *Coordinate community support groups with formal service systems.* Organized custodial grandparent support groups are often successful in gathering participants to discuss challenges and strategies of a particular caregiving issue. However, there is a need to have these issues coordinated with formalized services that could specifically address and alleviate some of the challenges. For example, if there is a support group that discusses several of the legal challenges and issues of intergenerational custody and caregiving, then connecting support group participants with a legal advocacy service or law office might benefit these grandparents.

2. *Examine ways of increasing participation in community programming.* Research has shown that low-level participation could come from low perception of benefits (Chandler, 2010). If grandparents raising grandchildren do not perceive that they can profit from educational programs or support groups, they will not prioritize attendance or even make an effort to sign up and attend community programs. In addition, educators and support group coordinators must examine practices that allow grandparents to attend regularly and stay undistracted. There needs to be more research and evaluation on the various on-site child care options, transportation needs and availability, and timing and locations of programming, in order to maximize the greatest participation and benefits for grandparents raising grandchildren.

3. *Connect programs to a strong/understandable theoretical base.* Over the years, community programming for grandparents raising grandchildren have lacked theoretical connectedness and direction (Thomas et al., 2000). Without being linked to a theory, program objectives and outcomes can sometimes be scattered and unorganized. In recent years, some programs have started using the life span development theory as an effective way to link theoretical concepts, principles, and assumptions to the lives and living situations of custodial grandparents. This theory allows family life educators to understand specific life stages and the things that make them unique and different, as well as to recognize that life often challenges us with nonnormative events to tackle, grandparents raising grandchildren being a relevant representation of a nonnormative event in many cultures.

4. *Focus on the physical and mental well-being of grandchildren.* Many of the programs targeting grandfamilies have understandably been directed toward meeting the needs and challenges of the grandparents. An additional direction and focus should be on the grandchildren themselves. Some of the grandchildren being cared for by their grandparents have seen their parents arrested and incarcerated, regularly abusing drugs and alcohol, and/or being abusive and neglectful to themselves or other family members. These grandchildren may benefit from programming to help them physically and mentally adjust to being raised by their grandparents.

5. *Design culturally responsive programs and ensure educators are culturally competent to meet the needs of all grandfamily program participants.* So much of family programming historically has been written for and by those of the white middle class (Hughes, 1994; Wiley & Ebata, 2004). The current emphasis on understanding diversity has started to change that precedent. In recent years, a primary goal of many family life educators is to reach audiences where they live and need help the most. This worthwhile objective also needs to be extended to the classroom. For many of African American heritage who are accustomed to living in extended family households, perhaps grandchildren being raised by grandparents is not such a nonnormative event as it is in other cultures. The same could be said for those of Latino or Native American heritage. Facilitators need to be trained to be aware of and sensitive to cultural differences so they can successfully reach and connect with diverse audiences of grandparents who find themselves as primary caregivers for their grandchildren.

6. *Examine ways in which grandfathers might provide unique contributions as custodial grandparents.* Little research has been done studying custodial grandfathers and whether their caregiving practices are similar or different from those of grandmothers (Bullock & Thomas, (2007). Related to that, more research is recommended in examining how two-grandparent custodial household activities and practices differ from single grandparent households.

7. *Grandparents raising grandchildren with disabilities.* Inviting professionals from the county health and community services to come and train grandparents on the rights of their special needs children and the specific community programs that might be available for their grandchildren is also recommended in the future. Along the same vein, tapping into someone from the school system who is knowledgeable about the rights and programming available for special needs children from the district would help grandparents become informed and more successful advocates for the grandchildren under their care.

REFERENCES

American Association of Retired Persons. (2007, October). *GrandFacts: A state fact sheet for grandparents and other relatives raising children.* Retrieved from http://www.grandfactsheets.org/doc/National%202007%20New%20Template.pdf

Bachman, H. J., & Chase-Lansdale, P. L. (2005). Custodial grandmothers' physical, mental, and economic well-being: Comparisons of primary caregivers from low-income neighborhoods. *Family Relations, 54*(4), 475–487.

Ballard, S. M., & Morris, M. L. (2005). Factors influencing mid-life and older adult's attendance at family life education programs. *Family Relations, 54*, 461-472.

Bigner, J. (2009). *Parent-child relations. An introduction to parenting* (8th ed.). Upper Saddle River, NJ: Prentice Hall.

Bjelde, K. (2004). Empowering grandparents raising grandchildren: A training manual for group leaders. *Journal of Extension, 42*(3). Retrieved from http://www.joe.org/joe/2004june/tt6.php

Brintnall-Peterson, M., Poehlmann, J., Morgan, K., & Shlafer, R. (2009). A web-based fact sheet series for grandparents raising grandchildren and the professionals who serve them. *Gerontologist, 49*, 276–282.

Brubaker, T. H., & Roberto, K. A. (1993). Family life education for the later years. *Family Relations, 42*, 212–221.

Bullock, K., & Thomas, R. L. (2007). The vulnerability for elder abuse among a sample of custodial grandfathers: an exploratory study. *Journal of Elder Abuse and Neglect, 19*, 133–150.

Bunch, S. G., Eastman, B. J., & Moore, R. R. (2007). A profile of grandparents raising grandchildren as a result of parental military deployment. *Journal of Human Behavior in the Social Environment, 15*, 1–12.

Butts, D. M. (2005). Kinship care: Supporting those who raise our children. *Elders as resources, Intergenerational strategies series.* Baltimore, MD: Annie E. Casey Foundation. Retrieved from http://www.aecf.org/upload/publicationfiles/kincare.pdf

Casey Family Programs. (2007, November). Supporting kinship care: Promising practices and lessons learned (Series No. 003). *Breakthrough series collaborative.* Seattle, WA: Author. Retrieved from http://www.casey.org/Resources/Publications/pdf/BreakthroughSeries_Kinship.pdf

Chandler, D. (2010). The underutilization of health services in the Black community. An examination of causes and effects. *Journal of Black Studies, 40*, 915–931.

Child Welfare League of America. (n.d.). *A tradition of caring (Kinship PRIDE): Information, resources, and support for kinship families.* Retrieved from http://www.cwla.org/programs/trieschman/pridetraditionofcaring.htm

Chitranshi, J., & Agarwal, S. (2010). Knowledge transfer: Do instructor characteristics matter? *Information Processing and Management, 70*, 648–655.

Conway, F., Magai, C., Springer, C., & Jones, S. C. (2008). Optimism and pessimism as predictors of physical and psychological health among grandmothers raising their grandchildren. *Journal of Research in Personality, 42,* 1352–1357.

Cooperative State Research, Education, and Extension Service. (2008). *Cooperative extension's educational responses to relative caregivers' needs and concerns: State and local networks and resource list.* Retrieved from http://www.csrees.usda.gov/nea/family/pdfs/grandfamilies_extension_resource.pdf

Cornelius, J. B., LeGrand, S., & Jemmott, L. S. (2009). African American grandfamilies' attitudes and feelings about sexual communication: Focus group results. *Journal of the Association of Nurses in AIDS Care, 20,* 133–140.

Cornell University. (2006). *New York parenting programs: Parenting a second time around (PASTA).* Retrieved from http://www.parenting.cit.cornell.edu/pp_pasta.html

Cox, C. B. (2002). Empowering African American custodial grandparents. *Social Work, 47,* 45–54.

Cox, C. B. (2007). Grandparent-headed families: Needs and implications for social work interventions and advocacy. *Families in Society: The Journal of Contemporary Social Services, 88,* 561–566.

Dannison, L. L., & Nieuwenhuis, A. (1994). *Second time around ... Grandparents raising grandchildren.* Retrieved from http://homepages.wmich.edu/~dannison/grandparents.html

Dellman-Jenkins, M., Blankemeyer, M., & Olesh, M. (2002). Adults in expanded grandparent roles: Considerations for practice, policy, and research. *Educational Gerontology, 28,* 219–235.

Dolbin-MacNab, M. L. (2006). Just like raising your own? Grandmothers' perceptions of parenting a second time around, *Family Relations, 55,* 564–575.

Dolbin-MacNab, M. L., & Keiley, M. K. (2009). Navigating interdependence: How adolescents raised solely by grandparents experience their family relationships. *Family Relations, 58*(2), 162–175.

Dolbin-MacNab, M. L., & Targ, D. B. (2003). Grandparents raising grandchildren: Guidelines for family life educators and other family professionals. In B. Hayslip & J. H. Patrick (Eds.), *Working with custodial grandparents* (pp. 213–228). New York: Springer.

Duay, D. L., & Bryan, V. C. (2008). Learning in later life: What seniors want in a learning experience. *Educational Gerontology, 34,* 1070–1086.

Duncan, S. F., & Goddard, H. W. (2005). Foundations and philosophies of outreach family life education. In S. Duncan & H. Goddard (Eds.). *Family life education: Principles and practices for effective outreach* (pp. 1–20). Thousand Oaks, CA: Sage.

Dunne, E. G., & Kettler, L. J. (2008). Grandparents raising grandchildren in Australia: Exploring psychological health and grandparents' experience of providing kinship care. *International Journal of Social Welfare, 17,* 333–345.

Edwards, O. W., & Daire, A. P. (2006). School-age children raised by their grandparents: Problems and solutions. *Journal of Instructional Psychology, 33,* 113–119.

Edwards, O. W., & Ray, S. L. (2010). Value of family and group counseling models where grandparents function as parents to their grandchildren. *International Journal for the Advancement of Counselling, 32*(3), 178–190.

Family Life Education Institute. (n.d.). *About family life education.* Retrieved from http://www.familylifeeducation.org/aboutflei.html

Family Strengthening Policy Center. (2007). *Strengthening grandfamilies through respite care* (Policy Brief No. 20). Washington, DC: National Human Services Assembly. Retrieved from http://www.nydic.org/fspc/documents/Brief20.pdf

Fields, J. (2003, June). *Children's living arrangements and characteristics: March 2002.* Current Population Reports (P20-547). Washington, DC: U.S. Census Bureau. Retrieved from http://www.census.gov/prod/2003pubs/p20-547.pdf

Fuller-Thomson, E., & Minkler, M. (2000). African American grandparents raising grandchildren: A national profile of demographic and health characteristics. *Health and Social Work, 25,* 109–110.

Generations United. (2007a). *Grandfamilies: Challenges of caring for the second family.* Washington, DC: Author. Retrieved from http://www.gu.org/LinkClick.aspx?fileticket=uvrG0WU45LY%3D&tabid=157&mid=606

Generations United. (2007b). *Grandparents and other relatives raising children: Respite care.* Washington, DC: Author. Retrieved from http://www.gu.org/LinkClick.aspx?fileticket=bgBQz wSAgvo%3D&tabid=157&mid=606

Generations United. (2010). *GrandFacts: Data, interpretation, and implications for caregivers.* Washington, DC: Author. Retrieved from http://www.gu.org/LinkClick.aspx?fileticket=Gaekl HcAIJ8%3D&tabid=157&mid=606

Giarrusso, R., Silverstein, M., & Feng, D. (2000). Psychological costs and benefits of raising grandchildren: Evidence from a national survey of grandparents. In C. B. Cox (Ed.), *To grandmother's house we go and stay: Perspectives on custodial grandparents* (pp. 71–90). New York: Springer.

Gibson, P. A. (2005). Intergenerational parenting from the perspective of African American grandmothers. *Family Relations, 54,* 280–297.

Gist, Y. I., & Hetzel, L. I. (2004, December). *We the people: Aging in the United States.* Census 2000 Special Reports (CENSR-19). Washington, DC: U.S. Census Bureau. Retrieved from http://www.census.gov/prod/2004pubs/censr-19.pdf

Gladstone, J. W., Brown, R. A., & Fitzgerald, K. (2009). Grandparents raising their grandchildren: Tensions, service needs and involvement with child welfare agencies. *International Journal of Aging & Human Development, 69*(10), 55–78.

Glass, J. C., & Huneycutt, T. L. (2002). Grandparents raising grandchildren: Extent of situation, issues involved, and educational implications. *Educational Gerontology, 28,* 139–161.

Goodman, C. C., & Silverstein, M. (2002). Grandmothers raising grandchildren: Family structure and well-being in culturally diverse families. *Gerontologist, 42,* 676–689.

Goodman, C. C., & Silverstein, M. (2006). Grandmothers raising grandchildren. Ethnic and racial differences in well-being among custodial and coparenting families. *Journal of Family Issues, 27,* 1605–1626.

Grant, R. (2000). The special needs of children in kinship care. *Journal of Gerontological Social Work, 33,* 17–33.

Grinstead, L. N., Leder, S., Jensen, S., & Bond, L. (2003). Review of research on the health of caregiving grandparents. *Journal of Advanced Nursing, 44,* 318–326.

Hayslip, B., & Goodman, C. C. (2007). Grandparents raising grandchildren: Benefits and drawbacks. *Journal of Interpersonal Relationships, 5,* 117–119.

Hayslip, B., & Kaminski, P. L. (2005). Grandparents raising their grandchildren. *Marriage and Family Review, 37,* 147–169.

Henderson, T. (2004). Grandparents rearing TANF: A study in Virginia. *Journal of Family and Consumer Sciences, 96,* 10–12.

Hughes, R., Jr. (1994). A framework for developing family life education programs. *Family Relations, 43,* 74–80.

Jendrek, M. P. (1994). Grandparents who parent with their grandchildren: Circumstances and decisions. *Gerontologist, 34,* 206–216.

Kaplan, M., Forthun, L. F., Kostelechy, K. L., Nochols, A., Johnston, J. H., Corbin, M., et al. (2008). *Rationale and recommendations for strengthening the intergenerational agenda within Cooperative Extension.* Retrieved from http://agexted.cas.psu.edu/FCS/mk/Docs/WhitePaper.pdf

Kaplan, M., Hanhardt, L., & Crago, N. (2002). *Grandparents raising grandchildren: Doubly stressed, triply blessed.* College of Agricultural Sciences, Agricultural Research and Cooperative Extension, Penn State. Retrieved from http://pubs.cas.psu.edu/FreePubs/pdfs/agrs84.pdf

Kolomer, S. (2008). Grandparent caregivers. *Journal of Gerontological Social Work, 50,* 321–324.

Kolomer, S., McCallion, P., & Overendyer, J. (2003). Why support groups help: Successful interventions for grandparent caregivers of children with developmental disabilities. In B. Hayslip & J. Patrick (Eds.), *Working with custodial grandparents* (pp. 111–126). New York: Springer.

Kreider, R. M. (2008). *Living arrangements of children: 2004.* House Economic Studies (Publication No. P70–114). Washington, DC: U.S. Census Bureau. Retrieved from http://www.census.gov/prod/2008pubs/p70-114.pdf

Kropf, N. P., & Burnette, D. (2003). Grandparents as family caregivers: Lessons for intergenerational education. *Educational Gerontology, 29,* 361–372.

Kropf, N. P., & Kolomer, S. (2004). Grandparents raising grandchildren: A diverse population. *Journal of Human Behavior in the Social Environment, 9,* 65–83.

Landry-Meyer, L., Gerard, J. M., & Guzell, J. R. (2005). Caregiver stress among grandparents raising grandchildren: The functional role of social support. *Marriage and Family Review, 37,* 171–190.

Landry-Meyer, L., & Newman, B. M. (2004). An exploration of the grandparent caregiver role. *Journal of Family Issues, 25,* 1005–1025.

Leder, S., Grinstead, L. N., & Torres, E. (2007). Grandparents raising grandchildren: Stressors, social support, and health outcomes. *Journal of Family Nursing, 13,* 333–352.

Marx, J., & Solomon, J. C. (2000). Physical health of custodial grandparents. In C. B. Cox (Ed.) *To grandmother's house we go and stay: Perspectives on custodial grandparents* (pp. 37–55). New York: Springer.

McCallion, P., Janicki, M. P., Grant-Griffin, L., & Kolomer, S. (2000). Grandparent carers II: Service needs and service provision issues. *Journal of Gerontological Social Work, 33,* 57–84.

McGowen, M. R., Ladd, L., & Strom, R. D. (2006). On-line assessment of grandmother experience in raising grandchildren. *Educational Gerontology, 32,* 669–684.

Messing, J. T. (2006). From the child's perspective: A qualitative analysis of kinship care placements. *Children and Youth Services Review, 28,* 1415–1434.

Minkler, M., & Fuller-Thomson, E. (2005). African American grandparents raising grandchildren: A national study using the Census 2000 American Community Survey. *Journal of Gerontology, 60,* S82–S92.

Moore, V. R., & Miller, S. D. (2007). Coping resources: Effects on the psychological well-being of African American grandparents raising grandchildren. *Journal of Health & Social Policy, 22,* 137–148.

Morris, M. L., & Ballard, S. M. (2003). Instructional techniques and environmental consideration in family life education programming for mid-life and older adults. *Family Relations, 52*(2), 167–173.

Mullen, F. (2000). Grandparents and welfare reform. In C. B. Cox (Ed.), *To grandmother's house we go and stay: Perspectives on custodial grandparents* (pp. 113–131). New York: Springer.

Musil, C. M., Schrader, S., & Mutikani, J. (2000). Social support, stress, and special coping tasks of grandparent caregivers. In C. B. Cox (Ed.), *To grandmother's house we go and stay: Perspectives on custodial grandparents* (pp. 56–70). New York: Springer.

Mutchler, J. E., Baker, L. A., & Lee, S. (2007). Grandparents responsible for grandchildren in Native-American families. *Social Science Quarterly, 88,* 990–1009.

Mutchler, J. E., Lee, S., & Baker, L. A. (2003). *Grandparent care in the African-American population.* Boston: Gerontology Institute, University of Massachusetts. Retrieved from http://www.mccormack.umb.edu/centers/gerontologyinstitute/pubAndStudies/GrandparentCareintheAfricanAmericanPopulation.pdf

National Council on Aging. (2007, Winter). *Maintaining participation of older adults in community-based physical activity programs* (Issue Brief No. 7). Washington, DC: Author. Retrieved from http://www.healthyagingprograms.org/content.asp?sectionid=73&ElementID=492

Ness, C. N., Dannison, L., & Smith, A. (2000). Grandparents raising grandchildren: A psychoeducational group approach. *Journal for Specialists in Group Work, 25,* 67–78.

Office of Services to the Aging. (2003, July). *Best practices manual: For service providers assisting kinship caregivers in the state of Michigan.* Lansing, MI: Author. Retrieved from http://www.michigan.gov/documents/miseniors/BestPracticeManual_208131_7.pdf

Park, H. (2005). Grandmothers raising grandchildren: Family well-being and economic assistance. *Focus, 24,* 19–27.

Patrick, J. H., & Tomczewski, D. K. (2007). Grandparents raising grandchildren: Benefits and drawbacks? Custodial grandfathers. *Journal of Intergenerational Relationships, 5,* 113–116.

Penn State Cooperative Extension. (2011). *Grandparents raising grandchildren—Doubly stressed, triply blessed.* Retrieved from http://www.extension.org/pages/32573/grandparents-raising-grandchildren-doubly-stressed-triply-blessed

Price, C. A., & Brosi, W. A. (2006). Resources for advancing family gerontology education and practice. *Family Relations, 55,* 649–662.

Pruchno, R. A., & McKenney, D. (2002). Psychological well-being of black and white grandmothers raising grandchildren: Examination of a two-factor model. *Journal of Gerontology: Psychological Sciences, 57B,* P444–P452.

Roberto, K. A., & Qualls, S. H. (2003). Intervention strategies for grandparents raising grandchildren: Lessons learned from the caregiving literature. In B. Hayslip & J. H. Patrick (Eds.), *Working with custodial grandparents* (pp. 13–26). New York: Springer.

Ross, M. E., & Aday, L. (2006). Stress and coping in African American grandparents who are raising their grandchildren. *Journal of Family Issues, 27,* 912–932.

Sahyoun, N. R. (2002). Nutrition education for the healthy elderly population: Isn't it time? *Journal of Nutrition Education and Behavior, 34,* S42–S47.

Sands, R. G., Goldberg-Glen, R., & Thornton, P. L. (2005). Factors associated with the positive well-being of grandparents caring for their grandchildren. *Journal of Gerontological Social Work, 45*(4), 65–82.

Scarcella, C. A., Ehrle, J., & Geen, R. (2003, August). *Identifying and addressing the needs of children in grandparent care* (Series B, No. B-55). Washington, DC: Urban Institute. Retrieved from http://www.urban.org/UploadedPDF/310842_B-55.pdf

Segrist, K. A. (2004). Attitudes of older adults toward a computer training program. *Educational Gerontology, 30,* 563–571.

Seltzer, M. (1976). Suggestions for the examination of time-disordered relationships. In J. F. Gubrium (Ed.), *Time, roles and self in old age* (pp. 111–125). New York: Human Sciences Press.

Silverstein, M. (2007). Benefits of grandparents raising grandchildren. *Journal of Intergenerational Relationships, 5,* 131–134.

Simmons, T., & Dye, J. L. (2003). *Grandparents living with grandchildren: 2000.* Census 2000 Brief (C2KBR-31). Washington, DC: U.S. Census Bureau. Retrieved from http://www.census.gov/prod/2003pubs/c2kbr-31.pdf

Smith, A. B., & Dannison, L. L. (2001). Educating educators: Programming to support grandparent-headed households. *Contemporary Education, 72,* 47–51.

Smith, A. B., & Dannison, L. L. (2003). Grandparent-headed families in the United States: Programming to meet unique needs. *Journal of Interpersonal Relationships, 1,* 35–47.

Smith-Ruiz, D. (2008). African American grandmothers providing extensive care to their grandchildren: Sociodemographic and health determinants of life satisfaction. *Journal of Sociology & Social Welfare, 35,* 29–52.

Stevenson, M. L., Henderson, T. L., & Baugh, E. (2007). Vital defenses: Social support appraisals of Black grandmothers parenting grandchildren. *Journal of Family Issues, 28,* 182–211.

Strom, R., Beckert, T., & Strom, S. (1996). Determining the success of grandparent education. *Educational Gerontology, 22*(7), 637–649.

Strom, R., Carter, T., & Schmidt, K. (2004). African-Americans in senior setting: On the need for educating grandparents. *Educational Gerontology, 30,* 287–303.

Strom, R., & Strom, S. (1992). Curriculum and instruction for grandparents. *International Review of Education, 38*(4), 436–438.

Strom, R., & Strom, S. (2000). Goals for grandparents and support groups. In B. Hayslip & R. Goldberg-Glen (Eds.), *Grandparents raising grandchildren: Theoretical, empirical, and clinical perspectives* (pp. 289–304). New York: Springer.

Strom, R., Strom, S., Fournet, L., & Strom, P. (1997). Cooperative learning in old age: Instruction and assessment. *Educational Gerontology, 23,* 581–599.

Thomas, J. T., Sperry, L., & Yarbrough, M. S. (2000). Grandparents as parents: Research findings and policy recommendations. *Child Psychiatry and Human Development, 31,* 3–22.

Truluck, J. E., & Courtenay, B. C. (1999). Learning style preferences among older adults. *Educational Gerontology, 25,* 221–236.

U.S. Census Bureau. (2000). *Grandparents living with own grandchildren under 18 years by responsibility for own grandchildren by length of time responsible for grandchildren for the population 30 years and over in households.* Retrieved from http://factfinder.census.gov/home/saff/main. html?_lang=en

U.S. Census Bureau. (2008). Selected social characteristics in the United States: 2006–2008. *In 2006-2008 American Community Survey.* Retrieved from http://factfinder.census.gov/servlet/ ADPTable?_bm=y&-geo_id=01000US&-qr_name=ACS_2008_3YR_G00_DP3YR2&-ds_ name=ACS_2008_3YR_G00_&-lang=en&-redoLog=false&-_sse=on

U.S. Census Bureau. (2009). *Living arrangements of children under 18 years and marital status of parents, by age, sex, race, and Hispanic origin and selected characteristics of the child for all children.* Retrieved from http://www.census.gov/population/www/socdemo/hh-fam/ cps2009.html

U.S. Department of Health and Human Services, Center for Disease Control and Prevention, National Center for Health Statistics. (2010). *Health, United States 2009: With special feature on medical technology.* Hyattsville, MD: Author. Retrieved from http://www.cdc.gov/nchs/data/hus/ hus09.pdf

U.S. Department of Health and Human Services, National Institute on Aging, National Institute of Health. (2007). *The health & retirement study: Growing older in America* (NIH Publication No. 07-5757). Bethesda, MD: Author. Retrieved from http://www.nia.nih.gov/NR/rdonlyres/ D164FE6C-C6E0-4E78-B27F-7E8D8C0FFEE5/0/HRS_Text_WEB.pdf

Waldrop, D. P., & Weber, J. A. (2001). From grandparent to caregiver: The stress and satisfaction of raising grandchildren. *Families in Society, 82,* 461–472.

Wallace, G. (2001). Grandparent caregivers: Emerging issues in elder law and social work practice. *Journal of Gerontological Social Work, 34,* 127–136.

Walsh, F. (2005). Families in later life: Challenges and opportunities. In Carter & McGoldrick (Eds), *The expanded family life cycle. Individual, family, and social perspectives* (pp. 307–326). New York: Pearson.

Watson, J. A. (1997). Factors associated with African American grandparents' interest in grandparent education. *Journal of Negro Education, 66*(1), 73–82.

Waycie, L. (2006). Groups for grandparents raising grandchildren. *Children & Libraries, 4,* 17–18.

Whitley, D. M., & Kelley, S. J. (2007). *Grandparents raising grandchildren: A call to action.* Administration for Children and Families, Region IV. Retrieved from http://www.statelibrary. sc.gov/docs/grandfamilies/grc_overview_call_to_action.pdf

Wiley, A. R., & Ebata, A. (2004). Reaching American families: Making diversity real in family life education. *Family Relations, 53,* 273–281.

Chapter 7

Family Life Education With American Indian Families

DIANNE DUNCAN PERROTE, CFLE, AND SAUL FEINMAN

We have both worked with American Indian/Alaska Native (AI/AN) people and lived on Indian reservations. Our experiences working with Native people have changed us and affected our lives and who we are as human beings. We have been influenced, challenged, and expanded by these encounters. To work and live in Indian country does not call for you to take on the norms and values of Native people or for them to take on yours. We view these experiences as a two-way street, as a fully human encounter in which you are as likely to be helped and influenced by the Native people you meet as you are to help and influence them. This is not just a technique or method but, rather, is a way of being. While living and working in Indian country does not change everyone, it has changed both of us, and we are not alone in being the beneficiaries of these outcomes.

More than any other work we have done, the people we met in Indian country were the most insistent upon us being real and heartfelt. To speak of "technique" or "method" falls short. In a class on diversity, a student asked, "How can you get Indian people to think you respect them?" "Respect them!" Truly, the lenses are turned on one's self. An essential requirement of family life educators is for them "to be in touch with their own feelings or biases" (Powell & Cassidy, 2000, p. 30). In this chapter, we share what we know about working with AI/AN populations in family life education settings.

DEFINING THE POPULATION

Prior to European contact, estimates of Native people ranged from 20 to 45 million (Allen, 1992). As can be seen by this large range, these are estimates, and there is little agreement on the true numbers. However, we do know that American Indians were people with complex societal structures that shaped the way they lived their lives and these complex structures have been reduced or removed over the years.

The discrepancy in numbers still exists today. While estimates in 2000 were that 1% of the total U.S. population (about 2.4 million) was American Indian, in 2008 it was estimated that 4.4 million AI/AN persons lived in the United States (BigFoot, 2008).

In addition to the lack of consensus on numbers, there is variation in terminology. In Canada, the aboriginal inhabitants are referred to as members of First Nations, or as Inuit or Metis; whereas in the United States, American Indian or Native American are more commonly used terms. In this chapter, we will use the term AI/AN people. Although the primary focus on the chapter is on American Indian families, we attempt to include information that would be relevant to Alaska Native, Pacific Islander, and other indigenous populations. When working with a particular tribe, the preference would be to refer to them by their individual name (i.e., what they call themselves in their own language).

There are 562 federally recognized tribes in the United States and 225 Alaska Native entities (BigFoot, 2008). These numbers fluctuate as tribes gain or lose federal recognition. The only ethnic group that has a specific legal relationship with the federal government via treaties is American Indians (Hildebrand, Phenice, Gray, & Hines, 2008). The Government-to-Government Tribal Consultation Policy from the U.S. Department of Housing and Urban Development (2001) states that, "The United States Government has a unique relationship with American Indian governments as set forth in the Constitution of the United States, treaties, statutes, court decisions, and executive orders and memoranda." The U.S. government maintains a government-to-government relationship with tribes. In addition, there are more than 200 Native American tribes, bands, or communities that, while not acknowledged by the federal government, are acknowledged by one or more state governments.

As a result of the Relocation Act, passed in 1952, more than 67,500 heads of households were relocated through a direct employment program. The intention of this legislation was to assimilate Native Americans into the mainstream population with promises of training and jobs if they would move to the cities (Hildebrand et al., 2008).

The impact of the Relocation Act (1972) and the Indian Child Welfare Act (ICWA) (1978) (described in more detail later in the chapter) on the population contributes to the variation in regard to American Indian numbers. Furthermore, there are other impacts that are not as visible. For example, there are a number of American Indian women who lost their federal Indian status when they married nonstatus or non-American Indian men. Between the 1890s and 1985, these women were forced to leave their home reserves, resulting in a slightly larger number of women than men migrating from rural reserves to urban areas (Krouse & Howard, 2009). Currently, there are still tribes that remove women from their tribal status if they marry outside the tribe.

While there are estimates from one source that suggest 60% to 65% of the American Indian population lives in urban areas (Hildebrand et al., 2008), there are other sources that suggest that due to recent economic hardships there has been a migration back to reservations where tribal communities and extended family offer much needed support. Because urban Indian communities are dispersed and based on relationships, AI/AN communities may be invisible or misunderstood to outsiders—meaning anyone but community members. It is incorrect to assume that urban AI/AN people live clustered in neighborhoods. The methodology of the U.S. census, based on the assumptions that this population lives clustered rather than being dispersed and network-based, is yet another contributing factor to census undercounts and miscounts of Indian people in urban settings (Lobo, 2009).

In 2009, the median family income was $37,348 for American Indian families, 23.6% of AI/AN individuals lived in poverty, and 24.1% lacked health insurance coverage (U.S. Census Bureau, 2009). Lower median incomes and the need to support larger families both contribute to high rates of poverty among American Indian families (Willeto & Goodluck, 2003). Between 27% and 31% of American Indian children experience poverty, compared to only 9% of non-Hispanic white children who live in poverty (Hildebrand et al., 2008).

Unique Aspects of Native American Families

Since European contact began in large part in 1492, paternalistic colonizers, governments, and religious institutions have attempted to reform the power structures of indigenous people and diminish the influence of Native women (Gilberg et al., 2003). Throughout indigenous societies, women had important rights and responsibilities. Iroquois women nominated and impeached chiefs within the clan. Whether foreigners or prisoners were adopted or sentenced to death was the decision of the Clan Mothers (Naybor, 2009). However, European settlers refused to recognize Indian women's leadership roles. By making war on Indian women—in other words, raping, abusing, and killing Indian women—colonizers seized the land and attempted to force assimilation (Gilberg et al., 2003). "Controlling women meant gaining control of the land" (Naybor, 2009, p. 3).

During the era of termination and assimilation in the early 1800s, the U.S. government imposed relocation of thousands of Native people. They were rounded up and force-marched across the country. One of the most well-known Indian treks is the "Trail of Tears" in which 17,000 Cherokees were relocated from their homeland in North Carolina to Oklahoma. It is estimated that more than 25% died of exposure, malnutrition, and disease along the way. Apaches were put in boxcars and sent from their home in the central United States and southwest to Florida. Inhospitable, remote lands were set aside for tribal people to be held until the government knew what to do with them. In his study of American history, Hitler hailed the U.S. government as being impressively efficient in their efforts to eradicate the indigenous people.

> Hitler's concept of concentration camps as well as the practicality of genocide owed much, so he claimed, to his studies of United States history. He admired the camps for the Indians in the Wild West; and often praised to his inner circle the efficiency of America's extermination—by starvation and uneven combat—of the red savages who could not be tamed by captivity. (Toland, 1976, p. 802)

Policies that may have posed the greatest challenges to AI/AN communities were those aimed at assimilating Native people via disruption of traditional family life (Fisher & Ball, 2002). It was estimated as of 1982 that, during the 1970s, 42% of Native American women were sterilized—many without their knowledge or consent (Gilberg et al., 2003). Historical degradation of Indian women is linked to the soaring domestic violence statistics in Indian country.

In 1978, the U.S. Congress passed the Indian Religious Freedom Act. Prior to that date, it was against the law to practice tribal spirituality (Gilberg et al., 2003). Medicine bundles were buried or burned. American Indians practiced their spirituality at great peril.

The ICWA was adopted by Congress in 1978. Prior to the passage of this act, many Indian children were being forcibly taken from their homes and placed with white foster and adoptive families where they were assimilated into white society (Hildebrand et al., 2008). As many as 25% to 35% of the Indian children were removed from their homes and placed in non-Indian homes by state courts, welfare agencies, churches, and private adoption agencies (Gilberg et al., 2003). Children were commonly transported to schools hundreds of miles from their homes and forbidden to speak their language or practice their spirituality. Boarding schools, run by both governments and religious institutions, were notorious for their abuse and brutality. The Meriam Report to Congress in 1928 outlined the harsh treatment of Native children in boarding schools and the brutality of authorities toward Indian children. Raised in institutions, multiple generations of Native people were subjected to inhumane treatment. As a result of children being forcibly removed from homes and communities, there was a loss of traditional cultural values, Native identity, and an internalization of oppression (Gilberg et al., 2003). This policy undermined the AI/AN family unit and intergenerational transmission of knowledge regarding cultural values, and childrearing was blocked (Fisher & Ball, 2002).

A disproportionate number of American Indians have experienced trauma (BigFoot, 2008). Trauma is a unique individual experience associated with an extremely shocking or distressing event or enduring conditions, which can involve an actual death or other loss, serious injury, or threat to a child's well-being. It is often related to the cultural trauma, historical trauma, and intergenerational trauma that have accumulated in AI/AN communities through centuries of exposure to racism, warfare, violence, and catastrophic disease. More specifically, trauma may be experienced as a single event (car accident, rape), a prolonged experience (historical events such as the removal from homelands, ongoing sexual abuse), cumulative effects (high rates and exposure to violence, such as domestic violence and community violence), personal events that impact several generations (boarding schools, massacres, forced relocation, early losses), violent deaths (homicide, suicide, unintentional injuries), and multiple victimization (two or more different types of victimizations) (BigFoot, 2008).

According to Maria Yellow Horse Brave Heart (as cited in Steinman, 2005), Native American history meets the 1948 Geneva Convention's definition of genocide, defined as the intent to destroy a national, ethnic, racial, or religious group. She asserted that the U.S. government never intended for the long-term survival of Native Americans. Intergenerational trauma or historical trauma generates responses such as survivor guilt, depression, low self-esteem, psychic numbing, anger, victim identity, death identity, thoughts of suicide, preoccupation with trauma, and physical symptoms, said Brave Heart (Steinman, 2005).

Strengths and Assets of Native American Families

The following quote sums up many of the strengths of AI/AN people:

To many people, portrayal of Indian people as victim, pure and simple, is the most compelling part of the contact story. There is a widespread belief that we, Native American and nonnative alike, have nothing to celebrate. All too many believe we should give forth with great trills of mourning. But it is of utmost importance to our continuing recovery that we recognize our astonishing survival against all odds; that we congratulate ourselves and we are congratulated by our fellow Americans for our amazing ability to endure, recover, restore our ancient values and life ways, and then blossom. Indeed there are many among us who realize the necessity of celebration of native life this year especially. (Allen, 1992, p. xi)

Time Life photographer Gordon Parks once said that if the truth in history is omitted no one will know how extraordinary the story of survival is. Strengths of AI/AN people include cultural resilience, extended family structures, and humor.

Resilience

Although the term *resilience* has only recently been linked with American Indians, resilience in the face of adversity has long been practiced (LaFromboise, Hoyt, Oliver, & Whitbeck, 2006, p. 194). A Lakota spiritual elder explained how resilience is inherent in his culture:

> The closest translation of "resilience" is a sacred word that means "resistance" . . . resisting bad thoughts, bad behaviors. We accept what life gives us, good and bad, as gifts from the Creator. We try to get through hard times, stressful times, with a good heart. The gift (of adversity) is the lesson we learn from overcoming it. (Graham, 2001, p. 1)

Despite many formidable risks, many AI/AN youth avoid problem behaviors. They engage in prosocial behavior such as interacting with family (helping out at home), engaging in school events and team sports, and participating in community events. These positive outcomes in the face of substantial adversity point to the resilience of American Indian youth (LaFromboise et al., 2006, p. 195). Specifically, factors that contribute to resilient outcomes for youth are positive self-esteem, maternal warmth, family structure, parental support, a strong sense of direction, and tenacity (Bergstrom, Cleary, & Peacock, 2003; LaFromboise et al., 2006). Additionally, active engagement in and positive feelings about tribal culture, such as involvement in traditional activities and ceremonies; adherence to traditional values; pride in one's culture; appreciation of the influences of elders, grandparents, and parents; and participation in school curricula that include Native history, language, and culture, lend to the resilience of Native American youth (Bergstrom et al., 2003; LaFromboise et al., 2006, p. 196).

Along with resilience, self-esteem is an important strength of AI/AN people. Four bases of self-esteem in traditional cultures were described by Brendtro, Brokenleg, and Van Bockern (1990): (1) belonging—caring adults look after the children from birth; the tribal community treats their relations with respect and concern; (2) mastery—through stories, AI/AN families provide nurturing and act as role models to foster balance in spiritual, mental, emotional, and physical competence; (3) independence—rewards are never offered for doing well; practicing appropriate self-management is in itself the reward; and (4) generosity—giving to others and giving back to the community are fundamental core values; generosity and unselfishness are stressed by adults.

Extended Family Structures

While it is true that many Native Americans have assimilated into mainstream society and have adopted family structures and roles similar to the dominant culture, as educators it is important to avoid making assumptions about family structure. Family structures, in many traditional AI/AN cultures, still differ from the nuclear family in mainstream American society. For example, AI/AN family networks are more structurally open. Several households can be included in the extended family representing significant relatives along both vertical and horizontal lines, thus assuming village-type characteristics (O'Shea & Ludwickson, 1992; Red Horse, Lewis, Feit, & Decker, 1978). Extended family members play important roles in facilitating the well-being of individuals within the tribe and the community. This may occur through shared resources, such as money, food, clothing, or services, such as child care or transportation for shopping or medical care (O'Shea & Ludwickson, 1992).

Another benefit of extended family support is that children are cared for by many relatives in addition to their parents. In 2009, 54% of AI/AN individuals age 30 and over lived with their grandchildren as compared to 40% in the general population (U.S. Census Bureau, 2009), indicating that grandparents are especially helpful in caring for children whose parents cannot or will not. Parents and relatives often engage in social activities with children, such as hand games, dances, feasts, and powwows (Abbott & Slater, 2000). Additionally, extended family members are important teachers for passing on traditional practices and values. Older generations of grandparents, great aunts, and great uncles (all considered grandparents in traditional Indian communities) are often as important as parents in serving as teachers and models (Hildebrand et al., 2008). The roles of teacher and disciplinarian are taken on by grandparents, aunts, and uncles while parents' primary focus is to give children unconditional love and support. For example, an aunt is considered a child's mother and an uncle is a child's father in the Lakota culture (Jones & Moomaw, 2002).

In addition to extended family, family structures, under some circumstances, include nonkin as well as kin. An important dimension of who constitutes Native American families includes face-to-face interactions. Families can be made up of individuals who are blood-related as well as nonblood-connected. Interactions convey more meaning than letters or phone calls (John, 1998, p. 330). It's very possible, in a school setting, that an uncle, aunt, or grandparent will attend events concerning the child.

The idea of extended family extends vertically and horizontally. Three strengths of American Indian families identified by Lewis (1981) were (1) helping systems that operate within the family; (2) courage and optimism obtained from spiritual life religion; and (3) respect for each other and personal relationships, which form the basis for later learning. These strengths often help Indian families face poverty and inadequate living conditions. For example, the multitude of forced relocations and outside threats, instead of making Indians evaporate or disappear as was the intention, served to strengthen the solidarity of the indigenous people. Consequently, connections extend over time, between generations and between tribes (Hildebrand et al., 2008).

Humor

Common strengths have been identified among the hundreds of tribes that exist in this country. Although each has unique features, they all include having a sense of humor. While there is no known research literature on humor, the descriptors chosen most often by the youth included the following: "friendly, kind, independent, smart, and funny/humorous." Most of these self-attributions closely parallel the American Indian cultural emphases on relationships, humor, and independence for children (Stiffman et al., 2007).

Once, at a friend's gathering, I (Perrote) was telling about an incident that had happened about 13 years earlier. The story goes that after having said goodbye to the family I was visiting, outside my Volkswagen was nowhere to be found! A bunch of kids had lifted the little car and carried it around the side of the house! "I was one of them!" a dinner guest piped up! Weaving of time and relationships is as important as storytelling. The telling and retelling of this hilarious story became a valuable link to our relationship.

FAMILY LIFE EDUCATION PRACTICES

Current State of Family Life Education

Head Start programs and Early Head Start programs embedded in many tribal communities are invaluable, and much of the family life education that occurs with AI/AN populations is in collaboration with Head Start programs. In one village, a community-wide survey identified the Head Start staff as a primary resource for information on parenting and child development. Head Start and Early Head Start federal regulations for family and community partnerships state that grantee and delegate agencies must work collaboratively with all participating parents to identify and continually access, either directly or through referrals, services and resources that are responsive to each family's interests and goals (U.S. Department of Health and Human Services [DHHS], 2006). These services and resources include emergency assistance, education and other appropriate interventions, information on mental health issues, such as substance abuse, child abuse and neglect, and domestic violence that place families at risk. Other opportunities include continued training for employment, health and nutrition information, and resources. Consequently, it is not unusual for Head Start and Early Head Start to be a leading community resource for information or classes in life skills, parenting, nutrition, and child development.

A key focus of Head Start has been involving fathers more meaningfully in the lives of their children. This became the Father Involvement Initiative embraced by many tribal programs. For example, the Red Cliff Band of Lake Superior Chippewa Early Head Start was awarded a Fatherhood Demonstration Grant to strengthen the parenting of young parents with a focus on fathers (Godfrey, 2002).

In Oregon "The Indian Family Wellness Project: An Application of the Tribal Participatory Research Model" was developed, implemented, and evaluated in collaboration with the Oregon Social Learning Center in Eugene and an AI/AN community that included Head Start as a key collaborator. Tribal participatory research (TPR) is based on an approach emphasizing participation of tribes and tribal members in all facets of the research process and incorporating cultural and historical factors essential to strengthening AI/AN families (Fisher & Ball, 2002).

Tribal colleges are a valuable resource and a common collaborator with many AI/AN Head Start programs to provide a location for life skills, parent education, child development, and other family life education classes. Tribal colleges and universities (TCUs) enroll students from over 250 federally recognized tribes. Those colleges vary in enrollment (size), focus (liberal arts, technical skills, sciences), location (woodlands, desert, frozen tundra, rural reservation, urban), and student population (all or mostly American Indian, many tribes represented, or only a few). However, tribal identity is the core of every tribal college, and they all share the mission of tribal self-preservation and service to their communities. There are tribal colleges in 14 states: Alaska (1), Arizona (2), Kansas (1), Michigan (3), Minnesota (3), Montana (7), Nebraska (2), New Mexico (3), North Dakota (5), Oklahoma (2), South Dakota (3), Washington (1), Wisconsin (2), and Wyoming (1). Child development and human services classes are offered at a number of sites. The White House Initiative on Tribal Colleges and Universities states the following:

> Tribal Colleges and Universities are both integral and essential to their communities. They are often the only postsecondary institutions within some of our Nation's poorest rural areas. Tribal Colleges and Universities serve a variety of people, from young adults to senior citizens, Indians and non-Indians. They also provide crucial services and add hope to communities that suffer high rates of poverty and unemployment. (U.S. Department of Education, 2011)

Women, Infants and Children (WIC) offices, available through 34 tribal organizations, are a source of valuable information for family wellness, health, and child development. The WIC target population is low-income, nutritionally at risk pregnant women, breastfeeding women, non-breastfeeding postpartum women, infants, and children up to their fifth birthday.

Benefits provided to WIC participants include supplemental nutritious foods, nutrition education, and counseling at WIC clinics and screening and referrals to other health, welfare, and social services.

The Indian Health Service (IHS), an agency within the U.S. Department of Health and Human Services (DHHS), is responsible for providing a comprehensive health service delivery system to AI/AN peoples. The provision of health services to members of federally recognized tribes grew out of the special government-to-government relationship between the federal government and Indian tribes that was established in 1787. IHS has a presence throughout a multitude of Native American communities; it is broken into 12 physical "areas" of the United States: Alaska, Albuquerque, Aberdeen, Bemidji, Billings, California, Nashville, Navajo, Oklahoma, Phoenix, Portland, and Tucson. IHS branches out to local clinics in communities, yet many are still located in remote locations. Retaining consistent medical staff is a challenge, and the remote location may limit access for many patients. For example, individuals in need of dialysis often have to move to a community where they can receive these services. The availability of medical care has an enormous impact on families.

AI/AN babies born in the northern tier of the United States are almost three times more likely to die from sudden infant death syndrome (SIDS) as are white babies. In response, the "Healthy Native Babies Project: Workbook and Toolkit" was developed. This project aimed at reducing sudden unexpected infant deaths (SUIDs), a category that includes SIDS, in AI/AN communities (Eunice Kennedy Shriver National Institute of Child Health and Human Development, 2010).

General Needs of This Population and Rationale for Family Life Education

According to the director of Behavioral Health at IHS, ". . . intimate partner violence poses a significant health threat across Indian Country. American Indians and Alaska Natives experience some of the highest rates of domestic violence and sexual assault of any population in the United States" (Weahkee, 2010, p. 1). One study found that its sample of Native American men and women reported a 91% lifetime incidence of interpersonal violence (Wasserman, 2005). Related to this, a 2008 Centers for Disease Control and Prevention report on health and violence found that 39% of Native women reported that they were victims of intimate partner violence some time in their lives—a rate higher than any other race or ethnicity surveyed. Intimate partner violence is a major public health problem that causes grave and lasting harm to individuals, families, and communities. Because most AI/AN individuals are seen at some point by a health care provider, the health care setting offers a critical opportunity for early identification and primary prevention of abuse.

In addition to intimate partner violence, there are many health issues that affect the well-being of AI/AN families. A 5-year IHS demonstration project indicates that risk factors for diabetes and cardiovascular disease can be reduced among the AI/AN population, who have the nation's highest rates of diabetes. Suicide prevention, depression, substance abuse, domestic violence, trauma, HIV prevention, and bullying are all areas on which IHS is diligently working to address, along with the health disparities of the American Indian population on a national and local level.

Urban school-based health centers (SBHCs) serving adolescents have the potential to be an excellent site for family life education. With the number of urban AI/AN children of mixed ethnicities constantly on the rise, urban school districts encounter new and unique challenges in serving American Indian families and children. Alcohol initiation at an early age is a strong predictor of later risk drinking (Zucker, Donovan, Masten, Mattson, & Moss, 2008), early onset of episodic drinking, subsequent sexual risk taking, and multiple sexual partners (Ramisetty-Mikler, Caetano, Goebert, & Nishimura, 2004). Culturally sensitive early interventions are poised to be implemented through SBHCs serving adolescents. A variety of strategies can be utilized to concentrate on prevention efforts regarding the reduction of alcohol/substance use among urban AI/AN youth. Collaborations between tribal, federal, state, and local public health institutions and the school have the capability of intervening and possibly reducing the disparities (Ramisetty-Mikler & Fernando, 2010).

"We Should Live Well Together: A Program to Improve Co-Parenting Relationships Within Native American Families" was developed and delivered by Michigan State University Extension and Michigan State University. A study of this program was conducted in order to identify perceptions of barriers and supports of positive coparenting within Native American households. Participants of the study wanted information and support related to healing from historical trauma, stress, anxiety, conflict, and anger; traditional parenting; traditional ways of gaining resources (financial, material, human); coparenting knowledge and supports through extended family; and tribal networks and traditional stories/quotes that provide wisdom for life today (Contreras & Silvey, 2010).

Marketing/Recruitment

Reservations are tight communities; this means it would be rare, if not impossible, that a family life education program could take place without extensive tribal support and groundwork. It is important to ensure that the proper approval from the governing body is in place before marketing and recruitment move forward on a reservation. Most likely the agency that is hosting the family life education event will have already addressed required protocols. While this may not be necessary, ignoring established protocols could result in an unexpected barrier. Conducting your program in conjunction with other events might be a good way to work within existing structures as well as gain visibility. For instance, if there is a health fair it would be an effective practice to have a table or booth where you could shake hands with people and personally invite them to the family life education presentation. Once tribal support is secured, methods of advertising a family life education event might include posters, flyers, Facebook posts, newsletters, announcements at other local events, or Listservs (if Internet is available). Texting individual reminders to participants can be another valuable method of marketing your program.

Despite some of these tech-savvy ways of marketing a family life education program, technology is not to be taken for granted. Many AI/AN communities are still lacking even the basic telephone networks. National reports examining the state of connectivity throughout Indian country found that the capabilities of telecommunications and information technology infrastructures in AI/AN communities fall far behind the rest of rural America (Early Head Start National Resource Center [EHSNRC] @ ZERO TO THREE, n.d.). Additionally, even if introduced, there are generations that are not comfortable with technology, and many will refrain from using it (EHSNRC @ ZERO TO THREE, n.d.).

Finally, be sure that marketing materials are culturally appropriate for your target audience. When inviting the family service workers from a Head Start in one American Indian community to look at materials developed through the Healthy Marriages Initiative, there was an outburst of protest. They explained that people were interested in "healthy relationship" information, and they did not want information on "marriage" because that was an institution of the dominate culture. At another site, there were individuals who embraced their traditional culture who emphatically stated that they believed in marriage and that information on building healthy marriages would be welcomed.

Barriers to Participation

Time, child care, transportation, and weather are potential barriers for any family life education audience; however, these factors may have unique aspects when working with AI/AN populations. Time is a demand for everyone these days, including American Indians. There are villages where people are at home by dark and don't go out again. This may be because of dangers in the community. In one area, there was a cougar spotted nearby so people were staying close to their homes.

Time is also an issue in regard to balancing work and family. One creative Head Start held "brown bag" lunches so that they could get the participation of a group of parents working in the tribal complex. Parents were already at the village, so attending the training during their lunchtime did not take extra gas or evening time away from family. If child care is needed, work with your hosts to address the child care needs of your audience. The best possible scenario is that a classic Head Start socialization could be held in conjunction with your family life education program.

Transportation is a key factor in the ability of participants to attend a family life education event. Of the federally recognized tribes, only 19 have a public transportation system funded by the Federal Transit Administration Section 18 program. Two thirds of reservation roads are unpaved and of poor quality, which has a major effect on highway safety. The highway fatality rate, according to the Federal Highway Administration, is four times the national average. Some tribal lands have tremendous geographic spread, which poses additional challenges to initiating and maintaining a transportation infrastructure (EHSNRC @ ZERO TO THREE, n.d.).

If people do have working vehicles, additional aspects to consider are distance and gas prices. One parent on the Navajo reservation explained her challenges regarding attending a meeting. "Once we drive 30 miles home, we can't afford to go out again. That'd be another 60 miles to go there and back. This gas has gotta last me all week."

Due to extreme isolated areas and lack of infrastructure, weather can be a barrier—the heat or the cold. If it's 110 degrees outside and the air-conditioning breaks down, there isn't going to be a class. If it's 30 degrees below zero, families may cancel their plans to attend an event. Families may not want to expose themselves to the risk of having to ask for help from outsiders should a crisis arise. This level of vulnerability is outside the comfort zone of many AI/AN people, and this population may want to avoid any risk; therefore they may refrain from coming out to a family life education event.

I (Perrote) was contracted to work on the Navajo reservation. One spring, after a particularly bad snow, the weather cleared up, the sky was blue, and the temperatures were rising. It was perplexing when everything didn't resume as usual. New to the vicinity, I didn't realize that it took a couple of weeks for the clay road surfaces to dry enough to support vehicles on hundreds of miles of dirt roads. A pickup truck could sink up to its axles.

Environmental Considerations

When going on-site to an AI/AN community to deliver family life education programming, the variations in environment and facilities are enormous. At one site, you might find state-of-the-art facilities with built-in projectors and screens that lower at the push of a button in a new tribal building. At another location, the wall may serve as a screen if there is an extension cord long enough to access electricity for the computer and projector. It would not be unusual to arrive with your equipment and find it necessary to launch into the presentation without technological support. Facilities available for a program at a rural location might include community tribal buildings, buildings at tribal colleges, parent rooms or classrooms at a Head Start, another program facility, meeting rooms at the tribal resort or casino, the hospital or clinic, the school, or a church.

If your program is directed to professional staff and being held in a tribal resort and casino as part of a conference there are professional people on site whose job it is to coordinate events. This coordination may include food, which can be a very important part of the event. At one training event, the hotel staff had removed the refreshments before it was time for the scheduled break. "I'm going to put that on your evaluations!" a participant teased. He did. While we laughed, it drove home the point that providing food and beverages is a basic to planning.

Conventional understanding of community is challenged by the mobility of Native people between urban and rural, as well as among social, cultural, and political spaces that define the urban AI/AN community. Movement is not just one way. For varying reasons and amounts of time, movement is back and forth. Women in these urban communities serve to both stabilize and facilitate local dynamics. Among the reasons women moved to the cities were greater opportunities and escaping domestic violence (Krouse & Howard, 2009).

Modes of Learning

The usual way for a child to learn a skill from an adult in the AI/AN community is to observe carefully over long periods of time and eventually the individual begins to take part in the activity. For example, an American Indian child learns the technology of fishing by going with adults on fishing trips, listening, and observing. He comes to know the places to go to find the fish, how to set nets, how to use a dip net, and how to prepare the fish to eat. Observation is used. There is minimal verbal preparation or interchange. Rarely would a child be asked to verbalize what has been learned. What the child learns becomes evident on the next fishing trips (Wyatt, 1978–1979). This mode of learning prevalent in childhood is still common among adults.

In addition to observation, storytelling is an important mode of learning for AI/AN populations. In community, storytelling is not limited to 20-minute sessions as it might be in an educational setting. A story begins during a fishing trip and might have many versions told in different contexts. Some information related to that story might come up during a discussion about the history of the area. In either case, once the story is started it might continue for hours during which time the listeners are expected to listen quietly (Wyatt, 1978–1979).

Individual achievement is in contrast to American Indian beliefs of cooperative interdependence and sharing and working together. Cultural traditions often inhibit American Indian children from being direct, verbal, or assertive, which can result in being misperceived and misunderstood. Generations of American Indians have experienced similar educational stresses (Hildebrand et al., 2008). To be successful in a majority school requires either becoming acculturated or balancing both the majority culture and the tribal culture. AI/AN youth are subject to acculturation stress—a psychocultural stress experienced during the process of encountering cultural differences between a host culture and the incoming culture (LaFromboise, 2009). For some, success in school is berated by their peers as looking down on their own people and acting like whites (Hildebrand et al., 2008). Consequently, educational methods that mimic those in a traditional classroom should be avoided by family life educators.

LaFromboise and colleagues (2006) advised using the skills-based approach of "American Indian Life Skills Development Curriculum," which follows well-established teaching methods, to develop social skills. Teachers and peers inform students of the rationale and components of a particular skill, model and demonstrate the skill for them, and later provide feedback on individual skill performance. The curriculum was developed in collaboration with students and community members from the Zuni Pueblo and the Cherokee Nation of Oklahoma in an effort to address suicide—a significant problem for many adolescents in Native American populations. Life skills that are addressed in the curriculum include communication, problem solving, depression, stress management, anger regulation, and goal setting.

In a research project conducted in partnership with the Jemez Pueblo and Arizona State University titled "Becoming Jemez: Early Childhood of Jemez Children," three questions were asked: (1) What should Jemez children learn in order to be "Jemez"? (2) How do they learn these things? (3) How does Head Start support or not support this learning? These three questions guided eight Walatowa Head Start parents and grandparents as they photographed the youngest members of the Jemez members beginning their linguistic, social, emotional, and spiritual development. Many familial and community events of daily life were represented in the Photovoice posters created as part of this project. "Guided by multifaceted oral traditions, children learn through participation, engaged observation and listening (peripheral learning), guided practice, trial and error, role modeling and direct and indirect instruction" (Romero-Little, 2009, p. 1).

The recurring themes demonstrated in these examples is that learning modes that are most useful and honoring of AI/AN people include shared experience, participation, storytelling, modeling, discussion, observation, listening, guided practice, role-playing, and offering information either directly or indirectly.

Educator Characteristics

Dr. Stephen Duncan, in his textbook *Family Life Education: Principles and Practices for Effective Outreach* (Duncan & Goddard, 2011), shared a story that illustrates important educator characteristics. When teaching a workshop on personal development on a Montana Indian reservation, he chose the metaphor of an apple to lead participants into an exercise where they would identify characteristics of their true or "core" selves. He opened the discussion by saying, "I'm like an apple, and at my core you will find…." Then he invited participants to complete the phrase by listing their core personal characteristics. Participants seemed amused, and when he asked them what they found funny, they were comfortable enough around him to be candid. Apples are red on the outside (at least many varieties) and white on the inside. So asking them to imagine they were an apple was like asking them to pretend they were American Indian only on the outside and white on the inside. They discussed which other possible metaphors would be more meaningful and found that metaphors representing human connection to the earth and other living things might be more appropriate (Duncan & Goddard, 2011).

Within this example of family life education delivery are several valued educator traits. Asking what participants found funny demonstrated a willingness to learn. Trust was displayed when the participants shared with the educator what they found funny and so the family life educator became a student of the participants' culture. This reciprocity between family life education and participants is essential when working with AI/AN families.

Building trust with the AI/AN population is paramount. Empathy, along with the willingness to understand and appreciate diversity, is essential. Additional characteristics critical to becoming a family life educator include general intellectual skills, self-awareness, emotional stability, maturity, awareness of one's own personal attitudes and cultural values, effective social skills, self-confidence, flexibility, verbal and written communication skills, and the ability to relate well with all ages and groups on a one-to-one basis (Powell & Cassidy, 2000). It is important to develop the ability to laugh at yourself. Being teased is a good sign (Hildebrand et al., 2008). Embrace the humor with a smile.

As a family life educator in an AI/AN community, in addition to the previously listed characteristics, it is important to "act with humility and quiet respect." In communicating, be honest and forthright with your answers. Be aware of "not talking too much" (Hildebrand et al., 2008). Personal questions may be interpreted as intrusive and may put people off. Invite input and opinions and then listen. Many AI/AN people are comfortable with silence. If the family life educator asks a group a family life educator while facilitating, then becomes anxious with the silence and fills the silence by answering his/her own question, participants will cease to offer anything of themselves.

Ethical Considerations

Reporting suspected abuse, like with any population, is an ethical consideration when working with AI/AN populations. In the ordinary course of your work, should you suspect or become aware of evidence that financial, physical, sexual, or other types of abuse have been observed or are suspected, or when there is evidence of neglect, knowledge of an incident, or an imminent risk of serious harm, it is important to follow a reporting procedure. However, the procedure for reporting such incidents in an AI/AN community may differ from reporting procedures in mainstream society. Work with the director of the agency who is sponsoring you to ask for recommended procedures for that community.

When among AI/AN people, it is essential not to participate in gossip or share confidential information. The communities are small and interconnected. You could be telling a story about an event back on the reservation, and someone in your audience will correct a detail of your story.

AI/AN people are very generous, and it is likely that you may be offered food or a gift. It is important to be gracious and respectful in your response to avoid offending anyone. From my experience, I've learned to take a little bit of food at each place so I won't get stuffed! You also may want to avoid certain types of praise. Among many tribes if you say something like, "I like your necklace," he/she may take it off and give it to you!

Misuse of research and the perception that American Indians were the most researched population led many tribes to impose a moratorium on "research," resulting in the lack of useful research on American Indian families. An example of "misuse" is the recent lawsuit of the Havasupai Tribe, as revealed in the April 22, 2010, issue of the *New York Times,* article in the "Tribe Wins Fight to Limit Research of Its DNA." In 2003, the Havasupai Tribe issued a "banishment order" to keep Arizona State University employees from their reservation in the red cliffs of the Grand Canyon. This ancient punishment was in response to the misuse by the university researchers of DNA samples tribal members had given beginning in 1990 with the hope of identifying clues to the tribe's devastating rate of diabetes. Unbeknownst to the tribe, their blood samples were used to study many other things from mental illness to theories of the tribe's geographical origins, which contradict their traditional stories.

Best Practices in Family Life Education Programming

The recent piece by Small, Cooney, and O'Connor (2009) on what they termed *evidence-informed program improvement* emphasizes the importance of using evidence and evaluation to improve programmatic efforts. While they reminded us of the wonderful comment made by Donald Campbell (1987)—that we should "evaluate no program until it is proud" (p. 347)—they also make it clear that, at some point, evaluation is a necessary component of any effective program. Evidence-based practices (EBPs) and programs have been incorporated after various funding agencies (governmental and private) insisted that financial support flows only upon evaluative evidence that the program is doing what it was designed to do.

The call for evidence-based programs has encountered special, perhaps even unique, difficulties within the context of interventions in AI/AN communities. For example, in discussing the use of a Talking Circle approach in an intervention to heal the wounds inflicted on Alaska Native communities by the *Exxon Valdez* oil spill in Prince Edward Sound in 1989, Picou (2000) noted that he could not use a systematic social survey to evaluate the impact of the intervention because such a method was culturally inappropriate. In its place, he employed the less rigorous technique of informal personal interviews, because this method was not considered offensive by the participants. Since quite a few programs and interventions with AI/AN people utilize spiritually based methods, it has been noted that the idea of doing evaluation research would be antithetical to an approach based in spirituality and religious practices.

In 2003, Oregon tribes and tribal communities voiced objections to the movement of federal, state, and county governments' requirement for funding requiring "evidence-based," "researched-based," "science based," and "best-practices." The linear approach to funding requirements is contrary to the circular worldview held by most Native people (Cruz & Spence, 2005). In response to emerging tribal concerns, the National Indian Child Welfare Association (NICWA) changed the theoretical term of EBPs to *Practice-Based Evidence: Building Effectiveness from the Ground Up* (Cruz & Spence, 2005).

In the context of being culturally insensitive or even offensive to core spiritual beliefs, it is significant to note what Brotherson (2008) found when reviewing available programs focused on parenting. Of the 12 programs examined, 11 had established evidence-based validity or were in the process of doing so through ongoing evaluation research. The only program for which this evidence was neither established nor forthcoming was Positive Indian Parenting, the one program that was aimed specifically at AI/AN audiences. The North Dakota State University report indicated that the Positive Indian Parenting was widely used and that there were anecdotal reports of its effectiveness, but evidence-based support was not available because the standard evaluative research had not been done. When Positive Indian Parenting was introduced it was cutting edge; it was designed for use with pan-Indian populations (i.e., across AI/AN nations). It was new and groundbreaking, for after 400 years of dismantling AI/AN families, this program showed value in parenting within AI/AN. It was claiming value in AI/AN culture.

Given that Positive Indian Parenting has been in use since 1987, the absence of the usual type of evidence-based assessment is quite striking. In response, Cross, Friesen, and Maher (2007) pointed out that most EBPs have not been evaluated with regard to their validity, cultural sensitivity, and efficacy for AI/AN populations. They argued that "little evidence exists that EBPs are effective for diverse groups and populations with different worldviews and values" (Cross et al., 2007, p. 11). Additionally, Cruz and Spence (2005) stated that government funding is often not available for tribal communities since initiatives developed in the "Indian way" cannot be found in listings of model or best practices approved by the federal government. The "Indian Way" of valuing the "unseen world," which can reflect disharmony in the "seen world," is not counted in the framework of science. In other words, what is valued is what is observed and counted (Cruz & Spence, 2005). This continues to result in significant disparity in the implementation of prevention and treatment programs for communities that need them the most.

Despite the cultural differences in regard to evidence-based programs and best practices, there are some programming efforts with AI/AN families that have been evaluated for effectiveness. These programs, described next, may serve as a basis for further family life education programming.

In 2002, seven AI/AN Early Head Start programs embarked on a partnership with the Brazelton Touchpoints Center. The Touchpoints Center provided tools to achieve goals to engage parents, increase parent involvement, and improve the self-esteem of both parents and teachers. The Touchpoints faculty taught and modeled the skills of self-reflection in the service of building relationships. This work was described as being a process of "mutual discovery," as all members of the collaborative effort developed deeper and more trusting relationships. Caregivers at the program reflected on parents' experiences, the child's experience, and their own experiences. Journaling was used by some programs, and some programs used journal exchanges between parents and teachers in reflective supervision sessions. Another key element was the use of language describing the child's behavior. The teacher described the behavior in a neutral way and then listened to the parent. The conversation would then follow where the parent wanted it to go. Touchpoints has been instrumental in sharing child development information and engaging parents in meaningful relationships (EHSNRC @ ZERO TO THREE, n.d.).

Schools are also a site for family life education programs. In one Northern Plains reservation community, a study for *Circle of Life*, an HIV/AIDS prevention intervention for AI/AN adolescents, was conducted. The curriculum was developed in response to the significant disparities in sexual health outcomes of AI/AN youth. Compared to their white counterparts, AI/AN youth have two to four times the rate of STDs (Centers for Disease Control and Prevention, 2003). With a focus on skill-building and role-playing, the 30-hour HIV/AIDS and STD prevention and health education curriculum promoted the development of overall wellness of students (Kaufman et al., 2010).

Another example of successful school-based programming is *American Indian Life Skills Development Curriculum.* In this curriculum, key issues in Native American Indian adolescents' lives are addressed, such as communication, problem solving, depression, stress management, anger regulation, sexuality, grieving, and goal setting. This program was successfully implemented at Sequoya High School in Tahlequah, Oklahoma (LaFromboise, 1996).

To address the problem of intimate partner violence, in partnership with faculty from Sacred Circle and Mending the Sacred Hoop Technical Assistance Project, the Family Violence Prevention Fund (FVPF) worked with more than 100 Indian, tribal, and urban health care facilities as well as domestic violence advocacy programs across the United States to improve the health system response to domestic violence. With funding from the IHS and Administration for Children and Families (ACF), the IHS/ACF Domestic Violence Project has trained thousands of health care providers and community advocates, identified and empowered national experts, instituted sustainable domestic violence response programs in hospitals and clinics, developed model policies and tools to better address abuse and prevent violence, and dramatically increased screening for domestic violence since it began in 2002. *Building Domestic Violence Health Care Responses in Indian Country: A Promising Practices Report* explains how that work that can be replicated (Family Violence Prevention Fund [FVPF], 2010).

Tribal communities have a history of using holistic approaches to address problems (Wasserman, 2005). Grants from the Office for Victims of Crime, tribal victim assistance programs, and a variety of tribal child abuse response projects are demonstrating a unique and powerful merging of traditional values and practices with mainstream efforts such as the multidisciplinary team meetings to provide support to child victims and their families, to assist victims with the healing process, and to assure that the non-Native justice systems are accountable for the needs of victimized children. It is also noted that non-Indian members of the team are able to improve their skills in working with tribal members, and the needs of the children of the tribe are more often met when the tribe takes the lead in the multidisciplinary team or child protection team (Wasserman, 2005).

FUTURE DIRECTIONS

It is an exciting time as a growing body of work and resources emerge, which incorporate two worlds: the world of research in prevention and intervention and the world of specific tribal cultural values and traditions. These two worlds are being integrated through the TPR model (Fisher & Ball, 2002). TPR has been informed by a community-sensitive approach to scientific inquiry called participatory action research (PAR) (Brydon-Miller, 1997). Community members are involved in all phases of the research process in PAR (Greenwood, Whyte, & Harkavy, 1993), and indigenous values and beliefs are used to form the core of interventions and as outcome variables (Park, 1999). The focus of TPR and PAR is not so much a set of procedures to follow for gathering data as it is a philosophy and approach to collecting and using data. TPR/PAR lends itself to the establishment of positive collaborative researcher–community relationships. Most PAR sets out to explicitly study something in order to change and improve it, thereby building and strengthening communities. There are countless tiny cycles of participatory reflection on action, learning about action and then new informed action that is in turn the subject of further reflection. Change does not happen at "the end"—it happens throughout (Wadsworth, 1998). TPR has the potential to guide and improve family life education programming and practices with AI/AN families. This approach is reflective of the life AI/AN people experience of "walking between two worlds." Family life educators can play an important role in building and strengthening families and communities by embracing their traditions in an evolving world.

REFERENCES

Abbott, D. A., & Slater, G. (2000). Strengths and stresses of Omaha Indian families living on the reservation. *Great Plains Research, 10,* 145–168.

Allen, P. (1992). *The sacred hoop: Recovering the feminine in American Indian traditions.* Boston: Beacon Press.

Bergstrom, A., Cleary, L., & Peacock., T. (2003). *The seventh generation: Native youth speak about finding the good path.* Charleston, WV: ERIC Clearinghouse on Rural Education and Small Schools.

BigFoot, D. S. (2008). Cultural adaptations of evidence-based practices in American Indian and Alaska Native populations. In C. Newman, C. J. Liberton, K. Kutash, & R. M. Friedman (Eds.), *A system of care for children's mental health.* Tampa: University of South Florida, Louis de la Parte Florida Mental Health Institute.

Brendtro, L., Brokenleg, M., & Van Bockern, S. (1990). *Reclaiming youth at risk: Our hope for the future.* Bloomington, IN: National Education Service.

Brotherson, S. (2008). *Parent Education Programs Summary NDSU Extension Service—2008.* Fargo, ND: NDSU Extension Service.

Brydon-Miller, M. (1997). Participatory action research: Psychology and social change. *Journal of Social Issues, 53*(4), 657–666.

Campbell, D. T. (1987). Problems for the experimenting society in the interface between evaluation and service providers. In S. L. Kagan, D. Powell, B. Weissbourd, & E. Zigler (Eds.), *America's family support programs: Perspectives and prospects* (pp. 345–351). New Haven, CT: Yale University Press.

Centers for Disease Control and Prevention. (2003). *Sexually transmitted disease and surveillance, 2002.* Atlanta, GA: U.S. Department of Health and Human Services.

Contreras, D., & Silvey, L. (2010, November). *We should live well together: A program to improve co-parenting relationships within Native American families.* Paper presented at the 72nd Annual Meeting of the National Council of Family Relations, Minneapolis, MN.

Cross, T., Friesen, B., & Maher, N. (2007). Successful strategies for improving the lives of American Indian and Alaska Native youth and families. *Focal Point, 21*(2), 10–13.

Cruz, C. M., & Spence, J. (2005). *Oregon tribal evidence based and cultural best practices.* Retrieved from http://www.oregon.gov/OHA/mentalhealth/ebp/tribal-ebp-report.pdf?ga=t

Duncan, S., & Goddard, H. (2011). *Family life education: Principles and practices for effective outreach* (2nd ed.). Thousand Oaks, CA: Sage.

Early Head Start National Resource Center @ ZERO TO THREE. (n.d.). *Honoring Cultural Traditions: Early Head Start program in American Indian and Alaska Native Communities.* Technical Assistance Paper 12. Retrieved from http://www.ehsnrc.org/PDFfiles/TA12.pdf

Eunice Kennedy Shriver National Institute of Child Health and Human Development. (2010). *Sudden Infant Death Syndrome (SIDS): Healthy Native babies.* Washington, DC: U.S. Government Printing Office.

Family Violence Prevention Fund. (2010). *Building domestic violence health care responses in Indian country: A promising practices report.* Retrieved from http://www.endabuse.org/userfiles/file/HealthCare/Promising%20Practices%20Report%20-%20Online%20version.PDF

Fisher, P., & Ball, T. (2002). The Indian Family Wellness Project: An application of the Tribal Participatory Research model. *Prevention Science, 3*(3), 235–240.

Gilberg, J., Nevilles-Sorell, J., Olson, T., Rock, B., Sandman, B., Skye, B., et al. (2003). *Addressing domestic violence in Indian country: Introductory manual.* Retrieved from http://www.mshta.org/Resources/Addressing%20Violence%20in%20Indian%20Country.pdf

Godfrey, C. (2002). Working with Native American fathers, *Child Mental Health.* Head Start Bulletin #73. DHHS/ACF/ACYF/HSB. Retrieved from http://eclkc.ohs.acf.hhs.gov/hslc/resources/ECLKC_Bookstore/PDFs/A6E18B91317C94E72DD233C75C4DBD7D.pdf

Graham, B. L. (2001). Resilience among American Indian youth: First Nations' youth resilience study. *Dissertation Abstracts International,* The Sciences and Engineering, *62* (3-B).

Greenwood, D., Whyte, W., & Harkavy, I. (1993). Participatory action research as a process and as a goal. *Human Relations, 46*(2), 175–192.

Hildebrand, V., Phenice, L., Gray, M., & Hines, R. (2008). *Knowing and serving diverse families* (3rd ed.). Columbus, OH: Merrill.

John, R. (1998). Native American families. In C. H. Mindel, R.W. Habenstein, & R. Wright Jr. (Eds.), *Ethnic families in America: Patterns and variations* (pp. 382–421). Upper Saddle River, NJ: Prentice Hall.

Jones, G., & Moomaw, S. (2002). *Lessons from Turtle Island: Native curriculum in early childhood classrooms.* St. Paul, MN: Redleaf.

Kaufman, C., Mitchell, C., Beals, J., Desserich, J., Wheeler, C., Keane, E., et al. (2010). Circle of life: Rationale, design, and baseline results of an HIV prevention intervention among young American Indian adolescents of the Northern Plains. *Prevention Science, 11*(1), 101–112.

Krouse, S. A., & Howard, H. A. (Eds.). (2009). *Keeping the campfires going: Native women's activism in urban communities.* Lincoln: University of Nebraska Press.

LaFromboise, T. D. (1996). *American Indian life skills development curriculum.* Madison: University of Wisconsin Press.

LaFromboise, T. D. (2009). American Indian life skills: A community driven model for suicide prevention. *Paradigm, 14*(4), 9–11.

LaFromboise, T. D, Hoyt, D., Oliver, L., & Whitbeck, L. (2006). Family, community, and school influences on resilience among American Indian adolescents in the upper Midwest. *Journal of Community Psychology, 34*(2), 193–208.

Lewis, R. (1981). Patterns of strengths of American Indian families. In F. Hoffman (Ed.), *The American family: Strengths and stresses* (pp. 101–111). Isleta, NM: American Indian Social Research and Development Associates.

Lobo, S. (2009). Urban Clan Mothers. *Keeping the campfires going: Native women's activism in urban communities* (pp. 1–21). Lincoln: University of Nebraska Press.

Naybor, D. (2009). *Women of the land: Women's leadership and protection of indigenous land rights.* Retrieved from http://povertyconference2010.files.wordpress.com/2010/09/women-of-the-land-deb-diver.doc

O'Shea, J., & Ludwickson, J. (1992). *Archaeology and ethnohistory of the Omaha Indians.* Lincoln: University of Nebraska Press.

Park, P. (1999). People, knowledge, and change in participatory research. *Management Learning, 30*(2), 141–157.

Picou, J. (2000). The "Talking Circle" as sociological practice: Cultural transformation of chronic disaster impacts. *Sociological Practice, 2*(2), 77–97.

Powell, L., & Cassidy, D. (2000). *Family life education: An introduction.* Mountain View, CA: Mayfield.

Ramisetty-Mikler, S., Caetano, R., Goebert, D., & Nishimura, S. (2004). Ethnic variation in drinking, drug use, and sexual behavior among adolescents in Hawaii. *Journal of School Health, 74*(1), 16–22.

Ramisetty-Mikler, S., & Fernando, S. (2010, November). *Youth at-risk: The emerging Urban American Indian/Alaska Native children.* Paper presented at the 72nd Annual Meeting of the National Council of Family Relations, Minneapolis, MN.

Red Horse, J., Lewis, R., Feit, M., & Decker, J. (1978). Family behavior of urban American Indians. *Social Casework, 59,* 67–72.

Romero-Little, M. E. (2009). *Becoming Jemez: The early childhood of Jemez children*: A Photovoice Research Project between Jemez Pueblo and Arizona State University. Retrieved from http://ece.aed.org/publications/naian/Becoming_Jemez.pdf

Small, S. A., Cooney, S. M., & O'Connor, C. (2009). Evidence-informed program improvement: Using principles of effectiveness to enhance the quality and impact of family-based prevention programs. *Family Relations, 58,* 1–13.

Steinman, E. (2005). *Native Americans suffer from historical trauma.* Retrieved from http://www.speroforum.com/site/article.asp?idCategory=33&idsub=134&id=1755

Stiffman, A., Brown, E., Freedenthal, S., House, L., Ostmann, E., & Yu, M. (2007). American Indian youth: Personal, familial, and environmental strengths. *Journal of Child and Family Studies, 16*(3), 331–346.

Toland, J. (1976). *Adolf Hitler: The definitive biography* (Vol. II). New York: Doubleday.

U.S. Census Bureau. (2009). *2009 American Community Survey for the American Indian and Alaska Native alone or in combination with one or more races.* Retrieved from http://www.census.gov/newsroom/releases/archives/facts_for_features_special_editions/cb10ff22.html

U.S. Department of Education. (2011). White House Initiative on Tribal Colleges and Universities home page. Retrieved from http://www2.ed.gov/about/inits/list/whtc/edlite-index.html

U.S. Department of Health and Human Services. (2006). *Federal regulations governing the Head Start program.* Washington DC: U.S. Government.

U.S. Department of Housing and Urban Development. (2001). *Government-to-government tribal consultation policy.* Retrieved from www.hud.gov/offices/pih/ih/regs/govtogov_tcp.cfm

Wadsworth, Y. (1998). *What is participatory action research?* Retrieved from http://www.scu.edu.au/schools/gcm/ar/ari/p-ywadsworth98.html

Wasserman, E. (2005). *Understanding the effects of childhood trauma on brain development in Native children.* Retrieved from http://www.unified-solutions.org/uploads/understanding_the_effects_of_childhood_trauma.pdf

Weahkee, R. (2010, June). Message from the Director, Division of Behavioral Health. *Indian Health Service Headquarters Division of Behavioral Health Newsletter*, 1–12.

Willeto, A., & Goodluck, C. (2003). *Native American kids 2003: Indian children's well-being indicators data book for 14 states.* Retrieved from http://www.nicwa.org/policy/research/2005/WellBeing.pdf

Wyatt, J. (1978–1979). Native involvement in curriculum development: The native teacher as cultural broker. *Interchange, 9*(1), 17–28.

Zucker, R., Donovan, J., Masten, A., Mattson, M., & Moss, H. (2008). Early developmental processes and the continuity of risk for underage drinking and problem drinking. *Pediatrics, 121,* 252–272.

Chapter 8

Family Life Education With Latino Immigrant Families

PAUL L. SCHVANEVELDT, CFLE, AND ANDREW
O. BEHNKE, CFLE

Providing family life education services to Latino populations requires the educator to consider the diversity and variation found in the group. Educators must take the time to fully understand the dynamics involved and be prepared to set aside stereotypes and traditional ideas. Strategies that may work with other majority cultural groups may not be as effective with Latino populations (Bairstow, Berry, & Driscoll, 2002). There are many factors to consider, such as language, acculturation, generational status, socioeconomic status, and life history. There are also many stereotypes and prejudices regarding Latino populations that may impede effective teaching. Effective family life educators must have a deep appreciation and understanding of the many complexities found within Latino culture that allow for culturally competent services.

We, the authors of this chapter, are both bilingual and have a variety of experiences working with Latino immigrant populations from which we have drawn in writing this chapter.

I (Schvaneveldt) have developed, directed, and implemented a variety of family life education programs with Latino audiences. Latino families are also a focus of much of my university teaching and research, including a recent Fulbright to Ecuador that informed family life education program development in the United States.

I (Behnke) have developed numerous programs to serve Spanish-speaking audiences over the past 12 years in addition to applied research in issues related to Latino immigrant families. I also oversee a collaborative of researchers and Latino-serving professionals in the South.

DEFINING THE POPULATION

Hispanic is a term that was adopted by the U.S. government in the early 1970s to identify persons from Latin American origin. The term originally referred to persons from Mexican, Puerto Rican, Cuban, Central and South American, or Spanish cultures. The term *Hispanic* does not refer to a specific racial group (European, African, or Asian racial ancestry) but refers to a person with ties to Spain (Súarez-Orozco & Páez, 2002). Recently, the term *Hispanic* has been criticized as a label because it conjures connections to Spanish colonialism. Subsequently, the term *Latino* has emerged as an alternative name for individuals who have ties to Latin America and the Spanish language, and this term is used throughout the chapter (Martín Alcoff, 2005).

The Latino cultural group is the largest ethnic minority group in the United States (Súarez-Orozco & Páez, 2002). In 2010, the Latino population in the United States numbered over 50 million people and comprised 16% of the U.S. population (U.S. Census Bureau, 2010). It is projected that the U.S. Latino population will grow to 132 million by the year 2050 (U.S. Census Bureau, 2009). Most Latinos in the United States are native born (61.9%); among the remaining two fifths who are foreign born, most were born in Mexico (24.3%), with 5.5% born in Central America, 4.4% born in South America, and 3.9% born in countries in the Caribbean (e.g., Cuba, Dominican Republic) (U.S. Census Bureau, 2009). The principal country of origin for Latinos residing in the United States is Mexico (63%), Puerto Rico (9.2%), Cuba (3.5%), El Salvador (3.3%), the Dominican Republic (2.8%), and Guatemala (2.1%); all other Spanish-speaking Central and South American countries combined comprise 16.1% of the U.S. Latino population (U.S. Census Bureau, 2010). Thus, the Latino population in the United States has many cultural variations and includes many diverse traditions.

We share these brief statistics to demonstrate that when working with a specific population, family life educators must be careful to hold in check personal biases. When working with Latinos, it is often helpful to know where they are from originally or with what country they identify. Some families may have lived in the United States for many years but still identify with their country of origin (e.g., Los Guatemaltecos—families from Guatemala) or families from Mexico by their state in Mexico (Los Sinaloenses—families from Sinaloa). There are millions of people of Spanish descent who do not speak Spanish and millions of people who speak Spanish (Latinos) but are not of Spanish descent (e.g., indigenous groups). Further, the Latino population includes people of various nationalities, races, religious traditions, socioeconomic levels, cultures, and customs. Though the majority of families may initially be from Mexico, over 20 different countries associate themselves with being part of Latin America, and the diversity among these groups is multifaceted.

Other demographic characteristics to consider are that Latinos report a much younger average age (27) than Caucasian (41), African American (32), or Asian American (36) groups, reflecting both the high fertility rate among Latinos and the lack of older aged Latinos currently in the United States (U.S. Census Bureau, 2009). In fact, there are more children under the age of 5 among Latinos than any other age category (17.5%). By contrast, just 5% of the Caucasian population is under the age of 5. Similar to the larger U.S. population, the median age at first marriage is 27.5 for males and 25.9 for females. While both English and Spanish are spoken in the majority of Latino households, 20.1% speak English only at home as their primary language compared to over 94% of the Caucasian population. The differences are even more distinct when considering whether a person is foreign-born or native to the United States. Over 72% of foreign-born Latinos report they speak English less than very well compared to 12.7% of native-born Latinos (Pew Hispanic Center, 2011).

Unique Aspects of Latino Families

It is important for family life educators to understand the roles of education and income in defining Latino families. Educational attainment is important to consider in promoting family strengths and child well-being among Latino populations. Nearly 13% of Latinos have earned a college degree. School dropout rates among Latinos are very high, with nearly 40% quitting school before earning their high school degree. Educational challenges are even greater for foreign-born Latinos with 34.4% of foreign-born Latinos ages 25 and older reporting less than a ninth grade education and only 10.2% having earned a college degree (Pew Hispanic Center, 2011).

In terms of income, median household incomes in 2008 showed Latinos earn $38,000 a year as compared to $66,000 by Asians, $56,000 by whites, and $47,000 by blacks. Median personal earnings were also lower with an average of $24,442 for native-born and $20,368 for foreign-born Latinos. By contrast, Asian Americans earned $35,542, Caucasians earned $31,570, and African Americans $24,951 in median annual income (U.S. Census Bureau, 2009). It is very important to note that many of the "unique" characteristics often attributed to Latino populations are confounded with income and educational disparities. We argue that many of the challenges and "deficits" identified among Latinos are often incorrectly attributed to cultural deficits. Many of the challenges identified within the Latino family can be attributed directly to limited educational attainment and income disparities that impact the well-being of the adults and children in families. Family life educators should use caution to avoid the mistake of attributing challenges and deficits within families based upon cultural aspects of the Latino culture and instead should look at ways to enhance educational and income opportunities for the families they serve.

It is necessary to recognize the social and economic diversity within the Latino population and to note that not all Latinos occupy the lower strata of the social hierarchy. At the same time, on nearly every measure of socioeconomic status, Latinos lag behind national averages on socioeconomic indicators (Vidal de Haymes & Kitty, 2007). While the majority of Latinos are native-born U.S. citizens, most have at least one immigrant family member, often residing under the same roof, who may not be a U.S. citizen (Vidal de Haymes & Kitty, 2007). Complicating things on another level, Latino clientele are less likely to own their homes or have health insurance, which can be associated with family instability. Government estimates show that 48.9% of Hispanics owned homes, compared to 74.9% of the Caucasian population (Kochhlar, Gonzalez-Barrera, & Dockterman, 2009),

Education and income may also be related to level of acculturation, which comprises another unique aspect of Latino families of which family life educators should be aware. Phinney and Devich-Navarro (1997) described U.S. ethnic groups as fitting into four major categories of acculturation. *Assimilated* refers to individuals who have adopted the majority cultural values and retain little to no cultural traditions unique to their original culture. *Separated* refers to individuals who reject the majority culture and retain most if not all of their original cultural traditions. Separated individuals tend to have little direct contact with the majority culture and may not learn English or mainstream American norms and customs. *Marginalized* refers to individuals who struggle to identify with either their traditional culture or the majority culture. *Acculturated* refers to persons who have developed a balance between their traditional culture and the majority culture. The acculturated view illustrates that many Latinos attempt to achieve a balance of living in the United States by maintaining their traditional culture while adapting to function within the majority U.S. culture. Not all Latinos fall into the same status of acculturation. Many are assimilated, being part of the majority American culture for many generations. Others are separated and have little to no contact with the majority culture. Many may feel marginalized and have difficulty connecting to either the majority or their Latino culture.

Some argue that understanding a Latino family's level of acculturation or their level of bicultural orientation is a useful strategy for helping them (Hispanic Healthy Marriage Initiative [HHMI], n.d.-a). However, there are many Latino families who have made the goal to return to their country of origin and may be less motivated to acculturate into the majority culture. In addition, migrant workers may stay in the United States seasonally and are often less motivated to adapt to the majority culture.

Another point of view regarding acculturation is that integration and acculturation into the majority culture is segmented or disjointed (Parra Cardona,

Busby, & Wampler, 2004). Thus, individuals may be more acculturated or integrated in some areas of life, such as education and occupation, but less integrated in other areas such as preference of music, food, and language spoken at home. Most likely, the majority of Latino immigrants have segmented levels of acculturation that vary with exposure to and integration into their communities. It is important for family life educators to understand that the individuals and families they serve may often have differing levels of acculturation and thus one should customize their curriculum to meet the needs of their population.

Strengths and Assets of Latino Immigrant Families

There are many unique aspects of Latino families that can be considered strengths or assets, including *familismo, simpatia, personalismo, machismo* and *marianismo*, and religion. An understanding of these aspects of Latino families can help family life educators to build upon the unique strengths of Latino families.

Familismo

Collectivism and individualism are important cultural themes to consider in understanding Latino culture (Triandis, 2001). Collectivism is defined as interdependency among in-groups (family, tribe, nation, etc.). Group goals may take precedence over individual goals, and behavior is communally shaped (Triandis, 2001). On the other hand, individualism is focused more on individual goals taking precedence over group goals. Latino culture leans more toward a collectivist cultural orientation. The more normative approach in collectivist cultures emphasizes family responsibilities and interdependence to maintain family groups.

The collectivist orientation, which is common among Latino families, is referred to as familismo, or familism. Familismo refers to a strong emphasis and connection to family members as a whole and reflects a willingness to put the needs of family members before individual needs (Falicov, 2007). Family life educators should recognize that the Latino culture tends to emphasize parenting, family activities, and family obligations more than the just the couple dynamics (HHMI, n.d.-b).

Many Latinos live in extended family groups, and children typically live at home until they get married (Falicov, 2007). Family members often care for elderly members as well as children. The U.S. Census Bureau (2009) reports that of all the racial and ethnic groups in the United States, Latinos are *much* more likely than the others to be living in a family setting and are least likely to have a household composed of a single person.

Simpatia

Another important cultural consideration to recognize is simpatia, or politeness. This refers to the importance of pleasant and polite social interactions and the avoidance of direct conflict or disagreement (Falicov, 2007). The cultural value of simpatia and respeto may make their Spanish-speaking clients less likely to disagree openly in a group setting, especially when it comes to recent immigrants or first-generation families. Thus, some individuals may be reluctant to express their true feelings about a topic or something they have learned. Approaches that involve direct and open communication and conflict resolution techniques may be viewed as rude and aggressive. Children are often taught to be "buen educado" or well-mannered (Rodriguez, 1999). Thus, children are taught to be polite, deferent to adults, and well-mannered. Children may be reluctant to engage in direct inter-action with adults outside the family and will refrain from being loud or boisterous.

Personalismo

Personalismo refers to the personal space and closeness that is expressed by shaking hands, giving hugs, or touching as manifestations of appreciation and affection (HHMI, n.d.-a). Thus, family life educators should recognize the importance of being friendly, engaging, and personal. Acting in a formal, brusque, or disengaged way will most likely be viewed as cold and uninviting. One common tradition among many Latino cultural groups (but certainly not all) is the use of the *besito,* or little kiss, which is done when people touch cheek to cheek while make a "kiss" sound with their lips. This is a sign of admiration or *cariño.* It is important to note that this only occurs between a man and a woman or between two women but never between two men.

Machismo and Marianismo

Gender roles are also an important consideration when working with Latino families. Machismo refers to notion of males being the patriarchal figures in the family and the primary decision maker (Falicov, 2007). Machismo is often misunderstood to refer to dominance over women. Historically, machismo referred to the chivalrous notion of providing for and protecting family members. Contemporary views of "macho" conjure views of physical strength, sexual prowess, withholding emotions, tolerating pain, and being "man enough" to transcend challenges. It also relates to the strength and work ethic that is characterized by Latinos (HHMI, n.d.-a). A contemporary view of machismo refers to a male who is a hardworking provider and protector and does not allow challenges to impact his ability to do so.

Marianismo refers to women being sexually conservative and focused on her children and family. A traditional view of female gender roles emphasizes the health and well-being of children and family members as the primary responsibility of the mother. Marianismo is sometimes viewed as women lacking power and being submissive to men. Women may have great influence in their family, although it may be exercised indirectly. Equity among men and women may not be obvious to an outside observer but is often present among Latino couples. The man's influence lies on making decisions that are pleasing to the woman and a woman's influence is based on her desire to show commitment to her husband and family (Gil & Vazquez, 1996; HHMI, n.d.-a).

Religion

Religion is an important component of Latino culture (Garzon & Tan, 1992). According to a recent Pew Hispanic Center (2007) survey, 68% of Latinos are Catholic, 15% are born-again or evangelical Protestants, 5% are mainline Protestants, 3% are identified as "other Christian," and 8% are secular. Because the majority of Latinos are Catholic, it would serve any family life educator working with this population to have an understanding of Catholic theology and doctrine. It is also important to understand that the Roman Catholic Church in many Latin American countries has traditions and customs that are unique to Latin America but that are very influential to family functioning and decision making.

One example of how religiosity may impact family dynamics is divorce. Divorce rates among Latinos are approximately 30% lower than for the general U.S. population (National Healthy Marriage Resource Center, n.d.). Many Latinas may be less likely to leave their husbands because of religious influences. Religious beliefs, combined with cultural factors of familismo, may strongly affect decisions made by family members in family life education programming. "When seen in this light of cultural reinforcement combined with the Catholic prohibition against divorce, one may better understand why the Hispanic woman may remain with a severely abusive husband for an extraordinary amount of time" (Garzon & Tan, 1992, p. 384).

FAMILY LIFE EDUCATION PRACTICES

Current State of Family Life Education

The field of family life education among Latino populations is relatively young; however, educators in the United States have been working with Spanish-speaking families in many capacities for decades. Promotoras de salud, or community health workers, have been working with migrant and farmworker families in the United States for over 70 years starting in the 1940s with the influx of migrant labor that occurred with the Bracero Program (May & Contreras, 2007). This program employed more than 4 million Mexican farm laborers during the 1940s and 1950s. The braceros (meaning "manual laborers" but literally meaning "one who works with his arms") came to work the fields of this nation during a period of relatively "open borders" and helped to convert the agricultural fields of the United States into some of the most productive on the planet (Massey & Durand, 2005). Much can be learned from the work of promotoras, who have sought to meet the needs of Spanish-speaking populations in the United States (May & Contreras, 2007).

Current trends have moved family life education as a field to be more mindful of the need for culturally competent education and resource delivery. For example, the National Alliance for Hispanic Families (2011) has encouraged a focus on programs that provide culturally relevant and community-based services to Latino children and families. They also advocate for programs that address challenges within the Latino community that focus on promoting stronger families and teaching problem-solving skills, communication skills, and conflict management skills. We have observed a heightened awareness for culturally competent programming that has led to numerous new parent education and family life education programs specifically targeting Spanish-speaking audiences. Historically, many programs were simply translations of evidence-based programs that were created for English-speaking audiences. However, over the past decade, a number of programs have been either completely reworked to be effective with Latino immigrant audiences or created from scratch with Spanish speakers in mind. This trend toward cultural adaptations rather than simply translations of English programs has allowed family life educators to more effectively serve wider Spanish-speaking audiences. Such trends have also led to more bilingual/bicultural trainers and educators working in the field of family life education.

General Needs of this Population and Rationale for Family Life Education

Research conducted with promotoras and other Spanish-speaking professionals has demonstrated five key concerns among immigrant Latino families in the United States (Aguinago et al., 2001; Behnke, 2008). These five major concerns are:

1. *Navigation through the U.S. legal and social systems (health care, immigration, driver's licenses, schools, courts, etc.).* Knowledge about available services and communication with service providers are common difficulties for newly immigrated Latinos.

2. *Educational success for their children.* For many families, improved educational opportunities for their children was the top reason why they chose to immigrate to the United States. These families often report that they are worried about their children's academics, and many are at a loss on how to help their children succeed in school.

3. *Language barriers.* Many families seek effective English as a second language (ESL) classes that meet the needs and busy schedules they face. Such educational opportunities help improve communication between parents and youth, increase access to community resources, and improve job prospects.

4. *Transportation issues.* In most states, immigrant Latinos have difficulties obtaining a driver's license because of policies requiring specific documents that not all Latinos possess. This is also hampered by a lack of public transportation in most suburban and rural areas where new immigrants are moving.

5. *Financial support is another area in which families would like help.* One reason for this is that they are often the first to be let go in hard economic times, due to language or documentation status. Many families seek ways to better manage the economic needs of their families and educational opportunities to help them secure better employment. Many Latinos are not eligible to receive most public services, like food stamps, Medicaid, unemployment benefits, or other services typically offered to families facing unemployment (Cohen, 2009).

All of these factors point to opportunities for family life educators to intervene and have a significant impact in the lives of Latino families.

Marketing/Recruitment

Marketing to Latino audiences should begin with needs and asset assessments at community, county, and state levels. Asset assessments help family life educators to identify and utilize available community resources and discover how best to implement resources. Needs assessments involve using existing data about a community and data collected directly from members of that community to assess perceived needs (Batsche, Hernandez, & Montenegro, 1999). Through conducting asset and needs assessments, family life educators can maximize their resources to provide services that are in greatest need. For example, you may find that Spanish-speaking Peruvian women ages 20 to 35 have issues with feeling isolated and are experiencing higher levels of anxiety. Subsequently, a program can be created to directly meet the needs of this population.

According to Valdés (2002), it is essential to build a "share of mind" or consumer awareness about the services you provide. For example, when Latinos think of needing services or programs they should think of you or your agency among those they would think of first. To do this, test materials with target segments, advertise in Spanish, and build familiarity through Latino community organizations and churches. It is also very important to consider cultural sensitivity in delivering your educational product. According to the National Latino Alliance for the Elimination of Domestic Violence, lack of cultural sensitivity and knowledge among service providers about the cultural dynamics of the women and families they serve results in discrimination and exclusion from services, thereby alienating and revictimizing the very people they intend to assist and support. They further explain that services that are based on European American values and life experiences often act as a barrier to access even in the absence of direct exclusion of discrimination (Low & Organista, 2000).

Other useful strategies include the use of Spanish radio advertisements to publicize the family life education program. For example, a program in North Carolina has developed relationships with the local radio, TV stations, and Spanish media producers. Subsequently, media blitzes, including radio and TV public service announcements, are utilized to reach many families who otherwise would not be aware of the family life education services. In most states, there is now United Way 211 or information service to provide a phone listing of resources where community members can find out about programs. The majority of Latino families (77%) have mobile phones and text messaging, which is a useful method of contact (Nielsen Company, 2010).

The digital divide of a few years ago is narrowing quickly. Regular Internet use is almost as common among Latinos (64%) as it is in the general population (72%) (Livingston, 2010). Web-based and multimedia sources of information are growing in popularity among Latino users, though families with lower literacy are still less likely to seek out information online. Internet use is much more common among native-born and younger Latinos, so other methods of contact may be more effective with foreign-born and older populations.

According to the Nielsen Company (2010), 66% of Latinos watch some Spanish language TV, and 86% watch some English language TV. Overall, 47% spend some time each day on the Spanish language Internet, defined as using e-mail, watching video, or listening to music in Spanish. Sixty percent listen to Spanish language radio, while 73% listen to English language radio. Utilizing these types of media can be a very effective tool in recruiting, but providing advertising in both English and Spanish is most effective.

Motivating families to take advantage of family life education services can be challenging. There are two common approaches: "incentivizing" participation and required participation. Some effective incentives commonly used include (1) focusing on the children (e.g., children's talent nights, youth programs); (2) providing meals; (3) providing incentives (e.g., door prizes, raffles, gift cards); (4) providing

ESL classes using the topic you're teaching; and (5) providing music, fun, and new opportunities to learn and interact with other people. Many immigrant Latinos come to the United States with a hope that their children will have increased opportunities for educational and occupational success. Therefore, when reaching out to Latino immigrant families and designing programs to address their needs, family life educators would do well to focus first on the children rather than the parents. Placing emphasis on engaging children will often help you engage the whole family and get more dedicated participation. Successful family life education programs should be dynamic, active, and family-focused. It is helpful to appeal to mothers and children to recruit fathers and to reach out to fathers individually by asking them to do something related to the program.

Other families are asked to participate in family life education programs to help them out of difficult situations. Some of the programs that require participation include (1) court-referred programs, (2) programs required by a school or state government entity, and (3) additional services being dependent on program participation. Our experience has shown that programs that require or mandate participation can be more difficult at first to engage participants; however, over time effective family life educators who validate and support the participants often see their clients choosing to engage in the program and voluntarily offering their experiences and ideas.

To enhance the success of any program serving Latino families, collaboration among program providers and participants is essential (Behnke, 2008). The effectiveness of programming and services depends on effectively involving partners with other institutions serving Latino populations, such as local churches with largely Latino congregants. For example, the Creciendo Unidos organization in Phoenix, Arizona, has a significant partnership with a local Catholic church that facilitates recruiting and offers a physical environment to hold classes and meetings (Creciendo Unidos, 2010). Another way to get connected with such groups is by volunteering or serving on advisory committees for other organizations with similar missions serving Latino clientele. It is also possible that you may need to organize a community committee to coordinate and serve Latino needs.

In our experience, when recruiting Latinos, personal invitations through visits or phone calls are most effective. We find that this recruitment by "word of mouth" incorporates the notion of "personalismo" and is much more effective than just sending home flyers. Often the families we most want to reach are those who are most burdened economically and least likely to just show up. Thus face-to-face visits, where the educator takes time to get to know the needs of the families and makes accommodations to meet those needs will often work best. We have also found that making short presentations to religious groups, school groups, and other community organizations can build trust and lead to effective results. During these meetings, introduce your organization's mission and goals and how they will benefit families.

It is also helpful to have culturally appropriate food and music as a way to create a welcoming atmosphere.

Fostering warm and trusting relationships will go a long way in enhancing recruitment and retention in family life education programming. Utilizing Spanish language materials is also very important. Keep the information clear by using generic terms that are not country-specific, unless targeting such groups. To retain families in a multiweek program, it is best to involve the entire family (possibly providing child care) and provide meals and transportation if possible. Make reminder phone calls prior to each session. A useful strategy to increase father involvement is to use "stealth education" by marketing your services as an activity that you (i.e., the parent) are doing for your children (Mulloney, 2009). By making programs child-focused or family-focused, many of the stigmas and barriers to father involvement are likely to be eliminated. It is valuable to recruit Latinos as advocates, mentors, recruiters, and volunteers. Involve parents in committees and advisory councils by reaching out personally to them. Be mindful of the time it takes to build trust; this trust with a known agency is crucial in developing a rapport with Latino families. By developing personal connections with Latino community leaders and directors, family life educators will be welcomed and more effective in their activities. As you continue to build trust and relationships with your target audience, look for ways to involve participants in the planning as this develops a sense of connection and investment in the program.

Barriers to Participation

Child care, transportation, language issues, and legal resident status may be significant barriers to participation in programs. Because Latino families often bring their children with them to events, it is important to consider the ages of all of the children. There may be a large age range present—from infants to teenagers. Obviously, different types of care and entertainment may be needed. If parents anticipate that their children will enjoy the event, the family is more likely to attend (Olsen & Skogrand, 2009). Additionally, if children enjoy coming to the program, it is more likely the parents will continue coming.

When targeting low-income populations, transportation may be a significant problem for families (Fidalgo & Chapman-Novakofski, 2001). You can plan programs in convenient locations and near public transportation systems. However, being able to provide transportation could help reduce some barriers to participation.

Translating materials from English into Spanish must be done with caution, and consideration of cultural differences should be recognized. All Spanish is not the same. Be wary of using slang, and attempt to learn the idioms and other idiosyncrasies of the different dialects of the Spanish language. Know what is acceptable and unacceptable to avoid offending individuals. Keep in mind that the English language can differ significantly as well depending on what part of the United States you are in (e.g., New York City versus South Carolina). Careful consideration to the differences within the Spanish language can prevent information from getting "lost in translation."

There are an estimated 11.1 million unauthorized immigrants residing in the United States (Pascal & Cohn, 2010). Our experience is that many people lacking legal documentation to reside in the United States will avoid attending family life education activities out of fear of being reported to legal authorities. Creating trust and confidence with people is critical in overcoming this barrier. Some of the ethical issues related to this barrier are discussed in greater detail later in this chapter.

Environmental Considerations

Where and how to deliver family life education are important considerations in planning such activities. Holding family life education activities in places and environments that are familiar and comfortable to your audience is most effective. Such places may be a trusted agency setting, such as a Head Start or a school. Additionally, in-home visits tend to be very effective (Delgado Gaitan, 1994). Given the importance of trust and possible concerns over immigration status, it is critical that services be provided in a location where people will feel safe and comfortable. Relationships develop more quickly when introduced by an already respected community member or agency (Escott, Mincemoyer, Nauman, Rodgers, & Sigman-Grant, 1996). Two examples include marriage education being provided at a local Head Start agency. Participants in the class trust the local agency in that they have a connection with the Head Start through their children. Also, the location of the class is often convenient and located in the neighborhood where the participants live. Many family literacy programs take advantage of in-home visits and offer parenting education and family literacy mentoring. The entire family is able to participate in these visits, and participants feel safe and secure in their own home. Some other factors to consider include holding events at a house of worship or community center. For example, holding a class or workshop in a neighborhood that is not familiar to your audience will likely yield little involvement. It is important to consider locations where the entire family will feel welcome and safe.

Latino labor force participation rates are higher than other ethnic groups in the United States. Even while working more, Latino household income has actually dropped since 2000 (U.S. Census Bureau, 2009). Considering that work schedules for family members will vary, programs should be somewhat flexible. For example, in one community where we have worked, families often work evening shifts due to the factory in town and the best time for classes were Sunday afternoons. Evening and weekend times may be best for classes targeting working families; for others, like new moms or parent involvement classes, sometimes mornings are best.

Modes of Learning

Delgado Gaitan (1994) showed that using small groups and less formal means of teaching are most effective. Classes should be interactive with fun activities, role-plays, music, videos, use of personal history, culturally relevant materials, and humor. It is valuable to allow for multiple face-to-face meetings to establish rapport with families. Another effective mode for family life education includes using ESL classes as the basis to facilitate deeper "stealth education"—where the family life educator teaches English vocabulary while also teaching topics like relationship education, money management, or parenting. This ESL approach is a good way to attract eager learners, while at the same time providing resources and opportunities for growth and beginning to establish personal relationships with members of the community. Without addressing the language barrier, relationships, access, and partnerships will continue to be slow and scattered. With this in mind, family life educators need to understand what types of programs and services Spanish-speaking clientele want, and create programs or have their programs culturally adapted and translated to use with these underserved audiences.

In addition to language, there are communication patterns common among Latino cultures that are important to understand when working with this target audience. Commonly, respeto, or respect, is shown by listening when a person is talking and by following his or her advice. Respect is shown for authority and to the elderly. Affection is used commonly. A hug, kiss on the cheek, or tap on the shoulder is usual. Individuals may not give you a direct or straight answer at times and tend to elaborate a lot in responses to questions. Given the cultural emphasis on being respectful, it is common to avoid confrontation and some find it hard to say "no." Understanding these cultural dynamics can shape the way family life education is presented to your audience.

Educator Characteristics

A challenge in providing effective family life education services is to identify bilingual/bicultural staff with the necessary experience to effectively provide family life education services (Uttal, 2006). When working with older or first-generation immigrants, educators may need to deliver their programs in Spanish and tailor them to slightly more traditional views on family and gender roles. Spanish-language educators must be willing to open themselves up to families and really give families the time and attention they need to build rapport and create a bond of trust. Often times Latino audiences may prefer certain educator characteristics. Lopez, Lopez, and Fong (1991) found that there was a preference for an ethnically similar counselor over an ethnically dissimilar counselor but that other characteristics such as individuals who were older and who had higher levels of education were preferred over ethnicity. This information is useful in placing staff within programs. Educators can do some preliminary research to determine what a specific group (25- to 30-year-old Cuban males, for example) look for and give credibility to in an educator.

In some communities, it may seem difficult to find qualified bilingual/bicultural educators. One strategy to bridge this leadership gap is to start "fishing schools" or "escuelas de pesca." Rather than simply teaching one parent how to fish, as the old saying goes, this approach helps parents become leaders and share with other groups of parents who in turn train and work with others. We find it easier to help Spanish speakers gain the necessary skills to be effective family life educators rather than teaching monolingual educators to speak Spanish. During the course of a Spanish language class or workshop, you might notice individuals who are very engaged in the topics. These individuals often make the best trainers/educators via "shadowing" or mentoring with another qualified family life educator. Many times Spanish-speaking individuals were just not aware of the monetary and social value of their skills to help their community. In our experience, hiring the right person or people is the most important and essential part of assuring program success with Spanish-speaking audiences.

An educator working with diverse populations should take time to self-reflect. In doing so, he or she can identify personal values and possibly biases. Knowing one's own degree of acculturation may help to identify with the targeted audience as well. "Culturally competent service providers need to understand their own level of acculturation and the extent to which they subscribe to traditional versus modern-Western values and behaviors" (Organista & Dwyer, 1996, p. 127).

Ethical Considerations

A major ethical issue to consider when providing family life education services to Latino populations is the possibility that some participants will lack legal documentation to reside in the United States. There are an estimated 11.1 million unauthorized immigrants residing in the United States (Pascal & Cohn, 2010). Reporting of undocumented immigrant status has been a major political and legal issue in the United States. Laws vary by state and local jurisdictions, which may or may not require the reporting of undocumented immigrants. In many cases, family life educators are not required to ask about documentation status and thus may not be required to report to local authorities regarding the potential immigrant status of a program participant. However, depending on funding and local policies, in some areas reporting may be required. Family life educators should carefully investigate guidelines regarding this matter as they plan and implement programming. Working out these details beforehand can help educators to avoid the possible implications and build trust in the agency providing services. If there is a perception among participants that program administrators will be reporting immigrant status to authorities, recruitment and retention to programs will be impacted.

Most children of unauthorized immigrants (73%) are U.S. citizens by birth as stipulated by the 14th Amendment of the U.S. Constitution. The number of children born in the United States in mixed-status families (unauthorized immigrant parents and citizen children) has expanded to 4 million children in 2008, up from 2.7 million in 2003 (Pascal & Cohn, 2010). As U.S. citizens, children from mixed-status families qualify for and are entitled to all programs and services provided to a U.S. citizen, which may include family life education services. Quite often, children are brought to the United States by their parents as legal minors and thus have little to no influence on their immigrant status. Subsequently, they may lack the legal documentation to attend some colleges and universities, enlist in the U.S. military, or perform other activities requiring legal resident status. In response to this issue, the Development, Relief, and Education of Alien Minors Act (i.e., DREAM Act) has been debated in the U.S. Congress. The purpose of the DREAM Act was to help those individuals who meet certain requirements to have an opportunity to enlist in the military or go to college and have a path to citizenship, which they otherwise would not have without this legislation. In order to qualify for this legislation, the child would have to have entered the United States before the age of 16, lived in the United States for 5 consecutive years, graduated from a U.S. high school, been accepted into a U.S. institution of higher education, and be of "good" moral character (DREAMActInfo, n.d.). While this legislation did not pass Congress at the time of publication of this article, it illustrates the ethical issues many mixed-status families and children face.

Best Practices in Family Life Education Programming

In the following section, we introduce a few successful programs used with Latino families. The FLAME family literacy program, serving Latino families in Chicago, based their program on the central role the family plays within the Latino culture. This cultural strength of close family relationships was used as a basis to increase daily parent–child literacy activities and reduce punitive parenting practices (Saracho, 2007). A key component of the success of this program is the focus on fostering a supportive home environment by regular home visits to mentor parents so they can provide children with literacy opportunities, act as literacy models for their children, and improve their relationships with their children's schools. Parents learn to select appropriate books and magazines for their children and how to use a library. Results show that parents do have a positive effect on their children's learning. Parents who are confident and successful learners are the most effective teachers of their children. Literacy is the subject most likely to be influenced by the social and cultural contexts of family.

A program serving the parents of Head Start children in Ogden, Utah, follows a similar model but focuses more on younger children and fostering healthy family dynamics (Schvaneveldt, 2008). The Weber State University Family Literacy Program serves primarily lower-income Latino families who have a child enrolled in Head Start. Trained family literacy facilitators who are fluent in Spanish and part of the Latino culture make frequent in-home visits to parents. An individualized educational approach is used that addresses the individual needs of each family. The trained family literacy facilitators first identify the current level of parental involvement in literacy activities and family interaction styles. Individualized lesson plans are then modified to meet the needs of the families. An in-home visit is made with the families approximately every 3 weeks to share information, model literacy involvement, create goals, and reinforce information. Major improvements are identified in the parents' daily literacy activities with their children, such as engaging with children in dialogic reading strategies, story telling, rhyming activities, letter and word identification, and many other literacy activities. Correspondingly, significant improvements are identified in the child's literacy activities, including reading a story with a parent and independent reading. Parenting behaviors are also positively impacted in the establishment of routines, contributing to family work, appropriate discipline, and most importantly creating a special time for reading each day (Schvaneveldt, 2008).

The Juntos Para Una Mejor Educación (Together for a Better Education) Program is a family program that brings together 8th through 12th grade youth, their parents, college-age mentors, and school staff to gain the knowledge and skills needed to help youth stay in school and bridge the gap from high school to college (Behnke & Kelly, 2011). This experiential program is taught in Spanish and meets for 2.5 hours once a week for 6 weeks in the evenings. Juntos also uses success coaches and college-age mentors to provide weekly afterschool clubs and activities with the target students before and after the 6-week program. The program brings together partners from Cooperative Extension, high schools and local community colleges, and college-age mentors to help youth acquire the skills to succeed in high school, to discover the benefits of higher education, and to attain a college education. A focus is on helping Latino families and community members come together as a support group to help each other realize their desires to get a higher education. The program has been carried out in 30 locations throughout the United States and program evaluation has shown a promising impact on the lives of Latino youth (Behnke & Kelly, 2011).

Similarly, a number of parenting education curricula have been designed and/ or culturally adapted for Latino audiences. One well-known program is the Los Niños Bien Educados (LNBE) curriculum (Center for Improvement of Child Caring [CICC], n.d.). This 12-week parenting education curriculum was developed for parents of 2- to 12-year-olds and has been culturally adapted to address issues of acculturation, language, childrearing customs and traditions, parenting roles, effective discipline, preventing abuse, and parenting involvement. Assessment of this program has found it to be culturally relevant and effective in promoting healthier and more positive parenting practices among Latino populations (CICC, n.d.). Other great parent education programs that have been culturally adapted for use with Spanish-speaking audiences include Parents as Teachers, The Incredible Years, Crianza con Cariño (Nurturing Parenting), Circulo de Padres (Circle of Parents) Program, and Parenting Wisely.

The Administration for Children and Families arm of the U.S. Department of Health and Human Services (DHHS) initiated the Hispanic Healthy Marriage Initiative (HHMI) in 2005 (HHMI, n.d.-b). The purpose of the HHMI is to provide culturally competent marriage and relationship education materials with the goal of improving child well-being through creating a healthier couple and family system. A major challenge for those providing marriage and relationship education services is finding culturally competent marriage education materials. In response to this challenge, the HHMI has produced a supplemental marriage education curriculum. The curriculum is not a comprehensive program but is designed to be used as a supplement to help facilitators and couples explore unique characteristics of the Hispanic culture on marriage and relationships. Topics include gender roles, acculturation and biculturalism, and communication with a Latino cultural focus (HHMI, n.d.-b).

An effective and culturally competent sexuality education program is ¡Cuídate!, a Latino youth health promotion program (Villarruel, Jemmott, & Jemmott, 2006). The goal of this program is to reduce HIV risk by teaching young people about STDs and choices. The program emphasizes the influence of family and gender role expectations on sexual behaviors. The course is taught by bilingual facilitators and teaches both abstinence and condom use as culturally acceptable. An evaluation of this program shows a reduction in the frequency of sexual intercourse, a reduced number of sexual partners, increased condom use, and a reduction in the incidence of unprotected sex (Villarruel et al., 2006).

Creciendo Unidos (growing together) provides family life education to a large Latino community. The mission of Creciendo Unidos is to build strong communities by empowering people to care for each other, develop leaders, and take responsibility for creating a healthy community that is worthy of their children. This vision is met by focusing on the family unit (Creciendo Unidos, 2010) and by providing family life education to the Latino community through a wide range of workshops, classes, and other learning activities. Programs are presented at a neighborhood Catholic school and church, and all materials are presented in Spanish. The program relies heavily on community volunteers for recruitment and operating the program. All presenters and facilitators are Latino and fluent in Spanish. Family life education programs, specifically designed to be culturally sensitive, include marriage education, family relationships, teens, foster care and adoption education, and men's groups. Program organizers are careful to clarify that the information presented in the programs is not therapy but instead is family life education. Each year, the Creciendo Unidos program serves thousands of Latino families in the Phoenix area.

A specific program offered by Creciendo Unidos is the Family Program (Todo es Posible), designed to help families develop close relationships (Creciendo Unidos, 2010). The program consists of three workshops and is followed by 18 weekly meetings, including community service projects and recreational activities. The training course requires a family commitment of 2 hours per week throughout the entire course. Topics focus on training parents to communicate and build relationships with their children. They also learn to strengthen their marital relationships. Adolescents learn to understand and improve relationships with their parents and siblings and also learn to practice the concept of responsibility. Younger children learn how to resist peer pressures.

Another program offered by Creciendo Unidos focuses on teens (Sin Límites) and attempts to strengthen cultural values, foster leadership skills, and to create positive future-oriented behaviors. The curriculum includes recreational, educational, and competitive activities. A marriage class (Curso De Relaciones Exitosas) attempts to help couples achieve healthier relationships. The course is a 16-hour retreat where participants learn about respect, love, unity, identity, and communication. Other topics include cultural integration, understanding generational gaps, communication, and leadership.

Finally, the FACE course focuses on foster care and adoption issues in families. The course was designed to address barriers that have typically prevented Hispanic families from embracing adoption and foster care. Families learn how to bring adoption and foster care issues to the forefront of the Latino community's consciousness by establishing partnerships with churches, schools, and other community resources (Creciendo Unidos, 2010).

FUTURE DIRECTIONS

Family life education with Latino populations is likely to include the continued development of programs from within the culture as opposed to simply using programs created for the majority culture. For example, a popular marriage education curriculum has simply been translated into Spanish from English as opposed to developing a marriage education curriculum specifically developed with a Latino cultural perspective. Though this approach attempts to serve this important audience, it may miss the mark in terms of actually meeting these families' needs. As we have said, the National Alliance for Hispanic Families (2011) encourages programming to be culturally relevant and community-based.

Another future direction will be greater recognition of the diversity within the Latino culture. For example, individuals from Mexico have unique cultural traditions and histories than do, for example, individuals from Puerto Rico or Ecuador. Also, there exists great diversity of educational experiences and income levels within the different Latino populations. Subsequently, family life educators need to recognize that not all Latino populations are homogeneous and that programming should be tailored to the cultural and social class characteristics of the population being served. Tailoring educational programs for differing populations and subpopulations will continue to be an area of growth. Indeed, increased training will be required for native speakers from diverse backgrounds to help them in gaining the skills and training to be effective family life educators. This will also require an expansion of research exploring cultural traditions from within the country of origin and then an examination of the acculturation processes impacting Latino families and their well-being.

Finally, there is a great need for the evaluation of effective programming and an analysis of the cost versus benefit of such programs in promoting healthy family dynamics and youth development. Specifically, family life educators need to identify which programs and practices are most effective in promoting strong and resilient families and youth. An analysis of the benefits and long-term savings of such programs relative to the initial costs is needed. For example, is the cost of providing for marital education programming recouped with subsequent savings in lowered divorced rates and the prevention of other family problems? Such cost-benefit analyses are essential in providing evidence to policy makers and agencies that provide funding for family life education services.

REFERENCES

Aguinago, A., Aragon, S., Bellmar, C., Chabo, J., Conrad, E., Diaz, J., et al. (2001). *Hispanic needs assessment field study.* Retrieved from http://www.sph.sc.edu/cli/documents/Hispanic%20Needs%20Assessment%20Field%20Study-DMSB_june01.pdf

Bairstow, R., Berry, H., & Driscoll, D. (2002). Tips for teaching non-traditional audiences. *Journal of Extension, 40*(2). Retrieved from http://www.joe.org/joe/2002december/tt1.shtml

Batsche, C., Hernandez, M., & Montenegro, M. (1999). Community needs assessment with Hispanic, Spanish-monolingual residents. *Evaluation and Program Planning, 22,* 13–20.

Behnke, A. (2008). Expanding the Latino market niche: Developing capacity and meeting critical needs. *Journal of Extension, 46*(5). Retrieved from http://www.joe.org/joe/2008october/rb5.shtml

Behnke, A., & Kelly, C. (2011). Creating programs to help Latino youth thrive at school: The influence of Latino parent involvement programs. *Journal of Extension, 49*(1). Retrieved from http://www.joe.org/joe/2011february/a7.php

Center for Improvement of Child Caring (n.d.). *CICC's Los Niños Bien Educados Program.* Retrieved from http://www.ciccparenting.org/LosNinosBienEdDesc.aspx#3

Cohen, M. (2009). Commentary: Undocumented women: Pushed from poverty and conflict, pulled into unjust disparity. *Journal of Public Health Policy, 30,* 423–426.

Creciendo Unidos. (2010). *Creciendo Unidos program overview.* Retrieved from http://www.creciendounidosaz.org/New_main.php

Delgado Gaitan, C. (1994). *Involving Latino families in schools: Raising student achievement through home-school partnerships.* Thousand Oaks, CA: Sage.

DREAMActinfo. (n.d.). *The DREAM Act.* Retrieved from http://dreamact.info

Escott, R., Mincemoyer, C., Nauman, D., Rodgers, M., & Sigman-Grant, M. (1996). Developing skills and expertise to program in Latino communities using satellite technology. *Journal of Extension, 34*(5). Retrieved from http://www.joe.org/joe/1996october/tt2.php

Falicov, C. (2007). Working with transnational immigrants: Expanding meanings of family, community, and culture. *Family Process, 46*(2), 157–171.

Fidalgo, G., & Chapman-Novakofski, K. (2001). Teaching nutrition to Hispanics at an English as a second language (ESL) center: Overcoming barriers. *Journal of Extension, 39*(6). Retrieved from www.joe.org/joe/2001december/a3.html

Garzon, F., & Tan, S. (1992). Counseling Hispanics: Cross-cultural and Christian perspectives. *Journal of Psychology and Christianity, 11*(4), 378–390.

Gil, R., & Vazquez, C. (1996). *The Maria paradox: How Latinas can merge old world traditions with new world self-esteem.* New York: Perigee Books.

Hispanic Healthy Marriage Initiative (n.d.-a). *Cultural adaptation and relationship dynamics.* Retrieved from http://www.acf.hhs.gov/healthymarriage/pdf/Cultural_Adaptation.pdf

Hispanic Healthy Marriage Initiative. (n.d.-b). *Curricula for Hispanics/Latinos.* Retrieved from http://www.healthymarriageinfo.org/marriage-curricula/curricula-for-hispanics-/-latinos1

Kochhlar, R., Gonzalez-Barrera, A., & Dockterman, D. (2009). *Through boom and bust: Minorities, immigrants, and home ownership.* Washington, DC: Pew Hispanic Research Center. Retrieved from http://pewhispanic.org/files/reports/109.pdf

Livingston, G. (2010). *The Latino digital divide: The native born versus the foreign born.* Retrieved from http://pewhispanic.org/reports/report.php?ReportID=123

Lopez, S., Lopez, A., & Fong, K. (1991). Mexican Americans' initial preferences for counselors: The role of ethnic factors. *Journal of Counseling Psychology, 38*(4), 487–496.

Low, G., & Organista, K. (2000). Latinas and sexual assault: Towards culturally sensitive assessment and intervention. *Journal of Multicultural Social Work, 8*(1/2), 131–157.

Martín Alcoff, L. (2005). Latino vs. Hispanic: The politics of ethnic names. *Philosophy & Social Criticism, 35,* 395–407.

Massey, D., & Durand, J. (2005). *Crossing the border: Research from the Mexican Migration Project.* New York: Russell Sage Foundation.

May, M., & Contreras, R. (2007). Promotor(a)s, the organizations in which they work and an emerging paradox: How organizational structure impacts promotor(a)s' work. *Health Policy, 82,* 153–166.

Mulloney, M. (2009, March). Stealth education. *Rensselaer Alumni Magazine, 11*(1). Retrieved from http://www.rpi.edu/magazine/march2009/stealth_education.html

National Alliance for Hispanic Families. (2011). Retrieved from http://www.hispanicfamily.org/

National Healthy Marriage Resource Center. (n.d.). *Hispanics and Latinos*. Retrieved from http://www.healthymarriageinfo.org/marriage-and-culture/hispanics-and-latinos#Hispanic%20 Marriage

Nielsen Company. (2010). *A snapshot of Hispanic media usage in the U.S.* Retrieved from http://www.nielsen.com/us/en/insights/reports-downloads/2010/snapshot-of-hispanic-media-usage-in-us.html

Olsen, C., & Skogrand, L. (2009). Cultural implications and guidelines for extension and family life programming with Latino/Hispanic audiences. *Forum for Family and Consumer Issues, 14*(1). Retrieved from http://www.ncsu.edu/ffci/publications/2009/v14-n1-2009-spring/olsen-skogrand.php

Organista, K., & Dwyer, E. (1996). Clinical case management and cognitive-behavioral therapy: Integrated psychosocial services for depressed Latino primary care patients. In P. Manoleas (Ed.), *The cross-cultural practice of clinical case management in mental health. Haworth social work practice* (pp. 119–143). New York: Haworth Press.

Parra Cardona, J., Busby, D., & Wampler, R. (2004). No soy de aqui ni soy de alla: Transgenerational cultural identity. *Journal of Hispanic Higher Education, 3,* 322–327.

Pascal, J., & Cohn, D. (2010). *U.S. unauthorized immigration flows are down sharply since mid-decade.* Washington, DC: Pew Hispanic Research Center. Retrieved from http://pewhispanic.org/files/reports/126.pdf

Pew Hispanic Center. (2007). *Changing faiths: Latinos and the transformation of American religion.* Washington, DC: Author. Retrieved from http://pewhispanic.org/files/reports/75.pdf

Pew Hispanic Center. (2011). *Statistical portrait of the foreign born population in the United States, 2008.* Washington, DC: Author. Retrieved from http://pewhispanic.org/factsheets/factsheet.php?FactsheetID=59

Phinney, J., & Devich-Navarro, M. (1997). Variation in bicultural identification among African American and Mexican American adolescents. *Journal of Research on Adolescence, 7,* 3–32.

Rodriguez, G. (1999). *Raising nuestros niños: Bringing up Latino children in a bicultural world.* New York: Fireside.

Saracho, O. (2007). Hispanic families as facilitators of their children's literacy development. *Journal of Hispanic Higher Education, 6*(2), 103–117.

Schvaneveldt, P. (2008, April). *Findings from Weber State University Family Literacy Project.* Paper presented at the Utah Governor's Early Childhood Summit, Capitol Building, Salt Lake City.

Suárez-Orozco, M., & Páez, M. (2002). *Latinos remaking America.* Berkeley: University of California Press.

Triandis, H. (2001). Individualism-Collectivism and personality. *Journal of Personality, 69,* 907–924.

U.S. Census Bureau. (2009). *U.S. Census Bureau 2005–2009 American Community Survey.* Washington, DC: Author. Retrieved from http://factfinder.census.gov/servlet/DTTable?_bm=y&-geo_id=01000US&-ds_name=ACS_2009_5YR_G00_&-mt_name=ACS_2009_5YR_G2000_B03001

U.S. Census Bureau (2010). The Hispanic population: 2010: 2010 Census Briefs. Washington, DC: Author. Retrieved from http://www.census.gov/prod/cen2010/briefs/c2010br-04.pdf

Uttal, L. (2006). Organizational cultural competency: Shifting programs for Latino immigrants from a client-centered to a community-based orientation. *American Journal of Community Psychology, 38,* 251–262.

Valdés, M. (2002). *Marketing to American Latinos: A guide to an in-culture approach.* New York: Paramount Market.

Vidal de Haymes, M., & Kitty, K. (2007). Latino population, growth, characteristics, and settlement trends: Implications for social work education in a dynamic political climate. *Journal of Social Work Education, 43*(1), 101–116.

Villarruel, A., Jemmott, J., & Jemmott, L. (2006). A randomized controlled trial testing an HIV prevention intervention for Latino youth. *Archives of Pediatrics & Adolescent Medicine, 160,* 772–777.

Chapter 9

Family Life Education With Asian Immigrant Families

Shann Hwa (Abraham) Hwang, CFLE

As the author of this chapter, I draw on my varied experiences in both research and family life education with the Asian immigration population. However, the more I study and interact with Asian immigrant families, the more I feel excited, fascinated, and surprised like a young jeweler examining diamonds. Each one shines differently from the others and has so much to offer. The moment I feel confident in what I know about Asian immigrant families, new research findings accumulated across disciplines and new insights given by Asian participants in family life education programs have shed additional light on these "diamonds" that fascinate me both personally and professionally. This chapter will not capture every facet of ethnic and cultural richness found among Asian immigrant families but rather will present important elements and relevant tools for family life educators when working with these families.

DEFINING THE POPULATION

The term *Asian immigrant families* refers to the collective group of Asian families who left their home countries and currently reside in America. Almost 70% of the total Asian American population is foreign born (Min, 2006). The number of foreign-born Asian Americans increased from 5 million in 1990 to 7.2 million in 2000 (U.S. Census Bureau, 2002). The U.S. Census Bureau (2010) reported that the five largest Asian immigrant groups, exceeding 1 million or more, are Chinese, Asian Indian, Filipino, Vietnamese, and, Korean, respectively. To set a consistent tone, Asian immigrant families, the target population of this chapter, are those who migrated to America after the Immigration and Nationality Act of 1965, which was the most liberal immigration law passed to date. Prior to this law, only a comparably small number of Asian immigrant families resided in America. Roughly 151,000 immigrants from five Asian countries (China, India, Japan, Korea, and the Philippines) were legally admitted to the United States between 1941 and 1964, and most of them were women (Min, 2006).

Unique Aspects of Asian Immigrant Families

Immigration experience, age distribution, education, employment, and family structure and values are unique aspects of Asian immigrant families that will be discussed in this section. A knowledge of these characteristics can help family life educators understand this population and thereby improve programming efforts.

Immigration Experience

A large group of Koreans from South Korea initiated their migration to the United States after the Korean War (1950–1953). A small number of them came as war brides, whereas the majority of South Koreans left unstable political and economic circumstances in their home country to secure a better life (Kitano & Daniels, 2001).

The Vietnam War (1955–1975), an example of the push and pull model of migration, forced many Southeast Asians, comprised of Vietnamese, Laotians, Hmong, and Cambodians, to leave their home countries (Kitano & Daniels, 2001). After 1975, a massive number of people from Southeast Asia fled to the United States. According to the 1990 U.S. Census, over 1 million Southeast Asians resided in various regions of the United States (Fong, 2008).

In June of 1989, the Chinese government attacked students during the students' democratic movement in Tiananmen Square, which led President George H. W. Bush to issue the Chinese Student Protection Act. At that time, roughly 48,000 Chinese foreign students and visiting scholars in the United States changed their status to permanent residents (Min, 2006).

The presence of political turmoil and challenging migration experience in conjunction with the absence of human and financial capitals during their initial stay in America made these Asian immigrants vulnerable. The ability to overcome numerous obstacles in the United States cannot be limited to these Asian Americans. Ironically, the immigrants previously mentioned would initially experience language barriers since English was not the spoken language in their countries (Kim, Lau, & Chang, 2006). Language barriers have a great potential to make their acculturation a long, challenging process that further impedes individual and family functioning. Given the trauma experienced by these groups of Asian immigrants in regard to government officials and public policies in their home countries, Asian immigrant families with war-related hardship tend to have marked difficulties in trusting government officials and maintain a hesitating attitude toward public policies (Kitano & Daniels, 2001).

From a different perspective, since 1965, many came to this country voluntarily as students who later sponsored other family members, particularly their parents (Treas, 2009). These foreign-born parents typically perform multiple tasks around the house for their grown children, such as cleaning, cooking, watching young children, instilling family values and traditions, and teaching ethnic language. Furthermore, other Asian immigrant families came as refugees due to political upheaval and dangerous living conditions in their home countries. Each immigrant family has intentionally or unintentionally brought with them collective values, traditions, and practices, which are an integral part of them. As a result, differing conditions of immigration and available resources separated Asian immigrant families when attempting to acculturate in the United States (Clark, Glick, & Bures, 2009), which widely emphasize individual autonomy and independence. Guion, Chattaraj, and Lytle (2004) pointed out that an individual's level of ethnic identity may associate with the variations found in individuals in the same ethnic group. Given the diverse background and migration experiences of Asian immigrants to the United States, family life educators are strongly encouraged to pay special attention to relevant historical, social, and cultural background along with empirical findings to understand within and between group differences while working with these families.

It is also suggested that Asian immigrant families are the second-fastest growing racial group, followed by Latino Americans, in the United States (Coles, 2006). Spanish language and the Catholic religion mark two commonalities for Latino ethnic groups in the United States (Min, 2006), whereas no common language and religion can be found among Asian ethnic groups. Variations within Asian population are evident. For examples, there are at least 32 different primary languages spoken among Asian immigrant families (Lee & Mock, 2005). Furthermore, there are many more dialects identified within each group (i.e., Chinese Americans).

Over half of Asian Americans resided in the West (51%), 19% lived in the South, 11% in the Midwest, and 19% in the Northeast in 2000 (Reeves & Bennett, 2003). Nearly 45% of foreign-born Asians lived in three metropolitan areas: (1) Los Angeles, (2) New York City, and (3) San Francisco. In fact, many new Asian immigrants—particularly ones with low acculturation desire, high language barriers, or limited available resources—may choose to reside in close proximity to their own ethnic group to seek social support when in need. This type of residential preference may provide tangible network opportunities or close family ties.

Age Distribution

In 2010, the median age of Asian Americans was 35.3 years, which was 1.5 years younger than the national median age of all Americans. Particular attention should be paid to Hmong, which was the youngest group with a median age of 16.3 years whereas Japanese was the oldest group with a median age of 42.4 years. Age can affect one's migration experience. Migrating from home countries to reside in the United States not only temporarily discontinues individual development in a familiar social context but also introduces added stress and changes to both the individual and the entire family to function in new social roles that are unfamiliar and challenging to them (Fong, 2008).

Education

Approximately 85% of all Asian Americans age 25 and over possessed at least a high school education (U.S. Census Bureau, 2011). In particular, 91% of Japanese had at least a high school education in 2000 (Reeves & Bennett, 2004). Additionally, 50% of all Asians, age 25 and over, had a bachelor's degree or higher compared to 28% for all adults in the United States. Furthermore, 20% of all Asians age 25 and over had an advanced degree (e.g., master's, PhD, MD, or JD) compared to 10% of the total population.

Attainment of a good education plays a significant part in Asian family life. Most Asian parents believe that academic success can be achieved through continuous hard work and determination in a good learning environment (Qin, 2008). Furthermore, many Asian parents associate children's academic success with their own child-rearing achievement. As a result, high expectations and pressure are intentionally added to their children to excel at school, which creates tension in parent–child relations. This all comes down to a common belief: One family member's success becomes the honor of the whole family (Lee & Mock, 2005).

Employment

Approximately 49% of Asian Americans hold managerial, professional, or related occupations. Interestingly enough, the general public widely holds the idea of Asians as the "model minority" (Fong, 2008), partly due to the perception of a high household income. This idea may be true for some but not for all. Reeves and Bennett (2004) stated that 29.3% of Cambodians and 37.8% of Hmong lived below the poverty line. Taking into account educational investments made by Asian immigrants, Zhou and Kamo (1994) pointed out that they do not get rewards for their educational capital investment equal to white Americans. Also, many college-educated Asian immigrants who received a college education in their home countries later migrated to America experiencing employment downward mobility (Kitano & Daniels, 2001) due to language barriers. Many of these Asian immigrants, particularly men who are fathers, are employed in low-status, low-paying occupations as taxi drivers or cleaners, and others operate in labor-intensive, long-hour small businesses that repeatedly take away their family time and involvement (Min, 2006). Doherty, Kouneski, and Erickson (1998) argued that the behaviors of fathers are extremely sensitive to changes taking place in the economic workforce. Their decreased ability to provide for their family, particularly related to children's education, may increase financial stress that in turn can affect family interactions. To illustrate this point, certain Asian immigrant men may display punitive behavior toward their wife or children (Kim et al., 2006) because of the decline in their social status and economic role (Min, 2006).

Family Structures and Values

Many educators, policy makers, mental health providers, and even the general public assume that Asian immigrant families share similar traditions, languages, belief systems, and family values, which has little validity (Min, 2006). In fact, individuals or families may share the same ethnic heritage and tradition, yet a certain degree of cultural variability still exists (Hildreth & Sugawara, 1993) within each ethnic group. However, there are some commonalities due to the fact that Confucianism, the dominant ethical and moral system in China, had a great influence in many other Asian cultures. For example, Confucianism emphasizes filial piety, loyalty to the group, conformity to societal expectations, and respect for one's superior (Fong, 2008), which significantly differ from the ideologies of Western culture. In this sense, individuals, particularly women, are informed, starting at a young age, to value the well-being of the family and to sacrifice individual dreams and aspirations.

In 2000, over 60% of all Asian Americans were married compared to 54% of the total population. In addition, the separation and divorce rates of all Asians were 1.3% and 4.2% respectively, which were substantially lower than the total population (2.2% and 9.7%). Past research suggests that the longer a person lives in the United States, the more likely his or her social and cultural characteristics reflect those of the mainstream society (Huang, 2005; Kim, Chen, Li, Huang, & Moon, 2009), which may suggest a higher divorce rate in the future.

Traditional Asian family structure remains patriarchal and often extended (Julian, McKenry, & McKelvey, 1994). Most Asian families highlight the importance of the family unit rather than individual well-being, whereas Western families emphasize independence and autonomy of individual family members. Roles and responsibilities in an Asian family are typically assigned from a hierarchical system that is generally based on gender, age, and social class (Huang, 2005). A great emphasis is typically placed on harmonious interpersonal relationships achieved through interdependence, loyalty, and conflict avoidance; personal dreams and development are sacrificed to maintain family harmony. For instance, couples in a more traditional Asian family typically place the well-being of the husband and his family members above and beyond the wife's own needs and well-being (Adler, 2003). In addition to gender roles, family members in many Asian immigrant families, particularly those of the younger generations, are intentionally socialized to embrace ethnic traditions, rituals, and beliefs that can be somewhat "out of place" and foreign to children who are mostly raised and educated in the United States. Consequently, many Asian immigrant families are constantly encountering value and belief system conflicts, particularly in the context of intimate relationships.

Generally speaking, the nuclear family structure emphasizes independence and autonomy whereas traditional Asian families value the family unit (Lee & Mock, 2005), which includes loyalty to the family. Committed obligations and shame-based responsibility are common mechanisms used to motivate women and children to honor the family. Shame and ridicule may be used when individuals fall short of family expectations (Lee & Mock, 2005). Furthermore, traditional Asian cultures are male-dominated, and women are consigned to subordinate roles. It is highly possible that the notion of honoring the family and harmony and social pressure may have kept many marriages together. Maintaining family harmony plays a significant part in family life, particularly for women, for which conflict and confrontation should be avoided at all cost. In close-knit Asian immigrant communities, rumor and gossip about one's family life, particularly one's marriage, can be widespread quite easily (Fong, 2008), which can bring shame and dishonor to the family. As a result, a wife's submission to the husband is necessary for a peaceful, harmonious marriage. However, Asian immigrant couples, especially those with traditional beliefs, constantly encounter challenges in regard to gender equality and autonomy promoted in the United States, which pose threats and stress to many marriages.

A high degree of marital conflict associated with money, along with acculturation stress, may arise for many Asian men with a refugee background who have low education levels, language barriers, and less transferable job skills (Kitano & Daniels, 2001). This group of Asian male immigrants may be compelled to take any low-paying, labor-intensive jobs that become available to provide for the family. On the other hand, women in these families, who did not work in their countries, may also be required to look for ways to make money for economic survival (Min, 2006). Over a period of time through improved language proficiency and job skills, the increased economic contribution made by Asian women in this situation along with the husband's decreased earning ability can heighten marital stress and conflict.

In addition to couple relationships, Asian cultures stress the importance of maintaining the respect and good opinions of others (Huang, 2005). Group harmony, such as family, is the central concern and displays of individualism are strongly discouraged (Min, 2006). Besides the issues relating to socioemotional development, common methods of discipline (e.g., shame and, behavior controlling) utilized by many Asian parents appear to be harsh and, perhaps, developmentally inappropriate according to mainstream American ideas (Larsen, Mikyong, & Nguyen, 2008).

Strengths and Assets of Asian Immigrant Families

I have found that diverse backgrounds, selective methods of migration, close family ties, resiliency, and recognized educational and vocational contributions to society make Asian immigrant families a valuable group. Diverse backgrounds of Asian immigrant families with multiple official spoken languages and rich cultural practices help these families appreciate people from multiple cultures.

Migration had an impact on individual and family interaction of Asian immigrants and this migration process, and resulting acculturation illustrates many strengths of this population. Adjusting to a new culture that differs from most Asian sociocultural practices and belief systems requires an open mind-set and continued resources to make this process manageable and effective. Generally speaking, individuals and families who arrived in America voluntarily after 1965 may embrace Western cultural values and practices positively. At the same time, this group of Asian immigrants possess more transferrable social capital (e.g., education, language skills, and employment experiences) that can be utilized upon arrival in America than did their earlier counterparts who came to America with low levels of education and language skills and fewer transferable job skills (Min, 2006). Reasons for migration, education level, language proficiency, employment history, individual and family life cycle, and available resources should be considered as vital elements of family life education.

Close family ties provide crucial social and psychological support to the survival and stability of new immigrant families in this country, particularly for Southeast Asians (Kitano & Daniels, 2001). Many of them may have experienced a level of postwar trauma, which can be difficult for others to comprehend. The support provided by their own people who have gone through similar circumstances can create a therapeutic effect upon arrival to the United States. In many circumstances, tangible support (e.g., money, shared household, and time) and intangible support (emotional and social needs) have become evident in many Southeast Asian immigrant families in various Asian-concentrated communities. For instance, multiple family members may contribute a portion of their wages to help a relative's family settle down by allowing this family to stay in the same household. Once this family saves sufficient funds to live on their own (e.g., renting their own apartment), this family will move out. This type of support not only provides space and resources to a new immigrant family during the initial transitional time but also decreases initial cultural shock and stress associated with adjustment experienced by adults who may be able to nurture a parent–child relationship. In reality, kinship support attempts to assist newcomers to secure a place where stable family life can be achieved (Kitano & Daniels, 2001).

Healey (2006) stated that for the 70% of Asian Americans who were foreign born, the immigration experience alone required periodic adjustments and changes (e.g., moving to a different city or state because of education or employment). Furthermore, a large number of Asian immigrants with a refugee background typically display a high degree of resiliency in order to survive and reestablish their family in a foreign land (Lee & Mock, 2005).

FAMILY LIFE EDUCATION PRACTICES

Current State of Family Life Education

Presently, family life education has not been a recognized professional credential among Asian Americans. Cassidy (2009) depicted that it may still take some time for this field to receive recognition. The demand for family life education by Asian immigrant families remains low. Wiley and Ebata (2004) argued that low demand should not be interpreted as lack of interest. In fact, low publicity may be a more accurate reason for low participation. A few possible reasons for low demand could be unfamiliarity with family life education, misconception of family life education with mental health problems, or feelings of shame and dishonor when disclosing family problems to outsiders.

As a discipline, family life education programs emphasize prevention through program design and implementation of content that would benefit participants' knowledge, skills, beliefs, or attitudes toward healthy family life (Hildreth & Sugawara, 1993). The notion of prevention deserves explanation and publicity among Asian immigrant families. Unfortunately, many traditional Asians do not accept Western biopsychological explanations of mental illness (Lee & Mock, 2005) due to the level of reluctance to share family problems with outsiders. By and large, Asian families are highly concerned about "saving face," and each family member will do whatever it takes to bring honor and glory to the family name (Kottler & Chen, 2008). By disclosing family problems and issues that may become widespread gossip and rumor in the community, Asians believe dishonor and shame are brought to the entire family. Feelings of shame and dishonor are the results of expressing vulnerability and disclosing a problematic family life to people who are not acquainted with the family. For instance, according to Chinese tradition, filial piety is heavily emphasized among Chinese Americans beginning in early childhood, particularly for sons. A filial son will attempt to achieve complete obedience to his parents during their time together and take good care of them as they grow older (Ikels, 2004), which is not necessarily a value in the Western culture.

The nature of the educational element in family life education results in greater receptivity among Asian immigrant families than do counseling or therapy, since Asian Americans value educational programs that benefit themselves and their families (National Healthy Marriage Resource Center, n.d.). Although some of these professionals might have attempted to provide workshops to Asian Americans, many are either not trained in the family sciences field or conduct their workshops through the teacher–student model, which differs from the fundamental principles and effective instruction methods rooted in family life education (Duncan & Goddard, 2011).

Family life educators who work at public schools have a great opportunity to work with students and families, particularly the ones dealing with family issues (Powell & Cassidy, 2001). A great example of a school-based, family-involved partnership program is Families and Schools Together (FAST). The aim of this program is to give participating parents the skills and confidence needed to work with children through empowerment (Families and Schools Together [FAST], n.d.). Establishing a mutually supportive partnership with public schools becomes an effective way to provide services to immigrant families (e.g., Asian immigrant families). It is vital to communicate through various means to Asian immigrant families the nature of family life education and how family relationships can be strengthened and enriched through education programs designed by qualified and well-trained family life educators. When explaining to the target population the nature of the program, the presenter needs to mention how family life educators receive their credential (certified family life educator, or CFLE) through the National Council on Family Relations as the professional organization, because credentials are highly valued by Asian Americans (Huang, 2005).

General Needs of This Population and Rationale for Family Life Education

Regardless of the types of program family life educators plan to deliver, a thorough needs assessment of the target population sets the stage to "meet needs" of families, a key principle of family life education proposed by Arcus, Schvaneveldt, and Moss (1993).

The traditional values of Asian culture, such as the strong emphasis on the family, unique marital beliefs, and parent–child interactions, are the needs that can be met by family life educators.

Many traditional Asian cultures stress the importance of the family over individuals. Family life educators should become aware of unique family interactions among family members for any given Asian ethnic group. The content of a program that tailors to the entire family may prove very appealing to Asian immigrant families.

Marital Relationships

Couple relationship education typically includes four components: (1) awareness, (2) feedback, (3) cognitive change, and (4) skills training (Halford, Markman, Kline, & Stanley, 2003). A vital goal of couple relationship education is to promote long-term marital satisfaction and stability. Incorporating long-term marital satisfaction and stability along with Asian cultural practices and family values in a program can convey a positive message to the participants to have a successful, balanced family life that values Asian traditions and heritage. A strong fear of losing heritage and traditions continues to be a major concern for many Asian immigrants when informed by credible educators to extensively adapt values and practices to those of the mainstream culture (Huang, 2005). Incorporation of Asian values into couple relationship programs may assist Asian immigrant couples in their adjustment to the mainstream culture.

By and large, Asian Americans hold a more traditional view toward couple relationships in which power and usage of resources rest with the males (Adler, 2003). This type of cultural practice poses increased levels of marital conflict when egalitarian roles, responsibilities, status, and opportunities become available for Asian immigrant women who are constantly encountering dilemmas in the United States (Min, 2006). Efforts made to educate Asian male immigrants to display loving, nurturing behavior toward other family members—particularly wives and children—should be emphasized. For instance, family life education programs might strive to provide Asian immigrant males with tools to create positive interactions with their family members. As a result, their lives in America may prove more stable and productive, which in turn might increase the likelihood of their children doing well in school.

Parent–Child Interaction

In Asian immigrant families, one important goal for many parents rests on establishing a stable family for the younger generation in order for them to get a good education (Qin, 2008), despite all the hardships and challenges they have experienced. Using the National Survey of Families and Households (NSFH) Wave 1 data to compare parenting practices of children ages 5 to 18, Julian and colleagues (1994) found that Asian parents were more involved in helping with reading and homework than were Hispanic parents. In some cases, parent–child interaction is sacrificed because parents work long hours or multiple jobs (Min, 2006). The importance of education and long work hours for the sake of their children demonstrate the emphasis on academic excellence. Consequently, many Asian immigrant parents maintain strict control and monitoring over their children's education (Qin, 2008), which heightens parent–child conflict because children assume that parents only care about school and homework.

On the other hand, young children spend a great deal of time at school interacting with children of a similar age. In the Western culture, emotional/verbal expressions of empathy and affect are encouraged in interpersonal relationships, which is uncommon to many Asian immigrants. Family life education programs may focus on specific skills to strengthen parent–child relations under the notion of helping their children to succeed. Asian immigrant parents need instruction as to how to encourage their children to pursue good education while building other important social skills (e.g., leadership, or community involvement).

Furthermore, parental involvement at school functions is an important indicator of support level to children in the United States. Performing this role well becomes a challenging task to some immigrant parents. Using data from the Early Childhood Longitudinal Study—Kindergarten Cohort, Turney and Kao (2009) found that language ability and time spent in the United States are significantly associated with the level of school involvement by Asian immigrant parents. The study revealed that Asian foreign-born parents were 2.8 times more likely than their white counterparts to report not feeling welcome at their child's school and 9.7 times more likely to indicate that language was a barrier to their involvement. Given the reported facts provided from this study, some Asian foreign-born parents may further decrease their involvement at school (Engstrom & Okamura, 2007) because of language barriers that in turn generated a negative impression of how parental involvement is perceived by their child and the school. Family life education programs may target culturally sensitive strategies to educate parents on ways to monitor children's education with flexibility. Parents need skills in positive communication strategies to discuss homework (Qin, 2008).

In terms of acculturation, different rates could happen in the same household. Typically, the rate of acculturation among young children to a new culture is much faster than older siblings and their parents. In the process of acculturation through interaction with and exposure to the mainstream culture, children in Asian immigrant families gradually adapt values and lifestyles that are similar to their peers because they want to fit in. Findings from Kim and colleagues (2009) argued that high levels of acculturation discrepancy in families along with the divergence of values between Chinese immigrant parents and their adolescents may weaken parent–child relationships. Adolescents in these families who are given less support from parents are more likely to experience depressive symptoms.

Along the same line of family values and tradition, Glenn and Yap (2000) explained that many Asian parents have attempted to get their children interested in their own culture and heritage language by sending them to language school. From a qualitative study, it was found that children in Chinese immigrant families reported learning their heritage language irrelevant and tended to resist parents' efforts on this matter (Zhang & Slaughter-Defoe, 2009). Unfortunately, mainstream values and life-styles may contradict with traditional Asian belief systems. Consequently, parent–child conflict may stem from cultural differences and distinct approaches between traditional and Western values on certain issues (e.g., respect, and dating) and high expectations of their children to excel in academic performance (Wong, 2006). Furthermore, stress associated with role reversal among family members leads family relationships to distress (Fong, 2008). For instance, parents who have language barriers heavily rely on English-speaking children as interpreters at grocery stores or school conferences, which may cause embarrassment and helplessness in parents who do not face this type of emotional distress in their home countries. Sometimes translators may be needed to reach this group of immigrants. In this case, family life educators may consider partnering with agencies that offer English classes or translation services to conduct workshops for new immigrants to provide helpful tips to assist their family adjusting to this culture.

Marketing/Recruitment

Pawel (2009) stated that marketing family life education programs is not to sell programs as a method of marketing. However, it is about "building relationships and an awareness about who you are, what you do, for whom, and why" (Pawel, 2009, p. 87). The attempts to utilize family life education programs to enhance, enrich, strengthen, and maintain healthy family life requires educators to acknowledge the unique aspect of cultural beliefs and practices that can influence their decision to participate and desire to learn.

Asian immigrant families comprise diverse ethnic groups with differing characteristics, such as spoken language, household income, education level, immigration experiences, and religious beliefs within and between each ethnic group. Family life education programs remain in low demand among Asian immigrant families. Duncan and Goddard (2011) proposed that educators should avoid a "one-size-fits-all" programming approach, which is particularly true when cultural variability among Asian immigrant families is evident.

Four dimensions of marketing (price, product, place, and promotion) proposed by Katz have been widely utilized by family life educators (Ballard & Morris, 1999; Duncan & Goddard, 2011; Powell & Cassidy, 2001). These four dimensions of marketing may work with groups that possess homogeneous characteristics along with a culturally sensitive needs assessment. Precautions should be critically taken when incorporating these dimensions in a diverse population. The author of this chapter proposes maintaining a certain level of flexibility and variation in marketing strategies when using them among Asian immigrant participants. For instance, the price associated with the exchange of service or family life education programs set by the educator may be perceived by some participants as a fair exchange of information that satisfies their needs. Conversely, the same fee may become a hindrance to families whose income may not allow them to afford such a service or program. In contrast, services free of charge may be perceived by many Asians as a way for the presenter to sell his or her own products which is common in many Asian communities (National Healthy Marriage Resource Center, n.d.). For this reason, a small, reasonable fee may be attached to a program that may convince the participants to think that it is worthy of their involvement.

With the idea that many Asian immigrant families operate from a collectivist approach, building a relationship or social connection through established organizations and social groups provides avenues for marketing family life education programs (Duncan & Goddard, 2011). Collaboration between educators and community organizations may create worthwhile relationships that will result in bringing positive changes to family relationships (Doherty & Anderson, 2005; Wiley & Ebata, 2004). Credible partnerships should be established through repeated interactions with community organization leaders. Partnerships with established social groups such as Chinese American associations, local churches, and ethnic language schools may be effective ways to reach families who are associated with these groups. In a similar way, church involvement has a long history in Korean American families. Educators can utilize available resources to partner with church leaders who have established trust within the community to promote healthy family life. For instance, Korean Churches for Community Development, a nonprofit, faith-based agency, aims to build loving and peaceful marriage and families for Asian Americans and Pacific Islanders, besides other programs and initiatives.

Another effective marketing strategy is to catch the attention of an ethnic minority group through local ethnic newspapers. Powell and Cassidy (2001) also proposed that TV educational campaigns can serve as an effective and popular information delivery method for new immigrants who may not be able to read printed materials. Nonetheless, these forms of campaigning and promotion may not reach all target populations due to the lack of access to these media, and the effects of behavior change via these methods are questionable (Doherty & Anderson, 2005).

In general, Asian immigrant families come from predominantly patriarchal societies that value seniority and social status (Kitano & Daniels, 2001). Explaining how family life education programs may assist new immigrant families to make smooth adjustments in this country, is more likely to gain support and participation from key players and leaders in the Asian American community. Education remains a top priority among many Asian immigrant families. Consequently, partnership with K through 12 schools in areas where Asian immigration families are highly concentrated can facilitate access to parents or guardians. Besides schools, gaining support and involvement from community agencies and organizations will create a community-wide family-focused effort on promoting healthy family life. Family life educators may seek assistance from English as a second language (ESL) teachers to send home program flyers with students. Promotional materials or flyers can be printed in their ethnic language along with English. In so doing, the publicity or promotional materials, with the support from schools, may increase initial trust from Asian immigrant families who may then consider participation.

Barriers to Participation

Four important barriers need to be considered when delivering family life education programs among Asian immigrant families; each will be addressed in this section. Carefully attending to these suggestions may retain participation rates.

First, with highly varied educational, socioeconomic, or linguistic characteristics, delivering family life education programs in English can potentially exclude many Asian Americans, particularly the ones who are not proficient in English. It was found that 79% of Asian Americans age 5 and over spoke a language other than English at home (Reeves & Bennett, 2004). Japanese immigrants were the only group in which 50% of them spoke only English at home. Approximately half of Chinese, Cambodian, Korean, Hmong, and Laotian spoke English less than very well. Promotional materials and flyers need to be clear in stating the language or languages in which sessions will be presented. This may reduce potential disappointments and frustration for some participants who do not understand or communicate in the presented language. English slang and adages should be either explained or avoided to minimize confusion to the audience. Given the diverse use of language among Asian immigrant families, a key element to increasing participation from diverse populations rests in helping the audience gain access to a program (Ooms & Wilson, 2005), which may not be delivered in a language that can be comprehended by the majority of the audience. Therefore, it is important to partner with key players in ethnic groups who may assist in promoting programs through major social gatherings and community events by using a language that can be understood by the target population.

Second, Asian Americans have a tendency to keep family issues within the family system. A common attitude held by most Asian immigrant families is that disclosing problems in family relationships brings disgrace and shame to the entire family (Fong, 2008). Additionally, the collective responsibility of taking care of a troubled family member for as long as possible is commonly accepted. Consequently, seeking professional help may be the last resort when family members can no longer accommodate the enduring demands of the troubled family member emotionally and socially. Therefore, raising the awareness of the educational component of family life education may help to minimize the reluctance associated with the notion of disgrace and shame brought to the entire family since family problems may not be disclosed. By doing so in a harmonious and nonconfrontational manner, the content of a program itself has the potential to educate and prepare the participants to deal with family issues in a preventative way.

Third, the issue of trust among families with refugee backgrounds may be a barrier to program participation. Doubt, mistrust, and suspicion may arise when programs are sponsored by city officials or state employees. As a result, gaining initial trust with participants who were previously mistreated by authority figures may prove extremely difficult.

Lastly, there is a common myth held by some Asian Americans that family-related workshops are associated with mental illness treatment (National Healthy Marriage Resource Center, n.d.). Ongoing efforts need to be made to clarify the principles and functions of family life education programs that fundamentally differ from intervention and therapy.

Environmental Considerations

Duncan, Box, and Silliman (1996) proposed that the maximum distance from home to the program site should be 15 miles. Locations should be arranged to give participants convenient accessibility, particularly for new immigrants, the elderly, and physically challenged individuals. In these cases, rooms on a lower level are preferred. Also, outside of the physical facility, a couple of program assistants, preferably Asian Americans who speak the ethnic language, may function as greeters to build initial rapport so participants feel at ease if the family life educator is not Asian.

Traditional classroom settings can sometimes intimidate the target audience who may have had negative school experiences in the past. The emphasis on the entire family is crucial to Asian immigrant families (Kitano & Daniels, 2001). With a combination of recreational outdoor activities designed for the whole family and family life education programs, the receptivity level may increase. In this case, programs are perceived as part of a family trip/activity. Also, the attendance rate seems to be fairly high when family life education workshops are offered at a familiar location (e.g., a local Asian community center) (Duncan & Goddard, 2011). Seasoned and culturally competent family life educators should explore several preferred settings prior to the program design phase so activities can be implemented according to the layout of a facility. On the other hand, web-based family life education programs may perfectly suit young Asian immigrants or professionals with busy schedules. However, this method of delivery might hinder individuals and families who have limited skills and knowledge about the Internet and computers, particularly when it is not effectively publicized.

Modes of Learning

The learning styles of the audience essentially dictate how educators design programs to achieve optimal outcomes. An experienced family life educator will adjust his or her delivery methods by keeping the core content of the program to meet the needs of families, particularly when working with ethnic groups. Powell and Cassidy (2001) suggested that the family life education method should be a group interaction rather than a lecture format. Mini-lectures, role-play demonstration, video clips, small groups, or experiential activities create an engaging atmosphere. Discussions in small group settings might work well with Asian immigrant families since speaking and asking questions in a formal setting is generally perceived as challenging the authority figure, which should be avoided in a traditional culture (Adler, 2003; Julian et al., 1994). Because familialism remains a core value for many Asian immigrant families (Medora, 2005), the focus of successful family life education programs should be designed on the family level instead of individual level. It is suggested that positive changes in family dynamics are likely to happen when the whole family is involved in a program (Duncan & Goddard, 2011).

Many college-educated Asian immigrants fall into the category of the "transaction perspective" (Thomas, Schvaneveldt, & Young, 1993) in which learners are active, autonomous, and capable participants in their thought and problem-solving processes. Factual knowledge and research findings embedded in the program may prove engaging to them. In this case, additional website links, book lists, or magazines on selected topics will satisfy their needs. Also, the benefits of web-based family life education programs might be appealing to this group of active learning participants.

To result in better program outcomes, it is necessary for family life educators to know the unique demographic makeup and needs prior to program design phase. Particularly, most Asian immigrant families may prefer information and advice (Huang, 2005), which falls under Level 2 of the family involvement model (Doherty, 2009), rather than disclosing family challenges and problems to an outsider. An information exchange time with the educator after the program might be arranged, which would then provide a great opportunity to discuss family issues with Asian immigrants in less threatening circumstances (Huang, 2005).

Educator Characteristics

Arcus and Thomas (1993) depicted that "the family life educator is the program, as it is the educator who selects, designs, and implements the program; selects and uses resources, materials, and activities; and responds to or ignores the interests and needs of the audience" (p. 26). Indeed, the success or failure of a program mainly depends on the familiarity of the family life educator with the audience. The way he or she handles cultural practices and traditions signals to the audience a level of acceptance. Initially, educators who are not of Asian descent or who are unfamiliar with the Asian immigrant community might consider partnering with other educators accustomed to Asian cultures or key players in Asian communities to deliver an effective program. Once a relationship has been established, other programs might become more acceptable to them.

Generally speaking, a family life educator presents his or her information with good intentions to the audience. Unfortunately, tension or unknowing contradiction with some aspects of family values perceived by the participants may cause resistance or total shutdown for the remainder of a program. When this happens, resistance to other family life education programs can occur. Medora (2005) suggested that Asian immigrant families highly value familialism over individualism, which deserves serious attention in program design and implementation. For instance, independence, autonomy, and assertiveness are highly valued in the mainstream culture, whereas interdependence, interconnectedness, and indirectness in communication appear to be on the other side of spectrum. When family life educators promote the mainstream values without taking cultural practices into account, the well-intended, empirically based information presented can create opposition in the participants.

Most Asian immigrant families view educational credentials as a crucial element found in educators (Fong, 2008), such as the CFLE. In hierarchical family structures, age and personal experience are additional critical indicators (Julian et al., 1994) of how receptive Asian immigrants view a program. For example, the level of receptiveness of a parent program remains low when it is presented by a young adult with an advanced degree who does not yet have children. In fact, the content of such programs may follow family life education design and methodology with the most current empirical findings. In reality, some Asian immigrants who are parents would question how much this young educator truly understands what parenting means in daily life.

As mentioned earlier, the issue of trust toward governmental officials or state employees (Kitano & Daniels, 2001) remains a barrier for families with a refugee

background to participate in programs and services provided through such chan-
nels. Educators need to gain trust with key players in these specific ethnic groups,
which may reduce doubt and concerns in regard to the intent of government- or
state-sponsored programs.

Ethical Considerations

Palm (2009) argued that one of the greatest challenges in working with diverse
populations is to identify a relevant and practical approach with the incorporation
of ethical principles to solve an ethical dilemma. Family life educators not only
need to be knowledgeable about ethical principles and guidelines practiced in the
profession but must also be held accountable for knowledge and skills presented
(Czaplewski & Jorgensen, 1993) when delivering a program that may impact the
lives of Asian immigrant families who possess distinct cultural values and beliefs.

A common belief has been widely promoted by the Western culture in regard to
assertion, independence, autonomy, and pursuit of personal dreams. For instance,
when an Asian woman learns assertiveness and practices it in her own marriage,
this may cause the husband to question a wife who talks like "an American." In
so doing, distress and disagreements in couple relationships may sometimes lead
to a heated discussion or hostile fights. A dilemma often exists for educators who
attempt to assist ethnic minority families in making a smooth adjustment by adopting views presented by the dominant culture without compromising their own
traditions and values.

An additional ethical consideration in regard to the idea of "model minority"
(Min, 2006) should be seriously revisited. A good number of Asian immigrant
families have been successful in educational attainment and occupational success.
Unfortunately, many more Asian immigrant families, particularly newcomers and
refugees, are constantly struggling with limited resources, language barriers, and
war-related trauma and may be disqualified for the services they need. Family life
educators should take particular care to meet the needs of these underserved Asian
immigrant families.

Best Practices in Family Life Education Programming

According to Huang (2005), Asians traditionally focus more on the parent–
child relationship than on the marital relationship because the couple relationship
is not commonly discussed in family interactions. Many Asian parents value the
notion of learning how to enhance a child's success. In this circumstance, parenting education programs offer a promising future that allows family life educators
to promote a healthy family life among Asian immigrant families in regard to
teaching children how to be successful in interpersonal relationships at school and
home. Small, Cooney, and O'Connor (2009) explained that effective programs

are presented to families as they are going through major transitions, such as the initial phase of immigration or a child's transition to high school. In spite of various types of parenting programs, designed either by the mainstream or ethnic groups, that are implemented by agencies and individuals among Asian immigrant families, a lack of empirically based parenting programs remains a pressing issue (Gorman & Balter, 1997).

A good example of a parenting program is Helping Youth Succeed: Bicultural Parenting for Southeast Asian Families (for a complete review, see Xiong, Detzner, Keuster, Eliason, & Allen, 2006) through the University of Minnesota Extension. This program was designed to be culturally sensitive. The organizers attempted to achieve five goals through parenting education to target four Southeast Asian groups (Cambodian, Hmong, Lao, and Vietnamese) in which adolescent children encounter various adjustment issues. These goals include: understanding the many different Southeast Asian family perspectives about parenting, understanding immigrant families and the differences among them, identifying and addressing problems of day-to-day parenting in a bicultural context, addressing issues affecting parent–child relationships in a foreign context, and understanding Southeast Asian issues and family strengths (University of Minnesota Extension, n.d.). In general, Southeast Asian families possess low levels of human and financial capital compared with other large Asian immigrant families (e.g., Chinese, Japanese, Korean, or Asian Indians), which make their acculturation challenging (Engstrom & Okamura, 2007).

Asian Youth Alliance (AYA) is a multilevel, ethnic-specific program developed for Chinese and Filipino youth living in Daly City, California, and was designed to decrease high-risk behaviors and substance use. A total of twelve 2-hour workshop sessions are implemented over a period of 6 to 7 weeks, covering important topics such as communication skills and self-esteem. This program was designated as a promising program and highly recommended by the Substance Abuse and Mental Health Services Administration (SAMHSA).

Contrasted to the common approach to parenting education found in Asian immigrant families, couple relationship programs or marriage education programs might remain less important to many Asian immigrant couples whose family dynamics heavily rests on raising children. Despite the low demand for marriage education, elements of couple relationships can be creatively blended into parenting education, especially the concept that healthy couple relationships ensure effective parenting skills and parent–child interactions (Huang, 2005).

A common finding in regard to the diversity of participants in marriage education showed that the content of many programs largely focused on the mainstream population with low consideration of the unique needs of ethnic minority families who could greatly benefit from services and programs to maintain healthy family life (Jakubowski, Milne, Brunner, & Miller, 2005). Halford and colleagues

(2003) suggested guidelines for best practice in marriage education, which included assessing the risk profile of couples, encouraging high-risk couples to attend relationship education, assessing relationship aggression, offering marital education at change points, promoting early presentation of relationship problems, matching content to couples with special needs, and enhancing accessibility of evidence-based marital education programs. In a similar fashion for implementing marriage education, incorporating five guidelines to a program designed for Asian immigrant families of any Asian ethnic group requires a high level of cultural sensitivity to terminologies and examples found in the Prevention and Relationship Enhancement Program (PREP).

FUTURE DIRECTIONS

Immigration itself disrupts individual development, redefines family roles, restructures family interactions, and requires families to establish new social support and resources in the receiving country (Clark, Glick, & Bures, 2009). With the rapid population increase and the diverse characteristics of many Asian immigrant groups documented by the U.S. Census Bureau, Asian immigrant families are constantly encountering both general and unique family issues at micro and macro levels in the midst of cultural shock and acculturative stress which may heighten their vulnerability level. At the family level, different rates of acculturation, amounts of available human and financial capital, and levels of language proficiency for each family member who progresses at distinctive phases of development may determine the level of family functioning. In addition, cultural practices and values, norms, and public policies also create challenges and changes to this emerging group, particularly with families that possess minimal resources and skills to navigate in the mainstream culture.

Future research may examine normative and nonnormative stressors for individuals and entire families associated with acculturation during the initial phase of immigration, which poses a high degree of unfamiliarity and cultural shock. Furthermore, data relative to acculturation and family relationships can be collected as family life educators conduct workshops among Asian immigrant families, which will increase the understanding of family dynamics in these groups. Colleges and universities through creative collaboration with public schools, community organizations, and social services, may strategically recruit and train Asian American students both at undergraduate and graduate levels to become certified family life educators to teach diverse Asian immigrant families. Furthermore, 79% of Asian Americans speak a language other than English at home, and it was over 90% for Cambodians, Laotians, Hmong, and Vietnamese

(Reeves & Bennett, 2004). Educators may consider feasible ways to promote family life education programs that are culturally sensitive and linguistically relevant to Asian immigrant families that speak many different languages. Finally, 2.6 million people listed their ethnicity as Asian and one other race in the 2010 U.S. Census (U.S. Census Bureau, 2011). What types of programming would be effective for Asian immigrants who identified themselves as more than one race? What issues might be encountered in interracial marriages, involving one Asian immigrant spouse? These are some important questions for family life educators to ask as they attempt to effectively assist and educate a diverse group such as Asian immigrant families to build a healthy family life in a foreign land.

REFERENCES

Adler, S. M. (2003). Asian American families. In J. J. Ponzetti Jr. (Eds.), *International encyclopedia of marriage and family* (pp. 82–91). New York: Macmillan Reference USA.

Arcus, M. E., Schvaneveldt, J. D., & Moss, J. J. (1993). The nature of family life education. In M. E. Arcus, J. D. Schvaneveldt, & J. J. Moss (Eds.), *Handbook of family life education: The practice of family life education* (pp. 1–25). Thousand Oaks, CA: Sage.

Arcus, M. E., & Thomas, J. (1993). The nature and practice of family life education. In M. E. Arcus, J. D. Schvaneveldt, & J. J. Moss (Eds.), *Handbook of family life education: The practice of family life education* (pp. 1–32). Thousand Oaks, CA: Sage.

Ballard, S. M., & Morris, M. L. (1999). Factors influencing midlife and older adults' attendance in family life education programs. *Family Relations, 54,* 461–472.

Cassidy, D. (2009). Challenges in family life education: Defining and promoting the profession. In D. J. Bredehoft & M. J. Walcheski (Eds.), *Family life education: Integrating theory and practice* (pp. 11–22). Minneapolis, MN: NCFR.

Clark, R. L., Glick, J. E., & Bures, R. M. (2009). Immigrant families over life course: Research directions and needs. *Journal of Family Issues, 30,* 852–872.

Coles, R. L. (2006). *Race and family: A structural approach.* Thousand Oaks, CA: Sage.

Czaplewski, M. J., & Jorgensen, S. R. (1993). The professionalization of family life education. In M. E. Arcus, J. D. Schvaneveldt, & J. J. Moss (Eds.), *Handbook of family life education: The foundation of family life education* (pp. 51–75). Thousand Oaks, CA: Sage.

Doherty, W. J. (2009). Boundaries between parent and family education and family therapy: The levels of family involvement model. In D. J. Bredehoft & M. J. Walcheski (Eds.), *Family life education: Integrating theory and practice* (pp. 253–260). Minneapolis, MN: NCFR.

Doherty, W. J., & Anderson, J. R. (2005). Community marriage initiatives. *Family Relations, 53*(3), 425–532.

Doherty, W. J., Kouneski, E. F., & Erickson, M. F. (1998). Responsible fathering: An overview and conceptual framework. *Journal of Marriage and the Family, 60*(2), 277–292.

Duncan, S. F., Box, G., & Silliman, B. (1996). Racial and gender effects on perceptions of marriage preparation programs among college-educated young adults. *Family Relations, 45,* 80–90.

Duncan, S. F., & Goddard, H. W. (2011). *Family life education: Principles and practices for effective education* (2nd ed.). Thousand Oaks, CA: Sage.

Engstrom, D. W., & Okamura, A. (2007). A nation of immigrant: A call for a specialization in immigrant well-being. *Journal of Ethnic & Cultural Diversity in Social Work, 16,* 103–111.

Families and Schools Together. (n.d.). Details information about parents' role. Retrieved from http://familiesandschools.org/about/?1#jajax

Fong, T. P. (2008). *The contemporary Asian American experience: Beyond the model minority* (3rd ed.). Upper Saddle River, NJ: Prentice Hall.

Glenn, E. N., & Yap, G. H. (2000). Chinese American families. In T. P. Fong & L. H. Shinagawa (Eds.), *Asian Americans: Experiences and perspectives* (pp. 277–292). Upper Saddle River, NJ: Prentice Hall.

Gorman, J., & Balter, L. (1997). Culturally sensitive parent education: A critical review of quantitative research. *Review of Educational Research, 67*(3), 339–369.

Guion, L., Chattaraj, S., & Lytle, S. S. (2004). Strengthening programs to reach diverse audiences: A curriculum to planning and implementing extension programs for ethnically diverse audiences. *Journal of Extension* [online], *42*(1). Available at: http://www.joe.org/joe/2004february/tt7.php

Halford, W. K., Markman, H. J., Kline, G. H., & Stanley, S. M. (2003). Best practice in couple relationship education. *Journal of Marital and Family Therapy, 29,* 385–406.

Healey, J. F. (2006). *Race, ethnicity, gender, and class: The sociology of group conflict and change* (4th ed). Thousand Oaks: CA: Pine Grove Press.

Hildreth, G. J., & Sugawara, A. I. (1993). Ethnicity and diversity in family life education. In M. E. Arcus, J. D. Schvaneveldt, & J. J. Moss (Eds.), *Handbook of family life education* (pp. 162–188), Thousand Oaks, CA: Sage.

Huang, W. R. (2005). An Asian perspective on relationships and marriage education. *Family Process, 44,* 161–173.

Ikels, C. (2004). *Filial piety: Practice and discourse in contemporary East Asia.* Stanford, CA: Stanford University Press.

Jakubowski, S. F., Milne, E. P., Brunner, H., & Miller, R. B. (2005). A review of empirically supported marital enrichment programs. *Family Relations, 53,* 528–537.

Julian, T. W., McKenry, P. C., & McKelvey, M. W. (1994). Cultural variations in parenting: Perceptions of Caucasian, African-American, Hispanic, and Asian-American parents. *Family Relations, 43,* 30–37.

Kim, I. J., Lau, A. S., & Chang, D. F. (2006). *Family violence among Asian Americans.* Retrieved from http://www.aasc.ucla.edu/policy/kim_lau_chang.pdf

Kim, S. Y., Chen, Q., Li, J., Huang, X., & Moon, U. J. (2009). Parent-child acculturation, parenting, and adolescent depressive symptoms in Chinese immigrant families. *Journal of Family Psychology, 23,* 426–437.

Kitano, H. H. L., & Daniels, R. (2001). *Asian Americans: Emerging minorities.* Upper Saddle River, NJ: Prentice Hall.

Kottler, J., & Chen, D. (2008). *Stress management and prevention: Application to daily life.* Belmont, CA: Thomson Wadsworth.

Larsen, S., Mikyong, K, G., & Nguyen, T. D. (2008). Asian American immigrant families and child abuse: Cultural consideration. *Journal of Systemic Therapies, 27,* 16–29.

Lee, E., & Mock, M. R. (2005). Asian families: An overview. In M. McGoldrick, J. Giordano, & N. Garcia-Preto (Eds.), *Ethnicity and family therapy* (pp. 269–289). New York: Guilford.

Medora, N. P. (2005). International families in cross-cultural perspective: A family strengths approach. *Marriage and Family Review, 38,* 47–64.

Min, P. G. (2006). *Asian Americans: Contemporary trends and issues.* Thousand Oaks, CA: Sage.

National Healthy Marriage Resource Center. (n.d.). *Engaging Asian Americans in marriage/relationship education.* Retrieved from http://www.healthymarriageinfo.org/docs/engagingasianamericans1.pdf

Ooms, T., & Wilson, P. (2005). The challenges of offering relationship and marriage education to low-income population. *Family Relations, 53,* 440–447.

Palm, G. (2009). Professional ethics and practice. In D. J. Bredehoft & M. J. Walcheski (Eds.), *Family life education: Integrating theory and practice* (pp. 191–197). Minneapolis, MN: NCFR.

Pawel, J. J. (2009). Marketing family life education programs by helping, not selling. In D. J. Bredehoft & M. J. Walcheski (Eds.), *Family life education: Integrating theory and practice* (pp. 87–99). Minneapolis, MN: NCFR.

Powell, L. H., & Cassidy, D. (2001). *Family life education: An introduction.* Mountain View, CA: Mayfield Publishing Company.

Qin, D. B. (2008). Doing well vs. feeling well: Understanding family dynamics and the psychological adjustment of Chinese immigrant adolescents. *Journal of Youth Adolescence, 37,* 22–35.

Reeves, T. J., & Bennett, C. E. (2003). *Asian and Pacific Islander population in the United States: March 2003* (P20-540). Washington, DC: U.S. Government Printing Office.

Reeves, T. J., & Bennett, C. E. (2004). *We the people: Asians in the United States* (CENSR-17). Washington, DC: U.S. Government Printing Office.

Small, S. A., Cooney, S. M., & O'Connor, C. (2009). Evidence-informed program improvement: Using principles of effectiveness to enhance the quality and impact of family-based prevention programs. *Family Relations, 58,* 1–13.

Thomas, J., Schvaneveldt, J. D., & Young, M. H. (1993). Programs in family life education development, implementation, and evaluation. In M. E. Arcus, J. D. Schvaneveldt, & J. J. Moss (Eds.), *Handbook of family life education* (pp. 106–130), Thousand Oaks, CA: Sage.

Treas, J. (2009). Four myths about older adults in America's immigrant families. *Generations, 4,* 40–45.

Turney, K., & Kao, G. (2009). Barriers to school involvement: Are immigrant parents disadvantaged? *Journal of Educational Research, 102,* 257–271.

University of Minnesota Extension. (n.d.). Helping youth succeed: Bicultural parenting for Southeast Asian families. Retrieved from http://www.extension.umn.edu/distribution/familydevelopment/00266.html

U.S. Census Bureau. (2002). *A profile of the nation's foreign-born population from Asia* (CENBR/01-3). Washington, DC: U.S. Government Printing Office.

U.S. Census Bureau. (2010). *Profile of general population and housing characteristics: 2010 demographic profile data.* Retrieved from http://factfinder2.census.gov/faces/tableservices/jsf/pages/productview.xhtml?pid=DEC_10_DP_DPDP1&prodType=table

U.S. Census Bureau. (2011). *Facts for features: Asian/Pacific American heritage month: May 2011* (CB11-FF.06). Washington, DC: U.S. Government Printing Office.

Wiley, A. R., & Ebata, A. (2004). Reaching American families: Making diversity real in family life education. *Family Relations, 53*(3), 273–281.

Wong, M. (2006). Chinese Americans. In P. G. Min (Eds.), *Asian Americans: Contemporary trends and issues* (pp. 110–145). Thousand Oaks, CA: Sage.

Xiong, Z. B., Detzner, D. F., Keuster, Z. H., Eliason, P. A., & Allen, R. (2006). Developing culturally sensitive parent education programs for immigrant families: The Helping Youth Succeed Curriculum. *Hmong Studies Journal, 7,* 1–29.

Zhang, D., & Slaughter-Defoe, D. T. (2009). Language attitudes and heritage language maintenance among Chinese immigrant families in the USA. *Language, Culture and Curriculum, 22,* 77–93.

Zhou, M., & Kamo, Y. (1994). An analysis of earnings patterns for Chinese, Japanese, and Non-Hispanic white males in the United States. *Sociological Quarterly, 35,* 581–602.

Chapter 10

Family Life Education With Arab Immigrant Families

LIBBY BALTER BLUME, CFLE, ANNITA SANI,
AND MENATALLA ADS

The portrait of Arab immigrant families presented in this chapter is intended to enhance family life educators' awareness and understanding of Middle Eastern family values, beliefs, and behaviors within the context of a strengths-oriented perspective. Our hope is to inform the development and implementation of culturally relevant family life education programs for Arab Americans. We begin by briefly identifying Arab populations and describing their migration patterns to the United States and then discuss Middle Eastern families more broadly. Next, we focus on the basic principles and processes that are critical for the implementation of culturally relevant family life education programs with Arab immigrant families. We conclude with recommendations for future research and practice to improve the well-being of Arab American families.

As chapter authors, we wish to acknowledge that our understanding of Arab family strengths has been informed by the scholarly literature on Middle Eastern culture and families, ongoing consultations with students and colleagues of Arab or Middle Eastern ancestry, and qualitative research with Arab and Arab American individuals and families over several years. Our understanding of Arab family patterns and strengths is influenced by Libby's research with Muslim American immigrant mothers and daughters in Michigan and by Mena's lived experience as a Muslim Arab American of Egyptian descent with both her immediate family and the cultural group as a whole. Annita, who has lived and worked in the United Arab Emirates (UAE) since 2001, has conducted home-based interviews with Arab families from several Middle Eastern countries and has provided family life education and counseling to individuals and families of Arab descent both in Michigan and the UAE over several years. Despite the authors' personal and professional work experiences with people of Middle Eastern ancestry, we also must acknowledge that we are writing this chapter through a Western cultural lens.

DEFINING THE POPULATION

Arab immigrant families are from countries with diverse ethnicities, religions, geographies, political systems, and economies (Abraham, 2009). The majority of Arab Americans are Christians (42% Catholic, including Roman Catholic, Maronite, and Melkite; 23% Eastern Orthodox, including Antiochian, Syrian, Greek, and Coptic; and 12% Protestant) and only about one quarter are Muslims (including Sunni, Shi'a, and Druze) (Prejudice Institute, 2010). They may come from one of the 22 Arabic-speaking countries in the Middle East—from Southwest Asia to North Africa, including Algeria, Bahrain, Comoros, Djibouti, Egypt, Iraq, Jordan, Kuwait, Lebanon, Libya, Mauritania, Morocco, Oman, Palestine, Qatar, Saudi Arabia, Somalia, Sudan, Syria, Tunisia, UAE, and Yemen. "Arab" immigrant families also may come from the non-Arab but primarily Muslim countries of Turkey (where they speak a language of Mongolian origin) or Iran, Pakistan, and Afghanistan (where they speak Aryan languages that are Indo-European) (Nydell, 2006). Although Iraqi Chaldeans speak a dialect of Aramaic, Arabic may be spoken as well (Hakim-Larson, Kamoo, Nassar-McMillan, & Porcerelli, 2007).

The lack of consensus about a definition of Arab ethnicity makes it difficult to obtain an accurate estimate of the number of Arab Americans, especially since the U.S. Census does not include a separate category for *Arab American* (U.S. Census Bureau, 2003). Data from the 2000 U.S. Census indicated that there were 1.2 million Arab Americans based on respondents' self-report of national origin; however, other estimates range from 3.5 million (Arab American Institute [AAI], 2010) to as high as 4.2 million (Arab American National Museum [AANM], 2010a). Some of this discrepancy is due to the fact that *Arab American* is an inclusive term (Ameri, 2007), but it may also reflect underreporting due to immigrant families' mistrust of government agencies asking personal questions (Abraham, 1994), especially in the wake of 9/11 and the consequent stigma attached with being identified as Middle Eastern (Baker et al., 2003).

Based on the American Community Survey (U.S. Census Bureau, 2011), 27% of Arab Americans live in the Northeast, while 26% live in the South, 24% in the Midwest, and 22% in the West. Approximately 576,000 Arab immigrants (48%) live in only five states: (1) California, (2) Florida, (3) Michigan, (4) New Jersey, and (5) New York. People reporting Arab ancestry number over 40,000 in five additional states: (1) Illinois, (2) Massachusetts, (3) Ohio, (4) Pennsylvania, and (5) Texas. About 94% of Arab Americans live in the metropolitan areas of Detroit, Chicago, Los Angeles, New York/New Jersey, and Washington, D.C. (AAI, 2010). Although California has the largest population of Arab immigrants, the highest concentration of Arab Americans live in the metropolitan Detroit area (AANM, 2010a).

Unique Aspects of Working With Arab Immigrant Families

The first recorded Arab American was a North African slave from Morocco, probably captured in 1511, who joined the 12 to 15 million other Africans sold into slavery over some 400 years (AANM, 2010a). The first modern wave of Arab immigrants to the United States arrived from the regions of present-day Syria and Lebanon, primarily for economic reasons, in the years from the late 1800s until World War I. A second wave of Arab immigrants followed after World War II through the mid-1960s, mostly settling in already-established Arab communities. This group included Egyptians, Iraqis, Yemenis, and refugees from Palestine after the State of Israel was established in 1948. They settled primarily on the East Coast and in the Midwest where jobs in industry were available. In addition, many immigrants from this period were professionals and university students who often chose to remain in the United States after completion of their education (Abraham, 2009). Today, half of Arab students studying in Europe and North America never return to their home countries (Asmar, 2003). The third wave of Arab immigration was aided by a 1965 change in U.S. immigration policy ending all restrictions based on national origin (AANM, 2010a). Among the more recent reasons for Arab emigration is the need for refuge from political unrest in the Middle East (Arab American and Chaldean Council [ACC] of Southeastern Michigan, 2006). The latest group to come to the United States in any significant numbers has been Iraqi, due to the Iraq–Iran War (1980–1988), the Iraqi invasion of Kuwait (1990), and the more recent U.S. war in Iraq. However, Arab migration to the United States has diminished dramatically since 9/11. In addition, increased travel restrictions between the United States and the Middle East post-9/11 have caused distress for many Arab Americans, especially for families with friends and relatives in their home countries (Nydell, 2006).

Family researchers and theorists agree that the emotional well-being of individuals and families is influenced by a complex interplay of multiple ecological factors that may include cultural norms, social attitudes, politics, economics, and other global issues (e.g., Bronfenbrenner, 1979; Clark, Glick, & Bures, 2009; Mourad & Abdella Carolan, 2010; Spiegel, 1982). For transnational immigrants to the United States, family ecosystems include factors in both the country of origin and the receiving country (Blume & De Reus, 2009b). Although the goal of most early immigrants was assimilation into American society (Abudabbeh, 2005), "a goal of ethnic preservation in the more recent waves of Arab Americans has fostered family trends of intra-ethnic marriage, cultivating larger families than average in America, continued use of the mother tongue, and the valuing of Arab traditions" (Hakim-Larson et al., 2007, p. 303). Research on the emotional well-being of Arab immigrants indicates that the combined pre- and post-migration stresses of exposure to war trauma in countries such as Lebanon, Palestine, and Iraq; traumatic dislocations from family members; loss of support systems; and disrupted kinship networks following migration are the primary concerns of Middle Eastern families (Clark et al., 2009; Faragallah, Schumm, & Webb, 1997). The stereotyping of Middle Eastern immigrants based on appearance (e.g., Muslim women who wear hijab, or headscarves) also has been a major stressor for Arab Americans (Ahmad, 2004; Baker et al., 2003). Since 9/11, the sociopolitical climate in the United States has attributed negative stereotypes to both Muslim and Christian Arab Americans, placing virtually all Middle Eastern immigrant families in the United States at risk for mental health problems, such as depression and anxiety, or—in the extreme—for victimization or physical violence (Hakim-Larson et al., 2007). Even though Arab Americans are classified as "white" by the U.S. Census, they may face discrimination that European Americans may not (Ahmad, 2004; Blume & De Reus, 2009a).

Generalizing from the scholarly research on Arab immigrant families in the United States is difficult. Because Arab Americans are not a monolithic group, the extent to which individuals in immigrant families may embrace their cultures of origin may differ. In addition, cultural practices that are displayed in the context of family interactions may not be observable in contexts outside of the family setting. Despite the diversity of this population (e.g., nationality, ethnicity, religion, and socioeconomic status), researchers have identified several Middle Eastern cultural attitudes, beliefs, and values that cross religious and country-of-origin boundaries (Nydell, 2006).

Strengths and Assets of Arab Immigrant Families

Because the focus of family life education is on prevention (Powell & Cassidy, 2007), family life educators who work with Arab immigrant families need not only to acquire an awareness of the ecological factors that impact family well-being but also need to identify, appreciate, and understand the family strengths that are present in Middle Eastern cultures. These family strengths are protective factors that can act as buffers for the acculturative stress that Arab immigrant individuals may encounter and can provide them with the support needed to develop to their fullest potential and contribute to American society (DeFrain & Asay, 2007). Despite the presence of multiple pre- and post-migration risk factors, Arab Americans have made achievements in all areas of American life—including professions, politics, and entertainment (for examples, see AANM, 2010b). Eighty-nine percent of Arab Americans have a high school diploma, and more than 46% of Arab Americans hold a bachelor's degree or higher, compared to 28% of Americans at large. Approximately 19% of Arab Americans have a post-graduate degree, nearly twice the American average (10%) (AAI, 2010).

Family strengths are those relationship qualities that contribute to the emotional health and well-being of families (DeFrain, 1999; Salabee, 2006). There are two reasons why the application of a family strengths conceptual framework to family life education with Arab immigrant families is important. First, Arab Americans are frequently characterized by negative portrayals in the sociopolitical context and in the media, which have significantly increased since 9/11 (Beiten, Allen, & Bekheet, 2010; Hakim-Larson et al., 2007; Jackson, 2010). For example, at the time of this writing, the constitutional freedom of Muslim American residents of New York and elsewhere in the country to erect community centers and mosques is being questioned by some U.S. politicians and American citizens (see Ghosh, 2010).

Second, the scholarly literature on Middle Eastern families found in most Western academic journals has focused on social problems and has paid little attention to the strengths of families of Arab ancestry (for a meta-analysis, see Beiten et al., 2010). A theoretical grounding in family strengths may help family life educators to challenge the validity of the negative stereotypes about Arab Americans in the popular media and scholarly literature (AANM, 2011). The following family strengths describe characteristics of strong Arab immigrant families: *commitment, roles and responsibilities, interdependence, courtship and marriage,* and *harmony.*

Family Commitment

A fundamental Arab American family strength is the feeling of commitment to family members or the family unit. Arabs and Chaldeans tend to have more children and live in larger households than members of the general population (Baker et al., 2003). Regardless of religious beliefs, national origin, and ethnicities, Middle Eastern households typically are comprised of at least two or three generations—usually the spouses, their children, and the parents of either spouse. Intergenerational families are an important social institution in Middle Eastern cultures that provide family members with the context and structure for multiple opportunities to enhance family strengths.

When families do not consist of more than two generations residing together, however, an extended family structure may provide Arab American families with a context for the development of protective factors, such as caring relationships, high expectations, and family support. Extended family interaction patterns offer opportunities for family members to provide assistance to one another with child care, reduction of financial constraints by shared housing and related expenses, help with chores, and emotional support. When family members are separated by transnational migration, opportunities to interact with other Arab Americans in religious and community center settings also can be a source of social support for Arab immigrant families whose extended family network may have been disrupted (see Stack, 2003).

Primary loyalty to the family also is important to Arab immigrants. Middle Eastern families place a high priority on remaining emotionally close, enhancing individual and family well-being (Ismael & Jabbra, 2004; Nydell, 2006). For example, continuity with extended families back home is maintained post-immigration by Arab Americans through telephone calls, travel abroad, and—more recently—the Internet (Daneshpour, 1998). The extended family provides ongoing contact and opportunities to assist one another and to demonstrate commitment over time. Commitment to family, in turn, fosters the development of family strengths, such as family cohesion, filial piety, and the intergenerational transmission of cultural values and traditions (DeFrain, 1999; DeFrain & Asay, 2007).

Family Roles and Responsibilities

The patriarchal family structure commonly found in Middle Eastern families provides family members with a clear idea of the roles and responsibilities of each family member (Baker, 2003). For example, Arab immigrant parents often rely on respect for authority in raising children (Diller, 2011; Haboush, 2006). Generally, Arab immigrant families are patriarchal and patrilineal, with highly differentiated gender roles. In traditional households, women take responsibility for children and home life, and children are expected to help with chores at an early age (Sharifzadeh, 2004). Culturally, the father is considered the head of the family and is responsible for providing the family's basic living needs and security, which is obligatory under Islamic law. Men also are responsible for mediating between the family and the community, with the eldest male in the family as the primary decision maker for affairs outside of the home (Nydell, 2006).

In the 21st century, however, as modernization brings economic prosperity and salaried work for men and women, "Middle Eastern families revise, improvise, and invent new family scripts for the organization of kin-work" (Stack, 2003, p. 9). For example, in some wealthy households in the oil-rich Middle East, hired domestic workers are increasingly performing the cooking, cleaning, caring for children, tutoring, and driving duties that were formerly reserved for mothers; however, Arab immigrant families where women work outside the home maintain traditional family values and practices (Stack, 2003; see also the United Nations Development Programme, 2005). Because they still take primary responsibility for instilling cultural values and customs in their children, many women may not be seeking the level of gender equity that most family life educators expect (Carolan, Bagherinia, Juhari, Himelright, & Mouton-Sanders, 2000). Nevertheless, family life educators need to pay particular attention to role strain in these Arab immigrant families. However, because roles and responsibilities for all Arab immigrant women may not have changed significantly after migration, family life educators may expect to work with both traditional and more acculturated Arab immigrant families (Mourad & Abdella Carolan, 2010).

Family Interdependence

Arab immigrant families in the United States are typically from countries with collectivist worldviews where individuals are expected to live by shared norms, values, and interests (Diller, 2011). For example, the idea of encouraging independence and freedom of choice in children is less common in Arab immigrant families than in many other American families (Haboush, 2006). Individuals in traditional Arab American families are socialized to believe that interdependence is a normal and healthy family interaction pattern. Family members are encouraged to maintain a collectivist worldview in which one's individual decisions and behaviors promote family well-being rather than striving for independence as an indicator of maturity and responsibility. As a result, most Arab American family members understand that individual well-being is related to family well-being. One's sense of identity, purpose, and self-esteem are derived from the achievements of all family members, not from one individual's accomplishments. For example, for many young adults the primary motivation for earning high grades in college is the honor that it brings to the family name, and as a result, they may feel pressure to live up to their parents' high educational expectations (Haboush, 2007). In addition, academic success raises the family's social status and is perceived to make one a more attractive potential spouse.

This collectivist attitude commonly found in Middle Eastern societies is often misunderstood as the idea that individuals are forced to forego or deny their personal dreams and aspirations for the sake of the family or group. Instead, individuals learn at an early age to evaluate the consequences of their behavior in terms of its impact on the reputation of the family and the honor that it brings or takes away. Rather than focus on the concept of interdependence as being a deficit trait, family life educators should understand interdependence as a condition of commitment and family strength. This interdependence allows individuals to make a conscious effort to remain aware and concerned about the full implications of their decisions and behaviors on the well-being of other family members, including the willingness to alter their plans for the good of all.

Courtship and Marriage

The Arab American family strengths of commitment, roles and responsibility, and interdependence are reinforced through two commonly misunderstood marriage practices: family-planned marriages, in which parents play a major role in selecting a spouse for their unmarried adult children, and endogamy, or marriage to relatives. Marriage to first cousins is a common practice in Middle Eastern societies and is believed to reinforce family strengths, such as commitment and interdependence, and provide an alternative solution to premarital dating, which is not permitted in Middle Eastern societies where Islam is the dominant religion (Haboush, 2007). Endogamy is believed to promote harmonious family relationships as the bonds between existing relatives are reinforced and respect between families is deepened.

Many families in Middle Eastern societies also believe that it is more important for the family members to know the family lineage and background of the person who will eventually become a member of their family than it is for individuals to become acquainted with one another on a personal level (Erickson & Al-Timimi, 2001). The importance given to knowledge of a potential spouse's family lineage over having established an interpersonal relationship between the potential spouses was expressed by a young adult female Arab student during a class discussion on culturally diverse marital customs. In response to her perception that it is a common belief in Western society that family-arranged marriages involve a Middle Eastern woman being forced to marry a man who she does not know, she asked: "Why do they say we marry people who we do not know? I'm marrying my cousin, and I know everything about him." The other students began cheering, "He makes the money, and you make the babies!" This is an example of the patriarchal family structure with gender roles and responsibilities clearly defined. The teacher remarked, "Oh, he must be tall like you." And she answered, "I don't know, I have never seen him." Such situations may occur after immigration as extended families become increasingly transnational (see De Reus & Blume, 2008).

Since it is acceptable for feelings of being in love and intimacy to develop after marriage, many young adults may not object to their parents' selection of a spouse and may prioritize complying with their parents' selection over any hesitancy they may feel. Ideally, family-arranged marriages will involve parental selection of candidates for a potential spouse, with the final choice being ultimately the daughter's decision after the young couple becomes acquainted during supervised "dates" (see Carolan et al., 2000). According to Islamic law, men and women can contract marriage directly; thus, contrary to popular belief, coerced arranged marriage violates Islamic principles (Daneshpour, 1998). Although family-arranged marriage is often negatively portrayed as a cultural practice in which young women are forced to marry their parents' choice, respect and awareness of the collective worldview held by Arab family members are critical to successful interventions with Arab immigrant families (Diller, 2011).

Family Harmony

The belief that family members should live in harmony with their surroundings rather than try to control events and circumstances is a common Middle Eastern family strength, termed *Al-Qadr*: the belief that life events are predetermined or the result of fate. Living in harmony involves acknowledging that individuals have little impact on changing the outcome of events. However, a common misconception is that a belief in Al-Qadr absolves individuals from taking personal responsibility for their actions and thus may inhibit participating actively in preventative programs. Rather, Al-Qadr should be viewed as a family strength that helps Middle Eastern family members manage and cope with inevitable stress and crises (Abi-Hashem, 2008a; DeFrain, 1999; DeFrain & Asay, 2007).

FAMILY LIFE EDUCATION PRACTICES

Family life educators who recognize the strengths of Arab immigrant families can begin to identify resources and develop programs to assist them during their adaptation to life in the United States (Dalla, DeFrain, Johnson, & Abbott, 2009). However, family life education programs for Arab immigrant families in the United States are not common, in part because in traditional Middle Eastern cultures, individuals do not seek help outside of the extended family network and leaders of their religious community. As previously mentioned, however, the potential for negative impacts of the accumulated pre- and post-migration stressors on family well-being for Arab immigrant families justifies family life education programs that focus on prevention. Although some of the programs described below deliver services to individual clients (i.e., evidence-based *practice*), all are "evidence-based programs with an identifiable curriculum and comprise an organized set of practices, activities, and strategies" (Small, Cooney, & O'Connor, 2009, p. 1).

Current State of Family Life Education

Despite the fact that young people in Arab countries have little access to family life education (El-Tawila, 2000), information about family life education programs, tutoring, and recreational services for youth is more often accepted by Arab immigrant families than are services to adults. For example, in an Israeli study of Arab teachers' attitudes toward the inclusion of a family life education program covering 18 different topics (some of these topics are sexuality, marriage, childbirth, emotional intimacy, interpersonal communication, gender roles in families, parent–child relationships, and friendships), results indicated a high degree of support for family life education in Arab schools; however, some subjects (e.g., sexuality and cross-sex friendships) were considered inappropriate for Arab students because of Qur'anic teaching, and parent involvement was considered essential. The author compared her findings to negative attitudes toward sex education among some religiously conservative families in North America (Oz, 1991).

For this chapter, we surveyed programs in the metropolitan Detroit area serving the Arab immigrant community and asked the following questions:

- What, if any, family life education services do you provide?
- How are they provided (i.e., seminars, lecture series, classes, youth programs)?
- How do you recruit participants, or how do you advertise?
- What is the ethnicity and religious affiliation of most of the providers or teachers?
- Is it acceptable for non-Arabs and/or non-Muslims to provide services on family life education?

Our survey results indicated that most family life education being delivered to Arab immigrant families is carried out in the context of other programs, such as schools, health centers, churches, or mosques. Overall, most family life education programs for Arab immigrant families are taught by providers of the same gender, religion, and ethnicity as program participants. Delivery of family life education programs is usually through weekly lectures, educational seminars, conferences, and workshops in cooperation with Islamic centers, universities, and schools. Most programs also disseminate educational publications, newsletters, and information on community resources. In addition, several websites that are consistent with Middle Eastern cultural and religious teachings exist for Arab immigrant families.

General Needs of This Population and Rationale for Family Life Education

Generally, family life education programs are available for Arab American children, adolescents, and adults, but the vast majority are for middle school or high school youth. Programs for young people in the Arab immigrant community typically emphasize healthy development, civic education and engagement, youth recreation and leadership, and self-enrichment through cultural activities. Family life programs for youth also frequently include mentoring, scouting, and participating in internship opportunities. Youth or adult programs involving mixed-sex classes on personal topics, such as sexuality, are culturally not acceptable to most Arab immigrant families, particularly if they are Muslim. However, when single-sex family life education with Arab Americans is conducted on personal topics, family life educators are the same sex as the students.

Topics often reflect a focus on Muslim or Arab family life, including classes on gender roles and relationships, financial literacy, premarital education, successful marriage, sexuality, marital discord, divorce and its impact on children and society, and domestic violence. In the past decade, programs emphasizing ways to counter prejudice have increased in the aftermath of 9/11, including diversity training, forums on immigration policy and legal rights, citizenship classes, courses in English language and literacy, and family life education curricula strengthening Arab immigrant families as they adapt to life in the United States. Overall, the programs in our survey offered family life education that reflected 8 of the 10 family life education Substance Areas (National Council on Family Relations [NCFR], 1994): Families in Society, Internal Dynamics of Families, Human Growth and Development, Human Sexuality, Interpersonal Relationships, Family Resource Management, Parent Education and Guidance, and Family Law and Public Policy. Understandably, the two areas not addressed are Family Life Education Methodology and Ethics since these prevention programs do not train family life educators.

Marketing/Recruitment

Since word of mouth seems to be the most effective way to market within a close-knit Arab immigrant community, representatives of family life education programs should identify community leaders and ask them for help with recruitment. It is certainly acceptable to solicit support from Arab or Middle Eastern religious leaders, such as the imam, minister, or priest (Nassar-McMillan & Hakim-Larson, 2003). Family life educators should work with their local Arab American communities to develop family life education programs with Arabic speakers as well as family life education resource guides that include culturally sensitive material in Arabic. With permission, make in-person visits to distribute brochures and flyers to Muslim immigrant families after Friday prayer at mosques or to Arab Christian families after Sunday church services. The following common marketing techniques are also appropriate for recruiting Arab American families:

- Direct mail (translate newsletters and fliers into Arabic and English)
- E-mail (send notices to schools, community organizations, and religious centers)
- Electronic posts (include subscribers to Listservs, Twitter, and Facebook).

- Websites (provide complete program descriptions, schedules, and registration information)
- Personal visits (include public and parochial schools, churches, and mosques)

Several national organizations are available to help family life educators find resources for Arab individuals and families in their local communities. Arab American organizations are an especially effective recruiting tool because these groups can effectively and quickly use existing community networks to get the word out about family life education programming. For example, the Arab Community Center for Education and Social Services (ACCESS) in metropolitan Detroit publishes a widely read e-newsletter; runs close to 100 health care and social service programs; sponsors the Arab American National Museum (AANM); and organizes community-wide educational forums, interfaith discussion groups, and music and art festivals—all of which provide opportunities for free publicity.

Barriers to Participation

Family life educators can anticipate that immigration status, gender, and age differences may be barriers to participation in family life education by Arab immigrants. For example, recent arrivals from Arabic-speaking countries may not be fluent enough in English to benefit from family life education programs that are delivered in English. This is especially true for women from traditional families or older adults of either sex who have not had much contact with Westerners before moving to the United States. One of the immediate goals is for many new immigrant parents *and* children to develop proficiency in reading and writing in the English language.

In addition to language differences, Middle Eastern cultural norms restrict—or sometimes even prohibit—discussion of personal or family issues with nonrelatives (see Baker, 2003). In most traditional Arabic cultures, older adults are consulted by family members to resolve disputes and are expected to provide sage advice for conflict resolution on marital issues, financial concerns, and child care.

> The population of the Arab world is characterized by a mixture of traditional and modern societies and sub-societies. The Arab family lives between its nuclear state, consisting of the married couple and their children, and its need for the support of the family of origin, the extended family, and sometimes of the whole clan, the *Hamula*. (Baker, 2003, p. 69)

Arab immigrant family members—especially elders—may believe that while non-Arab family life educators might be knowledgeable about the programs and services available in the United States, they have limited life experiences or understanding of Middle Eastern cultural traditions. Similarly, Muslim immigrants may have difficulty adjusting to American society where daily life is not accommodative to Islam (e.g., calls to prayer, holidays, and dietary restrictions) (Carolan et al., 2000). In addition, "the historical legacy of colonization and Western politics in the Middle East may further increase the difficulty of establishing a working alliance with certain families" (Haboush, 2007, p. 188).

Environmental Considerations

Religious centers (e.g., mosques, churches, and faith-based organizations) often serve as places where community networks are built and would likely be a setting in which Arab immigrant families would feel comfortable. Depending on the level of conservativeness among family members, family life educators should also consider seating arrangements that separate participants by gender or decide to offer separate sessions for men and women. Due to Middle Eastern cultural norms, Arab immigrant women may feel more comfortable in a female-only setting even if they are non-Muslim. In addition, scheduling of family life education workshops or classes for observant Muslim families must be sensitive to the timing of daily calls to prayer and religious holidays.

If a topic is sensitive or personal (e.g., sexuality or relationships), Arab immigrant families may be more comfortable with the home-based delivery of family life education programs. When shared concerns arise, family life educators could consider planning for several members to attend a program in one participant's home. Wherever information is disseminated, family life education professionals should make arrangements for young children to minimize disruptions. Educators may arrange for child development programs to run simultaneously to a program on a different topic.

The use of an interpreter is recommended not only for limited English-speaking participants but also to encourage participants to express their ideals without being self-conscious of their use of English and to encourage expressions that they can best communicate in their native language. Finally, expect that Arab immigrant families may arrive late to classes or workshops since in their home cultures the notion of time is more fluid than in the United States, possibly because in Arabic languages there are no clear grammatical distinctions between past and future (Al-Krenawi & Graham, 2000).

Modes of Learning

Middle Eastern cultures rely less on didactic communication than on learning through shared experience, history, and implicit messages (Chng & Collins, 2000). For example, many Arab societies have an oral tradition in which cultural norms and traditional values are passed on through storytelling and poetry. "Indirect means of communication include frequent allusions to proverbs and folk parables" (Daneshpour, 1998, p. 362). As a result, Arab immigrant family members may be more comfortable with learning by engaging in dialogues and discussions than in reading or listening to speakers. However, family life educators also should provide written handouts for information presented verbally to assist with strengthening comprehension of the English language.

Family life educators should also be aware that Arab immigrant family members may receive and send nonverbal cues and messages to one another. Meaning does not have to be communicated through words; instead, gestures may be critical determinants of one's true feelings. For example, males may avoid eye contact as a sign of respect (Springer, Abbott, & Reisbig, 2009). Although it is not necessarily disrespectful to establish eye contact with individuals, family life educators should judge how comfortable individual family members are with direct eye contact and not be offended if someone of the opposite sex avoids eye contact.

Equally important is the awareness that verbal communications may often be misinterpreted.

> For example, in interactions with professionals, respect requires that the family give the impression that they are not in conflict with the professionals' recommendations ... which may give the impression that they are in agreement but may not act on the suggested interventions. (Sharifzadeh, 2004, p. 405)

A training video titled *Multicultural Counseling: Working with Arab Americans*, available from the American Psychological Association (APA), demonstrates how to interact with family members, become aware of personal boundaries, and reconcile Middle Eastern traditions with American culture (Abi-Hashem, 2008b). The video includes an interview, demonstration, and case analysis by an Arab American family therapist in which he discusses the specific interpersonal communication strategies he employs in greeting, establishing rapport, and inquiring about the family immigration history of an Arab American young adult client— techniques that are all very relevant to family life education settings.

Educator Characteristics

The NCFR has articulated the personal qualities necessary to be successful as a family life educator (see NCFR, 1994). Among the most important for providing family life education to Arab immigrant families are *self-awareness, empathy, flexibility, compassion,* and the *understanding and appreciation of diversity* (Duncan & Goddard, 2005; Powell & Cassidy, 2007). Although it is certainly helpful in working with Arab immigrants to be of Arab descent and to share the same religious tradition as the students, it is not essential if family life educators are culturally sensitive and unbiased (Dwairy, 2006; Lynch & Hanson, 2004). In interviews with Muslim Americans, for example, the first choice of a family professional was found to be a person who was Muslim, followed by a non-Muslim known to the Muslim community as a culturally sensitive and caring professional (Carolan et al., 2000). In our experience, Muslim families are generally open to non-Muslim family life educators, but the best scenario would be for a non-Muslim to work in collaboration with a Muslim professional so that both what is acceptable and what is unacceptable according to Islamic law are represented.

Overall, to work successfully with Arab immigrant groups, family life educators need to develop the following specific skills and attitudes:

- Ability to communicate in a way that is consistent with traditional Middle Eastern family values and is responsive to Arab cultural perspectives
- Willingness to respect diverse views about gender roles in family and marriage
- Ability to accept diverse perspectives that may be in contrast to one's personal, cultural, religious, and political views
- Responsiveness to conflicting feelings and optimism about sociopolitical events in participants' countries of origin and sociopolitical discrimination against people of Arab descent in the United States
- Willingness to reflect on how their own privilege (e.g., social location and education) may unconsciously promote stereotypes by making generalizations about cultural groups

Perhaps the most critical quality for family life educators working with Arab immigrant families is a global orientation to understanding the issues affecting them (Darling, 2007). "Therefore, viewing families from an international context is not only important to increase our understanding of those beyond our borders, but also to gain insights about those who have recently immigrated to new countries" (Darling, 2007, p. 254).

Ethical Considerations

Ethical practice with any immigrant group involves respect for privacy and strict confidentiality, especially with refugee populations in cases where revealing identities could lead to retribution toward family members left behind in politically hostile countries (see Nassar-McMillan & Hakim-Larson, 2003).

To practice in an ethical manner, family life educators also must uncover and maintain an awareness of the varied sources of their own privilege as Americans when working with immigrant populations from Middle Eastern countries (Blume & De Reus, 2009b). Even when family life education practitioners think that they are unbiased, they may hold unconscious stereotypes about immigrant families, due in large part to the social construction of Middle Eastern ethnicities in the United States. It is important for family life educators to examine their personal values and beliefs about immigrants, and Arab Americans in particular, given the pervasively negative messages in U.S. media and TV. For example, immigrants may be viewed negatively by family life educators as needing to leave behind their cultural values and traditions in order to achieve assimilation to American society. However, family life educators are ethically bound to respect diversity and maintain a culturally relative view of the family values, beliefs, and behaviors of the families they serve (NCFR, 2009).

Ethics demand sensitivity to class differences among immigrant groups, depending on the country of origin how recent the migration. Researchers have found that a family's change in socioeconomic status, change in status as a minority, or change in professional status upon immigration often affects their adjustment to American life. For example, many immigrants held professional positions in their home countries only to be unable to practice law or medicine after migration (Abraham, 2009).

Best Practices in Family Life Education Programming

The application of a family strengths conceptual framework in working with Arab immigrant families requires that family life educators focus their attention on understanding healthy family interaction patterns, assisting family members to articulate their strengths, and then identifying ways to utilize these resources to cope with conflict and stress to promote family well-being. The most significant differences between Arab immigrant families and Western family life education practitioners often lie in the valuing of greater family connectedness, less flexible and more hierarchical family structures, and an implicit communication style (Daneshpour, 1998). Not all Arab immigrant family members will strictly adhere to the religious or cultural conventions of their faith or ethnic group; however, family life educators should try to conceptualize family values and practices for a culture that is different from their own as existing along a cultural continuum (see Lynch & Hanson, 2004). For example, "Some evidence suggests that many Arabs may find acculturation to be more difficult than have other immigrants, especially those affiliated with Islam.... [More] Middle Eastern subjects than other immigrants agreed with statements such as 'In the U.S., there is no place I really belong'" (Faragallah et al., 1997, p. 182). Such remarks are consistent with our qualitative research with immigrant women. When asked if she felt like an American, an interviewee who self-identified as a Muslim Arab answered as follows:

> I was older when I came, even though I have the American citizenship, I still can't feel that, you know? Because I didn't grow up in this culture maybe,

I haven't spent much time here maybe, even though it's been like 20 years, but I don't know. It doesn't feel like it. Is that bad to say? It doesn't feel like it, no, because, I don't know, even though I worked and I speak English, it doesn't feel like it. (Blume, Assar, Hadied, & De Reus, 2007)

No matter how many years immigrants have lived in the United States, bonds to their country of origin may remain strong.

Family life educators should assess the level of acculturation of family members, historical or contextual stressors affecting immigrant or refugee families, and cultural differences in communication styles between themselves and their clients (Berry, Phinney, Sam, & Vedder, 2006; Springer et al., 2009). If family life educators are unsure about the role of elders or extended family members, the propriety of mixed-sex interaction, or other cultural norms, it is better to ask the families with whom they are working than risk being culturally inappropriate (Springer et al., 2009). The following practical suggestions—based on our own extensive experiences with Arab immigrants in various settings—are not comprehensive or universal but may minimize cultural discomfort for family life educators and Arab immigrant participants:

- Dress conservatively. Women should wear long slacks or a skirt that at least falls to the knees and not wear low-cut blouses.
- Offer separate sessions by gender so men and women have the option of meeting with a same-sex family life educator.
- Offer a handshake to women only if their hand is extended. Avoid offering men a handshake unless they offer first.
- Offer food to participants for receipt in their right hand; the left hand is considered unclean.

When meeting with Arab immigrant family members in their home, do as follows:

- Enter the home only after being invited by an adult. Avoid being in the home alone with only one other adult. Female family life educators should not remain in the home alone with a male family member. Likewise, male family life educators should not remain in the home if the only other adult present is female. Ask upon entering what other family members are present, and if none are present, offer to return at a later date.
- After you enter the home and the door is closed, offer to remove your shoes before walking to your seat. Prepare for removing your shoes by wearing socks.
- Do accept a small snack if offered. It is acceptable to only take a small bite and not eat the snack entirely.

Effective family life practitioners need to have an awareness of Arab culture, recent history, and the family's migration experiences. They "should learn about the cultural values and experiences of Arab Americans and allow their clients to educate them about their individual cultural contexts" (Erickson & Al-Timimi, 2001, p. 325). It is also important for family life educators to consider how Arab immigrant families' worldviews can inform their own family life education practices, including the potential value of Arab indigenous ways of helping within the family (Erickson & Al-Timimi, 2001).

Exemplary Programs

The U.S. Agency for International Development (USAID) funded Family Health International's Youthnet program to develop family life education curriculum for Arab families worldwide. The Muslim curriculum, called "Teaching Adults to Communicate with Children," links health and religious lessons from the Qur'an (Esack, Moreau, & Pribila, 2007). Topics include Muslim family life education, sexual development, gender roles, and relationships and marriage. Although this program has not been evaluated formally, it was field-tested as part of an initiative to support faith-based institutions abroad and meets three of four categories for evidence-based programs: theory-driven, relevant to the community (there are Christian and Muslim versions), and developed by well-qualified staff (Small et al., 2009).

In the New York City area, the Arab American Family Support Center (AAFSC) serves the Arabic-speaking community with the overall goal of strengthening Arab immigrant families as they adapt to life in the United States.

> AAFSC provides comprehensive social services to Arab-American immigrant families and children as they adjust to a new culture and navigate American laws and cultural norms. AAFSC addresses language barriers, encourages positive leadership, and promotes a stronger and more united Arab-American community. (Arab American Family Support Center [AAFSC], 2011a, para. 1)

Its prevention program "is a strength based approach where families are involved in identifying their problems and challenges, setting goals, planning services and defining the desired outcomes" (AAFSC, 2011b, para. 2).

In the Detroit area, Muslim Family Services organizes the following:

> educational seminars and workshops in cooperation with Islamic centers, universities and schools [on topics such as] domestic violence, important of counseling and pre-marriage counseling, successful marriage, *Fiqh* [Islamic jurisprudence] of marriage, married and unmarried gathering (share experience), divorce and

its impact on children and society, marital discord and rules of engagement. (Muslim Family Services, n.d., para. 1)

The Arab American and Chaldean Council (ACC) is another community-based program with 40 outreach offices in southeastern Michigan that deliver "educational, employment and training, behavioral health, youth recreation and self-enrichment services, cultural activities, immigration, and health services." ACC's Youth Recreation and Leadership Center, for example, provides "educational activities to develop and enhance social skills while promoting responsible behavior and decision making." In addition, the Cultural Tapestry Program "enhances cultural awareness and promotes understanding while dispelling stereotypes." Handouts and lesson plans are available as a resource for family life educators (http://www.myacc.org/resources/cultural-tapestry-initiative).

Also in Michigan, ACCESS has been serving the Arab American community for 40 years, and is one of the nation's premier Arab American organizations. With 7 locations and over 90 programs, ACCESS offers services to a diverse population, regardless of ethnicity. Its mission is to advocate for and empower individuals, families, and communities. Started by a group of volunteers in 1971, ACCESS was originally created to assist the Arab immigrant population adapt to American life. It offers many family life education programs to improve family relations and family communication, including family financial literacy and domestic violence prevention (http://accfea.convio.net).

Finally, while web-based resources do *not* necessarily represent evidence-based family life education scholarship and practice, such sites can offer family life education practitioners an understanding of the diversity of Arab family values with which to begin a conversation about family life. Two such examples are Arab Family Life (http://www.arabfamilylife.org), a conservative Christian marriage and parent education site with a family life education curriculum available in Arabic, and A2 Youth (http://www.a2youth.com/articles/family_life), a website with an Islamic perspective on parenting (Alyas, 2010). Family experts caution, however, that we know little about the effectiveness of web-based family life education (Steimle & Duncan, 2004).

FUTURE DIRECTIONS

Currently, a dearth of existing family life education programs designed specifically for Arab immigrant families means that family life educators must draw from the available literature on Arab culture, family therapy with Muslim Americans, and best practices in working with diverse populations in schools to develop guidelines for effective practice (Haboush, 2007; see also Abi-Hashem, 2008b; Carolan et al.,

2000; Dwairy, 2006; Hakim-Larson et al., 2007; Nassar-McMillan & Hakim-Larson, 2003). For example, school psychologists tell us that "because of strong religious beliefs and emphasis on family honor, traditional families consider certain topics taboo for discussion.... Domestic violence and sexual issues, including birth control, homosexuality, and sexual abuse, are not openly discussed, especially among Muslim families" (Haboush, 2007, p. 193). Yet in a recent meta-analysis of research of families of Arab descent over the past 4 decades, domestic violence was the most studied, followed by family planning and contraception (Beiten et al., 2010). More importantly, the risk to Arab Americans' individual and family well-being is compounded by a lack of culturally relevant programs and services (ACC of Southeastern Michigan, 2006).

Equally important to keep in mind, however, are the distinctions among race/ethnicity, religion, and national origin (Blume et al., 2007; Blume & De Reus, 2009b). Individuals with the same ethnicity, including Arabs, may practice different religions. Likewise, a specific ethnic group can be made up of individuals who have migrated from different countries of origin. The future of successful family life education with Arab immigrant families, as with other ethnic minorities, depends on increasing the numbers of family life educators of Middle Eastern heritage, ethnicity, or religion. "Thus, it will take a multinational, multicultural, and multidisciplinary network of family professionals working together to enhance family well being worldwide" (Darling, 2007, p. 277). Until the pool of multiethnic family life educators increases, the need for family life educators who are culturally competent, internationally aware, and knowledgeable about the communities they serve is paramount.

REFERENCES

Abi-Hashem, N. (2008a). Arab Americans: Understanding their challenges, needs, and struggles. In A. Marsella, J. Johnson, P. Watson, & J. Gryczynski (Eds.), *Ethnocultural perspectives on disaster and trauma: Foundations, issues, and applications* (pp. 115–173). New York: Springer.

Abi-Hashem, N. (2008b). *Multicultural counseling video series: Working with Arab Americans.* Retrieved from http://www.apa.org/pubs/videos/4310843.aspx

Abraham, N. (1994). Anti-Arab racism and violence in the United States. In E. McCarus (Ed.), *The development of Arab-American identity.* Ann Arbor: University of Michigan Press.

Abraham, N. (2009). *Countries and their cultures: Arab Americans.* Retrieved from http://www.everyculture.com/multi/A-Br/Arab-Americans.html

Abudabbeh, N. (2005). Arab families: An overview. In M. McGoldrick, J. Giordano, & N. Garcia-Preto (Eds.), *Ethnicity and family therapy* (3rd ed., pp. 423–436). New York: Guilford.

Ahmad, N. M. (2004). *Arab-American culture and health care.* Retrieved from http://www.cwru.edu/med/epidbio/mphp439/Arab-Americans.htm

Al-Krenawi, A., & Graham, J. R. (2000). Culturally sensitive social work practice with Arab clients in mental health settings. *Health and Social Work, 25*(1), 9–22.

Alyas, A. M. (2010). *Parenting: An Islamic perspective.* Retrieved from http://www.a2youth.com/articles/family_life/parenting_an_islamic_perspective/2

Ameri, A. (2007, June). *Arab American families.* Presentation to the annual meetings of the Groves Conference on Marriage and Family, Detroit, MI.

Arab American and Chaldean Council of Southeastern Michigan. (2006). *Annual report, 2006.* Available from the Arab American and Chaldean Council, 62 West Seven Mile Road, Detroit, MI 48203-1967.

Arab American Family Support Center. (2011a). Retrieved from http://www.aafscny.org/Home%20Page

Arab American Family Support Center. (2011b). *Preventive services.* Retrieved from http://www.aafscny.org/Preventive%20Services

Arab American Institute. (2010). *Arab American demographics.* Retrieved from http://www.aaiusa.org/pages/demographics

Arab American National Museum. (2010a). *Arab Americans: An integral part of American society.* Dearborn, MI: AANM Educational Series.

Arab American National Museum. (2010b). *Making an impact.* Retrieved from http://www.arabamericanmuseum.org/Making-an-Impact.id.20.htm

Arab American National Museum. (2011). *Reclaiming our identity: Dismantling Arab stereotypes.* Retrieved from http://www.arabstereotypes.org

Asmar, M. (2003, December 29). Stop the brain drain from the Arab world. *Gulf News (Dubai).* Retrieved from http://www.aljazeerah.info/Opinion%20editorials/2003%20Opinion%20Editorials/December/29%20o/Stop%20the%20brain%20drain%20from%20the%20Arab%20world%20By%20Marwan%20Asmar.htm

Baker, K. A. (2003). Marital problems among Arab families: Between cultural and family therapy interventions. *Arab Studies Quarterly, 25*(4), 53–74.

Baker, W., Stockton, R., Howell, S., Jamal, A., Lin, A. C., Shryock, A., et al. (2003). *Detroit Arab American study.* Ann Arbor, MI: Inter-University Consortium for Political and Social Research. Retrieved from http://dx.doi.org/10.3886/ICPSR04413

Beiten, B. K., Allen, K. R., & Bekheet, M. (2010). A critical analysis of Western perspectives on families of Arab descent. *Journal of Family Issues, 31,* 211–233.

Berry, J. W., Phinney, J., Sam, D. L., & Vedder, P. (Eds.). (2006). *Immigrant youth in cultural transition: Acculturation, identity and adaptation across national contexts.* Mahwah, NJ: Lawrence Erlbaum.

Blume, L. B., Assar, I., Hadied, L., & De Reus, L. A. (2007). *Dialectics of ethnic identity.* Poster presented at the biennial meetings of the Society for Research on Identity Formation, Washington, DC.

Blume, L. B., & De Reus, L. A. (2009a). Resisting whiteness: Autoethnography and the dialectics of ethnicity and privilege. In S. Lloyd, A. L. Few, & K. Allen (Eds.), *Handbook of feminist family studies* (pp. 43–55). Thousand Oaks, CA: Sage.

Blume, L. B., & De Reus, L. A. (2009b). Transnational families and the social construction of identity: Whiteness matters. In R. L. Dalla, J. DeFrain, J. Johnson, & D. Abbott (Eds.), *Strengths and challenges of new immigrant families: Implications for research, policy, education, and service* (pp. 71–90). New York: Lexington.

Bronfenbrenner, U. (1979). *The ecology of human development.* Cambridge, MA: Harvard University Press.

Carolan, M. T., Bagherinia, G., Juhari, R., Himelright, J., & Mouton-Sanders, M. (2000). Contemporary Muslim families: Research and practice. *Contemporary Family Therapy: An International Journal, 22*(1), 67–79.

Chng, C. L., & Collins, J. R. (2000). Providing culturally competent HIV prevention programs. *American Journal of Health Studies, 16*(1), 24–33.

Clark, R. L., Glick, J. E., & Bures, R. M. (2009). Immigrant families over the life course: Research directions and needs. *Journal of Family Issues, 30,* 852–872.

Dalla, R. L., DeFrain, J., Johnson, J., & Abbott, D. A. (Eds.) (2009). *Strengths and challenges of new immigrant families: Implications for research education, policy, and service.* Lanham, MD: Lexington.

Daneshpour, M. (1998). Muslim families and family therapy. *Journal of Marital and Family Therapy, 24*(3), 355–368.

Darling, C. A. (2007). International perspectives in family life education. In L. H. Powell & D. Cassidy, *Family life education: An introduction* (2nd ed., pp. 253–277). Long Grove, IL: Waveland Press.

DeFrain, J. (1999). Strong families around the world. *Family Matters, 53,* 8–13.

DeFrain, J., & Asay, S. M. (2007). *Strong families around the world: Strengths-based research and perspectives.* New York: Taylor & Francis.

De Reus, L. A., & Blume, L. B. (2008). A note from the guest coordinators: Special collection on transnational families. *Family Relations, 57,* 415–418.

Diller, J. V. (2011). Working with Arab and Muslim American clients: An interview with Marwan Dwairy. In J. V. Diller, *Cultural diversity: A primer for human services* (4th ed., pp. 289–302). Belmont, CA: Brooks/Cole.

Duncan, S. F., & Goddard, H. W. (2005). *Family life education: Principles and practices for effective outreach.* Thousand Oaks, CA: Sage.

Dwairy, M. A. (2006). *Counseling and psychotherapy with Arabs and Muslims: A culturally sensitive approach.* New York: Teachers' College Press.

El-Tawila, S. (2000). *Youth in the population agenda: Concepts and methodologies, Regional Paper No. 44.* Cairo, Egypt: Population Council.

Erickson, C. D., & Al-Timimi, N. R. (2001). Providing mental health services to Arab Americans: Recommendations and considerations. *Cultural Diversity and Ethnic Minority Psychology, 7*(4), 308–327.

Esack, F., Moreau, L., & Pribila, M. (2007). *Family life education: Teaching adults to communicate with youth from a Muslim perspective.* Arlington, VA: Family Health International.

Faragallah, M. H., Schumm, W. R., & Webb, F. J. (1997). Acculturation of Arab-American immigrants: An exploratory study. *Journal of Comparative Family Studies, 28,* 182–203.

Ghosh, B. (2010, August 10). Does America have a Muslim problem? *Time Magazine.* Retrieved from http://www.time.com/time/nation/article/0,8599,2011798,00.html

Haboush, K. L. (2006). Lebanese and Syrian families. In M. McGoldrick, J. Giordano, & N. Garcia-Preto (Eds.), *Ethnicity and family therapy* (3rd ed., pp. 468–486). New York: Guilford.

Haboush, K. L. (2007). Working with Arab American families: Culturally competent practice for school psychologists. *Psychology in the Schools, 44*(2), 183–198.

Hakim-Larson, J., Kamoo, R., Nassar-McMillan, S. C., & Porcerelli, J. H. (2007). Counseling Arab and Chaldean American families. *Journal of Mental Health Counseling, 29*(4), 301–321.

Ismael, J., & Jabbra, N. (2004). Introduction. *Journal of Comparative Family Studies, 35*(2), 133–137.

Jackson, L. (2010). Images of Islam in U.S. media and their educational implications. *Educational Studies: Journal of the American Educational Studies Association, 46,* 3–24.

Lynch, L. W., & Hanson, M. J. (2004). *Developing cross-cultural competence: A guide for working with children and their families* (3rd ed.). Baltimore: Paul H. Brookes.

Mourad, M. R, & Abdella Carolan, M. T. (2010). An ecological approach to culturally sensitive intervention for Arab American women and their families. *Family Journal, 18,* 178–183.

Muslim Family Services. (n.d.). *Education.* Retrieved from http://www.muslimfamilyservices.org/education

Nassar-McMillan, S. C., & Hakim-Larson, J. (2003). Counseling considerations among Arab Americans. *Journal of Counseling and Development, 81,* 150–159.

National Council on Family Relations. (1994). *Standards and criteria for the certification of family life educators, college/university curriculum guidelines, and an overview of content in family life education: A framework for planning life span programs.* Minneapolis, MN: Author.

National Council on Family Relations. (2009). *Tools for ethical thinking and practice in family life education* (2nd ed.). Minneapolis, MN: Author.

Nydell, M. K. (2006). *Understanding Arabs: A guide for modern times* (4th ed.). Boston: Intercultural Press.

Oz, S. (1991). Attitudes toward family life education: A survey of Israeli Arab teachers. *Adolescence, 26,* 899–912.

Powell, L. H., & Cassidy, D. (2007). *Family life education: An introduction* (2nd ed.). Long Grove, IL: Waveland Press.

Prejudice Institute. (2010). *Arab Americans: Factsheet #5.* Baltimore: Author. Retrieved from http://www.prejudiceinstitute.org/Factsheets5-ArabAmericans.html

Salabee, D. (2006). *Strengths perspective in social work* (4th ed.). Boston: Allyn & Bacon.

Sharifzadeh, V. S. (2004). *Families with Middle Eastern roots.* In E. W. Lynch & M. J. Hanson (Eds.), *Developing cross-cultural competence: A guide for working with children and their families* (3rd ed., pp. 373–407). Baltimore: Paul H. Brookes.

Small, S. A., Cooney, S. M., & O'Connor, C. (2009). Evidence-informed program improvement: Using principles of effectiveness to enhance the quality and impact of family-based prevention programs. *Family Relations, 58*(1), 1–13.

Spiegel, J. (1982). An ecological model of ethnic families. In M. McGoldrick, J. K. Pearce, & J. Giordano (Eds.), *Ethnicity & family therapy.* (pp. 37-49) New York: Guilford.

Springer, P. R., Abbott, D. A., & Reisbig, A. M. J. (2009). Therapy with Muslim couples and families: Basic guidelines for effective practice. *Family Journal, 17*(3), 229–235.

Stack, C. B. (2003). Frameworks for studying families in the 21st century. In N. S. Hopkins (Ed.), *The new Arab family* (pp. 5–15). Cairo, Egypt: American University in Cairo Press.

Steimle, B. M., & Duncan, S. F. (2004). Formative evaluation of a family life education website. *Family Relations, 50,* 67–76.

United Nations Development Programme. (2005). *Arab human development report 2005: Empowerment of Arab women.* Retrieved from http://hdr.undp.org/en/reports/regional/arabstates/name,3403,en.html

U.S. Census Bureau. (2003). *The Arab population: 2000.* Retrieved from http://www.census.gov/prod/2003pubs/c2kbr-23.pdf

U.S. Census Bureau. (2011). *American community survey 3-year estimates (2007–2009).* Retrieved from http://www.census.gov/acs/www/index.html

Chapter 11

Family Life Education With Black Families

EBONI J. BAUGH, CFLE, AND DEANNA R. COUGHLIN

As chapter authors, we have unique academic and professional preparation in addition to volunteer experience with black families, both in the United States and abroad. Eboni has a family life education and marriage and family therapy background, working with black families as both a therapist and a state extension specialist. She has presented and published in the areas of culturally sensitive research methods and working with diverse populations. DeAnna has worked and volunteered countless hours with the Boys & Girls Clubs of America (BGCA), gaining experience with black families. In the international arena, DeAnna has traveled to Kenya and worked with Kenyan parents and children. Based on knowledge gained through these varied experiences, we will discuss family life education with black families in the United States.

DEFINING THE POPULATION

The terms *black* and *African American* are used interchangeably throughout the literature. The U.S. Census Bureau classifications of black and African American refer to people with origins from black racial groups of Africa, those of non-African black heritage, and those who identify as Negro, Afro American, Kenyan, Haitian, or Nigerian (U.S. Census Bureau, 2007). In addition, *African American* can refer to anyone who has emigrated from Africa, including those who identify as some other race (i.e., white, Asian). As such, this chapter will use the term *black* to refer to people with African and non-African black racial characteristics and those who personally identify with the black race. *African American* will only be used when referring to a specific program, organization, or institution that uses that term in the title.

There are currently 38.9 million black people in the United States today, which accounts for 13% of the total population and makes up the second largest minority group following the Hispanic/Latino population (Humes, Jones, & Ramirez, 2011; U.S. Department of Health and Human Services [DHHS], 2009; U.S. Census Bureau, 2007). Blacks constitute the largest minority group in 23 states, including Alabama, Arkansas, Delaware, Georgia, Illinois, Indiana, Kentucky, Louisiana, Maine, Maryland, Michigan, Minnesota, Mississippi, Missouri, New York, North Carolina, Ohio, Pennsylvania, South Carolina, Tennessee, Virginia, West Virginia, and Wisconsin, as well as the District of Columbia (U.S. Census Bureau, 2007). The majority reside in the South while the West represents the smallest percentage with approximately 5% of the population (U.S. Census Bureau, 2007; U.S. DHHS, 2009).

According to the U.S. Census Bureau's American Community Survey (2007), blacks have a larger percentage of younger people (31%) and a smaller percentage of older people (8%) when compared to the non-Hispanic white population (22% and 15%, respectively) (U.S. DHHS, 2009). Additionally, in the United States there are 8.6 million black households comprised of 44% married couples (U.S. Census Bureau, 2007). Approximately 30% of black households are maintained by women alone (U.S. Census Bureau, 2007), and the average household size is three individuals (U.S. Census Bureau, 2007).

In 2009, the annual median income for black households was $32,584, which is 4% lower than the previous year (DeNavas-Walt, Proctor, & Smith, 2010). Furthermore, 25.8% of black households were at or below poverty compared to non-Hispanic white families with 8.2% below poverty (DeNavas-Walt et al., 2010). Of those families below the poverty line, 13.6% had children under the age of 18, and 17% had children under the age of 5 (U.S. Census Bureau, 2007). The rates of poverty increased to 26.5% when the family consisted of a female head of household with no husband present. Within those single female-headed households, 34.3% had children under the age of 18 and 46.4% had children under the age of 5 (U.S. Census Bureau, 2007). Also, 21% of blacks lacked health insurance, which was an increase from 19% the previous year (DeNavas-Walt et al., 2010).

A disproportionate number of black grandparents are raising grandchildren when compared to their white and Hispanic counterparts (Mutchler, Lee, & Baker, 2006). Approximately 1.3 million black grandparents live with grandchildren under the age of 18, with 50% being the primary caregivers of these children (U.S. Census Bureau, 2007). Support networks of extended kin are a unique feature and strength of the black family. Extended kin networks, such as grandparents, provide both tangible support (finances) and intangible support (emotional closeness) for children in need of care (Stevenson, Henderson, & Baugh, 2007). See Chapter 6 in this volume for more specific information on family life education with grand-parent-headed households.

Unique Aspects of African American Families

Black families have a variety of unique aspects that differentiate them from other racially and ethnically diverse families. Historically, the black family's uniqueness has been viewed through a pathological lens (Barnes, 2001; Bell-Tolliver, Burgess, & Brock, 2009; Fine, Schwebel, & James-Myers, 1987; Perkins-Dock, 2005). The pathological model deemphasizes the strengths of the black family, while emphasizing the white family's experience as the standard, viewing uniqueness as a deficiency and believing that racism has led to extreme damage that requires structural change (Barnes, 2001; Fine et al., 1987). However, over time the complex structure that defines the black family is beginning to be viewed through alternative lenses (Barnes, 2001). An additional model that has been used to view the black family includes the cultural equivalent (also known as the structural–functional) model (Barnes, 2001; Fine et al., 1987). The cultural equivalent model claims that when socioeconomic conditions are controlled for (with the exception of slavery), black and white families are more similar than they are dissimilar (Barnes, 2001; Fine et al., 1987). Finally, the emergent model emphasizes the importance of the black family's African heritage and claims that the black family must be studied independent of other heritages (Barnes, 2001; Fine et al., 1987; Perkins-Dock, 2005; Waites, 2009). Overall, these models provide three distinct views of the unique aspects of the black family. While each model has a specific focus, this chapter will view the black family using a strengths perspective. The unique aspects of interest include the influence of African heritage, the legacy of slavery, family structure, the influence of religion, and the resiliency of the black family.

African Heritage

African heritage continues to have influence on the black family today. As a collectivist culture, Africans work for the good of the group rather than focusing on the individual (Harvey, McCullough-Chavis, Littlefield, Phillips, & Cooper, 2010; Scannapieco & Jackson, 1996). Therefore, African culture emphasizes the importance of a group of people working together. This includes giving support to families by raising children and pooling resources. The collectivist nature of the African culture is still common among black families as reliance on extended family networks for support and resources continues to occur (Fine et al., 1987; Perkins-Dock, 2005; Scannapieco & Jackson, 1996; Waites, 2009). Furthermore, the African culture also focuses on the importance of spirituality and hope. Likewise, many black families view religion and spirituality as influential and important aspects of daily life (Barnes, 2001; Fine et al., 1987; Perkins-Dock, 2005).

Legacy of Slavery

The legacy of slavery is unique to the black family's history (Goodman & Silverstein, 2006; Scannapieco & Jackson, 1996) and is one of the largest impacts on how black families operate today. With an emphasis on the group as a whole, the African culture promoted many survival strategies implemented by slaves, particularly within the family structure (Scannapieco & Jackson, 1996). When slaves were first brought to the United States against their will, it was common for the traditional family to be separated. This separation from the family of origin forced slaves to form alternative family structures that included both blood relatives and nonblood relatives (Scannapieco & Jackson, 1996). After emancipation, the black family experienced additional changes in family structure. People began attempting to reconnect with family members they had been separated from and also began migrating North in search of jobs (Armstrong & Crowther, 2002; Scannapieco & Jackson, 1996). This migration caused the black family to rely on extended family and nonblood relatives for financial support, emotional support, and assistance with caregiving (Goodman & Silverstein, 2006; Scannapieco & Jackson, 1996). The family structure was once again reliant on external sources of support as family members attempted to build a solid foundation with which their family could benefit and prosper.

Family Structure

The impact of slavery caused the black population to adapt to new and challenging situations over hundreds of years and continues to influence the structure of the black family today. The black family continues to make use of extended family networks, including nonblood relatives, for both tangible and intangible resources (Barnes, 2001; Bell-Tolliver et al., 2009; Goodman & Silverstein, 2006; Hamilton-Mason, Hall, & Everett, 2009; Harvey et al., 2007; Jarrett, Jefferson, & Kelly, 2010; Lamborn & Nguyen, 2004; McCrae & Fusco, 2010; Perkins-Dock, 2005; Riina & McHale, 2010; Scannapieco & Jackson, 1996; Thomas, Sperry, & Yarbrough, 2000; Tolson & Wilson, 1990; Waites, 2009). Resources such as financial and emotional support; assistance with caregiving; providing food, clothing, cleaning, and transportation, in addition to encouragement and advice (Barnes, 2001; Goodman & Silverstein, 2006; Hamilton-Mason et al., 2009; Jarrett et al., 2010; Lamborn & Nguyen, 2004; Perkins-Dock, 2005; Scannapieco & Jackson, 1996; Waites, 2009) are received from family members who reside both inside and outside of the nuclear family system. Another unique feature of the black family structure is the respect and reverence of older generations. Grandparents and great-grandparents are integral resources, especially with regard to caregiving of children and ailing or sick family members (Antonucci & Jackson, 2007; Armstrong & Crowther, 2002; Goodman & Silverstein, 2006; Thomas et al., 2000; Waites, 2009). Additionally, it is common for black families to include nonblood relatives in their family circles, such as additional members of the community, neighbors, and the church family (Armstrong & Crowther, 2002; McFadden, 2005; Perkins-Dock, 2005).

Religion

Another unique theme that consistently emerges from the literature is the importance of religion and spirituality (Armstrong & Crowther, 2002; Barnes, 2001; McFadden, 2005; Perkins-Dock, 2005). Religion and spirituality provide messages of hope and a way to connect to one's past (Barnes, 2001). The church provides a safe place where individuals and families can freely express themselves (Perkins-Dock, 2005). Also, the church may provide resources to families similar to that of the extended kin networks, helping to support the family in times of need (Armstrong & Crowther, 2002; Perkins-Dock, 2005). The importance of religion and spirituality can be traced back to African heritage, as a coping mechanism for families during the time of slavery, and it continues to be important to black families today (Armstrong & Crowther, 2002; Barnes, 2001; Perkins-Dock, 2005).

Resiliency

Finally, all of the aforementioned aspects of the black family contribute to the rich uniqueness therein and provide mechanisms of resiliency. Despite a history of oppression, the black family has survived and acquires strength through the utilization of resources such as extended kin networks, spirituality, and the church community (Barnes, 2001; Bell-Tolliver et al., 2009; Harvey et al., 2007; Jarrett et al., 2010; Riina & McHale, 2010). The black family remains strong despite larger systemic barriers such as poverty, racism, and discrimination (Brody et al., 2008; Hamilton-Mason et al., 2009; Harvey et al., 2007; Jarrett et al., 2010).

Strengths and Assets of African American Families

Black families have a diverse array of strengths and assets that have helped them remain strong throughout history. There are a number of studies that view the black family's struggles as weaknesses and claim that these struggles have inherent deficiencies. However, current research has refuted this claim and no longer views the black family through a pathological lens. Instead, more recent ideologies that emphasize the black family's resiliency are coming to the forefront. Focusing on the strengths of close-knit support networks both within the immediate and extended family, coping techniques, religious affiliations, and the development of a positive racial identity are all cited as increasing and contributing to the strength of black families.

Extended Support Network

The black family's use of extended support networks continues to be cited as one of its most vital assets (Barnes, 2001; Bell-Tolliver et al., 2009; Goodman & Silverstein, 2006; Hamilton-Mason et al., 2009; Harvey et al., 2007; Jarrett et al., 2010; Lamborn & Nguyen, 2004; McCrae & Fusco, 2010; Perkins-Dock, 2005; Riina & McHale, 2010; Scannapieco & Jackson, 1996; Thomas et al., 2000; Tolson & Wilson, 1990; Waites, 2009). Barnes (2001) suggested that regardless of the family structure, most black families consider themselves to be successful and will often reach out to extended support networks. Relationships formed with blood relatives as well as nonblood relatives provide essential resources during difficult times. Jarrett et al. (2010) suggested that kin networks, or extended support networks, provide care, connections, and resources that helped to protect members from the effects of hunger, illness, alienation, and hardship. The authors went on to discuss the kinship network's role in providing normative safety nets that attempt to help the black family flourish instead of flounder (Jarrett et al., 2010). This extended support network reminds families that they are not alone and that there are others who are able and willing to assist them in their times of need.

Religious Community

The religious community provides a safe and welcoming place where individuals and families can express themselves freely, hence the reason why the church remains as a source of strength for the black family (Perkins-Dock, 2005). Church members and church leaders are considered a part of the extended support networks for black families. The church community provides emotional support in the forms of hopeful messages, low-cost day care, and ways of coping such as prayer, music, and fellowship, with which the black family can look to for strength during times of need as well as day-to-day functioning (Barnes, 2001; Perkins-Dock, 2005).

Work and Educational Achievement

Work and educational achievement are valued highly in the black community. In comparison to their white counterparts, black parents view education, namely higher education, as a necessary stepping stone for success (Immerwahr & Foleno, 2000).

In 2009, 84% of blacks age 25 and older had at least a high school diploma, and 19% had either a bachelor's degree or higher level of education (U.S. Census Bureau, 2007). Additionally, in 2007 there was approximately $137.4 billion in receipts for black-owned businesses, which is a 55% increase from 2002 (U.S. Census Bureau, 2007). Moreover, there were approximately 1.9 million black-owned businesses in 2007, representing a 60.5% increase (U.S. Census Bureau, 2007).

Resiliency, Coping Techniques, and Racial Identity

Although the black family has extended support networks, church communities, and increases in education and business numbers, it continues to face many challenges. In the face of these challenges, the black family draws on resiliency, coping techniques, and racial identity. Racism and discrimination have long been a part of the black experience and has been linked to numerous health effects, including stress-related health problems and depressive symptoms (Brody et al., 2008). Hamilton-Mason et al. (2009) found in their review of the literature that black females use internal strategies (religious and spiritual resources), external strategies (utilizing the extended support network), and roles flexing (adapting appearance, avoiding certain people or situations, or confronting the issues) to cope with difficulties. Additionally, Harvey et al. (2007) discussed that black parents who promote a positive racial identity along with a sense of racial pride help equip their children with resources needed to deal with problems in manageable ways, thereby increasing resiliency in their children and the family as a whole.

FAMILY LIFE EDUCATION PRACTICES

Current State of Family Life Education

Many educational programs for black families occur at or in conjunction with a faith-based organization. Black churches occupy a powerful and prominent role within the community (Chandler, 2010; National Healthy Marriage Resource Center, 2008; Waites & Urieta, 2008) and have provided instruction on a wide variety of topics since the abolishment of slavery (Isaac & Rowland, 2002). The church continues to be a major influence in the spiritual, educational, social, economic, and political lives of black people (Woodson & Braxton-Calhoun, 2006) by providing a safe haven and teaching survival techniques needed to cope in a world that is often unfriendly and unfair (Adkison-Bradley, Johnson, Sanders, Duncan, & Holcomb-McCoy, 2005).

Although churches and other faith-based organizations provide many educational and community programs, they have been criticized for lacking the capacity to address specific needs. Many programs at black churches are adept at handling the emergency needs of the congregation (e.g., food, child care, and shelter) but may fail to provide adequate social programs (Myers, 2005) that address other issues of well-being. In a study of the culture of 1,236 black churches, only 10% to 20% offered social programming such as relationship education programs or counseling and rehabilitation services (Myers, 2005). Churches may lack the ability or expertise to handle complex social and relational issues, making family life education for the black community a top priority.

Outside of the faith community, government-based programs have emerged in response to the needs of the black population. The Children, Youth, and Families at Risk (CYFAR) program within the National Institutes of Food and Agriculture (NIFA) funds research and community programs created and disseminated by extension service faculty and land-grant universities (U.S. Department of Agriculture, 2011). As a result, extension-based programs have been created and/ or revised to deliver relevant services regarding issues that are found in the black community.

The African American Healthy Marriage Initiative (AAHMI) is the result of a collaborative effort between the Administration for Children and Families (ACF), the U.S. Department of Health and Human Services (DHHS), national and regional civic leaders, and organizations within the community to encourage and strengthen healthy marriages and relationships within the black community (AAHMI, 2010). In order to complete this task, the AAHMI seeks to (1) increase the numbers of responsible fathers, (2) promote healthy marriages, (3) improve the well-being of children, and (4) strengthen black families and communities (U.S. DHHS, 2003) through education, collaboration, and resource allocation AAHMI, 2003).

General Needs of This Population and Rationale for Family Life Education

According to a recent report from the Black Community Crusade for Children (Children's Defense Fund, 2011), black communities have and continue to face adversity. Many current challenges facing the black family include but are not limited to the following:

- Economic hardships and high rates of unemployment
- Racial injustice and an imbalanced legal system
- Violence, drug abuse, and related issues
- Negative images in the media and their influence
- Inadequate education
- Broken relationships within the family and the community (Children's Defense Fund, 2011)

Although many of the previously cited issues are systemic and sociocultural in nature, they can be addressed when educational programs make use of the coping strategies and resilient nature found within black families (Mehta, West-Olatunji, Sanders, & Goodman, 2007).

Determining how to strengthen and stabilize the black family has been a significant challenge for many family life educators (Hildreth, Boglin, & Mask, 2000). Historically, most family life education programs were created based on the experiences of middle-class Caucasian participants and have used blacks as examples of dysfunction, poverty, and ineffective parenting (Hughes, 1994). Contemporary programs strive to be more representative of diversity and focus on strengths-based methods to draw on the unique cultural history found within this group. For example, Coard, Wallace, Stevenson, and Brotman (2004) conducted focus groups with black mothers to examine specific cultural practices that should be included in parenting programs. The mothers reported that racial socialization was a fundamental aspect of parenting and discussions on racial pride, equality, and achievement were very important (Coard et al., 2004) and should be addressed within educational programs for parents.

Marketing/Recruitment

Effective marketing and recruitment techniques for programs that target black participants utilize personal contacts with the community. Educators must foster strong working relationships with faith-based organizations, the black media, historically black colleges and universities, civic and social organizations, fatherhood and other community outreach programs, and black Greek sororities and fraternities (AAHMI, 2003; Bell, Butler, Herring, Yancey, & Fraser, 2005; National Healthy Marriage Center, 2009).

Guion, Chattaraj, Lytle, Broadwater, & Goddard (2003) outlined the following strategies for marketing programs aimed at the black community:

- Use positive examples of black people in the design and dissemination of marketing materials.
- Personalize your marketing techniques (e.g., use phone calls and face-to-face delivery methods).
- Recognize the importance of family values by including extended family members.
- Demonstrate how your program will strengthen the community by attending and supporting other community events.
- Do not give the impression that your program will *rescue* participants or *fix* their problems.

- Acknowledge the ethnicity of those working with the program and its effect on participants.
- Encourage participants to ask questions about the program.

Marketing strategies must be sensitive to the cultural and historical context in which black lives exist. Suggested advertising methods for targeting this population include (1) radio and public access television, (2) community newspapers, (3) ads on buses, (4) street teams that hand out information, (4) beauty and barber shops, (5) kiosks at shopping centers, (6) schools, (7) historically black sororities and fraternities, and (8) health care clinics (National Healthy Marriage Resource Center, 2008).

Barriers to Participation

Isaac and Rowland (2002) conducted focus groups to determine institutional barriers encountered in faith-based education. The authors reported that participants were less likely to attend educational programs due to (1) perceived irrelevance of program, (2) lack of variety in topics, (3) confusing or absent information, (4) variation in viewpoints of leaders, (5) issues with instructor, and (6) ineptitude of instructor. Because of the strong connection between family life education programs and faith-based institutions among black families, these barriers are helpful to family life educators as they are designing and implementing programs for this population.

Additional research has examined determinants of the lack of participation of blacks in research, health-related community programs, and clinical trials (Bonner, Ferrans, Moore-Burke & Gorelick, 2005; Sadler et al., 2010; Vesey, 2002). These barriers to participation can be divided into three main categories (*sociocultural, economic,* and *individual*) as outlined by Swanson & Ward (1995):

Sociocultural

Decreased participation has been attributed to what appears to be the most prevailing barrier: a historical distrust of educational, social, and medical institutions (Chandler, 2010; Livingston et al., 2010; Russell, Maraj, Wilson, Shedd-Steele, & Champion, 2008; Sheely & Bratton, 2010; Vesey, 2002). Stories of unethical medical practices, discrimination, and the lack of equal treatment passed down through generations (Dancy, Wilbur, Talashek, Bonner, & Barnes-Boyd, 2004) have resulted in a pessimistic and suspicious view of those who reside outside of the black community.

Economic

Other factors impeding participation include issues with accessing services such as transportation and cost (Livingston et al., 2010). Relying on extended family members and navigating public forms of transportation can keep some from regular attendance (Russell et al., 2008). Programs not within walking distance or those unable to provide transportation may find attendance can be an issue. Low-income and/or rural residents face additional economic stress when they have to miss work and travel in order to receive services (Davis & Ford, 2004).

Individual

Blacks report being unaware of the existence of many programs and how to access them stemming from a lack of communication with agencies (Livingston et al., 2010). They also report that age and educational level (Isaac & Rowland, 2002) can deter their participation.

Environmental Considerations

As a number of educational and social programs take place in or in conjunction with a faith organization, educators can utilize many specific strategies that are used in black churches in family life education programs. To create a welcoming environment, programs can be housed within the black community at locations familiar and accessible to participants (Vesey, 2002). Programs should provide incentives (Murry & Brody, 2004), transportation, child care (Livingston, et al., 2010; Russell et al., 2008), and meals when possible. Program sessions should have flexible schedules (i.e., nights and weekends) (Livingston et al., 2010), allot time for peer interaction, center around cultural and ethnic practices, and provide peer mentors (Waites & Urieta, 2008). Other important practices that should be borrowed from black churches are the use of prayer and music. Both are used in black churches to uplift and revive: prayer as a coping mechanism (Chandler, 2010) and music as a tool of expression (Adkison-Bradley et al., 2005) and a culturally specific learning strategy (Shaw, 1993).

Additional suggestions for creating a comfortable setting include (1) using both Afrocentric and Eurocentric worldviews, (2) encouraging critical analysis of information to foster empowerment, and (3) emphasizing the practical application of material (Shaw, 1993). Above all, it is necessary that educators establish trust with black participants (Russell et al., 2008), acknowledge the effects of discrimination (Chandler, 2010), and convey the value and purpose of family life education programs.

Modes of Learning

Distinct cultural practices resulting from historical experiences with discrimination have shaped the manner in which many in the black community learn. Economic issues of poverty and substandard living conditions coupled with psychological feelings of inferiority and discomfort in learning environments (Neely, 2003) influence the educational experiences of many. As a result, the path to learning is shaped differently for black children and adults. In order to address these differences, Willis (1989) identified four major domains of black learning: (1) social interaction and social learning, (2) focus on and respect for community, (3) creative expression, and (4) nonverbal communication.

In addition, Guion et al. (2003) suggested using the following in programs based on the unique styles of learning of black people:

- Imagination and humor
- Independent activities to demonstrate self-sufficiency
- Physical actions
- Hands-on experiences
- Focus on people instead of things
- Oral and kinesthetic information

Educator Characteristics

Teachers who have experienced success in working with black students value experiential learning activities over other methods (Shaw, 1993) of instruction. Participants prefer instructors who are knowledgeable, professional, energetic, and flexible, and who encourage group interaction (Isaac & Rowland, 2002). Those who demonstrate cultural competence and sensitivity (Chandler, 2010) are perceived better than those who ignore differences or assume no bias exists. Educators must recognize their own bias and cultural perceptions (Shaw, 1993) and how they may affect interactions with the black community.

Neely (2003) discussed individual characteristics and pedagogy of teachers who succeed in working with black students of varying ages. The author insists that instructors must first consider their own biases and then find ways to increase their interactions with black people. Other more specific classroom strategies include the following:

- Using the Socratic method and visual cues
- Being personable and tolerant
- Believing in their own positive impact on students
- Using positive reinforcement in verbal and physical forms (e.g., smiling, nodding, and patting on the back)

- Connecting with and motivating students
- Linking course content to real life

Ethical Considerations

Family life educators respect and value the experiences of all those served, including those from diverse backgrounds. Yet there can be a discrepancy that exists between personal perceptions of conventional behavior and that of someone from another culture. The cultural practices of a community may deviate from those customary to the dominant culture (Denby & Alford, 1996), leaving educators questioning their role and responsibility. One such issue within the black community is spanking.

Spanking has historically been used as a form of discipline within many black families. Intergenerational transmission of religious and cultural ideals (Lassiter, 1987), residing in poverty, and rural locations (Berlin et al., 2009; Giles-Sims, Straus, & Sugarman, 1995), and the legacy of slavery (Lassiter, 1987), have substantiated its use as a normative practice. In an attempt to teach children respect for elders, prepare them for racial inequality, and instill cultural behavioral expectations, physical punishment is valued (Berlin et al., 2009). While some black parents (e.g., middle-class, and less conservative) are forgoing spanking for less punitive methods of discipline (Dodge, McLoyd, & Lansford, 2005; Horn, Cheng, & Joseph, 2004), it still remains a common practice for others. Due to the disparity of opinions on spanking based on many contextual factors (Flynn, 1996), educators must not only be aware of the use of corporal punishment as a discipline technique but also develop the ability to decipher when behaviors become abusive and to help provide black families with guidelines for effectively using spanking as a discipline technique.

Best Practices in Family Life Education Programming

As mentioned previously, faith-based institutions play an integral part in the lives of the black community. Therefore, family life educators should partner with the faith community during planning, implementation, and delivery of programs. Woodson & Braxton-Calhoun (2006) provide the following instruction for establishing relationships with the black faith community:

- Increase knowledge of your local faith community.
- Learn appropriate protocol for church operations.
- Visit worship services frequently.
- Discuss scheduling classes with appropriate church personnel.
- Advertise classes based on church procedures.
- Confirm availability for program.
- Maintain relationships with key contact people.

In addition, the authors suggest when partnering with the faith community that educators should schedule programs months in advance, keep programs short (4–6 weeks), and focus on the benefit of program content and not on research (Woodson & Braxton-Calhoun, 2006).

Along with the faith community, educators should maintain partnerships with community leaders and representatives from social service agencies. Community leaders can serve as advocates and role models for participants (National Healthy Marriage Resource Center, 2009), identify other members of the community to provide support and leadership (Mehta et al., 2007), and increase opportunities to recruit others.

Guion et al. (2003) highlighted the following behavioral/informational and historically relevant best practices during program delivery:

Behavioral/Informational	Use expressive language.
	Incorporate humor.
	Include music.
	Maintain direct eye contact.
	Be informal and flexible.
	Value group effort.
	Use Ebonics (i.e., "Black English") and slang for some (Ogbu, 1999).
Historical	Appreciate heritage and history.
	Utilize oral language traditions.
	Respect the role of elders.
	Connect with other black people.
	Promote education as a way to a better life.
	Value historically black colleges and universities.
	Recognize dual existence (majority vs. minority culture).
	Collaborate with religious organizations.
	Use extended family networks.

Family life education programs for the black community should include efforts to strengthen the family using the principles of (1) unity, (2) cooperative work and accountability, (3) principles, (4) creativity, (5) autonomy, (6) cooperative economics, and (7) acknowledgement of previous struggles (Logan, 1996). Examples of successful family life education programs that incorporate many of the previously listed characteristics are found in Appendix A.

It is important to draw upon the strong community and familial connections in the lives of black people. Programs must collaborate with extended family members, churches, historically black colleges and universities, and other community networks (Hildreth et al., 2000) to provide a mechanism of holistic support for black families. Educators should also respect the importance of religion and previous experiences with discrimination and also address the subsequent mistrust of institutions (Chandler, 2010) inherent in the black community.

FUTURE DIRECTIONS

Future family life education programming with black families should address six core areas. These six areas are discussed next.

First, create strong working relationships with community and faith-based organizations. Historically, programs for the black community have been housed within the community itself. Community-based organizations and black churches provide education, assistance, and a safe haven for members of the black community. Family life educators should increase their presence within the black community by participating in community events, coordinating programs with community gatekeepers, and engaging families in programming from start to finish.

Second, design culturally competent interventions, and revise those currently in use. Cultural competence, more so than cultural sensitivity, is needed in family life education. Instead of using materials created for white, middle-class audiences, new materials should be created, which capture the most salient aspects of black family life (racial socialization, historical impact of slavery, extended family support, etc.). Black families should be involved in the process of programming, from conception to delivery. Culturally competent and relevant programs can reduce mistrust with institutions and should improve participation rates. Educators must also be aware of their own cultural biases and recognize their impact on program delivery.

Third, explore ways to increase the participation of black men and boys. Most research on black families focuses on mothers and grandmothers with less emphasis given to the role of the black male. Viewed as absent, incarcerated, or derelict in responsibilities, black men have been omitted from many programming efforts in community, health, and educational organizations. Family life education programs should provide information and mentorship that support the efforts of black men, while highlighting the importance of their role in the community.

Fourth, utilize the resilient nature of the black family. A great asset to the black family is its strong kinship bonds. Relationships with family members and non-relatives serve as protective factors that provide financial, social, and emotional support. Strengths-based programming that includes people outside of the nuclear family system is needed.

Fifth, address the overall well-being of black children. Statistics on black children report disproportionally high rates of poverty, violence, drug abuse, teen pregnancy, imprisonment, poor academic achievement, and abuse (Hart Research Associates, 2011). Black children are at higher risk for negative mental, physical, and emotional outcomes than their white peers. Therefore, programming to reduce and/or address these needs is paramount.

Sixth, family life educators should work to increase rigor in program implementation, delivery, and evaluation. To adequately address the needs of black families, there should be more scholarship on community and family life programs. Programs must demonstrate the use of theory-driven, research-based materials and report the outcome of interventions. Evaluating existing programs and services to increase effectiveness can also provide scholarly information for the creation of future programs.

REFERENCES

Adkison-Bradley, C., Johnson, D., Sanders, J. L., Duncan, L., & Holcomb-McCoy, C. (2005). Forging a collaborative relationship between the black church and the counseling profession. *Counseling and Values, 49,* 147–154.

African American Healthy Marriage Initiative. (2003, June). *African American healthy marriage initiative. A targeted strategy for working effectively with African American communities.* Retrieved from http://www.aahmi.net/docs/factsheet.pdf

African American Healthy Marriage Initiative. (2010). *Mission initiatives.* Retrieved from http://www.aahmi.net/mission.html

Alvy, K. T. (1994). *Parent training today: A social necessity.* Studio City, CA: Center for Improving Child Care.

Antonucci, T. C., & Jackson, J. S. (2007). Intergenerational relations: Theory, research, and policy. *Journal of Social Issues, 63,* 679–693.

Armstrong, T. D., & Crowther, M. R. (2002). Spirituality among older African Americans. *Journal of Adult Development, 9,* 3–12.

Barnes, S. L. (2001). Stressors and strengths: A theoretical and practical examination of nuclear, single-parent, and augmented African American families. *Families in Society: The Journal of Contemporary Human Services, 82,* 449–460.

Beach, S., McNair, L., Fincham, F., & Hurt, T. (n.d.). Program for strong African American marriages. University of Georgia Institute for Behavioral Research, Center for Family Research. Retrieved from http://www.uga.edu/prosaam/index.html

Bell, L., Butler, T. L., Herring, P., Yancey, A. K., & Fraser, G. E. (2005). Recruiting Blacks to the Adventist health study: Do follow-up phone calls increase response rates? *Annals of Epidemiology, 15,* 667–672.

Bell-Tolliver, L., Burgess, R., & Brock, L. J. (2009). African American therapists working with African American families: An exploration of the strengths perspective in treatment. *Journal of Marital and Family Therapy, 35,* 293–307.

Berlin, L. J., Ispa, J. M., Fine, M. A., Malone, P. S., Brooks-Gunn, J., Brady-Smith, C., et al. (2009). Correlates and consequences of spanking and verbal punishment for low-income White, African American, and Mexican American toddlers. *Child Development, 80,* 1403–1420.

Blackman, L. C. (n.d.). *African American marriage enrichment program.* African American Family Life Education Institute. Retrieved from http://www.aafle.org/aafle/index.php/AAFLE/aafle-classes-for-couples.html

Bonner, G. J., Ferrans, C. E., Moore-Burke, E. F., & Gorelick, P. (2005). Determinants of trust and mistrust in physicians identified by African American caregivers. *African American Research Perspectives, 10,* 89–102.

Brody, G. H., Chen, Y., Kogan, S. M., McBride-Murry, V., Logan, P., & Luo, Z. (2008). Linking perceived discrimination to longitudinal changes in African American mothers' parenting practices. *Journal of Marriage and Family, 70,* 319–331.

Chandler, D. (2010). The underutilization of health services in the Black community. An examination of causes and effects. *Journal of Black Studies, 40,* 915–931.

Children's Defense Fund. (2011). *The state of black children and families: Black perspectives on what black children face and what the future holds.* Washington, DC: Hart Research Associates. Retrieved from http://www.childrensdefense.org/programs-campaigns/black-community-crusade-for-children-II/bccc-assets/the-state-of-black-children.pdf

Coard, S. I., Wallace, S. A., Stevenson, H. R., & Brotman, L. M. (2004). Towards culturally relevant preventive interventions: The consideration of racial socialization in parent training with African American families. *Journal of Child and Family Studies, 13*(3), 277–293.

Dancy, B. L., Wilbur, J., Talashek, M., Bonner, G., & Barnes-Boyd, C. (2004). Community-based research: Barriers to recruitment of African Americans. *Nursing Outlook, 52,* 234–240.

Davis, S., & Ford, M. (2004). A conceptual model of barriers to mental health services among African Americans. *African American Research Perspectives, 10,* 44–55.

DeNavas-Walt, C., Proctor, B. D., & Smith, J. C. (2010). *Income, poverty and health insurance coverage in the United States: 2009* (Current Population Reports P60-238). Washington, DC: U.S. Census Bureau. Retrieved from http://www.census.gov/prod/2010pubs/p60-238.pdf

Denby, R., & Alford, K. (1996). Understanding African American discipline styles: Suggestions for effective social work intervention. *Journal of Multicultural Social Work, 4,* 81–98.

Dodge, K. A., McLoyd, V. C., & Lansford, J. E. (2005). The cultural context of physically disciplining children. In V. C. McLoyd, N. E. Hill, & K. A. Dodge (Eds.), *African American family life. Ecological and cultural diversity* (pp. 245–263). New York: Guilford.

Fine, M., Schwebel, A. I., & James-Myers, L. (1987). Family stability in black families: Values underlying three different perspectives. *Journal of Comparative Family Studies, 18,* 1–23.

Flynn, C. P., (1996). Normative support for corporal punishment: Attitudes, correlates and implications. *Aggression and Violent Behavior, 1,* 47–55.

Giles-Sims, J., Straus, M. A., & Sugarman, D. B. (1995). Child, maternal, and family characteristics associated with spanking. *Family Relations, 44,* 170–176.

Goodman, C. C., & Silverstein, M. (2006). Grandmothers raising grandchildren: Ethnic and racial differences in well-being among custodial and coparenting families. *Journal of Family Issues, 27,* 1605–1626.

Guion, L. A., Chattaraj, S., Lytle, S. S., Broadwater, G., & Goddard, H. W. (2003). *Culturally Relevant Resources List: Developing Programs to Effectively Work with Multi-Need, Diverse Audiences (Diversity Project).* Gainesville: Florida Cooperative Extension, University of Florida.

Hamilton-Mason, J., Hall, J. C., & Everett, J. E. (2009). And some of us are braver: Stress and coping among African American women. *Journal of Human Behavior in the Social Environment, 19,* 463–482.

Hart Research Associates. (2011). *The state of black children and families. Black perspectives on what black children face and what the future holds.* Washington, DC: Children's Defense Fund. Black Community Crusade for Children. Retrieved from http://www.childrensdefense.org/programs-campaigns/black-community-crusade-for-children-II/new-research-and-data.html

Harvey, A. R., McCullough-Chavis, A., Littlefield, M. B., Phillips, A. D., & Cooper, J. D. (2007). A culturally competent family enhancement and empowerment model for African American parents. *Smith College Studies in Social Work, 80,* 70–87.

Hildreth, G. J., Boglin, M. L., & Mask, K. (2000). Review of literature on resiliency in black families: Implications for the 21st century. *African American Research Perspectives*, 6, 13–21.

Horn, I. B., Cheng, T. L., & Joseph, J. (2004). Discipline in the African American community: The impact of socioeconomic status on beliefs and practices. *Pediatrics, 113,* 1236–1241.

Hughes, R., Jr. (1994). A framework for developing family life education programs. *Family Relations, 43,* 74–80.

Humes, K. R., Jones, N. A., & Ramirez, R. R. (2011). *Overview of race and Hispanic origin: 2010.* 2010 U.S. Census Bureau Brief C2010BR-02.

Immerwahr, J., & Foleno, T. (2000). *Great expectations: How the public and parents—White, African American and Hispanic—view higher education.* National Center for Public Policy and Higher Education, Public Agenda, Consortium for Policy Research in Education, National Center for Postsecondary Improvement. Report 00-2. Retrieved from http://www.highereducation.org/reports/expectations/expectations.pdf

Isaac, P., & Rowland, M. (2002). Institutional barriers to participation in adult education within religious institutions. *Journal of Research on Christian Education, 11*(2), 101–120.

Jarrett, R. L., Jefferson, S. R., & Kelly, J. N. (2010). Finding community in family: Neighborhood effects and African American kin networks. *Journal of Comparative Family Studies,* 299–328.

Lamborn, S. D., & Nguyen, D. T. (2004). African American adolescents' perceptions of family interactions: Kinship support, parent-child relationships, and teen adjustment. *Journal of Youth and Adolescence, 33,* 547–558.

Lassiter, R. E. (1987). Child rearing in black families: Child-abusing discipline? In R. L. Hampton (Ed.), *Violence in the black family: Correlates and consequences* (pp. 39–53). Lexington, MA: Lexington Books.

Livingston, J. N., Eaton, S., Singleton, D., Farrell, P., Wells, V., Brown, C., et al. (2010). Early childhood education and services for all children: A call to action for social science and human service professionals. *African American Research Perspectives, 11,* 127–137.

Logan, S. L. M. (1996). *The black family: Strengths, self-help, and positive change.* Boulder, CO: Westview Press.

McCrae, J. S., & Fusco, R. A. (2010). A racial comparison of family group decision making in the USA. *Child and Family Social Work, 15,* 41–55.

McFadden, S. H. (2005). Points of connection: Gerontology and the psychology of religion. In R. F. Paloutzian & C. L. Park (Eds.), *Handbook of the psychology of religion and spirituality* (pp. 162–176). New York: Guilford.

Mehta, S., West-Olatunji, C., Sanders, T., & Goodman, R. (2007). *Recommendations for working with African American parents of primary school children in low-resourced schools.* Retrieved from http://www.eric.ed.gov/PDFS/ED498991.pdf

Molgaard, V. (2001). *The strong African American families program.* Athens: Center for Family Research, University of Georgia. Retrieved from http://www.cfr.uga.edu/saaf2

Murry, V. M., & Brody, G. H. (2004). Partnering with community stakeholders: Engaging rural African American families in basic research and the Strong African American Families Preventative Intervention Program. *Journal of Marital and Family Therapy, 30,* 271–283.

Mutchler, J. E., Lee, S., & Baker, L. A. (2006). *Grandparent care in the United States: Comparisons by race and ethnicity.* Retrieved from http://www.mccormack.umb.edu/centers/gerontologyinstitute/pubAndStudies/DiversityinGrandparentCareHouseholds.pdf

Myers, V. L. (2005). Black church culture, social programs and faith-based policy: Using organization theory to reconcile rhetoric and reality. *African American Research Perspectives, 10,* 116–138.

National Healthy Marriage Resource Center. (2008). *Effective marketing messages for African American couples.* Retrieved from http://www.healthymarriageinfo.org/docs/marketingaacouples.pdf

National Healthy Marriage Resource Center. (2009). *Supporting an African American healthy marriage initiative.* Retrieved from http://www.healthymarriageinfo.org/docs/supportinganaahmi.pdf

Neely, A. (2003). *Teaching African American students: A look at instructional methods and cultural differences.* Williamsburg, VA: College of William and Mary. Retrieved from http://imet.csus.edu/imet11/portfolio/smiley_k/WebQuest/Neely.pdf

Ogbu, J. U. (1999). Beyond language: Ebonics, proper English, and identity in a Black-American speech community. *American Educational Research Journal, 36,* 147–184.

Perkins-Dock, R. E. (2005). The application of Adlerian Family Therapy with African American families. *Journal of Individual Psychology, 61,* 233–249.

Riina, E. M., & McHale, S. M. (2010). Parents' experiences of discrimination and family relationship qualities: The role of gender. *Family Relations, 59,* 283–296.

Russell, K. M., Maraj, M. S., Wilson, L. R., Shedd-Steele, R., & Champion, V. L. (2008). Barriers to recruiting urban African American women into research studies in community settings. *Applied Nursing Research, 21,* 90–97.

Sadler, G. R., Gonzalez, J., Mumman, M., Cullen, L., LaHousse, S. F., Malcarne, V., et al. (2010). Adapting a program to inform African American and Hispanic American women about cancer. *Journal of Cancer Education, 25,* 142–145.

Scannapieco, M., & Jackson, S. (1996). Kinship care: The African American response to family preservation. *Social Work, 41,* 190–196.

Shaw, C. (1993, Winter). Multicultural teacher education: A call for conceptual change. *Multicultural Education,* 22–26.

Sheely, A., & Bratton, S. C. (2010). A strengths-based parenting intervention with low-income African American families. *Professional School Counseling, 13,* 175–183.

Stevenson, M. L., Henderson, T. L., & Baugh, E. (2007). Vital defenses: Social support appraisals of Black grandmothers parenting grandchildren. *Journal of Family Issues, 28,* 182–211.

Swanson, G., & Ward, A. (1995). Recruiting minorities into clinical trials: Toward a participant-friendly system. *Journal of the National Cancer Institute, 87,* 1747–1759.

Thomas, J. L., Sperry, L., & Yarbrough, M. S. (2000). Grandparents as parents: Research findings and policy recommendations. *Child Psychiatry and Human Development, 31,* 3–22.

Tolson, T. F. J., & Wilson, M. N. (1990). The impact of two- and three-generational Black family structure on perceived family climate. *Child Development, 61,* 416–428.

U.S. Census Bureau. (2007). *The American community—Blacks: 2004* (American Community Survey Reports ACS-04). Retrieved from http://www.census.gov/prod/2007pubs/acs-04.pdf

U.S. Department of Agriculture. (2011). *Communities at risk. CYFAR program overview.* Retrieved from http://www.csrees.usda.gov/nea/family/cyfar/overview.html

U.S. Department of Health and Human Services. (2003). *African American healthy marriage initiative.* Washington, DC: African American Healthy Marriage Initiative. Retrieved from http://www.aahmi.net/docs/aahmibrochure1.pdf

U.S. Department of Health and Human Services. (2009). *The Office of Minority Health: African American profile.* Retrieved from http://minorityhealth.hhs.gov/templates/browse.aspx?lvl=2&lvlid=51

Vesey, G. A. (2002). A successful strategy for recruitment and retention of Black elders in applied research. *African American Research Perspectives, 8*(2), 41–56.

Waites, C. (2009). Building on strengths: Intergenerational practice with African American families. *Social Work, 54,* 278–287.

Waites, C. C., & Urieta, D. M. (2008). Health promotion activities in six African American churches in a southeastern community. *African American Research Perspectives, 10,* 130–149.

Willis, M. G. (1989). Learning styles of African American children: A review of the literature and interventions. *Journal of Black Psychology, 16,* 47-65.

Wilson, P., & Ekulona, A. (n.d.). *Exploring relationships and marriage with fragile families.* Baltimore: Center for Fathers, Families and Workforce Development.

Woodson, J. M., & Braxton-Calhoun, M. (2006). Techniques for establishing educational programs through the African American faith community. *Journal of Extension, 44.* Retrieved from http://www.joe.org/joe/2006february/tt3.php

APPENDIX A

Title	*Primary Goal(s) and Content Areas*
Effective Black Parenting Program Center for the Improvement of Child Care Alvy (1994) http://www.ciccparenting.org/ EffBlackParentingDesc.aspx	Culturally specific parenting techniques, discipline, racism, family rules, praise, and communication
Exploring Relationships and Marriage with Fragile Families Wilson & Ekulona (n.d.) Center for Urban Families http://www.cfuf.org/relationships_marriage	Low-income mothers and fathers in strengthening their relationships, exploring marriage, and providing healthy and safe environments for their children
Program for Strong African American Marriages (ProSAAM) PREP, Inc. Beach, McNair, Fincham, & Hurt (n.d.) http://www.prepinc.com/Content/CURRICULA/ ProSAAM.htm	Effective communication, problem solving, and intimacy
African American Marriage Enrichment Program: How to Make Your Good Thing Better© Blackman (n.d.) African American Family Life Education Institute, LLC www.aafle.org	Purposes of marriage, causes of relationship disillusionment and divorce, elements of highly satisfying marriages, strategies for improving marital stability and satisfaction, and increasing racial and gender fairness in the family and society
Strong African American Families Project (SAAF) Moolgard (2001) Center for Family Research University of Georgia http://www.cfr.uga.edu/saaf2	Family-based program encourages positive choices for adolescents and strengthens racial pride and family communication

Chapter 12

Family Life Education With Lesbian, Gay, Bisexual, and Transgender Families

Lis Maurer, CFLE

Growing up in a rural community during a time when few mentors and role models existed for lesbian, gay, bisexual, or transgender young people, I, the author, bring a complex and sometimes conflicting array of lived experiences to my writing. From isolation, harassment, and bold acts of discrimination to the sheer joy of finding others who honored or shared the richness of diversity regarding sexual orientation and gender identities, I have known both the best and worst of how individuals, institutions, and laws can impact the lives of lesbian, gay, bisexual, and transgender (LGBT) people. I draw upon the framework of social justice education introduced by Adams, Bell, and Griffin; the determination and resilience of Rustin, Milk, Lorde, Hooker, Martin & Lyon, Rivera, Kameny, Gittings; and all those who acted on behalf of the LGBT population in much more dangerous times. Classically trained as a sexuality educator, I find inspiration in a diverse array of people and works and count Parker Palmer, Margaret Wheatley, and all my students as guiding influences in my work. As a professional, I work to bring compelling data, research, and hope for creating more spaces in which gentle and spirited inquiry, common humanity, dignity, and respect become the norm.

DEFINING THE POPULATION

One of the first challenges of serving families of diverse sexual orientations and gender identities is the basic matter of finding and reaching out to them because of regional and community variations in the use of language and terminology. Determining what sexual and gender minority people call themselves is an important first step toward serving these families. LGBT is the preferred term in some areas of the United States, yet in others, the accepted acronym is GLBT, or gay, lesbian, bisexual, and transgender. At times, additional identities are included in acronyms such as LGBTTQQIA for lesbian, gay, bisexual, transgender, transsexual, queer, questioning, intersex, and ally. There is also is an emerging trend among young people to make up new words to describe their identities or to choose no label at all (Savin-Williams, 2005). Thus, the question of outreach to LGBT families may become even more complicated when today's young people mature and begin families of their own.

To review, the basic concepts of sexual orientation and gender identity terminology are as follows:

Sexual Orientation—*to whom one is attracted (e.g., heterosexual, gay, lesbian, bisexual, queer). A heterosexual person is attracted to people of a different sex. A gay or lesbian person is attracted to people of the same sex. A bisexual person is attracted to people of a different and the same sex.*

Gender Identity—*one's internal sense of gender (e.g., conventionally gendered, transgender, transsexual, and genderqueer). A transgender person has a gender identity that is not congruent with the sex he or she was pronounced at birth or whose gender identity is different from the one society associates with he or she.*

Coming Out—*a process with multiple layers; coming out to oneself by recognizing and accepting one's sexual orientation, and making decisions about how, whether, and when to share that information with others (Gay & Lesbian Alliance Against Defamation [GLAAD], Inc., 2010).*

Words and their definitions also change over time. Some words once considered universally disrespectful (such as "queer" and other terms formerly used as insults) have been reclaimed and embraced by some LGBT people. However, for others, these words are still highly charged and inappropriate. Words describing LGBT people are also highly influenced by culture, age, class, and other factors, so a common lexicon may never be collectively adopted. An excellent resource for the most authoritative and up to date terminology is the *Gay & Lesbian Alliance Against Defamation (GLAAD) Media Reference Guide* GLAAD, 2010).

For the purposes of this chapter, the term *LGBT* is used to describe all those people who experience same-sex attraction or fall somewhere on the gender identity continuum in a place not wholly congruent with the sex they were pronounced at birth.

How many people are LGBT in the United States? There are several answers, and most have to do with the way the question was asked and who did the asking. Demographers estimate a range of 4% to 9% adults are LGBT (Harris Interactive, 2011). Initial tabulations of same-sex couples released during summer 2011 were found to have some coding errors involving accurately recording the sex of a proportion of unmarried partners/spouses. Census 2010 and Census 2000 same-sex household data results were then re-analyzed. Preferred estimates of same-sex couples released by the Census Bureau are considered to be more accurate than the initial tabulations (Williams Institute, 2011). The 2010 U.S. Census data show about 1.3 million adults report living together as same-sex couples (O'Connell & Feliz, 2011). This represents a significant increase from 2000 Census data that showed 358,390 couples (or slightly more than 700,000 people) living together as same-sex couples. Census data undercounts LGBT people and families because it counts only those people living together in relationships in a single household; and it only counts those willing to report their status truthfully—not those who might be fearful or concerned about disclosing their sexual orientation. This increase in reporting likely reflects the efforts of a proactive public education campaign aimed at LGBT people by the U.S. Census, as well as increased willingness of LGBT people to reveal this information to the government.

Consistently since 1992, about 5% of the population has self-identified in election exit-polling as LGBT (Smith & Gates, 2001). Kinsey's research identified 10% of men who were predominantly gay and 4% who were exclusively gay from adolescence onward through the time of the study (Kinsey, Pomeroy, & Martin, 1948). Savin-Williams's research demonstrates 15% to 20% of adolescents have some degree of same-sex orientation, yet only 3% to 4% embrace a LGBT identity (Savin-Williams, 2005).

Unique Aspects of LGBT Families

One of the most important pieces to understanding how LGBT people may differ from non-LGBT people is their vulnerability to a host of negative situations and consequences. This is particularly true during their adolescent years (Garofalo, Wolf, Kessel, Palfrey, & DuRant, 1998). LGBT youth are at particular risk not because of their LGBT status but primarily because of societal stigma and its effects (Hart & Heimberg, 2001). Areas that have received extensive attention include isolation (Garofalo et al., 1998), stress (Hart & Heimberg, 2001), violence (D'Augelli, 2002), depression (Hart & Heimberg, 2001), alcohol and substance use (Garofalo et al., 1998; Marshal et al., 2008; Remafedi, 1987), suicide (Garofalo et al., 1998; Hart & Heimberg, 2001; Russell, 2003), and estrangement from family and friends (D'Augelli, 2002). Research on LGBT youth has also highlighted significant disparities in risk-taking behavior (Busseri, Willoughby, Chalmers, & Bogaert, 2008), tobacco use (Garofalo et al., 1998; Ryan, Wortley, Easton, Pederson, & Greenwood, 2001), and homelessness (Ray, 2006). There is also a high incidence of unintended teen pregnancy (Saewyc, Poon, Homma, & Skay, 2008) among LGBT youth, which is especially unusual in light of overall declining trends in teen pregnancy (McKay, 2006).

Another unique aspect is the diversity and variation in the experiences of LGBT people. There are different norms and cultural values about sexual orientation and gender identity. In some places, LGBT people are persecuted (O'Flaherty & Fisher, 2008); in others, they are treated similarly to other people (Ottosson, 2006), and in some cultures they are revered (Roscoe, 1991). In the United States, it's a complex picture. Many of the unique concerns of LGBT families have to do with their unequal legal status. Without access to the economic benefits of heterosexual marriage, partners and children of LGBT parents cannot access the federally provided resources or state-conferred rights of both parents: employment benefits like dependent health care, family leave, and pension benefits; the right of both parents to make emergency medical decisions; access to family support programs such as Social Security; veteran's benefits; equal taxation; military service benefits; pathways to legal immigration; inheritance; and access to courts for matters such as wrongful death and worker's compensation (Defense of Marriage Act, 1996). At least 1,138 federal rights and privileges are extended only to heterosexual married couples (U.S. Government Accounting Office, 2004) and hundreds more at the state level. This unequal status extended all the way to the bedroom until 2003, when the U.S. Supreme Court *Lawrence et al. v. Texas* (2003) decision ruled that consensual adult sexual behavior was protected under the Fourteenth Amendment, thus decriminalizing private consensual sexual activity between same-sex adults.

In some jurisdictions and states, there are laws and public policies designed to provide LGBT people with freedom from discrimination. In other places there are laws specifically designed to try to prevent LGBT people from fully participating in society—including those that have to do with adoption, child custody, visitation rights, and decision making when a child or partner is ill. At the federal level, there is currently just one piece of pro-LGBT legislation—the Matthew Sheppard and James Byrd, Jr., Hate Crimes Prevention Act, signed into law in 2009. This expanded existing federal hate crimes legislation to include crimes motivated by the victim's sexual orientation, gender identity, or disability status.

(The most up-to-date maps illustrating the patchwork of state and local laws addressing LGBT people and nondiscrimination, foster care, relationship recognition, adoption, and other issues can be found at the National Gay and Lesbian Task Force website [http://www.thetaskforce.org/reports_and_research].)

Americans can also be fired or denied a job because of their sexual orientation (or perceived orientation) in 29 states and because of their gender identity in 37 states. This has a profound impact on LGBT families, especially with regard to economically supporting LGBT families and accessing health care and other benefits usually conferred through an employer or a partner's employer. For instance, in the largest nationally representative sample, key differences in health insurance coverage and access to care were found between gay and lesbian couples and heterosexual couples (Buchmueller & Carpenter, 2010).

A life span approach is helpful in discerning other unique aspects of LGBT individuals and families that provide important context for family life education programs. Unique aspects of LGBT youth and young adults, LGBT-headed families with children, midlife adults, and older adults are discussed in the next sections.

LGBT Youth and Young Adults

In addition to the previously mentioned challenges facing LGBT youth, LGBT youth report more sexual partners than heterosexual youth (Blake et al., 2001) and higher rates of alcohol use before last sex (Blake et al., 2001). However, LGBT youths in schools with LGBT-inclusive curricula reported fewer sexual partners, less recent sex, and less substance use before last sex than did LGBT youths in schools without this instruction (Blake et al., 2001). A Minnesota study of 9th and 12th grade teen parents found one in three teen fathers reported same- or mixed-sex sexual partners in the past year, as did one in eight teen mothers (Forrest & Saewyc, 2004). LGBT youth also use contraceptives less frequently than their heterosexual peers when engaging in sexual behavior that can lead to pregnancy (Goodenow, Netherland, & Szalacha, 2002; Robin et al., 2002).

The relationship of these youth to their families and their sense of connectedness at school also play a role. LGBT young people who experienced rejection by their families were about three and a half times more likely to have engaged in unprotected sex (Ryan, Huebner, Diaz, & Sanchez, 2009). Connectedness to family or school has been linked to lower rates of teen pregnancy, but many sexual LGBT youth feel less connected to these than their heterosexual peers. LGBT youth may be more apt to seek caring connections through parenthood as a result of having fewer support resources upon which to draw (Kirby, Lepore, & Ryan, 2005).

Discrimination can play a role early in their lives, as LGBT adolescents are also 40% more likely to be stopped or arrested by police and more likely to be expelled from school and convicted by courts than heterosexual peers with the same level of misconduct (Himmelstein & Brückner, 2010).

In adulthood, LGBT people must master a number of developmental tasks (e.g., finding and creating community, career decisions) that are typical of all young adults; however, LGBT individuals face several added dimensions when achieving these tasks. The desire to remain in relative proximity to family/family of choice or to seek comfort with rural versus urban life may trump dreams of moving to gay "meccas" in urban areas. Career aspirations include issues from deciding where to live (which may be based on locating LGBT-friendly communities and employers with LGBT-friendly policies) to which career fields are options to an individual based on how successfully they navigated their K through 12 schooling and beyond. Young adults seeking employment have to master interview skills *and* decisions about how and whether to come out during the interview process and also ways to determine whether a company is LGBT-friendly *and* a good fit.

In terms of seeking a partner and dating, opportunities for meeting a partner have moved beyond bars and private house parties, which were common in the past when being gay was criminalized. Less stigmatized views of LGBT people mean that the potential to meet friends and partners extends into LGBT and non-LGBT worlds—sports leagues, work, reading groups, PTAs, church, online dating sites, and more. Overall, research has found similarities and differences between gay and lesbian and heterosexual couples' dating behavior. Rose and Zand (2000) found lesbian dating more free from traditional notions of gender roles. Another study demonstrated that unlike heterosexual people, education and earnings were not significant predictors of being in a cohabitating relationship for lesbians and gay men. But similar to heterosexual people, race, employment status, and geography were similar predictors of relationship status (Strohm, Seltzer, Cochran, & Mays, 2006).

Other unique aspects that affect LGBT people of all ages but that may cause additional stress at this time are negotiating families of origin and issues of estrangement (LaSala, 2000), building families of choice (Hunyady, 2008), reconciling sexuality and spirituality (Davidson, 2000), and navigating in a complex world where some individuals are always assumed to be LGBT, while others are all but invisible (Cashore & Tuason, 2009; Shulman, Horne, & Levitt, 2003).

LGBT-Headed Families With Children

According to the 2000 U.S. Census, families with children headed by gay and lesbian couples live in 99.3% of all counties in the United States (Gates & Ost, 2004; U.S. Census Bureau, 2003). Overall, U.S. Census data reveal that 33% of female same-sex households and 22% of male same-sex households reported having children under 18 living in the home (U.S. Census Bureau, 2003). Preliminary data from the 2010 U.S. Census indicate findings similar to those of the 2000 Census.

An estimated 6 to 14 million children had a gay or lesbian parent in 1990 (National Adoption Information Clearinghouse, 2000; Sullivan, 1995).

Despite the stereotype that LGBT people and families live only in a few specific urban areas, data show that LGBT-headed households are present throughout the United States. Same-sex couples with children often live in states and areas not known for large LGBT communities (Gates & Ost, 2004). States with the highest concentration of same-sex couples with children are Mississippi, South Dakota, Alaska, South Carolina, Louisiana, Alabama, Texas, Kansas, Utah, and Arizona (Gates & Ost, 2004).

There are many paths to parenthood for LGBT families. LGBT people may have children from previous or current heterosexual relationships or through surrogacy, donor insemination, and assistive reproductive technology. They may build their families through adoption or fostering, with some seeking the services of specific LGBT family building projects. And similar to their non-LGBT peers, their families represent a range of diversity in terms of their composition—couples, single parents, extended families, family webs, and blended families (Telingator & Patterson, 2008).

Kids of LGBT parents have their own lexicon, too; *queerspawn* is one word used by some people with an LGBT parent(s) to describe their own identity. "This term asserts that people with LGBTQ parents are part of the queer community because of their family and/or cultural experience, regardless of their own sexual orientation or gender identity" (Canfield-Lenfest, 2008). *COLAGEr*—a reference to the national group Children of Lesbians and Gays Everywhere—is another term used by some people with LGBT parents. *Second Generation* is used to describe LGBT adult children who also have LGBT parents (COLAGE, n.d.); *Kids of Trans,* or KOT, describes people with [a] transgender parent(s) (Canfield-Lenfest, 2008). A *bothie* has both a lesbian mother and gay father (COLAGE, 2004).

Midlife Adults

At midlife, LGBT and non-LGBT people face some similar challenges, as well as some that are unique. For LGBT people with children, one parent almost always has unequal legal standing or status that can change based on in what city or state the family lives. In addition, LGBT adult children may be expected to take on a disproportionate amount of caregiving for a parent or other relative, as LGBT people may be viewed as "single" even if they live with a partner and children of their own. This caregiving role may include more hours of care, higher levels of assistance to their care recipients, a higher level of stress, and a greater possibility of job loss as compared with their peers in different sex relationships (Fredriksen, 1999). LGBT caregivers may also be put in the unique position of being expected to care for a relative who has treated them disrespectfully because of their LGBT status (Coon, 2003). Some LGBT adults also care for "families of choice" in addition to families of origin, which may hone their skills but can also contribute to the risk of causing caregiver burnout. And though LGBT people may have fewer kin-based supports especially in midlife, ways they develop friendships/social supports remain largely unexplored (Barker, Herdt, & deVries, 2006).

Older Adults

An estimated 2 to 7 million Americans over 65 are LGBT (Grant, 2010). LGBT elders are more likely to live in poverty than their heterosexual peers (Albelda, Badgett, Schneebam, & Gates, 2009), partly due to private and federal programs that exclude people with same-sex partners (including Social Security, Medicare, and Meals on Wheels). Compared to heterosexual elders, LGBT elders may experience isolation from both heterosexual and younger LGBT communities, have no family to care for them, are more likely to live alone (New York City Department of Health & Mental Hygiene, 2008; Rosenfeld, 1999), and are five times less likely to access services (Cahill, South, & Spade, 2000; Hollibaugh, 2004; Plumb, 2003).

LGBT elders also have unique strengths. They share a common culture, have cultivated skills in self-reliance and resilience throughout life, have learned to create support networks, and have developed coping skills in dealing with a hostile environment (Grossman, D'Augelli, & Dragowski, 2007; MetLife Mature Market Institute & the Lesbian and Gay Aging Issues Network of the American Society on Aging, 2010). Nearly 40% believed that being LGBT helped them prepare for aging (MetLife Mature Market Institute, 2006).

Strengths and Assets of Gay and Lesbian Families

Research comparing same-sex and different sex couples is an emerging area. Research comparing same-sex couples who had civil unions, those who did not, and heterosexual married couples found that same-sex couples reported greater relationship quality, compatibility, and intimacy and lower levels of conflict than heterosexual married couples (Balsam, Beauchaine, Rothblum, & Solomon, 2008).

Research on LGBT parents finds those in committed relationships were generally indistinguishable from their heterosexual peers, with the exception that lesbians were particularly skilled at working together well (Roisman, Clausell, Holland, Fortuna, & Elieff, 2008) and that lesbian couples were more likely to divide paid and unpaid labor evenly as compared to heterosexual couples (Patterson, Sutfin, & Fulcher, 2004). The first study of lesbian couples' relationship quality during the transition to parenthood showed love decreased across the transition and conflict increased (Goldberg & Sayer, 2006), consistent with research on heterosexual couples making this same transition (Belsky, Spanier, & Rovine, 1983).

Gay fathers have been found to have parenting skills similar to heterosexual fathers and showed higher attentiveness to children's needs, paternal nurturing, and communication as compared to their heterosexual counterparts (Bigner & Jacobsen, 1989). Gay families may provide insight regarding parenting and masculinity free from traditional gender norms and a reconceptualization of family that could expand "role norms in novel ways that may serve as alternative models for all families" (Schacher, Auerbach, & Silverstein, 2005, p. 31). At the same time, the experience of gay men who are considering family building is greatly influenced by their experiences and negotiations with adoption agencies, reproductive technology, families, partners, and stereotypes (Berkowitz & Marsiglio, 2007). The many negotiations and relationships (e.g., institutions as well as birth mothers, parents, and partners) these men may have to enter into and negotiate can have a profound effect on their paths to parenthood.

Children of LGBT families have been studied extensively, particularly to answer the "litmus test" question of LGBT parent suitability: Do children of LGBT parents grow up to be LGBT themselves? A substantial body of research has shown that children of lesbian/gay parents are as likely (or unlikely) as those of heterosexual parents to be gay or lesbian (Patterson, 2006; Stacey & Biblarz, 2001; Telingator & Patterson, 2008). Few other differences have been found (Stacey & Biblarz, 2001), and each type of family, whether with parents of different or same gender, has specific advantages and disadvantages (Biblarz & Stacey, 2010). "Research has shown that the adjustment, development, and psychological well-being of children is unrelated to parental sexual orientation and that children of lesbian and gay parents are as likely as those of heterosexual parents to flourish" (Paige, 2005, p. 496).

The first study to examine delinquent behavior, substance abuse, and victimization in adolescents with same-sex versus different sex parents found no differences—risk behaviors were associated with the quality of relationship with the parents, not their family structure (Wainwright & Patterson, 2006). Likewise, another study found adolescents whose parents described closer relationships with them reported higher quality peer relations and more friends in school (Wainwright & Patterson, 2008). Another probed the relationships and attachment of gay, lesbian, and straight adoptive parent couples and found no significant differences in happiness, attachment, or overall relationship satisfaction (Farr, Forssell, & Patterson, 2010).

The body of research showed few significant differences between the children of heterosexual and LGBT parents, until a new piece of research spanning 20 years tracking children from birth through adolescence showed an unexpected difference—children of lesbian mothers had fewer behavior problems than their peers. In this study, the largest longitudinal study of same-sex-parented families, children were rated higher in social, academic, and overall competence and significantly lower in social problems, rule-breaking, and problem behavior than their peers from non-lesbian families (Gartrell & Bos, 2010).

The issue of resilience is just beginning to be explored (Hunter, 1999; Russell, 2005). The concept of resilience identifies strengths. LGBT people and their families are enmeshed in stressful situations throughout their lives. Yet most survive and might be viewed as prototypes for resiliency. LGBT youth, as Savin-Williams (2005) terms them, are "positive, resilient, and diverse," (p. 190) perhaps due to having had to acquire many developmental assets as a result of navigating and negotiating the sheer number and types of risks they face.

Several studies have explored the impact of homophobia on children of lesbian/gay parents, but only a few examine factors that promote resilience in these same youth. Attending a school that provides a curriculum inclusive of LGBT issues and opportunities to socialize with other children of LGBT families were some factors that showed increased resilience (Van Gelderen, Gartrell, Bos, & Hermanns, 2009). The motivation for a significant amount of research on children with LGBT parents has been family law research for use in custody and adoption cases seeking to determine whether children's well-being is affected by their parent's sexual orientation (Arnup, 1999; Settersten, 2008).

In short, most of the challenges children of LGBT parents face relate to homophobia and stigma about sexual orientation from the larger society rather than any inherent differences in upbringing or family structure (Bos, van Balen, & van den Boom, 2005). And perhaps more importantly most children survive and thrive having had this unique experience. Abigail Garner (2002) said, "It wasn't having a gay father that made growing up a challenge, it was navigating a society that did not accept him, and by extension, me."

Children of LGBT parents who share their family status with others are harassed at school at about the same rate as LGBT youth (Ray & Gregory, 2001). And LGBT families who are from nondominant ethnic or racial minority groups must negotiate the ideas, values, and beliefs regarding sexual orientation and gender expression of both the dominant culture and their own minority cultures. However, children of LGBT parents can also learn important strategies from their families for living in a world that may ignore their experience and discriminate against them. They must learn to navigate and negotiate within several different communities and spheres; in some ways, these children may be viewed as bicultural or tricultural if they are also negotiating the norms of an additional nondominant heritage or background.

There is also a multifaceted picture of experiences for K through 12 students with LGBT parents. LGBT parents are more likely than heterosexual parents to be actively engaged with their child's school. They were more likely to volunteer (67% vs. 42%), attend parent–teacher conferences (94% vs. 77%), be members of the parent–teacher organization, and contact school about their child's academic performance. This suggests LGBT parents are potential assets for schools, but many LGBT parents report feeling ignored or mistreated by their school communities—especially by other parents. Students with LGBT parents also reported challenges—30% reported feeling that they could not fully participate in school because they had an LGBT parent, while 36% felt that schools did not acknowledge their LGBT family (for instance, not permitting one parent to sign a school form because he/she was not the student's legal parent). Twenty-two percent said they had been discouraged from talking about their family at school by a teacher, principal, or other school personnel (Kosciw & Diaz, 2008).

FAMILY LIFE EDUCATION PRACTICES

Current State of Family Life Education

Other than the groundbreaking 2006 work *An Introduction to GLBT Family Studies* (Jerry Bigner, Editor) and the interdisciplinary *Journal of GLBT Studies,* the bulk of literature and resources regarding family life education and LGBT families lies in multidisciplinary and other fields—for instance sociology, family studies, gerontology, psychology, social work, education, health, public policy, statistics, and economics. That weakness may also be a significant strength, however, as it encourages students, practitioners, and researchers to view LGBT people and families through a multidimensional lens that may reflect their diverse lives more accurately and authentically.

There are very few family life education programs specifically designed for LGBT individuals and families at all life stages. Of those that do exist, few are integrated within a family life education framework or delivery system. Instead they may be found in a variety of other specific disciplines—the child welfare system, local LGBT community centers, legal and advocacy organizations, and sexuality services. These can be difficult to find and access, and in many areas of the country, there is not a community-based LGBT center available to inquire about accessing such services.

The oversight of LGBT issues in many types of programming and curricula remains pervasive at present. And due to the 1996 Defense of Marriage Act, nearly all marriage education efforts by definition specifically exclude LGBT populations because of the federal definition of marriage. Other family living or marriage prep classes may be restricted to heterosexual couples only, depending on the sponsoring organization.

The National Council on Family Relations (NCFR) issued a fact sheet on same-sex marriage in 2004 and periodically includes information about LGBT people and families in its publications and journals. There have been several LGBT parenting magazines over the past few decades, although these usually are produced by and for LGBT people without interest or support from non-LGBT family life education or parenting organizations. Some organizations also provide LGBT parenting classes (e.g., Rainbow Families of Staten Island Play & Parenting Group, Charleston's Alliance for Full Acceptance Parenting Group, Boston's Lesbian/ Gay Family & Parenting Services, New York City's Family Program of the LGBT Community Center, the California Parenting Institute, and the national organization Family Equality Council), childbirth classes (e.g., Childbirth Education for LGBTQ Families at Maia Midwifery, Oakland, California), or intentionally or unintentionally integrated classes for LGBT and heterosexual parents. However, the onus is usually on LGBT people to request inclusion rather than finding existing programs or services that proactively address their needs.

General Needs of This Population and Rationale for Family Life Education

The needs of the LGBT community have long been overlooked, and educators have a real opportunity to design programs that address the specific needs of LGBT people. The current state of family life education regarding LGBT individuals and families in some ways reflects that of society at large—it is an area of increasing conversation and research, an area of great promise and limited understanding, and one that has the potential to impact many more people (e.g., LGBT people, and their families, friends, coworkers, and children) than was previously understood.

Based on the existing research that describes the challenges of this population, there are a number of specific needs toward which family life education programs could direct efforts. Programming opportunities include information about specific issues facing LGBT people—youth, prospective parents and parents, couples, and the unique issues of older adults.

Youth are coming out as LGBT at younger ages than ever before. LGBT K through 12 students encounter widespread harassment and alienation, with profound effects—including lower grades and the desire to not pursue college (Kosciw, Diaz, & Greytak, 2008), both of which directly impact future goals and future earning potential. LGBT people of all ages must navigate complicated issues regarding their careers. LGBT people must take additional steps to secure their relationships, rights, and families; sometimes it is expensive, impossible, or against the law for them to do so. Children of LGBT parents are harmed by restrictions on parenting, foster parenting, and adopting. And finally, and perhaps most obviously, all people deserve to be treated with dignity and respect. LGBT people have the right to expect that their needs will be understood and addressed by culturally competent family life professionals. An excellent first step might include revisiting the NCFR Family Life Education Content and Practice Areas, to explore areas that could be enhanced with specific information/resources to be more responsive to the needs of LGBT families.

A developmental approach is used next. In this section, this approach provides a framework for further describing the needs of LGBT individuals and families.

Youth and Young Adulthood

Family life education programs can do many things to address the needs of LGBT young adults—for instance, programming about family building, foster parent, and adoption issues that includes information all parents need to know, as well as the specific information LGBT parents and prospective parents will need. Therefore, family life education could be used to provide information about the rights of LGBT parents in the local jurisdiction, which agencies will work with LGBT parents, and information about where second-parent adoptions or surrogacy are legal. Because the needs of LGBT parents can be so different from those of heterosexual parents due to local, state, and federal law, family life education programs might need to be more detailed and perhaps separate or in addition to those offered to heterosexual parents.

Family resource management workshops could include information about securing some basic rights and finances through legal paperwork. Parent education and guidance curricula and sessions could incorporate areas of particular interest to LGBT parents—for instance, programs for LGBT parents to help their children cope with discrimination and parent–child communication programs.

The realm of heterosexual parents raising LGBT youth is also one of great importance but with little service provision. Therefore, family life education professionals are well positioned to provide concrete skills to parents toward cultivating increased knowledge and acceptance. Some will be very similar to those for all parents, while others are unique (such as highlighting the research linking parental rejection to negative health outcomes). Family life education programs with catchy titles such as "So Your Kid Just Came Out to You—Now What?" a program developed and implemented by the author, present an area of growth to a population of parents who may feel isolated and ill-equipped even in today's world.

Parents can also be an important conduit to reaching LGBT youth directly to provide life-enhancing and risk-reducing family life education. Given the research earlier in this chapter, LGBT youth have significant needs that could be addressed by family life education in the areas of drug and alcohol education, educational and vocational programs, sexuality education, communication, decision making, risk reduction, peer pressure, pregnancy prevention, and building healthy relationships.

An additional area of great need falling within the family life education context is addressing unintended pregnancy and teen parenthood in LGBT youth. LGBT youth may try to cope with stigmas through heterosexual dating and sexual behaviors as they may feel more "camouflaged" in an attempt to avoid being identified (Saewyc, Bearinger, Blum, & Resnick, 1999). Thus, sexuality education efforts to prevent unintended teen pregnancy—programs almost exclusively designed to address heterosexual teen behavior—have not been effective for LGBT youth (Saewyc, Pettingel, & Skay, 2004), and more effective strategies that actively name and address the needs of LGBT youth may be seen as more relevant to their lives (Saewyc et al., 2008). Parent–child communication programs might also provide skills to enhance connectedness that could counteract these trends.

Additional issues, including access to education, safety from physical or verbal harm from peers and others, safe schools, and interest in continuing on in secondary education and college, can have lifelong impacts on access to earning potential. Given the research about youth in the juvenile justice and child welfare systems, family life education could be used to address this issue and help LGBT youth by providing programs on a variety of basic necessary skills—setting up and running a home, budgeting and managing resources, and performing other life skills as these youth age and set out on their own.

Midlife

There are many common experiences LGBT and non-LGBT people at midlife share. LGBT people approaching midlife may be juggling responsibilities of caring for their own children as well as caring for elderly parents. Therefore, family life education could be used to address this issue and help LGBT families by providing enhanced caregiver skills and tools that take into account the unique stresses they face and could also further explore financial planning and family resource management issues that are unique to LGBT families. Likewise, content about the internal dynamics of families and healthy family functioning for LGBT families and the impact of family stress, both normative as well as crisis, should be addressed. As their children grow, families will benefit from youth development, self-esteem, interpersonal relationships, and human sexuality family life education programs to support their children's healthy development just as heterosexual parents can benefit from this same information.

Older Adulthood

Since many LGBT elders experienced coming of age before the modern LGBT rights movement, they may not be "out" to friends, family, or providers, and their life experience likely differs profoundly from that of younger LGBT people (Fassinger, 1997; Kimmel, 1995). As a result, family life education professionals may not realize they are serving LGBT elders or recognize their needs. LGBT elders might be particularly unlikely to participate in family life education programs since the majority believe they are not welcome in mainstream senior services programs (Berkman, 2006). Therefore, family life education could be used to address this by first cultivating sensitivity to gain trust and demonstrate how family life education may enhance their lives. As illustrated earlier in this chapter, issues of money and finances loom particularly large at this stage of life; therefore, family life education offerings like nutrition education and financial counseling may serve critical needs at a time when LGBT people may feel most vulnerable and alone. Fostering understanding among LGBT elders of how law and public policy issues may disparately impact them is another important role for family life education programs. And as the area of human sexuality education for elders of all orientations becomes increasingly more common, family life education professionals can begin to think about ways such programs can be inclusive of the needs of LGBT elders. Some recent attention has centered on addressing family life education needs of elders of all orientations and HIV/AIDS. Making sure LGBT people of all ages, even older adults, receive accurate, appropriate information about HIV/AIDS remains ever important. It is equally important that family life education professionals remember to educate and address LGBT people and themes not only in terms of disease, disaster, and discrimination but from a perspective that avoids reducing all LGBT people to one issue (risking further marginalization and stereotyping) and instead honors each individual's needs, risks, and future.

Marketing/Recruitment

Educating family life education students and practitioners is essential—as is recognizing marketing and recruitment issues and opportunities. Effective promotion of programs that serve the needs of LGBT families, or families with LGBT members, must address several key themes. Efforts at transparency of purpose and philosophy, as well as specific and informed outreach, will be required.

As consumers, LGBT people have proven to be fiercely brand-loyal to companies that specifically market to them (Harris Interactive, 2007). The power of this characteristic can be harnessed to great effect and can be a key tool in marketing and outreach. Likewise, LGBT culture is rich with symbols (e.g., pride flags and other rainbow items, pink triangles, and the "equal" sign), a significant but often hidden history, and specific language and terminology. Family life education providers who understand LGBT culture, symbols, and themes can more effectively seek out LGBT people confidently, credibly, and competently.

Engaging with LGBT leaders in local communities and enlisting their assistance in marketing is another strategy for success. Collaborating or volunteering in existing events planned by and for LGBT people (e.g., LGBT pride events) may contribute to a sense of credibility, commonality of purpose, and goodwill. In some areas, it may be challenging to engage with LGBT people if the overall climate is still stigmatizing or perceived to be unsafe.

Barriers to Participation

Several important factors can influence participation. LGBT youth might not attend family life education programs if they are available within their community because of fear of being "outed" to parents or friends, concern about confidentiality issues, or skepticism that the presenter or sponsoring organization may not be welcoming and inclusive of LGBT youth. And should LGBT youth attend, challenges educators may encounter in encouraging them to participate may include similar issues.

As a group, LGBT people also contend with the legacy of being pathologized at best, vilified at worst. Thus, LGBT people may distrust educators or providers until they prove themselves culturally competent. LGBT people also generally have rich word-of-mouth networks through which information about which professionals and business to trust and which not to trust are shared.

Family life education curricula must provide information that is accurate, useful, and nonjudgmental. However, since the literature reveals a complex reality, a key barrier to participation may simply be that LGBT people may fear family life education programs that make assumptions about their lives.

Environmental Considerations

Given some of these barriers to participation, some relatively small changes to the environment (physical, psychological, actual, and virtual) may improve the attendance, popularity, and learning that can occur in family life education programs and settings.

Providing ample information in online formats, when possible, can serve to allay potential participants' worries. A website that includes family life education offerings, as well as statements that clearly state the educator's or organization's rationale for and interest in serving LGBT people and families well (and one that includes the organization's nondiscrimination statement, when applicable), may be the first point of contact that many LGBT people will use to decide how and whether to utilize family life education services. Other online services—resources for download, Listservs, and social networking pages one can join, and even online family life education learning modules and services when possible—can also address confidentiality concerns of youth, parents of LGBT youth, and LGBT people of all ages. These can also serve as remarkably effective marketing tools, once LGBT people begin sharing the positive experiences they've had with a particular family life education program or educator.

In the physical environment of family life education settings and programs, conducting an inclusion audit (discussed in the next section) to explore how effective program materials, offerings, required forms, and even posters on the walls are at communicating a welcoming, culturally competent program, is an important process. Attention to other details that are more audience-specific, such as providing books and magazines that are inclusive of LGBT families and experiences or comfortable furniture and furnishings for LGBT youth (perhaps in the "rainbow" palette or with recognizable LGBT signs and symbols), will also serve to communicate a sense of belonging. For parents of LGBT children, readily available resources and a recognition that each parent may be in a different place regarding his or her own journey (uncertainty, acceptance, understanding, support, etc.) are important.

Modes of Learning

There are several ways in which family life education can be conducted to acknowledge the complexities of LGBT families while serving people of *all* orientations well. One strategy is to incorporate information about all orientations into existing family life education programs. Integrating LGBT content and themes can be relatively simple and is a key strategy for family life educators. Family life education efforts should strive for inclusive language at all times, not just when an LGBT person may be in the room. For instance, consider using terms like *parents* rather than mother and father, *partner* rather than husband or wife, *boyfriend* or *girlfriend* rather than just one gender-specific word in teaching situations, scenarios and handouts, and even forms such as evaluations and intake forms where demographic information is requested. Many people appreciate the use of inclusive language because they have an LGBT parent, sibling, or child. Incorporating inclusive pronouns or nongendered names into examples in family life education sessions also can serve as a simple but powerful model that such relationships exist in everyday life. Family life educators can leave it up to the audience to discuss whether "Chris" or "Pat" in a role-play scenario is male or female and if it matters.

While some LGBT people, especially youth, are at risk for very negative outcomes, family life educators can help participants put information into a realistic context. Society is overtly hostile to LGBT people; responding to stigmatization, stress management, internalized oppression, the desire to fit in, managing parental disapproval, and sheer survival all play a role in behaviors that may yield increased risk. Yet, previous research is being reexamined to seek additional information about survey design and sampling. In some cases, earlier research that highlighted negative outcomes was conducted only on very specific subsets of LGBT people, such as those already in the juvenile justice system (Savin-Williams, 2001). Family life educators can help people of all orientations learn that LGBT people are not "doomed" to sad or dangerous lives by illuminating existing research and examining the process by which some topics receive study, while others do not.

Family life education programs may also conduct an "inclusion audit" (find one example at http://www.outforhealth.org/files/all/out_for_health_lgbt_inclusion_audit.pdf) to explore what barriers and supports exist within a program regarding serving LGBT people/families. Are LGBT people and experiences reflected in agency materials and forms? Are resources, services, and referrals inclusive and sensitive to the needs of LGBT families? Imagine an LGBT family in the office or waiting room reading pamphlets/handouts or accessing services. Evaluate whether agency settings and services are congruent with messages of pluralism, diversity, and respect of LGBT people/families.

Educator Characteristics

Family life educators can prepare for sessions with LGBT-specific groups, as well as adapt or modify existing program content and models for greater inclusiveness. The first step is being adequately prepared. There are many high-quality sources of information and training locally and online, to address knowledge gaps about LGBT families. In some communities, a conversation about locating resources and expertise may lead to professional development opportunities for family life educators. Community-based and campus-based LGBT centers may also be sources of resources, training, and like-minded colleagues.

A family life educator doesn't have to be an LGBT person to do quality work around family life education and LGBT families, issues, and themes. Conversely, not all LGBT people are knowledgeable and skilled in this area. Family life education organizations should avoid assuming an LGBT person will be responsible for all LGBT efforts or outreach or delegate this role to an LGBT person without a clear rationale for doing so. Family life educators can prepare by becoming familiar with the facts, laws, and policies LGBT people must know about and navigate. For those family life educators who are not LGBT themselves, consider what it may be like to think about the things LGBT people might have to think about, worry about, and plan for in a typical day.

If a family life professional has deeply held beliefs that are at odds with LGBT people's well-being, safety, or right to exist with respect and dignity free from harm, they should discuss this with a supervisor. A grievance policy and nondiscrimination policy should also exist for both employees and clients, so incidents can be reported, investigated, and addressed.

Ethical Considerations

LGBT people are unique in that they have been the focus of efforts to attempt to change their sexual orientation; no exploration of the topic of ethics is complete without acknowledgment of this reality. Historically, LGBT people were sometimes forcibly treated with shock treatment, psychiatric drugs, brain surgeries, aversion therapy, chemical castration, and other methods to try to change their sexual orientation (Fornstein, 2002). Efforts and organizations seeking to change a person's sexual orientation to heterosexual have been discredited, and such efforts were found to be ineffective and in some cases caused harm (APA Task Force on Appropriate Therapeutic Responses to Sexual Orientation, 2009). Nevertheless, these attempts provide a troubling and burdensome legacy—and one that may have profound impact on the interest of LGBT people in participating in family life education programs. Whether they themselves have experienced this or not, LGBT people may seek signs from well-meaning providers to assure that they will be treated with dignity and respect.

The NCFR *Ethical Principles and Guidelines for Family Scientists* 1.01 and 1.02 specifically address issues of avoiding discrimination based on sexual orientation and extending dignity and respect to all (Adams, Dollahite, Gilbert, & Keim, 2001). Additional ethical principles and guidelines provide guidance on other key issues discussed in this chapter, such as confidentiality, diversity, and law and policy issues.

Best Practices in Family Life Education Programming

Best practices and successful programming for LGBT families with regard to family life education are still limited at this time. This is partly due to lack of data that include sexual orientation and gender identity. Ignorance about LGBT people and families and how services and service delivery must consider their unique needs also plays a role in this lack of information. Sometimes professionals may work in direct opposition of the needs of LGBT families because they fear the loss of support (from supervisors, the organization, other clients, or donors) or simply are unwilling to meet the needs of LGBT families, perhaps due to preconceived beliefs. There are, however, a number of model programs that incorporate key themes and issues facing LGBT families into their design and implementation. As Small, Cooney, & O'Connor (2009) noted, such programs need to be socioculturally relevant. LGBT people and families are used to, but frequently weary of, "translating" information, program materials, and resources into what is accurate, useful, and appropriate for their needs. Some existing programs do the "translating" for them by offering culturally competent services, professional development training for staff, and in some cases programs actually designed and tailored to their unique needs. Several examples are highlighted here.

Out for Health, Planned Parenthood of the Southern Finger Lakes LGBT Health &Wellness Project in central New York State (www.outforhealth.org) provides outreach, education, and information to LGBT people, their providers, and the community at-large about the importance of including and welcoming LGBT people. This initiative includes a comprehensive website, training for providers, social and support groups for LGBT people and their families, and ongoing evaluation components. Using a multidimensional model of wellness, offerings include a COLAGE group, sessions for medical and social service professionals, nationally recognized speakers, support groups, a book group, and a knitting circle. Sexual and reproductive medical care, provided by trained staff, is also available.

Gay–Straight Alliances, or GSAs, are groups at the high school and sometimes middle school level that support the needs of LGBT and allied students. They are frequently a safe "home base" for kids of LGBT parents as well. The first school-based GSA was established in 1988, and since that time, more than 4,000 GSA groups have been created throughout the country. GSAs "seek to improve school climate by addressing and reducing anti-LGBT bullying and harassment in school" (Gay Lesbian and Straight Education Network, 2007). The effects of these GSAs have been far-reaching—LGBT students in schools with GSAs are less likely to miss school because they feel unsafe compared to students in schools without a GSA and are significantly more likely than students in schools without a GSA to be aware of a supportive adult at school (84% compared to 56%). LGBT students who report having supportive faculty and other school staff report higher grade point averages and are more likely to say they plan to pursue postsecondary education than LGBT students who do not have supportive school staff (Kosciw & Diaz, 2006).

Lambda Legal's kit *Take the Power—Tools for Life and Financial Planning* (http://www.lambdalegal.org) provides tools for LGBT individuals and families to protect their children, relationships, financial assets, and health care wishes. Lambda Legal also collaborated with the Child Welfare League of America to create the *Getting Down to Basics* tool kit for those working in child welfare and juvenile justice systems. Since LGBT young people are in America's child welfare and juvenile justice systems in disproportionate numbers, the tool kit gives guidance on an array of issues affecting them and the adults and organizations who provide them with out-of-home care.

The Family Acceptance Project develops family education materials, including the booklet *Supportive Families, Healthy Children: Helping Families with Lesbian, Gay, Bisexual & Transgender Children*. This resource is designed for parents/caregivers to support their LGBT children, reduce the risk of negative outcomes, and promote their well-being. It is available in English, Spanish, and Chinese.

The Ferre Institute Lesbian and Gay Family Building Project (http://www .prideandjoyfamilies.org/) offers educational programs (though they don't currently publish curricula); information and referral; and support for LGBT parents, prospective parents, and their children. They publish the *Directory of Family Building Services for LGBT People*, which lists welcoming human services providers. The project sponsors groups in several cities with educational and social activities and a Listserv for discussions of family building and parenting issues and hosts provider trainings, including "Straight Talk about LGBTQ Lives: Working with LGBTQ Families in Professional Settings."

God Loves Each One Ministry (http://www.godloveseachone.org/index.htm) creates resources for people of faith interested in creating a dialogue about sexual orientation and gender in congregations and families. Current publications include *All God's Children: Teaching Children about Sexual Orientation and Gender Diversity,* a guide to caring conversations with young children that offers practical guidance, children's sermons, and classroom activities; *And God Loves Each One: A Resource for Dialogue about Sexual Orientation,* a starting point for dialogue in families and faith community; *Dios Nos Ama por Igual: Una Invitación al Diálogo sobre la Orientación Sexual* for Spanish-speaking families; and *Made in God's Image: A Resource for Dialogue about Gender Differences* that provides information about transgender and intersex experience.

The National Coalition of Anti-Violence Programs (NCAVP) (http://www .ncavp.org/about/default.aspx) addresses the issue of violence committed against and within LGBT and HIV-affected communities and advocates for victims of violence/harassment, domestic violence, sexual assault, and police misconduct. Their most recent research-based publication with the National Center for Victims of Crime, *Why It Matters—Rethinking Victim Assistance for LGBTQ Victims of Hate Violence & Intimate Partner Violence*, documents extensive gaps in service provision. Through this new collaboration, the organizations aims to better serve individuals and communities whose victimization has largely been unseen, unreported, and underserved.

Because basic awareness and cultural competence about LGBT families is often a first step toward extending service provision, traveling photo exhibits can powerfully depict the strength and diversity of LGBT families and individuals and serve as important tools for community building, family life education continuing education, and as cosponsorship opportunities for family life educators to partner with LGBT organizations. Love Makes a Family: Portraits of LGBT Parents and Their Families (http://www.familydiv.org/lovemakesafamily.php) seeks to challenge and change myths and stereotypes about LGBT people and their families. *Fearless,* by photographer Jeff Sheng, documents LGBT high school/collegiate athletes who are "out" to their teammates and coaches. It was most recently displayed at the 2010 Winter Olympics. These are sometimes evaluated by local sponsors to measure changes in knowledge and behavior of attendees.

Locating and accessing support can be difficult, especially for LGBT elders. One program, a telephone support group in rural North Carolina for partners of people who have Alzheimer's disease, addressed some of these challenges (Moore, 2002). Successful elements identified included utilizing alternate delivery methods to address geographic and economic challenges, recognizing ways existing programs were structured from a heterosexist perspective that left needs unmet, and using inclusive language and providing validation to participants' unique experiences. Several of these components are similar to other family life education programs addressing LGBT families' needs.

Upon exploring the best practices and model programs, an interesting mix of non-LGBT organizations and LGBT-specific organizations are represented. Poverny (1999) explored the case for and against mainstreaming services and outlines a strategy for service delivery models promoting family life education for LGBT people. Key themes include recognition that LGBT families live in two different worlds (LGBT and the dominant society), that they are more familiar with non-LGBT organizations than most of those organizations are with them, and that attitudes and behaviors of staff must change for LGBT families to have equal access to culturally competent services to meet their needs.

Although guidelines and best practices for successful family life education with LGBT populations are still in the early stages, suggested guidelines for successful programming can be gleaned from existing literature and the limited programming that has been successfully implemented. Here is a list of these guidelines for successful LGBT-inclusive family life education programming.

- Know general definitions and terminology.
- Establish "safe space" (supportive, confidential, knowledgeable) for LGBT families and LGBT youth to be authentic and for heterosexual parents of LGBT children to express their concerns, hopes, and questions.
- Avoid assumptions—not all people are heterosexual and not all LGBT youth are struggling. LGBT people come in all sizes, abilities, ages, religions, and backgrounds.

- Incorporate inclusive language and culturally competent service delivery into programming.
- Create new programs and curricula when current offerings do not meet the needs of LGBT people.
- Involve LGBT people at all levels—create an advisory board and partner with LGBT organizations.
- Know how to locate key resources. Things do change; seasoned professionals will want to keep up with the latest research, too. Young people especially are expanding boundaries, challenging assumptions, and constructing identity and community in exciting new and different ways.
- Conduct an inclusion audit.
- Provide professional development opportunities to insure cultural competence in understanding and serving LGBT people and families.
- Identify other community resources for collaboration and referral.
- Create policies and processes that are inclusive of LGBT families and LGBT staff.
- Respond to bias and misinformation in participants and colleagues.
- Include LGBT-themed information in all sessions/settings, and infuse the curriculum with content about sexual orientation and gender identity—ideally not as a separate, compartmentalized topic but as another important aspect to every topic.

FUTURE DIRECTIONS

One emerging area of research is the impact that sexual orientation has on human development over the life span, and this new research will likely take place across disciplines and across the world (Patterson, 2008). Another theme that will impact the future is the current generation of LGBT youth. These young people have several unique experiences. They are the first generation to have been able to connect with other LGBT youth in rather simple and direct ways—through GSAs in their schools and online. LGBT youth will arrive at future destinations—college, adoptive fertility agencies, family management and resource programs, relationship education programs, family life education preparation and credentialing processes—no longer experiencing delight *if* a professional or agency demonstrates LGBT expertise but *expecting* knowledgeable services that address their unique needs.

Dominant-culture curricular models are common. For instance, LGBT people and families do not appear directly in the NCFR curriculum guidelines or family life education content areas; rather, they fall under the nebulously described "understanding of lifestyles of minority families." There are rich opportunities for existing curricula and standards to be updated and for ethnonational curricula across all aspects of diversity to be created (Wiley & Ebata, 2004). Evidence-based curricula for LGBT individuals/families are rare and lacking a network regarding LGBT themes for family life education to access, difficult to locate, or replicate. As with other dimensions of diversity, access, appropriateness/fit, and relevance will be factors in the success of any program.

Despite much literature about negative outcomes, little research has been done regarding possible positive outcomes of strategies LGBT people learn to overcome societal stigma. Topics include further investigating resilience; the creation and definitions of community; and the skills of adaptation, creativity, and communication. Work on resilience and family networks encourages integration of current knowledge of sexual orientation and family strengths to inform future research (Oswald, 2002). Horn, Kosciw, and Russell (2009) suggested an approach that is not entirely risky or resilient but that is a recognition of the social context of each youth and the dramatic effect parental response and support can have on identified risks. These will surely influence future directions for education and research in a field primed for opportunities for growth.

Finally, continued and increased data collection about the needs of LGBT people/families is recommended. Information, particularly regarding LGBT ethnic and racial minority families, families across class dimensions, and families of bisexual and transgender people, will help inform future directions for research and practice.

REFERENCES

Adams, R., Dollahite, D., Gilbert, K., & Keim, R. (2001). The development and teaching of the ethical principles and guidelines for family scientists. *Family Relations, 50*(1), 41–48.

Albelda, R., Badgett, M., Schneebam, A., & Gates, G. (2009). *Poverty in the lesbian, gay and bisexual community*. Los Angeles: Williams Institute. Retrieved from www.law.ucla.edu/williamsinstitute/pdf/LGBPovertyReport.pdf

APA Task Force on Appropriate Therapeutic Responses to Sexual Orientation. (2009). Report of the Task Force on Appropriate Therapeutic Responses to Sexual Orientation. Washington, DC: American Psychological Association.

Arnup, K. (1999). Out in this world: The social and legal context of gay and lesbian families. *Journal of Gay and Lesbian Social Services, 10*(1), 1–25.

Balsam, K., Beauchaine, T., Rothblum, E., & Solomon, S. (2008). Three-year follow-up of same-sex couples who had civil unions in Vermont, same-sex couples not in civil unions, and heterosexual married couples. *Developmental Psychology, 44*(1), 102–116.

Barker, J., Herdt, G., & de Vries, B. (2006). Social support in the lives of lesbians and gay men at midlife and later. *Sexuality Research and Social Policy, 3*(2), 1–23.

Belsky, J., Spanier, G., & Rovine, M. (1983). Stability and change in marriage across the transition to parenthood. *Journal of Marriage and the Family, 45*, 567–577.

Berkman, B. (Ed.). (2006). *Handbook of social work in health and aging*. New York: Oxford University Press.

Berkowitz, D., & Marsiglio, W. (2007). Gay men: Negotiating procreative, father, and family identities. *Journal of Marriage and Family, 69*(2), 366–381.

Biblarz, T., & Stacey, J. (2010). How does the gender of parents matter? *Journal of Marriage and Family, 72*(1), 3–22.

Bigner, J., & Jacobsen, R. (1989). Parenting behaviors of homosexual and heterosexual fathers. *Journal of Homosexuality, 18,* 173–186.

Blake, S., Ledsky, R., Lehman, T., Goodenow, C., Sawyer, R., & Hack, T. (2001). Preventing sexual risk behaviors among gay, lesbian, and bisexual adolescents: The benefits of gay-sensitive HIV instruction in schools. *American Journal of Public Health, 91*(6), 940–946.

Bos, H., van Balen, F., & van den Boom, D. (2005). Lesbian families and family functioning: An overview. *Patient Education and Counseling, 59,* 263–275.

Buchmueller, T., & Carpenter, C. (2010). Disparities in health insurance coverage, access, and outcomes for individuals in same-sex versus different-sex relationships, 2000–2007. *American Journal of Public Health, 100*(3), 489–495.

Busseri, M., Willoughby, T., Chalmers, H., & Bogaert, A. (2008). On the association between sexual attraction and adolescent risk behavior involvement: Examining mediation and moderation. *Developmental Psychology, 44*(1), 69–80.

Cahill, S., South, K., & Spade, J. (2000). *Outing age: Public policy issues reflecting gay, lesbian, bisexual and transgender elders.* Washington, DC: National Gay and Lesbian Task Force.

Canfield-Lenfest, M. (2008). *Kids of trans resource guide.* San Francisco: COLAGE. Retrieved from http://www.colage.org/wp-content/uploads/2010/12/KOT-Resource-Guide-Draft-2.pdf

Cashore, C., & Tuason, T. (2009). Negotiating the binary: Identity and social justice for bisexual and transgender individuals. *Journal of Gay & Lesbian Social Services, 21*(4), 374–401.

COLAGE. (2004). *Tips for medical professionals for making better/safer environments for children with LGBTQ parents.* Retrieved from http://www.colage.org/resources/tips-for-medical-professionals-for-making-bettersafer-environments-for-children-with-lgbtq-parents/

COLAGE. (n.d.). *Making GSAs inclusive of youth with LGBTQ parents.* Retrieved from http://www.colage.org/resources/making-gsas-inclusive-of-youth-with-lgbt-parents/

Coon, D. (2003). *Lesbian, gay, bisexual and transgender (LGBT) issues and family caregiving.* San Francisco: Family Caregiver Alliance. Retrieved from http://caregiver.org/jsp/content/pdfs/op_2003_lgbt_issues.pdf

D'Augelli, A. (2002). Mental health problems among lesbian, gay, and bisexual youths ages 14 to 21. *Clinical Child Psychology and Psychiatry, 7,* 433–456.

Davidson, M. (2000). Religion and spirituality. In R. M. Perez, K. A. DeBond, & K. J. Bieschke (Eds.), *Handbook of counseling and psychotherapy with lesbian, gay and bisexual clients* (pp. 409–433). Washington, DC: American Psychological Association.

Defense of Marriage Act, Pub. L. No. 104-199. (1996, September 21). Washington, DC: U.S. Government Printing Office. Retrieved from http://frwebgate.access.gpo.gov/cgi-bin/getdoc.cgi?dbname=104_cong_public_laws&docid=f:publ199.104

Farr, R., Forssell, S., & Patterson, C. (2010). Gay, lesbian, and heterosexual adoptive parents: Couple and relationship issues, *Journal of GLBT Family Studies, 6*(2), 199–213.

Fassinger, R. (1997). Issues in group work with older lesbians. *Group, 21,* 191–210.

Fornstein, M. (2002). Overview of ethical and research issues in sexual orientation therapy. In A. Shidlo, M. Schroeder, & J. Drescher (Eds.), *Sexual conversion therapy: Ethical, clinical, and research perspectives* (pp. 167–180). New York: Haworth Medical Press.

Forrest, R., & Saewyc, E. (2004). Sexual minority teen parents: Demographics of an unexpected population. *Journal of Adolescent Health, 34*(2), 122.

Fredriksen, K. (1999). Family caregiving responsibilities among lesbians and gay men. *Social Work, 44*(2), 142–155.

Garner, A. (2002, February 11). Don't protect me, give me your respect. *Newsweek.* Retrieved from http://www.newsweek.com/2002/02/10/don-t-protect-me-give-me-your-respect.html

Garofalo, R., Wolf, R., Kessel, S., Palfrey, J., & DuRant, R. (1998). The association between health risk behaviors and sexual orientation among a school-based sample of adolescents. *Pediatrics, 101*(5), 895–902.

Gartrell, N., & Bos, H. (2010). US national longitudinal lesbian family study: psychological adjustment of 17-year-old adolescents. *Pediatrics, 126*(1), 1–9.

Gates, G., & Ost, J. (2004). *The gay & lesbian atlas.* Washington DC: Urban Institute.

Gay & Lesbian Alliance Against Defamation, Inc. (2010). *GLAAD media reference guide* (8th ed.). Retrieved from http://www.glaad.org/document.doc?id=99

Gay Lesbian and Straight Education Network. (2007). *GLSEN releases research brief showing benefits of Gay–Straight Alliances.* Retrieved from http://www.glsen.org/cgi-bin/iowa/all/news/record/2216.html

Goldberg, A., & Sayer, A. (2006). Lesbian couples' relationship quality across the transition to parenthood. *Journal of Marriage and Family, 68*(1), 87–100.

Goodenow, C., Netherland, J., & Szalacha, L. (2002). AIDS-related risk among adolescent males who have sex with males, females, or both: Evidence from a statewide survey. *American Journal of Public Health, 92,* 203–210.

Grant, J. (2010). *Outing age: 2010 public policy issues affecting lesbian, gay, bisexual and transgender elders.* Washington DC: National Gay and Lesbian Task Force. Retrieved from http://www.thetaskforce.org/downloads/reports/reports/outingage_final.pdf

Grossman, A., D'Augelli, A., & Dragowski, E. (2007). Caregiving and care receiving among older lesbian, gay, and bisexual adults. *Journal of Lesbian and Gay Social Services, 18*(3–4), 15–38.

Harris Interactive. (2007). The gay, lesbian, bisexual and transgender population at-a-glance. Retrieved from http://www.witeckcombs.com/pdf/glbt-market-research-highlights.pdf

Harris Interactive. (2011). *Surveying among gays & lesbians.* Retrieved from http://www.witeckcombs.com/pdf/hi_white_paper_surveying_gays_and_lesbians-01-2011.pdf

Hart, T., & Heimberg, R. (2001). Presenting problems among treatment-seeking gay, lesbian, and bisexual youth. *Journal of Clinical Psychology, 57,* 615–627.

Himmelstein, K., & Brückner, H. (2010). Criminal-justice and school sanctions against nonheterosexual youth: A national longitudinal study. *Pediatrics, 127*(1), 49–57.

Hollibaugh, A. (2004, September 1). *The post-Stonewall/baby boomer generations' impact on aging in gay, lesbian, bisexual & transgender communities.* (Services and Advocacy for Gay, Lesbian, Bisexual & Transgender Elders [SAGE], Performer). Listening Session for the 2005 White House Conference on Aging (WHCoA), Washington, DC.

Horn, S., Kosciw, J., & Russell, S. (2009). Special issue introduction: New research on lesbian, gay, bisexual, and transgender youth: Studying lives in context. *Journal of Youth and Adolescence, 38,* 863–866.

Hunter, J. (1999). Beyond risk: Refocus research on coping. *Journal of the Gay & Lesbian Medical Association, 3*(3), 75–76.

Hunyady, M. (2008). We are family: I got all my sisters with me! *Journal of Lesbian Studies, 12*(2–3), 293–300.

Kimmel, D. (1995). Lesbians and gay men also grow old. In L. Bond, S. Cutler, & A. Grams (Eds.), *Promoting successful and productive aging* (pp. 289–303). Thousand Oaks, CA: Sage.

Kinsey, A., Pomeroy, W., & Martin, C. (1948). *Sexual behavior in the human male.* Philadelphia: W. D. Saunders.

Kirby, D., Lepore, G., & Ryan, J. (2005). *Sexual risk and protective factors. Factors affecting teen sexual behavior, teen pregnancy, childbearing, and sexually transmitted disease: Which are important? Which can you change?* Washington, DC: National Campaign to Prevent Teen Pregnancy.

Kosciw, J. G., & Diaz, E. M. (2006). *The 2005 National School Climate Survey: The experiences of lesbian, gay, bisexual and transgender youth in our nation's schools.* New York: Gay, Lesbian, and Straight Education Network.

Kosciw, J. G., & Diaz, E. M. (2008). *Involved, invisible, ignored: The experiences of lesbian, gay, bisexual and transgender parents and their children in our nation's K-12 schools.* New York: Gay, Lesbian, and Straight Education Network.

Kosciw, J., Diaz, E., & Greytak, E. (2008). *2007 National school climate survey: The experiences of lesbian, gay, bisexual and transgender youth in our nation's schools.* New York: Gay, Lesbian, and Straight Education Network.

LaSala, M. (2000). Lesbians, gay men, and their parents: Family therapy for the coming-out crisis. *Family Process, 39*(1), 67–81.

Lawrence et al. v. Texas, 539 U.S. 558 (2003).

Marshal, M., Friedman, M., Stall, R., King, K., Miles, J., Gold, M., et al. (2008). Sexual orientation and adolescent substance use: A meta-analysis and methodological review. *Addiction, 103,* 546–556.

McKay, A. (2006). Trends in teen pregnancy in Canada with comparisons to U.S.A. and England/ Wales. *Canadian Journal of Human Sexuality, 15,* 157–161.

MetLife Mature Market Institute. (2006). *Out and aging: The MetLife study of lesbian and gay baby boomers.* Retrieved from http://www.metlife.com/assets/cao/mmi/publications/studies/ mmi-out-aging-lesbian-gay-retirement.pdf

MetLife Mature Market Institute & the Lesbian and Gay Aging Issues Network of the American Society on Aging. (2010). Out and aging: The MetLife study of lesbian and gay baby boomers. *Journal of GLBT Family Studies, 6,* 40–57.

Moore, W. (2002). Lesbian and gay elders: Connecting care providers through a telephone support group. *Journal of Gay & Lesbian Social Services, 14*(3), 23–41.

National Adoption Information Clearinghouse. (2000). *Gay and lesbian adoptive parents: Resources for professionals and parents.* Retrieved from http://www.childwelfare.gov/pubs/f_ gay/f_gay.pdf

New York City Department of Health & Mental Hygiene. (2008). *Community Health Survey. NYC Community Health Survey, 2005 through 2007.* Bureau of Epidemiology Services.

O'Connell, M., & Felix, S. (2011). *Same-sex Couple Household Statistics from the 2010 Census.* Fertility and Family Statistics Branch, Social, Economic and Housing Statistics Division. U.S. Bureau of the Census.

O'Flaherty, M., & Fisher, J. (2008). Sexual orientation, gender identity and international human rights law: Contextualizing the Yogyakarta principles. *Human Rights Law Review, 8*(2), 207–248.

Oswald, R. (2002). Resilience within the family networks of lesbians and gay men: Intentionality and redefinition. *Journal of Marriage and Family, 64*(2), 374–383.

Ottosson, D. (2006). *LGBT world legal wrap up survey.* Brussels, Belgium: International Lesbian and Gay Association.

Paige, R. (2005). Proceedings of the American Psychological Association for the Legislative Year 2004: Minutes of the Annual Meeting of the Council of Representatives, February 20–22, 2004, Washington, DC, and July 28 and 30, 2004, Honolulu, Hawaii, and Minutes of the February, April, June, August, October, and December 2004 meetings of the board of directors. *American Psychologist, 60*(5), 436–511.

Patterson, C. (2006). Children of lesbian and gay parents. *Current Directions in Psychological Science, 15,* 241–244.

Patterson, C. (2008). Sexual orientation across the life span: Introduction to the special section. *Developmental Psychology, 44*(1), 1–4.

Patterson, C., Sutfin, E., & Fulcher, M. (2004). Division of labor among lesbian and heterosexual parenting couples: Correlates of specialized versus shared patterns. *Journal of Adult Development, 11*(3), 179–189.

Plumb, M. (2003). *SAGE: National needs assessment and technical assistance audit.* New York: SAGE.

Poverny, L. (1999). It's all a matter of attitude: Creating and maintaining receptive services for sexual minority families. *Journal of Gay & Lesbian Social Services, 10*(1), 95–113.

Ray, N. (2006). *Lesbian, gay, bisexual and transgender youth: An epidemic of homelessness.* New York: National Gay and Lesbian Task Force Policy Institute and the National Coalition for the Homeless.

Ray, V., & Gregory, R. (2001). School experiences of the children of lesbian and gay parents. *Family Matters, 59,* 28–34.

Remafedi, G. (1987). Adolescent homosexuality: Psychosocial and medical implications. *Pediatrics, 79*(3), 331–337.

Robin, L., Brener, N., Donahue, S., Hack, T., Haie, K., & Goodenow, C. (2002). Associations between health risk behaviors and opposite-, same-, and both-sex sexual partners in representative samples of Vermont and Massachusetts high school students. *Archives of Pediatric and Adolescent Medicine, 156,* 349–355.

Roisman, G., Clausell, E., Holland, A., Fortuna, K., & Elieff, C. (2008). Adult romantic relationships as contexts of human development: A multimethod comparison of same-sex couples with opposite-sex dating, engaged, and married dyads. *Developmental Psychology, 44*(1), 91–101.

Roscoe, W. (1991). *The Zuni man-woman.* Albuquerque: University of New Mexico Press.

Rose, S., & Zand, D. (2000). Lesbian dating and courtship from young adulthood to midlife. *Journal of Gay and Lesbian Social Services, 11*(2–3), 77–104.

Rosenfeld, D. (1999). Identity work among lesbian and gay elderly. *Journal of Aging Studies, 13*(2), 121-144.

Russell, S. (2003). Sexual minority youth and suicide risk. *American Behavioral Scientist, 46,* 1241–1257.

Russell, S. (2005). Beyond risk: Resilience in the lives of sexual minority youth. *Journal of Gay & Lesbian Studies in Education, 2*(3), 5–18.

Ryan, C., Huebner, D., Diaz, R., & Sanchez, J. (2009). Family rejection as a predictor of negative health outcomes in White and Latino lesbian, gay, and bisexual young adults. *Pediatrics, 123,* 346–352.

Ryan, H., Wortley, P., Easton, A., Pederson, L., & Greenwood, G. (2001). Smoking among lesbians, gays, and bisexuals: A review of the literature. *American Journal of Preventive Medicine, 21*(2) 142–149.

Saewyc, E., Bearinger, L., Blum, R., & Resnick, M. (1999). Sexual intercourse, abuse and pregnancy among adolescent women: Does sexual orientation make a difference? *Family Planning Perspectives, 31,* 127–131.

Saewyc, E., Pettingel, S., & Skay, C. (2004). Teen pregnancy among sexual minority youth in population-based surveys of the 1990s: Countertrends in a population at risk. *Journal of Adolescent Health, 34,* 125–126.

Saewyc, E., Poon, C., Homma, Y., & Skay, C. (2008). Stigma management? The links between enacted stigma and teen pregnancy trends among gay, lesbian, and bisexual students in British Columbia. *Canadian Journal of Human Sexuality, 17*(3), 123–139.

Savin-Williams, R. (2001). A critique of research on sexual-minority youths. *Journal of Adolescence, 24*(1), 5–13.

Savin-Williams, R. (2005). *The new gay teenager.* Cambridge, MA: Harvard University Press.

Schacher, S., Auerbach, C., & Silverstein, L. (2005). Gay fathers expanding the possibilities for us all. *Journal of GLBT Family Studies, 1*(3), 31–52.

Settersten, R. (2008). Postcards from the edge of American family life. *Family Focus on Adoption, National Council on Family Relations,* F12–F14.

Shulman, J., Horne, S., & Levitt, H. (2003). To pass or not to pass: Exploration of conflict splits for bisexual-identified clients. In J. S. Whitman & C. J. Boyd (Eds.), *The therapist's notebook for lesbian, gay and bisexual clients: Homework, handouts and activities for use in psychotherapy.* Binghamton, NY: Haworth Press.

Small, S., Cooney, S., & O'Connor, C. (2009). Evidence-informed program improvement: Using principles of effectiveness to enhance the quality and impact of family-based prevention programs. *Family Relations, 58,* 1–13.

Smith, S., & Gates, G. (2001). *Gay and lesbian families in the United States: Same-sex unmarried partner households.* Retrieved from http://www.urban.org/UploadedPDF/1000491_gl_partner_households.pdf

Stacey, J., & Biblarz, T. (2001). (How) does the sexual orientation of parents matter? *American Sociological Review, 66*(2), 159–183.

Strohm, C., Seltzer, J., Cochran, S., & Mays, V. (2006, August). *Couple relationships among lesbians, gay men, and heterosexuals in California: A social demographic perspective.* Paper presented at the Annual Meeting of the American Sociological Association, Montreal, Quebec, Canada. Retrieved from http://www.allacademic.com//meta/p_mla_apa_research_citation/1/0/4/9/1/pages104912/p104912-1.php

Sullivan, A. (1995). *Issues in gay and lesbian adoption: Proceedings of the Fourth Annual Pierce-Warwick Adoption Symposium.* Washington, DC: Child Welfare League of America.

Telingator, C., & Patterson, C. (2008). Children and adolescents of lesbian and gay parents. *Journal of the American Academy of Child and Adolescent Psychiatry, 47*(12), 1364–1368.

U.S. Census Bureau. (2003). Married-couple and unmarried-partner households: 2000. *Census 2000 Special Reports.* Retrieved from http://www.census.gov/prod/2003pubs/censr-5.pdf

U.S. Government Accounting Office. (2004, January 23). *Defense of Marriage Act: Update to prior report.* GAO-04-353R. Retrieved from http://www.gao.gov/new.items/d04353r.pdf

Van Gelderen, L., Gartrell, N., Bos, H., & Hermanns, J. (2009). Stigmatization and resilience in adolescent children of lesbian mothers. *Journal of GLBT Family Studies, 5*(3), 268–279.

Wainwright, J., & Patterson, C. (2006). Delinquency, victimization, and substance use among adolescents with female same-sex parents. *Journal of Family Psychology, 20,* 526–530.

Wainwright, J., & Patterson, C. (2008). Peer relations among adolescents with female same-sex parents, *Developmental Psychology, 44*(1), 117–126.

Wiley, A., & Ebata, A. (2004). Reaching American families: Making diversity real in family life education. *Family Relations, 53*(3), 273–281.

Williams Institute. (2011). Census snapshot: 2010. Retrieved from http://www3.law.ucla.edu/williamsinstitute/home.html

Chapter 13

Preparing Family Life Educators to Work With Diverse Populations

Alan C. Taylor, CFLE, and Sharon M. Ballard, CFLE

The United States has frequently been likened to a "melting pot" of people hailing from a wide array of backgrounds, cultures, and ethnicities. Preparing family life educators to work with culturally diverse populations and increasing their cultural awareness have become increasingly important in today's society (Powell & Cassidy, 2007). In order for family life educators to effectively meet the needs of their diverse audiences, they must be equipped with essential skills, relevant knowledge, and valuable experiences. Too often, new educators are not provided with adequate opportunities to gain knowledge and skills that will prepare them to work with these populations.

The overriding purpose of this chapter is to discuss in more depth the role of the family life educator in relation to the *Framework for Best Practices in Family Life Education* that was introduced by Ballard and Taylor in the first chapter of this book. We will first discuss the growing need and importance for educators to be culturally competent. Next, we will provide specific suggestions and directions for those educators who are looking to strengthen their abilities in working with multicultural populations. Finally, we will discuss the specific skill sets, knowledge bases, and experiences that will strengthen the family life education practices of both the seasoned educator and future educators alike.

THE CULTURALLY COMPETENT FAMILY LIFE EDUCATOR

With the United States having such a diverse population, it is essential that those working with families and individuals in the community be understanding and sensitive to many different cultural beliefs and practices. Becoming culturally competent is a frequently addressed topic in university classrooms and has become a fundamental focus of family studies and community services programs over the past couple of decades. More specifically, the term *cultural competence* means having the ability to respond respectfully and effectively to cultural differences and similarities (Camacho, 2001).

Over the past several decades, in relation to working with diverse populations, specific fields of study in human services have identified the need for culturally competent practitioners. For example, the American Psychological Association (APA) Ethical Principles and Code of Conduct (American Psychological Association [APA], 1992) require that psychologists be aware of differences due to race, ethnicity, language, socioeconomic status, gender, and national origin. The counseling and mental health fields also have identified the importance of implementing culturally competent practices when working with diverse populations (Jencius & Duba, 2002; Siegel et al., 2000). Specific to the field of family life education, a code of ethical principles and guidelines was originally established by the Minnesota Council on Family Relations in the 1990s for all parent and family life educators (National Council on Family Relations [NCFR], 2010a). These principles have since been officially accepted as the guiding code of ethics for all certified family life educators through the National Council on Family Relations (NCFR). One particular ethical principle relates to cultural competency: "We will respect cultural beliefs, backgrounds and differences and engage in practice that is sensitive to the diversity of child rearing values and goals" (NCFR, 2010a, p. 1).

Allen and Blaisure (2009) also provided several suggestions for family life educators striving to become more culturally competent. One approach is to use a "diversity lens" to build cross-cultural understanding within family life education practices. Using this lens, specifically in conjunction with the *Framework for Life Span Family Life Education* (Bredehoft, 2009), allows educators the ability to be multicultural, gender-fair, and aware of the special needs of their participants. Another suggestion made by Allen and Blaisure in regard to cultural competence is for family life educators to continually develop a personal awareness or their own cultural beliefs and then to use reflexivity. Reflexivity is the process by which family life educators become increasingly aware of themselves and their own cultural experience and the effect that has on how they relate to others.

With the globalization of our economy and the ease of worldwide communication, it is imperative that individuals working with children and families in the community have the ability to synthesize knowledge and cultural awareness into effective practices that support and sustain the health and well-being of the individual and family (McPhatter, 1997). In order for family life educators to be most successful while working with diverse populations, they must strive to possess a sense of cultural competence as an essential trait in their professions. However, cultural competence moves beyond simply an understanding of diversity. This understanding must be translated into practice. For family life educators to become better prepared to implement community education to diverse audiences, they first must be equipped with the necessary *skills, knowledge,* and *experiences* to help them be successful. Skills, knowledge, and experiences are essential ingredients for culturally competent family life educators. The next sections will discuss these three components (skills, knowledge, and experiences) in more detail.

PREPARING AND STRENGTHENING THE FAMILY LIFE EDUCATOR

Related to the importance of a well-prepared family life educator, one of the operational principles of family life education established by Arcus, Schvaneveldt, and Moss (1993) was that "qualified educators are crucial to the successful realization of the goals of family life education" (p. 20). No matter how effective a program design, without someone to implement it well, even the most well-planned family life education program may "flop." Small, Cooney, and O'Connor (2009) also recognized the importance of "well-qualified, trained, and supported staff" (p. 8) to program effectiveness. The field of family life education has made great strides in the provision of guidelines regarding this operational principle. The Certification in Family Life Educators (CFLE) program through the NCFR was established in 1984, and there are currently more than 120 approved accredited academic programs in the United States and Canada (NCFR, 2011a, 2011b). However, this is still an area of concern, because despite the certification, there are still many who are teaching family life education who are not properly trained.

In addition to training, the personal characteristics and attributes of the educator are important to the success of family life education programs. In 1993, Arcus and Thomas posited that "...the family life educator *is* the program, as it is the educator who selects, designs, and implements the program; selects and uses resources, materials, and activities; and responds to or ignores the interests and needs of the audience" (p. 26). Daro (2000) emphasized the importance for educators to have the ability to effectively establish rapport, to gain trust, and to remain nonjudgmental to a program's effectiveness.

The NCFR (2011c) identified traits, skills, and abilities necessary to be a successful family life educator. Those applicants pursuing the full CFLE must have an employer rank them on the traits, skills, and abilities. They include the following:

- Works well with diverse audiences
- Engages in ethical decision making
- Exhibits professionalism and maintains appropriate boundaries
- Possesses problem-solving skills
- Has an overall skill in educational methodology (e.g., needs assessment, planning, implementing, and evaluating curricula and programs)
- Has interpersonal communication skills
- Possesses public speaking skills
- Demonstrates written communication skills
- Works well one-on-one
- Works well in groups
- Has an awareness of one's own personal attitudes and cultural values
- Accepts and integrates constructive feedback
- Possesses emotional stability and maturity, empathy, self-confidence, and flexibility

Several of these attributes are connected to specific skills family life educators must possess in order to be effective, while others are related directly to one's knowledge base or experiences. Some of these qualities were also mentioned in previous chapters as important traits when working with diverse populations. For example, for family life educators working with Arab immigrant families (Chapter 10), self-awareness, empathy, flexibility, and compassion were all qualities identified by Blume, Sani, and Ads as being most important and critical for educators to possess. Another particular educator quality discussed in Chapter 10 was the desire of Arab immigrant families for a family life educator who has global orientation to understanding issues affecting them (Darling, 2007). In addition, Olsen and Archuleta, in Chapter 2, reported research that found that family life educators are more successful when they show empathy and have credibility in the eyes of rural families (Rogers, 2003). These are qualities that will prove beneficial in any family life education setting.

There are several different approaches family life educators may take when working with diverse populations. Myers-Walls (2000) introduced a continuum that includes three distinct modes or approaches that family life educators take when providing community education. These modes refer to the range or roles the educator has and the location of power utilized within a community program.

The first mode on one end of the continuum is called the "expert" approach. This approach involves the educator possessing information and skills that the participants do not have but would benefit from learning. When working with diverse populations, educators must be equipped with sufficient knowledge, being true "experts" on the topic being discussed.

On the other side of the continuum, the second mode is entitled the "facilitator" approach. This approach refers to the needs and desires of the participants. In this mode, the participants are the ones who have the power to select what information and skills they feel are most relevant and essential to them at that time. In this approach, the educator is a true catalyst, directing the participants to their own desired learning experiences. When providing family life education to various populations, educators must be knowledgeable about the topics the participants might be interested in exploring.

Finally, the "collaborator" approach is located in the middle of this continuum and represents the understanding that shared responsibility for program direction and learning come from both the educator and the participants. Both parties have important information and perspectives to contribute.

For an educator to use any of these three educator modes and be effectively successful, their preparation and their content information must go beyond just the knowledge and skills of family life curriculum. Their expertise, research, and experience must also encompass information pertaining to the specific cultural beliefs and practices of the population with which the educator is working. Ultimately, family life educators must understand their target audience, their preferred educational setting, and how the participants will interpret the educator's style of interaction (Myers-Walls, 2000). For example, Hwang explained in Chapter 9 that when interacting with some Asian immigrant populations, regular eye contact with new acquaintances is often interpreted as disrespectful. However, a communication technique that is often recommended in educational settings is to connect with your audience by making eye contact. These two expectations of eye contact contradict one another. It's the responsibility of the educator to resolve this contradiction, by finding other culturally appropriate ways to connect with the audience. For another example, it's important for family life educators to recognize that building a culture of self-disclosure in the classroom does not always work well with some Asian immigrants, who may interpret self-disclosure of a family problem as a reason for disgrace or shame (Fong, 2002), or as Hwang explained in Chapter 9, Asian immigrants may be hesitant to self-disclose to a person in authority.

What are specific suggestions family life educators can do to better prepare themselves to work with diverse populations? Myers-Walls (2000) explained that there are several steps educators can take to respond to diversity in respectful and growth-producing ways. First, it is important for educators to know who they are as an individual, which reinforces the idea of reflexivity. Becoming self-aware allows family life educators the ability to gain insights into their own ethnicities and an understanding of how their backgrounds may impact their professional practice. Related to this, educators must discover to which groups they personally affiliate and how they feel about themselves and others. Second, family life educators can benefit from discovering what they know about themselves and other groups of people. Educators will profit from assessing their own values and attitudes and determining how they feel about them. Finally, family life educators are encouraged to be flexible rather than rigid. Following these suggestions may increase comfort with self and others and help educators to feel better prepared to work with diverse populations. Suggestions specific to skills, knowledge, and experience are shared in the following sections.

Skill Building

The goal of family life education is to enrich the lives of the individual and the family through prevention and education (Powell & Cassidy, 2007). There are several different methods of delivery that a family life educator can employ when developing family life education programs, including a traditional classroom setting, focus groups, newsletters, pamphlets, online discussion boards, and even distance education (Duncan & Goddard, 2011; Powell & Cassidy, 2007). Most university family life education programs have a course in family life education methodology, and this course is required for those pursuing the CFLE through the abbreviated application process with NCFR. A typical course in methodology covers skills in planning, implementing, and evaluating programs. Future family life educators may learn the mechanics of programming, but in order to effectively relay material and, more importantly, connect themselves to their target audiences, family life educators need to possess essential proficiencies or skills that relate to interpersonal relationships (Powell & Cassidy, 2007). More specifically, family life educators should be competent in having (1) an understanding of self and others; (2) interpersonal communication skills, such as listening, being empathetic to others, having the ability to self-disclose, decision making, problem solving, and conflict resolution; (3) an understanding of intimacy, love, and romance; and (4) the ability to relate to others with concern, respect, sincerity, and responsibility (Olson-Sigg & Olson, 2009). In addition, because many community agencies rely on collaboration and teamwork, family life educators need to demonstrate flexibility and the ability to work as a valuable member of a group.

According to West and Turner (2006), interpersonal skills are those skills that allow us to interact and relate to people. They are learned and refined through our interactions with others. These skills include empathy, active listening, problem solving, and effective communication. Empathy involves identifying with and understanding another person's point of view (West & Turner, 2006). Active listening involves the ability to attend to the speaker fully, while maintaining eye contact and observing the speaker's nonverbal cues (Martin, 2010). Nonverbal cues include both facial expressions and body language and can be just as effective in understanding a client's needs as his or her words.

Utilizing interpersonal skills may help family life educators better connect with diverse populations. Family life educators must learn to be confident with their own interpersonal communication styles and must be taught specific skills to help them effectively connect with those whom they will serve. Future family life educators currently being trained at many universities or colleges are given opportunities to learn these interpersonal skills. When group projects and assignments are required as part of course assignments, the need to collaborate with other students encourages interpersonal communication and promotes teamwork. Group assignments expose individuals to differing opinions and different methods of accomplishing tasks. These are skills that will translate well when family life educators are required to collaborate with other professionals to build and deliver the best programs for the populations in question.

There were many excellent examples throughout Chapters 2 through 12 that illustrated the importance of interpersonal skills. As discussed by Baugh and Coughlin in Chapter 11, Neely (2003) is quoted as having found that those family life educators who were tolerant, personable, who used positive reinforcement, and were able to connect with and motivate the target audience were more successful in working with black families. All of these qualities can be attributed to an educator demonstrating appropriate interpersonal skills during educational activities. Similarly, in Chapter 6, "Family Life Education With Grandfamilies: Grandparents Raising Grandchildren," Baugh, Taylor, and Ballard reported research that older adults preferred their family life educators to be respectful, enthusiastic, and understanding (Duay & Bryan, 2008). These authors also found that participants were more likely to consistently attend and later return for future programs when qualities such as these were implemented by their family life educators. These qualities are not just specific to working with an older adult population, but will build connections in many diverse family life education settings.

A related skill for effective family life educators that is often overlooked is the ability to communicate effectively with their target audience. In order to communicate effectively, family life educators need to have strong written and verbal communication skills. Verbal skills are the ability to use language to convey thoughts, feelings, and emotions—an important component in any family life setting. Written communication skills are the ability to articulate and write our thoughts and ideas in a clear and concise manner (West & Turner, 2006). This is especially relevant now that many family life education programs are offered online or through written media.

Knowledge Building

There have been several studies conducted that have identified those areas of knowledge considered most important in community services and education (Boltuck, Peterson, & Murphy, 1980; Prerost & Reich, 1984). The NCFR Committee on Standards and Criteria for Certification of Family Life Educators identified 10 content areas as being essential for preparing family life educators. They include (1) interpersonal relationships, (2) families and individuals in societal contexts, (3) internal dynamics of families, (4) parenting education and guidance, (5) family resource management, (6) human sexuality, (7) human growth and development over the life span, (8) family law and public policy, (9) professional ethics and practice, and (10) family life education methodology (NCFR, 2010b). These standards and criteria have been an important mechanism in helping family life education program developers determine appropriate curriculum content for age-specific programs. In addition, these criteria have been used as a valuable measuring stick by university and college programs to determine the necessary comprehensive curriculum standard for preparing future certified family life educators.

These 10 areas can be examined in more depth, using a cultural and diversity lens to aid family life educators in becoming more culturally knowledgeable about the populations whom they will teach. Although each content area was discussed in detail in Chapter 1 as each relates to diversity, it is important to note the role of knowledge as a whole in programming. A common theme discussed in several previous chapters of this book is the necessity of family life educators to have a strong knowledge relative to both their content and their population. For example, grandparents in grandfamilies (Chapter 6) expressed an interest in new research and wanted their existing knowledge enhanced and fortified (Duay & Bryan, 2008). Therefore, family life educators should be able to handle concerns and provide participants with applicable resources that will help them immediately. Family life educators working with prison inmates and their families (Chapter 3) will be more successful if they possess a working knowledge of child development and family systems theories and knowledge of substance abuse recovery and mental disorders (Frye & Dawe, 2008; Greenberg, 2006; Magaletta & Herbst, 2001).

Experience Building

Competence as a family life educator, as well as cultural competence, comes with practice and experience. Varied real-world experiences help to prepare capable family life educators. The more opportunities family life educators have to interact and provide services for diverse populations, the more competent and effective they will be in their future programming.

In Chapter 5, "Family Life Education With Military Families," Carroll, Smith and Behnke found that there is a strong preference among military audiences and leaders for family life educators who have had experience with the military way of life. Personal history and experience with the unique lifestyle of the military brings a perspective that is appreciated by many military families. Educators who have previously served in the armed forces, been married to a service member, or been children of a service member bring credibility to program information and activities that other family life educators may have a difficult time achieving.

Spending time and sharing experiences with members of the target audience can be a very informative means of helping a family life educator design and select content for programming. Understanding through experiencing the traditions and culture of audiences will aid educators in knowing what might be appropriate and effective means of interaction in a family life education setting. An example of this is given by Perrote and Feinman in Chapter 7. The authors explained that when family life educators ask personal questions to Native American audiences, the questions may be interpreted as being intrusive and may put people off. "Native Americans are comfortable with silence, therefore, educators need to be good listeners." In addition, if family life educators become anxious with silence and fill it by answering their own questions, "participants will cease to offer anything of themselves." The more familiar family life educators are with their audience's culture and traditions, the greater the likelihood an open, trusting interpersonal relationship can be developed.

There are several ways future family life educators are prepared to gain experience working with diverse populations to achieve cultural competence. Unfortunately, some novice family life educators are placed into a new educational program with very little training or preparation working with diverse populations. This method incorporates a "learn-as-you-go" approach and usually does not build the educator's confidence or immediate cultural competence. For future family life educators at a university or college, service learning and internships are two vehicles for gaining experience and enhancing one's understanding of culture.

Service Learning

Service learning is a credit-bearing educational experience in which students participate in organized service activities that meet identified community needs and which actively engage students as a way to gain further understanding of course content, a broader appreciation of the discipline, and an enhanced sense of civic responsibility (Bringle & Hatcher, 1995). The goal of service learning is to promote learning through active participation, during which time the student is able to use the skills and knowledge they have learned in the classroom in real-life scenarios.

Service learning provides students with time to reflect on their experiences and potentially develop a sense of caring for others (Corporation for National and Community Service, 2010).

For students, service learning emphasizes the reciprocal and beneficial relationship between individuals and the community, while also teaching students the value of knowledge through application. Service learning compels students to consider how they and the people they serve exist in a social context (Roschelle, Turpin, & Elias, 2000). Service learning also is a means of gaining a more comprehensive understanding of human diversity and challenges students to connect the critical thinking goals of the classroom with their own personal value systems (Mintz & Hesser, 1996). Through service learning, future family life educators are exposed to a diversity of cultures and life experiences. Confronting and being challenged by the issues of others brings future educators face-to-face with a reality that is difficult to replicate in a classroom setting (Bass, Barnes, Kostelecky, & Fleming, 2004).

Service learning often benefits the community by having future family life educators help reach underserved individuals and families (Green, 1998). Community partners have acknowledged the unique contributions of student service learners and have supported the belief that many agency activities would not be possible without the added support of schools and universities (Lamson, Ballard, & LaClaire, 2006). Finally, students' awareness of key issues and community needs may increase as a result of their service with community agencies.

Internships

Duncan and Goddard (2011) make the case for the difference between teaching family life education content areas at a college or university and "outreach family life education." This distinction is important and, to date, universities have done more to prepare new PhDs to be university teachers than to be effective outreach family life educators. For those programs whose focus is on preparing future family life educators to enter a community outreach setting, internships can prove a successful means of training and an important rite of passage. Internships, which are typically facilitated by an academic program or institution, typically take place after the student has completed their general education and major coursework requirements. Research has found that many universities are using internships within their curriculum (Ballard & Carroll, 2005), and they are a required component for those students applying for the CFLE credential through the abbreviated application process (NCFR, 2011b). The internship experience allows students to implement what they have learned in the classroom in a real-life work setting. Internships may facilitate career maturity and contribute to the development of lifelong skills by helping students apply classroom-learned family life education principles (Ballard & Carroll, 2005). According to Smart and Berke (2004), students reported that their internships provided them with valuable learning experiences, helped clarify career choices, helped develop interpersonal skills, and provided an avenue for personal growth (Bell & Haley, 1995; Davis, Steen, & Rubin, 1987; Eyler, 1995; Karasik & Berke, 2001). Having close supervision by a qualified professional is vital for the family life education intern to learn expectations, problem solving, and other aspects of the job.

In addition to the various ways internship experiences benefit future educators, universities profit as well. For university programs, family life education internships have been found to validate curriculum in a working environment and provide new educators with real-life learning experiences that cannot be attained through case studies/scenarios and lecture. These internship experiences typically expose future family life educators to diverse populations they would not have had access to within the classroom.

Community agencies in which future family life educators work during their internships also benefit from internship programs. Internships provide an avenue for employers to try out and test newly trained family life educators before officially hiring them. Internships can be part of a cost-effective model for community agencies, as they allow agency directors to employ personnel at no cost or low cost. Agencies rely on family life education interns to provide the labor and on-hand personnel necessary to run their various family life education programs. Without interns, some valuable programs might be discontinued due to funding cuts. Finally, some community agencies find that newly trained family life educators contribute fresh ideas and new energy to the workplace. This enthusiasm is not just felt among fellow agency workers but also among the children, adults, and families with whom the agency serves.

Internships and service-learning experiences that contribute the most to the development of qualified family life educators provide direct exposure to diverse populations and actual family life education programming experiences rather than being assigned menial and non–family life education related tasks. At their best, family life education internships provide students with the opportunity to utilize best practices in working with diverse audiences. In general, all family life educators, new and seasoned, must find experiences in real-world settings that will allow them to develop a sound sense of cultural competence for the populations they are serving.

MIXED POPULATIONS

As the title states, this book was intended to help family life educators discover the best practices that are known and utilized when working with diverse populations.

Each chapter within the book was designed to address a specific diverse population and the family life education practices that can be used effectively with this particular group. We believe this information will prove helpful but also acknowledge that there are intersecting dimensions of diversity that may result when teaching family life education programs with a mixture of families (e.g., black family; lesbian, gay, bisexual, and transgender [LGBT] family; and grandfamily) in the audience.

It is important that educators prepare to meet the needs of their audiences, and an important step in doing so is to administer a needs assessment to potential participants prior to or at the beginning of each family life education program (Arcus et al., 1993). Educators designing and implementing programs within communities where mixed populations will participate must recognize that "needs" may change from one program to another. In other words, the determined needs of one particular mixed group might not be the same needs for a subsequent mixed group. Additionally, once the needs are assessed, the family life educator is accepting and respectful to all who attend. Making sure that respect and acceptance exist in the classroom does not solely lie on the shoulders of the family life educator. Family life educators also may need to encourage those attending to be tolerant and accepting of differences as well. This will take planning, especially if participants with differing cultural backgrounds and dissimilar beliefs and values regarding family life, enroll in the same family life education program.

Although an emphasis is often made to celebrate the differences among diverse groups and to design family life education programs specifically to address these differences, it is helpful to acknowledge the similarities that exit among diverse families and individuals. The next section will introduce some of the interesting similarities that exist among the specific populations presented in previous chapters of this book. Having knowledge of these similarities may provide family life educators with opportunities to develop program content that will meet the needs of a mixed population. In addition, family life educators may also use this information to insightfully structure their family life education program design in a manner that will create a comfortable learning environment in which participants will actively participate and grow. Finally, family life educators may be able to use this information to strengthen their own educator role as they focus on the interpersonal attributes and skills necessary to successfully connect with a mixed population.

Collectivism as a Family Strength

Several of the diverse populations in previous chapters were reported as being collective in nature. In other words, families are interdependent and interconnected, in regard to living arrangements, the sharing of resources and emotional support. Within American Indian populations (Chapter 7), extended family support structures are used often, as extended family members play important roles in facilitating the well-being of individuals, families within the tribe, and community. Likewise, Blume, Sani, and Ads (Chapter 10) discussed that members in Arab immigrant families view interdependence as a normal and healthy family interaction pattern. Strong collectivism ideals were also reported within black families (Chapter 11), Latino immigrant families (Chapter 8), and Asian immigrant families (Chapter 9). Collectivism is a common thread woven through many of the diverse populations discussed, but that often differs from the larger, majority culture in the United States. Family life educators will need to carefully navigate through the collectivism vs. individualism ideologies when addressing a mixed population.

Leadership Support as a Family Strength

For both American Indian families and military families, leadership support is viewed as a valuable and important resource. Carroll, Smith, and Behnke (Chapter 5) discussed the important role assigned to military leaders. Leaders are charged with being responsible for everything under their command, extending to the responsibility of the well-being of service members and their families. Families rely on these leaders to connect them with military base resources, community resources, and other families with similar needs. Similarly, Perrote and Feinman (Chapter 7) reported that tribe leaders play a comparable role to military commanders. Tribe and other senior community leaders play a significant role in providing American Indian families with needed resources such as money, food, clothing, and services such as child care and transportation (O'Shea & Ludwickson, 1992). These resources are often shared among tribe members. It would benefit family life educators to acknowledge these additional support levels (formal or informal) that interact closely with the families in their audiences.

Religion as a Family Strength

Families from several diverse populations report incorporating religious practices and beliefs in their family life. Schvaneveldt and Behnke (Chapter 8) reported that family functioning and decision making among Latino immigrant families from Central and South America are greatly influenced by the Roman Catholic Church's ideology, beliefs, and practices. Religious beliefs, combined with cultural factors of *familismo,* may strongly affect decisions made by family members in family life education programming (Falicov, 2007). For Arab immigrant families, black families, and rural families, religion also plays an important role in their family functioning and decision making. In a target audience containing a mixed-diverse group, it is important for family life educators to acknowledge that religious beliefs and practices may influence some, if not all, participants' attitudes, behaviors, and values regarding family functioning.

Recruiting Based on Family Strengths: Connecting to Communities

Nearly all of the chapter authors discussed the importance of family life educators to connect with cultural leaders and other influential people in the community when recruiting program participants. Baugh and Coughlin (Chapter 11), in particular, found that effective marketing and recruitment techniques targeting black participants utilize personal contacts within the community. These contacts include strong working relationships with faith-based organizations and other community outreach programs as well (National Healthy Marriage Resource Center, 2009). Similarly, Olsen and Archuleta (Chapter 2) also found that connecting with community professionals who have trusted relationships with rural families is advantageous in marketing a program (Bailey & Paul, 2008). Other populations, in which community connections are deemed important for recruitment, include military families (Chapter 5), Latino immigrant families (Chapter 8), American Indian families (Chapter 7), Asian immigrant families (Chapter 9), Arab immigrant families (Chapter 10), and LGBT families (Chapter 12).

As with any combination of participants, whether they are homogeneous to a single diverse population or mixed, family life educators who adhere to the previously discussed code of ethics (NCFR, 2010a) and who are equipped with the necessary content knowledge, skill set, and experience should feel better prepared to meet the needs of the people they teach. As has been emphasized throughout this book, planning an effective family life education program to meet the needs of a diverse population is important. However, even more vital for those educators working with diverse populations is the focus on developing valuable interpersonal skills, effective communication strategies, and a rich knowledge base. These important skills and attributes will help family life educators find success with any population they service.

FINAL THOUGHTS

There is an ever-present divide between research and practice; however, there also is a disconnect between preparation and practice. Currently, there are only three textbooks that specifically address family life education practices: Duncan and Goddard (2011), Powell and Cassidy (2007), and Bredehoft and Walcheski (2009). Beyond these three publications (and the now classic *Handbook of Family Life*

Education), there are few resources available for preparing future family life educators or for practicing family life educators to draw upon. This book takes steps toward bridging these divides and makes an important contribution to the family life education literature.

In this book, we presented the *Framework for Best Practices in Family Life Education*, which includes program content, program design, and the family life educator situated in the context of culture and strengths and needs of the target population. These components are interdependent and are all crucial to successful family life education. The role of the family life educator is central; yet, if there is not appropriate content or effective delivery methods, then the program will not be successful. Similarly, an evidence-based program that includes both content and design may not work if there is not a skilled family life educator implementing the program. Therefore, we have advocated for a best practices approach, and each chapter in this book highlighted best practices related to program content, program design, and the family life educator.

Overall, experienced family life educators have pulled together the current state of best practices in working with 11 populations. The need for a more empirical study of what makes effective programming is apparent. Because of the limited research that has been conducted in family life education, it has been necessary for family life educators to draw from other related areas such as health promotion or adult education to inform effective family life education practice. However, these chapters are a starting point and provide an important advance in the field of family life education. Family life education continues to develop as a profession, and efforts are continually made to raise the visibility and credibility of family life education. As family life education continues to develop as a profession, it is imperative that we build a more extensive knowledge base specific to family life education. It is through these efforts that not only will the credibility and visibility of family life education increase but also that family life educators will be better able to strengthen and enrich all different types of families.

REFERENCES

Allen, W. D., & Blaisure, K. R. (2009). Family life educators and the development of cultural competency. In D. J. Bredehoft & M. J. Walcheski (Eds.), *Family life education: Integrating theory and practice* (pp. 209–220). Minneapolis, MN: National Council on Family Relations.

American Psychological Association. (1992). *Ethical principles of psychologists and code of conduct*. Washington, DC: Author.

Arcus, M. E., Schvaneveldt, J. D., & Moss, J. J. (1993). The nature of family life education. In M. E. Arcus, J. D. Schvaneveldt, & J. J. Moss (Eds.), *Handbook of family life education: Foundations of family life education* (pp. 1–25). Newbury Park, CA: Sage.

Arcus, M. E., & Thomas, J. (1993). The nature and practice of family life education. In M. E. Arcus, J. D. Schvaneveldt, & J. J. Moss (Eds.) *Handbook of family life education: The practice of family life education* (pp. 1–32). Newbury Park, CA: Sage.

Bailey, S., & Paul, L. (2008). Meeting the needs of rural caregivers: The development and evaluation of an Alzheimer's caregiving series. *Journal of Extension, 46*(1). Retrieved from http://www .joe.org/joe/2008february/a1.shtml

Ballard, S., & Carroll, E. (2005). Internship practices in family studies programs. *Journal of Family & Consumer Sciences, 97*(4), 11–17.

Bass, B., Barnes, H., Kostelecky, K., & Fleming, M. (2004). Service learning and portfolios: enhancing the scholarship of integration and application. *Journal of Teaching in Marriage and Family, 4*(1), 79–99.

Bell, A., & Haley, E. G. (1995). Internships spell success for students. *Journal of Family & Consumer Sciences, 8*(4), 61–64.

Boltuck, M., Peterson, T., & Murphy, R. (1980). Preparing undergraduate psychology majors for employment in the human service delivery system. *Teaching of Psychology, 7*(2), 75–78.

Bredehoft, D. J. (2009). The framework for life span family life education revisited and revised. In D. J. Bredehoft & M. J. Walcheski (Eds.), *Family life education: Integrating theory and practice* (pp. 3–10). Minneapolis, MN: National Council on Family Relations.

Bredehoft, D. J., & Walcheski, M. J. (Eds.) (2009). *Family life education: Integrating theory and practice* (2nd ed.). Minneapolis, MN: National Council on Family Relations.

Bringle, R. G., & Hatcher, J. A. (1995). A service-learning curriculum for faculty. *Michigan Journal of Community Service Learning, 2,* 112–122.

Camacho, S. (2001). Addressing conflict rooted in diversity: The role of the facilitator. *Social Work with Groups, 24,* 135–152.

Corporation for National and Community Service. (2010). *What is service learning?* Retrieved from http://www.learnandserve.gov/about/service_learning/index.asp

Darling, C. A. (2007). International perspectives in family life education. In L. H. Powell & D. Cassidy, *Family life education: An introduction* (2nd ed., pp. 253–277). Long Grove, IL: Waveland Press.

Daro, D. (2000). Linking research to practice: Challenges and opportunities. *Journal of Aggression, Maltreatment, & Trauma, 4,* 115–137.

Davis, J., Steen, T., & Rubin, S. (1987). A study of the internship experience. *Journal of Experiential Education, 10*(2), 22–24.

Duay, D. L., & Bryan, V. C. (2008). Learning in later life: What seniors want in a learning experience. *Educational Gerontology, 34,* 1070–1086.

Duncan, S. F., & Goddard, H. W. (2011). *Family life education: Principles and practices for effective outreach* (2nd ed.). Thousand Oaks, CA: Sage.

Eyler, J. (1995). Graduates' assessment of the impact of a full-time college internship on their personal and professional lives. *College Student Journal, 29*(2), 186–194.

Falicov, C. (2007). Working with transnational immigrants: Expanding meanings of family, community, and culture. *Family Process, 46*(2), 157–171.

Fong, T. P. (2002). *The contemporary Asian American experience: Beyond the model minority.* Upper Saddle River, NJ: Prentice Hall.

Frye, S., & Dawe, S. (2008). Interventions for women prisoners and their children post-release. *Clinical Psychologist, 12*(3), 99–108.

Green, D. (1998). Student perceptions of aging and disability as influenced by service-learning. *Physical and Occupational Therapy in Geriatrics, 15,* 39–55.

Greenberg, R. (2006). Children and families: Mothers who are incarcerated. *Women & Therapy, 29*(3/4), 165–179.

Jencius, M., & Duba, J. D. (2002). Creating a multicultural family practice. *Family Journal: Counseling and Therapy for Couples and Families, 10*(4), 410–414.

Karasik, R. J., & Berke, D. L. (2001). Classroom and community: Experiential education in family studies and gerontology. *Journal of Teaching in Marriage and Family, 1*(4), 13–38.

Lamson, A., Ballard, S., & LaClaire, S. (2006). Creating an effective intergenerational service-learning experience: Components of the UGIVE program. *Journal of Teaching in Marriage and Family, 6,* 186–205.

Magaletta, P., & Herbst, D. (2001). Fathering from prison: Common struggles and successful solutions. *Psychotherapy, 38*(1), 88–96.

Martin, M. E. (2010). *Introduction to human services: Through the eyes of practice settings.* Boston: Allyn & Bacon.

McPhatter, A. R. (1997). Cultural competence in child welfare: What is it? How do we achieve it? What happens without it? *Child Welfare, 82,* 103–124.

Mintz, S., & Hesser, G. (1996). Principles of good practice in service-learning. In B. Jacoby (Ed.), *Service-learning in higher education* (pp. 26–52). San Francisco: Jossey-Bass.

Myers-Walls, J. A. (2000). Family diversity and family life education. In D. H. Demo, K. R. Allen, & M. A. Fine (Eds.), *Handbook of family diversity* (pp. 359–379). New York: Oxford University Press.

National Council on Family Relations. (2010a). *Family life educators code of ethics.* Retrieved from http://www.ncfr.org/sites/default/files/downloads/news/CFLE_CODE_OF_ETHICS_2010_0 .pdf

National Council on Family Relations. (2010b). *Family life education content areas: Content and practice guidelines.* Retrieved from http://www.ncfr.org/sites/default/files/downloads/news/ CFLE_Content_and_Practice_Guidelines_2010_0.pdf

National Council on Family Relations. (2011a). *Academic program approval.* Retrieved from http://www.ncfr.org/cfle-certification/academic-program-approval

National Council on Family Relations. (2011b). *Standards and criteria for the certified family life educator (CFLE) designation.* Retrieved from http://www.ncfr.org/sites/default/files/downloads /news/Standards_2011.pdf

National Council on Family Relations. (2011c). *Certified family life education employer work experience assessment and validation form.* Retrieved from http://www.ncfr.org/sites/default/files/ downloads/news/Employer_Assessment_and_Verification_Form_2011.pdf

National Healthy Marriage Resource Center. (2009). *Supporting an African American healthy marriage initiative.* Retrieved from http://www.healthymarriageinfo.org/docs/supportinganaahmi .pdf

Neely, A. (2003). *Teaching African American students: A look at instructional methods and cultural differences.* Williamsburg, VA: College of William and Mary. Retrieved from http://imet. csus.edu/imet11/portfolio/smiley_k/WebQuest/Neely.pdf

Olson-Sigg, A., & Olson D. H. (2009). Interpersonal relationships. In D. J. Bredehoft & M. J. Walcheski (Eds.), *Family life education: Integrating theory and practice* (pp. 153–162). Minneapolis, MN: National Council on Family Relations.

O'Shea, J., & Ludwickson, J. (1992). *Archaeology and ethnohistory of the Omaha Indians.* Lincoln: University of Nebraska Press.

Powell, L. H., & Cassidy, D. (2007). *Family life education: Working with families across the life span.* Long Grove, IL: Waveland Press.

Prerost, F., & Reich, M. (1984). Factors affecting evaluation of undergraduate job applicants: Urban vs. rural human service delivery systems. *Teaching of Psychology, 11*(4), 218–220.

Rogers, E. M. (2003). *Diffusion of innovations* (5th ed.). New York: Free Press.

Roschelle, A. R., Turpin, J., & Elias, R. (2000). Who learns from service learning? *American Behavioral Scientist, 43*(5), 839–847.

Siegel, C., Davis-Chambers, E., Haugland, G., Bank, R., Aponte, C., & McCombs, H. (2000). Performance measures of cultural competency in mental health organizations. *Administration and Policy in Mental Health, 28*(2), 91–106.

Small, S. A., Cooney, S. M., & O'Connor, C. (2009). Evidence-informed program improvement: Using principles of effectiveness to enhance the quality and impact of family-based prevention programs. *Family Relations, 58,* 1–13.

Smart, L., & Berke, D. (2004). Developing professional standards in family science internships. *Journal of Teaching in Marriage & Family, 4*(1), 101–126.

West, R., & Turner, L. H. (2006). *Understanding interpersonal communication.* Belmont, CA: Thomson Wadsworth.

Index

Note: page numbers followed by "f" and "t" indicate figures and tables, respectively.

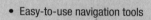